READINGS
in
STATE
and
LOCAL
GOVERNMENT

Joseph F. Zimmerman, 1928 -   ed.

State University of New York, Albany

Holt, Rinehart and Winston, Inc.

New York   Chicago   San Francisco   Toronto   London

February, 1967

PREFACE

State and local government is an important area of study that unfortunately is often overshadowed by some of the dramatic activities of the federal government in the fields of foreign affairs, national defense, and outer space. The fifty states, approximately 3,000 counties, 17,000 municipalities, 17,000 townships 34,000 school districts, and 19,000 other special districts employ over seven million persons and spend sixty-six billion dollars annually. They affect the activities of the average citizen daily in a multitude of ways, whereas the federal government has relatively little daily direct contact with the average citizen.

Several good state and local government textbooks are presently obtainable. However, they tend to be primarily descriptive and do not adequately bring out the importance and controversial nature of many of the current issues. The purpose of this reader is to make readily available to students of state and local government significant readings dealing with major problems and issues. These readings serve to supplement and not supplant the textbooks. Consequently, an effort has been made to avoid the inclusion of readings that contain material customarily found in textbooks.

An examination of the standard state and local government textbooks reveals differences of opinion concerning the organization of a state and local government textbook. The selections included in this reader have been arranged in such a manner that they can be used with any standard textbook.

An editor is always faced with the difficult task of selecting readings. Plenteous readings of quality are available in some areas of state and local government while a shortage exists in other areas. In addition, space limitations forced the editor to leave out a number of articles worthy of inclusion. Nevertheless, an attempt has been made to include readings indicative of the great variety of institutions, problems, and proposed solutions found in the realm of state and local government.

The views expressed in the various selections do not necessarily reflect those of the editor. The readings were not selected to represent a particular viewpoint, but rather to present a wide array of opinions. In fact, most readers undoubtedly will disagree with some of the views contained in the readings.

Worcester, Massachusetts
February 1964

J.F.Z.

CONTENTS

Part 7: STATE AND LOCAL ACTIVITIES

Part 8: STATE-LOCAL PERSONNEL AND FINANCE

part one

DEVELOPMENT
OF THE AMERICAN
FEDERAL SYSTEM

1

DEVELOPMENT
OF THE AMERICAN
FEDERAL SYSTEM

Any study of state and local government should
logically start with a consideration of the development of the
American federal system. Without a knowledge of its development students will experience difficulty in acquiring a proper
understanding of its current status and problems.

Concern with the status of federal-state relations led to the
creation in 1953 of the Commission on Intergovernmental Relations, a bipartisan commission of twenty-five members, to study
problems of federal-state-local relations. The excerpt from the
Commission's 1955 report traces the development of our federal
system of government and considers the issue of national supremacy, the impact of the fourteenth amendment, and recent changes
in the system.

1. Evolution of the American Federal System*

THE PROBLEM OF FEDERALISM

The proper division of labor and authority between the Nation and the States is the key to maintaining the federal nature of our system of government. The lines of division are not static. They have been controversial from the beginning of our life as an independent country. They remain so today.

The American federal system began as an experiment. It was the third try for a solution on this continent to the age-old problem of striking a satisfactory balance between the needs for central strength and central regulation on the one hand and the values of local freedom of action on the other. The framers of our Constitution had joined in a revolution that cut them loose from the old British imperial system, because that system imposed unwelcome controls from a remote center. They had also lived under the "league of friendship" established by the Articles of Confederation. They met under the reluctant auspices of the Congress of that Confederation, to seek "a more perfect union," and began their work by discarding the Articles.

The federal system devised by the framers of the Constitution was the product of necessity rather than doctrine. There was no dictionary definition of federal government to apply nor any working model to copy. They found the classical examples from Greece and the medieval unions of European cities too remote in time and circumstance to be suitable. Their experience under the Articles of Confederation had taught them what to strive for and what to avoid. They were content to keep the States substantially as they knew them, but they deplored certain economic and fiscal tendencies in some States. Chiefly, they felt a very practical need for a central government of much greater strength and potentialities than the Articles provided.

MIDDLE COURSE CHOSEN

Characteristically, they took a middle course to met that need—in retrospect probably the only course that was both "adequate to the exigen-

---

* Commission on Intergovernmental Relations. From *A Report to the President for Transmittal to the Congress.* (Washington, D.C.: U.S. Government Printing Office, June 1955), pp. 9–12 and 20–30.

cies of government and the preservation of the union" and capable of winning majority support. They rejected summarily the advice of those few, like Hamilton, who sought to build a unitary authority, to abolish the States as autonomous units, and to provide for the appointment of governors from the National Capital. They also overruled decisively the considerably greater number who wanted to keep the union a mere confederation, with a few strengthening amendments to the Articles. Instead, they adopted in substance the Virginia Plan.

The Virginia Plan left the States unchanged so far as their domestic institutions were concerned, though the new Constitution expressly forbade some practices the framers thought would be undesirable—State taxes on exports and imports, the issuance of State currency, the impairment of contract obligations, separate agreements with foreign nations or with each other unless with National consent, and other matters now mainly of historical interest. But the Virginia Plan envisaged and the Constitution erected a new National Government, deriving its powers also from the people, capable of dealing with the people directly rather than exclusively through the State governments, and fitted out with a full complement of executive, legislative, and judicial institutions, with powers delegated by the terms of the Constitution. By implication the States were excluded from regulating interstate and foreign commerce and other subjects thus committed to National control. The framers spelled out a list of enumerated powers, including the "necessary and proper" clause, in order to give the National Government what the Virginia Plan had broadly described as:

> power to legislate in all cases to which the separate States are incompetent or in which the harmony of the United States may be interrupted by the exercise of individual legislation.

In a secondary series of decisions the framers modified the Virginia Plan somewhat to compromise, in the composition of the two Houses of Congress, the rival claims of the large States and the small. They also hit upon a device, the electoral college, for extending that compromise while notably increasing the strength and independence of the executive. By means of the "supreme law of the land" clause they introduced a National judicial control over unconstitutional State action. But in leaving the States to define the voting franchise, to conduct National elections along with their own, to choose Senators, and to pass on constitutional amendments, they guaranteed the indispensability of the States to the National Government. And in leaving to the States all powers not delegated to the National Government or otherwise prohibited to them, the Constitution recognized their vital role in the domestic affairs of government. . . .

This system has characteristically been very flexible, leaving a great deal of room for argument and adjustment. The division of powers between the Nation and the States leaves substantial authority with each, but the use and relative importance of powers may shift. The Constitution cannot be formally amended by either level of government without the participation of the other, but interpretation and usage may expand or contract the powers at either level. The National Government deals with the people directly, but it may also utilize the States to reach them indirectly. The States can write and change their own constitutions, but they must meet minimum requirements of the National Constitution. The States are equal in legal status, but not in size, wealth, and influence. In all these essentials the federal relationship is adjustable, within limits. It is affected by controversies over what any government in the system should do, as well as by concepts of what no government should do. Historically, the invocation of States rights has sometimes been as much a sign of opposition to a specific National policy as of attachment to local action as such. . . .

CONSTITUTIONAL DOCTRINE AND PRACTICE

The structure of the new National Government established in 1789 reflected closely the intent of the framers of the Constitution, for the Federalists controlled the Congress during the first decade. Issues of National-State relations that had been fought out in the Convention were re-opened, however, in the very first Congress. Anti-Federalists urged that the National Government should have little administrative machinery of its own, outside the realm of foreign affairs, and instead should use the State courts, the county tax collectors and law enforcement officials, and the State militia to serve its needs. The key vote in Congress in 1791, defeating the tax collector proposal, was close but decisive. The principle was confirmed that where the National Government had constitutional power it would act through its own agents. The division of power, in other words, would determine the division of labor.

This proposition was generally accepted, and in the main governed the administrative relations between the Nation and the States through the 19th century: the post office, the revenue services, and the United States district courts were National establishments. But the principle was never absolute. A major exception from the beginning was the States' control of elections. Minor ones followed. For example, when the first prisoner was convicted and sentenced by a Federal court under Federal law, there was no place to keep him but in a county jail. . . .

THE ISSUE OF NATIONAL SUPREMACY

The basic constitutional question for the federal system from 1789 to 1865 was the issue of National supremacy: whether the National Government was entitled to enforce, over State objections, decisions reached through its own constitutional processes. At bottom this was the same issue posed by the Virginia Plan, and apparently settled by the framers, but it kept reappearing. The first open challenge after 1789 came in 1798 when Jefferson and Madison inspired the Virginia and Kentucky resolutions denouncing the alien and sedition acts. They invited the other State legislatures to instruct their Senators to vote for repeal of the acts, and went on to intimate that the States had a right to resist the enforcement of Federal acts they deemed unconstitutional.

In 1814, at the Hartford Convention, New England leaders talked of secession if the Embargo Act were enforced. A few years afterward, Maryland and Ohio took official action to prevent branches of the Nationally-chartered Bank of the United States from operating within their borders; Ohio went so far as to seize the office and the cash on hand. In Jackson's administration, Georgia defied the Supreme Court and the requirements of a Federal treaty by convicting and hanging a Cherokee Indian under State law. South Carolina threatened nullification over the tariff issue. Among the efforts of northern States to nullify the Fugitive Slave Act of 1850 was the action of the Wisconsin courts in issuing a writ of *habeas corpus* to free a man convicted in a Federal court, after the Supreme Court had specifically denied their authority to do so.

All these challenges from various parts of the country were disposed of peaceably, except for the slavery controversy. Over that issue and secession the North, behind Lincoln's leadership, finally settled by force the ultimate issue of National supremacy. After the war it could no longer be maintained that the Union was only a creature of the States, or a compact among them, liable to be thwarted or dissolved at the will of any of them. From then on, the interpretation of National powers was to be determined, in the main, by some National authority.

WHO FIXES THE BOUNDARIES?

What those powers were, and which National authority was to be the judge of them, were questions not so conclusively settled. Chief Justice Marshall asserted emphatically in 1803 that it was the power and duty of the judiciary to say definitively what the law—including the Constitution —means, when a question is raised in a proper case. But his successor,

Chief Justice Taney, found in the doctrine of "political questions" some limits on the judicial power to interpret the supreme law. Further limits are inherent in the nature of the process of judicial review over legislation, confined as it is to cases and controversies. Andrew Jackson and Abraham Lincoln expanded the role of the President in ways the Court could not control, ways that sometimes give that office a decisive voice in determining the scope of National power as well as the direction of National policy. Finally, there are occasions when a congressional enactment is the dominant fact in the settlement of a constitutional controversy, at least for a period of years. This may happen because the congressional action is never subjected to a judicial test; or because the test comes only after the enactment has been in force for a long period of time; or because even when the courts bar one method of achieving an end, Congress finds another way. The Compromise of 1850, the Reconstruction Acts, the Agricultural Adjustment and Fair Labor Standards Acts of 1938, and most recently the legislation leaving the regulation of insurance with the States and the settlement of the Tidelands dispute illustrate such congressional determinations.

From time to time all three branches of the National Government have shown varying attitudes on issues of federalism. On the record of over a century and a half the Supreme Court, except when dealing with slavery, has probably taken the most consistently Nationalist position. While Congress has extended the sphere of National action, it has in many ways responded to locally held sentiments. Mindful of the impact of National action on the institutions of State and local governments, Congress has frequently taken affirmative action to protect their interests. Successive Presidents have taken sharply contrasting positions; some have been forthright advocates of strong National action, while others have been at pains to protect what they thought were the prerogatives of the States.

NATIONAL SUPREMACY UPHELD BY MARSHALL

Supreme Court doctrine on the boundaries of National and State powers illustrates judicial flexibility. Chief Justice Marshall took a strong Federalist line in vindicating National supremacy and in developing the doctrine of implied powers. He marked out a broad area for exclusive National jurisdiction. He sustained congressional authority when it was used, as in chartering the Bank of the United States or in regulating the coastwise trade. Even in the absence of congressional action, he blocked State entry into the National sphere, as by a tax, nondiscriminatory though it might be, on imported goods in their original packages. Marshall also took a stern view of State acts that violated the spirit, if not the letter, of express constitutional restrictions, or that threatened vested property rights. On the other hand, he found no difficulty in concluding on historical grounds that the Bill of Rights (the first eight amendments) was a restraint only on the National Government and not on the States, despite the ambiguity in phraseology of all but the First Amendment.

Chief Justice Taney, who came to the Court in 1835 from Jackson's Cabinet, did not depart radically from Marshall's positions. Nevertheless, he found noticeably more leeway for State action. A corporate charter was a contract not to be impaired, but its terms would be construed strictly to give the State the benefit of any doubt about the extent of the privileges conferred in the charter. A State could not issue paper currency, but it could charter a State-owned bank empowered to issue notes for circulation. And in a variety of situations where Congress had not legislated, he sanctioned a concurrent power in the States to regulate aspects of interstate commerce that were of special local concern. But when he ruled that Congress had no power to regulate slavery in the territories, popular opinion refused to accept the Court's word as final. This particular controversy had to be resolved by resort to arms.

New administrative undertakings of the war and postwar years introduced the National Government permanently into fresh areas of activity. Among these were the first Morrill Act of 1862, which made land grants for agricultural and mechanical colleges in each State; the establishment of a Commissioner (later Secretary) of Agriculture in the same year, and of a Commissioner of Education in 1867; and in 1870 the creation, under the Attorney General, of a Department of Justice to supervise from Washington the activities of the United States attorneys in the field. More important for the business world was the establishment of a National banking system in 1863. This created for the first time a corps of National bank examiners. In a follow-up move, Congress used the taxing power to oust the States from the field of chartering banks of issue. Soon thereafter there was a uniform currency.

THE FOURTEENTH AMENDMENT

The adoption of the Fourteenth Amendment in 1868 overshadowed all these moves in its long-term significance for National-State relations. It announced a national definition of citizenship, something the framers in 1787 had studiously avoided. Many thought the amendment authorized Congress to regulate civil rights generally all over the country, but the Congress soon lost its relish for that assignment. As it turned out, the amendment subjected to the possibility of judicial review in the Federal courts a broad range of State legislation over which the State courts had previously had the final word. By implication, it portended, too, a social revolution in the South. Many years passed, however, before judicial review afforded Negroes much of the protection that was the first and principal object of the amendment. Indeed, for a decade and a half the amendment seemed to have made surprisingly little change. The Supreme Court invalidated the last Civil Rights Act, but was otherwise at pains to stay aloof from most of the constitutional controversies over Reconstruction; and it declined at first to expand the field of its review of State legislation. Indeed, except for the abolition of slavery and of the supposed right of secession, the Reconstruction period ended with the federal balance apparently not far from its position in 1860. . . .

RESTRICTIONS ON ECONOMIC REGULATION

The details of constitutional interpretation since Reconstruction are too complex for recital here. One persistent trend was the judicial protection of property rights against the growing volume of State legislative and administrative action that attempted to regulate railroads, grain elevators, and other forms of business enterprise. The Supreme Court first recognized corporations as "persons" with standing to invoke the Fourteenth Amendment, and then broadened the meaning of the due process clause of the amendment to give it a substantive, and not merely a procedural, content. What had once been a phrase in the Bill of Rights intended to guarantee the historic forms of trial in criminal cases became by the end of the 19th century a significant constitutional barrier against legislation restricting the liberty of adults to make business contracts. The issue of constitutionality turned on the Court's views as to the reasonableness of the legislation. So a law limiting hours of labor was valid if applied to underground mining, but not to a bakery. Anti-union stipulations in labor contracts could not be allowed. Price regulations were restricted to public utilities, and subject to a judicial review of their reasonableness.

State regulation was cramped by the commerce clause, too. Illinois was prevented from limiting railroad transportation charges on interstate traffic (1886), and Iowa from stopping the sale of intoxicating liquors coming in from neighboring States (1890), although Congress had not yet expressed a national policy on either subject.

Judicial interpretation of the commerce clause and of the due process clause of the Fifth Amendment also put limits on congressional regulation of business activities. The Sherman Anti-Trust Act of 1890 was constitutional, but for a long time it was held not to apply to manufacturers, on the ground that manufacturing was not commerce; its regulation was, therefore, the province of the States. An attempt to outlaw the "yellow dog" contract in railroad employment was an unconstitutional deprivation of liberty without due process.

To the same general end the Tenth Amendment, reserving to the States or to the people all powers not delegated to the National Government, was sometimes made the basis for a narrow construction of congressional powers. Since child labor and agriculture were not mentioned in the list of enumerated powers, their regulation, it was said, was reserved to the States and could not be reached indirectly by the taxing or commerce powers of Congress.

A corollary doctrine led to the recognition of intergovernmental immunities from taxation, both on the salaries of public officials and on the interest on government bonds.

WHERE REGULATION WAS ALLOWED

While the lines of interpretation just sketched tended to limit both State and National regulation of economic enterprise, other regulations during the late 19th and early 20th centuries were receiving the Court's approval. Public health grounds justified compulsory vaccination of people and sanitary inspection of food. Public safety supported building codes and fire precautions. Humanitarian considerations justified limits on work hours for women in factories. Welfare and social justice sustained workmen's compensation laws altering the common law liabilities of master and servant. The need to protect real estate values supported zoning regulations. Revenue needs validated license taxes on carriers. Thus a considerable area was kept open for the States in spite of the Fourteenth Amendment.

Similarly, the powers of Congress were not always narrowly construed. The Court allowed use of the Federal taxing power to drive out colored oleomargarine and to control narcotics. After 1895 and until the Sixteenth Amendment, an income tax was unconstitutional, but a tax on corporate income was permitted when it was called an excise. During the first two decades of this century, the commerce power was extended to cover railroad holding companies, to enable the Interstate Commerce Commission to bring discriminatory intrastate railroad rates into line, to hamper lotteries, and to attack the white slave traffic. Later, the Court sanctioned the use of this power to pursue kidnapers, stolen property, and fugitives from justice across State lines. To use judicial figures of speech, Congress could "clear interstate commerce of obstructions," could "cleanse it of harmful use," and could control anything in "the stream of commerce." Congress also found a way to divest interstate liquor shipments of their immunity from State law. The treaty power opened the way to the regulation of migratory gamebird hunting. The war power was enough to sustain the first National prohibition law, as well as selective service. The postal power became the basis for fraud orders and bans on obscene publications.

RECENT CHANGES

Two related premises regarding the federal system underlay the judicial interpretation of National and State powers for a full half century after 1880. One was that workably clear and distinct boundaries between their respective realms of activity could be drawn in terms of constitutional powers. The other was that the Supreme Court was the final arbiter of the system. Experience showed both assumptions to be illusory. So many judicial precedents of contrary tendency accumulated that the boundary lines became unpredictable and, indeed, a zone of governmental no man's land sometimes appeared to lie between them. On the major issues of National and State power, the Supreme Court during the early 1900's often had a free choice in decision. Having such a choice, the Court was exposed again, as it had been on some earlier notable occasions, to a crossfire of political criticism. The clash culminated in 1937 when the Court began a series of sweeping reversals or modifications of former decisions.

Since 1937, judicial doctrine has recognized the emergence of a new concept of National-State relations, sometimes labelled "cooperative federalism" in contrast with the separatism of the previous era. The concept rests constitutionally on a broad view of National authority, on the abandonment of the due process clause as a source of substantive restraints on State regulation of economic affairs, and on the Court's refusal to entertain taxpayers' suits challenging exercises of the spending power. Coming full circle after 125 years by the route of implied powers, the Supreme Court now gives to the list of powers delegated to Congress in Article I, Section 8, of the Constitution approximately the same broad sweep of meaning conveyed by the Virginia Plan, as quoted earlier. At the same time, the Court has generally refused to invoke the prerogative of review over economic policy that it exercised for 40 years prior to 1937. State and National laws touching economic affairs are no longer held to be deprivations of due process because they conflict with natural rights of property or liberty of contract. The Court has accepted a reading of the general welfare clause that places no discernible judicial limits on the amounts or purposes of Federal spending, although it does not follow that the power to spend carries with it unlimited power to regulate. The potentialities of the spending power were only dimly apprehended before the income tax and the Federal Reserve System opened up new reservoirs of Federal revenues and credit. Grants-in-aid are only one characteristic use of the power, along with many other direct spending and lending programs. Finally, the Court has directed the lower Federal courts to follow State law in handling litigation based on diversity of citizenship, so as to minimize conflicts in the applicable rules of decision.

JUDICIAL REVIEW TODAY

Under judicial doctrine since 1937 the Supreme Court has largely removed itself as a practical factor in determining the economic policies of the States and the Nation. It has not, however, eliminated the historic role of judicial review in our federal system. Two remaining functions are noteworthy here, apart from its task of promoting uniformity of interpretation and filling in the gaps in Federal law. One is the duty of judging when the States have overstepped and encroached on whatever area should be the exclusive domain of Federal regulation, if any, or have actually legislated in conflict with Federal law. The exercise of this function is as old as the Court itself and as recent as the 1955 decision that only the Interstate Commerce Commission, and not a State, can revoke the license of an interstate trucking concern to use the highways.

The other function is very recent in its present-day significance, dating only from 1925, though its roots go back to the Fourteenth Amendment. This is the guardianship of civil liberties. In the face of its withdrawal from supervision over economic policies, the Court during the past 30 years has become noticeably more stern in construing State responsibilities under the Fourteenth Amendment to protect civil and political rights. Beginning in 1925, earlier doctrine has in effect been reversed, and the guarantees of freedom of speech, press, and religion, as well as some (but not all) of the procedural safeguards in criminal cases written in the Bill of Rights against the National Government, have been read also into the due process clause of the Fourteenth Amendment against the States. More recently, racial discriminations have been brought further under the ban of the equal protection clause of the same amendment. In this whole area, in contrast to the field of economic affairs, the Congress has moved slowly, and the Supreme Court has become the principal instrument of Federal surveillance. There is a surface paradox in this extension of National judicial power at the very time the Court is emphasizing its deference to State legislative policy. But the paradox disappears in a view of the purposes of our federal system which puts the strengthening and preservation of basic personal freedoms among the first objects of the Union. . . .

part two

CONSTITUTIONAL
FOUNDATIONS

2
CONSTITUTIONAL FOUNDATIONS

In contrast to the federal constitution that has proved to be amazingly flexible and durable, many state constitutions have proved to be rigid. This rigidity has made it extremely difficult for state and local governments to adjust to changing conditions.

The typical state constitution is too long, too detailed, and contains much material of a statutory nature. The restrictive nature of many of the constitutional provisions hampers the effective and efficient functioning of most state governments. In recent years a trend has started towards constitutional revision. The two newest states, Alaska and Hawaii, entered the Union in 1959 with brief constitutions that emphasized fundamentals and reversed the trend towards longer constitutions.

Dr. Harvey Walker, professor of political science at The Ohio State University, performs a valuable service by examining the validity of ten myths that have developed in conjunction with our state constitutional system; he urges constitution makers to emulate the scientist in challenging myths.

The constitutional commission has been used with increasing frequency since 1941 to facilitate the amending of a state constitution. Dr. Bennett M. Rich, professor of political science at Rutgers University, presents a case history of the 1941–1942 New Jersey constitutional commission and compares its proposals to those drafted by the 1947 New Jersey constitutional convention.

He also assesses the influence the 1941–1942 commission had upon the new constitution ratified by the voters on November 4, 1947, and concludes that the chief advantage of the commission is its educational value.

The civil liberties guaranteed by state constitutions are very similar to the civil liberties guaranteed by the federal constitution. Professor Robert S. Rankin, chairman of the Department of Political Science at Duke University, focuses attention upon the newer civil liberties and problems including discrimination, bureaucracy, labor unions, and subversion.

Harvey Walker
2. Myths and Realities of the State Constitutional System*

Every political and legal system develops a mythology or rationale which purports to explain and justify its existence and usefulness in a logical and convincing manner. In this, the American system differs little from others. Although Americans pride themselves on being realists in such matters, the stock explanations of how the system is constructed and how it works often represent a large element of oversimplification, or even wishful thinking. Like all social institutions, nations, states, and governments change, and explanations need frequent revision if they are to be kept up to date.

There are many examples of this mythology in the American scene. A few which relate to government and its activities will be examined in the light of contemporary knowledge. The case of the separation of powers doctrine has already been discussed. Others which affect constitution-drafting and revision include: (1) the concept of state sovereignty, (2) the constitution as fundamental law, (3) the concept of majority rule, (4) the independence of the judiciary, (5) the relation of legislative form to legislative product, (6) democracy and local self-government, (7) the democratic objectivity of the constitutional convention, (8) the desirability of universal suffrage, (9) the responsibility of political parties, and (10) the place of the expert in government. There are many others, but these should suffice. Obviously, space will permit only a brief statement of each stereotype and the evidence which impeaches it, and a hint of what is required for a realistic approach to the problem.

1. Theoretically, the idea that the states continue to be sovereign and independent as to those functions reserved to them under the Tenth Amendment is unassailable. Actually, the policy of the United States Supreme Court in encouraging the expansion of national power by broad construction of the vague grants made to the national government by the Constitution is resulting in a progressive centralization of governmental authority in Washington. Of prime importance today is the indefinitely expansible character of the taxing clause for the promotion of the gen-

* From *Major Problems in State Constitutional Revision* edited by W. Brooke Graves. (Chicago: Public Administration Service, 1960). pp. 12–17. Reprinted with permission of publisher.

eral welfare. State sovereignty becomes a shadow when political reality demands acceptance of federal grants on the terms laid down by the Congress. While it is true that the states cannot be abolished without constitutional amendment agreed to by all of them, their sovereignty means little if they are reduced to skeletons of their former dignity.

2. We are accustomed to describe our constitutions as the fundamental law and to make them harder to establish or to change than ordinary statutes. But the truth is that constitutions, particularly those of the states, contain many provisions which fall far short of being fundamental in character. Such particulars have been inserted in these documents for various reasons, but most of them add up to a lack of confidence in the legislative organs of the government. Since these constitutional provisions cannot readily be changed to harmonize with the changes in society and culture, they become an incubus preventing the adoption of modern legislation and tying the living present to the dead past. We must learn to distinguish what is fundamental and lasting in value from what is temporary and include only the fundamentals in our constitutional documents, leaving other matters to be acted upon by properly constructed and competent legislatures.

3. Americans are accustomed to assert that theirs is a real democracy where public questions are decided by vote, where the majority rules and the minority cheerfully bows to and follows the decisions thus reached. It is true that a larger proportion of the total population is legally qualified to participate personally in the choice of public officers and the decision of governmental issues in the United States than in many other countries. But many persons, nearly half, who live under the American system of government are disqualified from voting because they are under age or lack an adequate period of residence or citizenship. An even greater proportion fails to participate because of indifference or neglect. It is a rare election that brings out as many as 75 or even 50 per cent of those qualified to vote. More commonly the proportion is much smaller. A vote of 40 per cent is not particularly impressive as an expression of the public will. This situation underlines the importance of great care in further extensions of the suffrage and further education of the people to encourage them to inform themselves on public questions and to participate in elections.

4. The independence of the judiciary is a carefully fostered myth that has some substance but is exaggerated in the public mind. In the national government, where appointees to the bench serve during good behavior, there is more validity in the assumption of independence than in the states in which judges are elected, often for short terms, making the courts painfully dependent upon a public opinion that may be misguided

by journalistic emphasis upon occasional errors rather than upon general competence. Judges are almost universally required to be attorneys today, and thus all are bound by the lawyer's ethical code; but in many states they must depend upon the favor of political parties for their nomination or election and they share the fate of the whole party ticket, rather than being independent of it. Party influence also enters into the choice of federal judges through the custom of senatorial courtesy in confirmation and the natural preferences of a politically chosen chief executive. Although, in general, judges consciously make an effort to be impartial and to seek justice for those who come before them, there are subconscious influences of education and station in life that tend to lead them toward conservative economic and social views which are reflected in their opinions. These considerations need to be kept in mind by those who are charged with the writing or revision of state constitutions. There is no certain remedy for shortcomings in the independence of the judiciary, but it seems clear that there is ample room for improvement.

5. Another persistent myth affecting state government, which is carefully fostered by those who benefit from its continuance, that a legislature organized into two houses that possess substantially equal powers and whose concurrence is required in the enactment of legislation best preserves individual rights. Careful studies by competent scholars show that there is little truth to the assertion that a second house provides a valuable check against the follies of the first. Few bills, indeed, are passed by one house only to be defeated by the other. Where such action occurs it is more likely to be traceable to the fact that one house or the other is gerrymandered to give representation which does not reflect fairly the opinions of the electorate. In fact, because of bicameralism and gerrymandering our state legislatures are likely to be unrepresentative of the people they are designed to serve. This is one of the most serious problems facing state constitution-makers today. Only by making legislatures both representative and efficient can this branch of the government regain the public confidence which is so essential to the discharge of its functions. Many believe that these ends can be achieved best through the adoption of unicameralism, such as exists in Nebraska, in the provinces of Canada, and in virtually all local governments in this country.

6. Local-self-government, home rule for local units, freedom from state legislative control—these have long been the rallying cries of local government officials. The ineptitude of state legislatures in dealing with local problems, the unconscionable waste of time involved in the enactment of special legislation, the tendency toward political manipulation of urban populations for state and national ends have given great impetus to these demands. Yet, under modern conditions they are almost as

anachronistic as the divine right of kings. The reality is that few local governments can operate at all today without state-collected, locally shared taxes. The local units simply do not have an adequate tax base. It would be unrealistic to expect such aid without some measure of state control. What is needed is not freedom from control, but more intelligent exercise of it—better legislatures, better laws, and more expert and less political administration on the part of the states. The growth of immense urban agglomerations into metropolitan areas requires rationalization even at the expense of so-called local autonomy. And state constitution-makers will be called upon to use every ounce of ingenuity they possess to reconcile the general public interest with the local interest.

7. As pointed out earlier, the constitutional convention is a distinctively American contribution to political theory and action. Mythologically, it is the personification of the sovereign people assembled for the discharge of the solemn duty of framing their fundamental law.[1] It is supposed to be above politics and to have no peers among governmental agencies. Yet, experience has shown that the convention rarely rises above the legislature in the quality and experience of its membership and that pressure groups and political parties have significant influence upon its deliberations. The cost of convening and holding a constitutional convention has become practically prohibitive. Many states in recent years have turned from conventions to constitutional commissions that consist of experts who report to the governor and legislature and whose handiwork is submitted for popular vote, if approved by these political organs of the government. The saving in time and expense and the gain in the quality of the work done should commend this new American institutional device to constitution-framers as a replacement for the constitutional convention.

8. It has long been assumed by the devotees of the democratic myth that universal suffrage is devoutly to be desired. There is little doubt that in a democracy the participation of as many intelligent citizens as possible in the choice of officials and the decision of issues strengthens the government and the society. In practice, however, with few exceptions the extensions of the suffrage in this country have not been surrounded by the safeguards needed to insure that this privilege is exercised only by those who are able to use it intelligently. Political intelligence has little direct relationship to chronological age or to citizenship. It does have a relationship to education. It has no relationship to residence, but it does have a relationship to abstract and social intelligence. The consti-

---

[1] Harold M. Dorr, "The Myth of the Constitutional Convention," *Michigan Alumnus Quarterly Review* 22–23 (December 6, 1947).

tution-makers of the future should give careful consideration to the problem of defining those qualified to exercise the privilege of voting. The suffrage is mythologically thought of and spoken of as a right. In a well ordered state it is, rather, a privilege conferred upon those who are competent and willing to exercise it.

9. One of the most carefully documented and earnestly observed myths of our political society is that all or nearly all the evils from which it suffers may be traced to the fact that political parties are not responsible. Those who support this view point to the lack of party discipline in the United States, to the frequent inclusion on party tickets of persons nominated by direct primary of whom the party organization does not approve, and to the refusal of party members in legislative bodies to follow the party platform as evidence to support their contentions. The facts are that the major parties differ little in their platforms, that the direct primary encourages independence of the candidate from the party, and that party leadership, by and large, is not of a caliber that inspires public confidence. Parties have been largely free from control by the state. We are inclined to think and speak of them as private associations of citizens. Yet both common reason and the United States Supreme Court inform us that they are quasi-governmental entities, subject to control in the public interest. State constitution-drafters need to keep this fact in mind in preparing their documents to serve as fundamental law for the new age.

10. A frequent cliché of the professional politician and the political office holder is that "the expert should be on tap, never on top." Jacksonian democracy was based on the myth that the requirements of public posts were so simple that any reasonably intelligent citizen could discharge them to the satisfaction of the public. It may be that the simpler requirements of that less complex age made such a doctrine tolerable, but the development of science and technology, the great expansion of knowledge, and the enormous extension of public education during the last century have made it invalid today. There is no public administrative job in the present-day world that can be filled satisfactorily on a purely political basis. Mayors, county commissioners, governors, and even presidents can no longer discharge the administrative duties of their positions without professional assistance. The myth that an executive can successfully coordinate the activities of 50 or more separate agencies, each theoretically reporting directly to him, has been thoroughly exploded. The whole organization of the machinery of state administration, so far as it is dealt with in the state constitution, needs to be completely revised and reworked by the constitution-makers so that it will square with sound theory and experience in management. In fact, the less said about administrative organization and procedure in the constitution the better will be the

probability that they can be kept abreast of social changes. The state laws dealing with state and local administration need a similar review and revision. It seems safe to say that the place of the expert in modern government is a central one. Unless the political executive follows expert advice, it may be that the expert should be "on top," not merely "on tap."

SUMMARY

So ends the review of a few of the important myths of our state governmental organization and operation as they affect and are influenced by state constitutional development. Others that might have been included were passed over for lack of time and space. The scissors-and-paste-pot type of constitution-drafting so often followed in this country must be challenged if realities rather than myths are to be reflected in our constitutional documents. The framers of constitutions need to emulate the scientist who accepts no event as a fact, or no collection of similar events as obeying natural law, unless it can be observed, analyzed, classified, and subjected to experimental verification. Natural science has progressed and has grown more exact because myths have been challenged and scientific theories have been modified in the light of new discoveries. The social sciences, and particularly political science, are in sad need of similar questioning, rational doubt, and research. State constitution-making is in this sense a field ripe to the harvest.

Bennett M. Rich

3. Convention or Commission?*

Constitutional revision is a live issue in at least a third of the states. In many the problem of how to obtain constitutional reform obscures, and in some instances seems to outweigh, the substantive issues.

One procedural device, the appointive constitutional commission, has been seized upon during the past few years by California, Georgia, Michigan, Minnesota, New Jersey and Tennessee as the means to achieve revision. This procedure is not new. The constitutional commission has been used for almost a century.

Ordinarily the commission has its origin in a resolution of the legislature authorizing appointment of a small group by the chief executive, or

* From *National Municipal Review*. March 1948, pp. 133–139. Reprinted with permission of publisher.

jointly by the governor and the legislature, to consider constitutional revision in whole or in part.

A variation of this procedure is for the governor on his own authority to appoint a commission. Michigan's 32-member commission of 1942 was appointed in this manner.

Another variation is for the legislature to act without reference to the governor at all. California's Legislative Constitutional Revision Committee of 1947, made up of ten assemblymen and ten senators, illustrates this type.

Proponents of the appointive commission cite an impressive list of advantages:

1. The commission is inexpensive.
2. It is small, permitting informal discussion and thorough deliberation.
3. Experts and oustanding public and private leaders of the state can be selected without being forced to seek election to a constitutional convention.
4. The commission is not so susceptible to political pressures and to logrolling as a convention.
5. It can work more expeditiously than a convention.
6. It can study more effectively the experiences of other states.
7. Since continuous sessions are not held the commission has greater opportunity to reflect on problems.
8. The final product of the commission is superior to that of a convention.[1]

It is the purpose of this paper to examine the case history of the 1941–2 constitutional commission in New Jersey and to compare its proposals to the new constitution drawn up in convention at Rutgers University, June 12—September 10, 1947. New Jersey, incidentally, has had greater experience with the commission than any other state. Of 24 known commissions in fourteen states, seven were in New Jersey.[2] . . .

COMMISSION'S ACTIVITIES

The seven-man commission appointed in 1941 was composed of a county freeholder and a judge appointed by the speaker of the House, a

---

[1] See W. Brooke Graves, *American State Government* (3rd edition), page 76; Arthur W. Bromage, *State Government and Administration*, page 82.

[2] New Jersey 1852, 1854, 1873, 1881, 1894, 1905, 1941–2; California 1929; Georgia 1943; Michigan 1873, 1942; Maine 1875; North Carolina 1913, 1932; New York 1872–3, 1890; Pennsylvania 1919–20; Rhode Island 1897, 1912; Tennessee 1946; Vermont 1908–10; Virginia 1927; Washington 1934; West Virginia 1929. In addition, commissions are presently at work in Minnesota and California

state senator and the director of the Princeton Surveys, appointed by the president of the Senate, a state senator and a prominent legal and political figure appointed by Governor Charles Edison, and the editor of a leading newspaper, chosen by the six appointed members. The commission appointed a secretary and two assistants, one in public relations and one in research and drafting. All three non-members participated in discussions.

The commission first considered its approach to the problem, whether to propose a series of amendments or to draft a new document. Because of the number of amendments involved and the difficulty of working them into the old constitution, it was decided to draft a new constitution —notwithstanding the realization that authorization for preparation of a draft constitution was lacking in the law creating the commission.

The commission did most of its work at the University Club in New York, where the members spent Friday afternoons and evenings and Saturday mornings and afternoons over a three-months period in intensive study. It held no public hearings although it invited written suggestions and on a few occasions persons were asked to testify. Technical assistance was furnished by the Princeton Surveys. The commission report was issued in May 1942.

The legislature blocked the commission's suggestion that a public referendum be held on the question of permitting the legislature to submit a revised constitution at the general election of 1942. Instead, it held lengthy hearings and came to the conclusion that because of the war it was inadvisable to do anything.

A year later, as a result of pressure from Walter E. Edge, Republican candidate for governor, the legislature placed before the people the proposal that it sit as a constitutional convention. The proposal carried by a large majority in the general election of 1943.

The legislature then dusted off the commission report and, after certain modifications, presented the proposed constitution to the people in November 1944. This constitution was defeated after a bitter partisan battle.

Governor Alfred E. Driscoll revived the issue and, in his inaugural address in January 1947, called for a limited convention, popularly elected. At the primary election on June 3 the people approved a convention and selected 81 delegates. The convention met at Rutgers University on June 12 and by September 10 had drafted a new document. On November 4, 1947, the new constitution was accepted by an overwhelming majority, to become effective January 1, 1948.[3]

---

[3] See also the *Review*, September 1947, page 452; October 1947, page 513; and December 1947, page 633.

COMMISSION'S INFLUENCE

In attempting to assess the impact of the 1941-2 commission upon the new constitution, it should be pointed out that not every proposal made by the commission and later made a part of the new constitution may fairly be attributed to the commission's influence.

New Jersey's constitution had been subjected to no substantial change since 1875, when a series of amendments were adopted. These amendments, incidentally, were proposed by one of the state's seven commissions, the only one, in fact, whose efforts were crowned with almost complete success. . . .

There can be little doubt, however, that the proposals of the commission of 1941-42 made a deep impression on the thinking of the 1947 convention delegates.

First of all, the language of the two in some respects is identical. The legislative article of the commission report recognized the right of labor to organize and bargain collectively. The Bill of Rights of the new constitution states that persons in private employment shall have the right to organize and bargain collectively, and that persons in public employment shall have the right to organize and make known their grievances through representatives of their own choosing.

The commission report's prohibition on the legislative election or appointment of any executive, administrative or judicial officers is carried into the new constitution almost verbatim, as are prohibitions on certain special laws.

The commission's recommendation that gubernatorial elections be held in odd-numbered years is carried over; so also are the clauses authorizing the governor to investigate state officers and to appoint all officers whose election is not otherwise provided by law. Numerous other instances might be cited.

But a follow-up of language is obviously much less important than a follow-up of basic ideas. Here the influence of the commission is in some respects quite pronounced. Probably the most important carryover is in the judiciary article where the basic principles of court unification and centralized administration were recommended by the commission. Vehemently denounced in 1942, these ideas were accepted without much argument in 1947. . . .

EXECUTIVE PROVISIONS

The commission set the stage also for administrative reform by giving the governor wide powers to reorganize the state's sprawling administrative structure. The challenge which they threw out was accepted only partially by the convention. The commission proposed that the governor be authorized to allocate, by executive order, all agencies among nine named departments.

The convention balked at this as being a usurpation of the legislative function and adopted instead the proposal that only if the legislature refused to act by a given time should the governor act. Even then he was limited to presenting to the legislature, in a special session, his plans for reorganization.

In the matter of appointing department heads also, the convention was unwilling to take the commission's advanced position. Rather than permit the governor to appoint single executives to head all departments, the convention made possible the preservation of certain politically powerful commission-governed agencies by providing that all departments should be headed by a single executive "unless otherwise provided by law."

The commission's proposals were in some cases more advanced than the corresponding provisions of the new constitution. For example, the commission's draft allowed the legislature to provide for absentee voting at any time. The new constitution prohibits civilian absentee voting by its assertion that the legislature may provide for absentee voting by the military in peacetime. Also the legislative council was spelled out by the commission while the new constitution is silent on the subject.

In a surprising number of instances the proposals of the commission were less advanced than the position adopted by the convention. Outstanding failures of the commission to represent the best thinking were its recommendations: (1) prohibiting a second term for the chief executive and (2) requiring limited biennial sessions of the legislature.

The commission repeated a mistake in the old constitution by proposing a definite sum, $1,500, to be paid legislators. It provided for the election of the treasurer, as well as the comptroller, by the legislature. It named the departments among which the administrative agencies were to be allocated. It retained as constitutional officers the county clerk, sheriff, surrogate and coroner. The coroner, incidentally, is not mentioned in the new constitution. . . .

In some instances the commission took no action at all despite obvious need. The $100,000 debt limitation was retained, for example, notwithstanding the growth of the state's budget from $100,000 in 1844 to $150,000,000 a hundred years later.

The commission is open to criticism for an undiplomatic display of political one-sidedness. Membership of the commission consisted only of anti-Hague representatives.

HAGUE OFFENDED

When the report was released, the Hague faction took immediate offense at certain clauses which, they argued, were specifically designed to harass them. One would have overthrown a decision of the Hague-dominated top court, which seriously hampered the legislature in its efforts to investigate cities. Another would have denied a position on the new Supreme Court to Hague's son, by requiring ten years' experience as a member of the bar. At the time the report was issued he was a member of the top court, having been appointed by the previous governor because "it would please his daddy."

Perhaps the greatest weakness of the commission was in its failure to question, let alone attack, what were referred to in the recent convention as the "hot potatoes" of the constitution. The convention was prohibited by law from considering the problem of rural versus urban representation in the legislature—people versus acres. There was no prohibition upon the commission, but the problem was untouched. Nor was the true value tax clause disturbed. This requirement that property be assessed at true value had for years been a subject of intense controversy. The clause on gambling, which permitted big time betting at horse races yet forbade a church or firemen's bingo game, was unchanged.

It is difficult to avoid the conclusion that the commission report was something less than a complete overhauling of the constitution. It attacked vigorously and well certain of the basic weaknesses of the constitution. Much credit is due the commission for its work on the executive and the courts. On the other hand, its omission of important problems, its obvious effort to embarrass the Hague forces, its outdated proposals, its avoidance of controversial issues—all these must be placed to the debit side of its ledger.

On the credit side, however, in addition to the commission's substantive contributions must be recorded its educational value. The commission report was a challenge. It kept the revision issue alive. It set more people to talking about the constitution. It stepped up the educational campaign to make the people constitution-conscious. Had it not been for the commission, it is doubtful whether New Jersey would have a new constitution or one so far ahead of the old as it has today. . . .

CONVENTION ZEALOUS

. . . Fired with an extraordinary zeal to produce a progressive constitution and put an end to seven years of bickering, the delegates worked vigorously and with an unusual degree of harmony. Then, having completed their task, they appropriated a considerable part of the money set aside for the convention to publicize the new constitution. More than that, the delegates themselves worked arduously after the convention adjourned to sell the new document to the people.

All this is beyond the appointive commission. The acceptance or rejection of its proposals is strictly a legislative matter. The commission can pressure the legislature by stirring up public interest through timely press and radio releases. The New Jersey commission did precisely that. Citizens' organizations helped out. But it was not enough. The fact that the commission must report to the legislature is almost certain to be an insurmountable handicap to thorough-going revision.

Nor do many of the advantages claimed for the commission stand up under analysis. A commission is inexpensive, for example, only if its efforts prove successful. The appropriation for the New Jersey commission of 1941-42 was only $5,000; the appropriation for the convention was $350,000. But the one failed; the other succeeded. . . .

As a device for recommending incidental changes, especially those of a technical character, its record is better. Georgia illustrates the recent successful use of the commission as a means of effecting fairly numerous and important modifications short of a general revision. Governor Arnall, who writes glowingly of the commission, observes nevertheless that if a wholly new constitution were to be written, "the commission method would be undesirable and, perhaps, impractical."[4]

The commission has a second function, the importance of which has not been sufficiently appreciated. The commission can be of extraordinary value in stimulating public discussion of constitutional issues and of helping in the formation of policy. This was the one great value of the New Jersey commission. If the commission were freed of the fear of a legislative veto of its proposals, it would be in a position to perform a valuable service for the state. . . .

AN EDUCATIONAL DEVICE

Aside from its use as a device for recommending incidental changes, the chief asset of the commission is educational in nature. It can be used to explore the subject of revision, to examine the best thinking and experience of the country, to assist in stimulating popular discussion, and in formulating and crystallizing public opinion. If the commission is used to perform these services, rather than to act as a substitute for a

---

4 Ellis Arnall, "25 Study Georgia Basic Law," the *Review*, January 1944, page 12.

convention, it can help the state take a firm step toward the ultimate goal of a modern constitution.

This, in the end, is what the 1941 commission did for New Jersey. To that extent the commission was a great success, although it failed in its immediate objective. In fact, it is proper to go even further and to say that the 1947 convention, with only three months in which to work, could not possibly have succeeded as it did had it not been for the commission and the five-year discussion of its work. Without the preliminaries a 1947 convention in New Jersey would certainly have needed many months and the outcome would still have been doubtful.

Robert S. Rankin

4. Our Changing Bills of Rights*

WHY CHANGES OCCUR

Probably fewer alterations are made in a bill of rights than in any other section of a state constitution. This is not difficult to understand. In fact, the question may be raised why any change in a bill of rights is necessary. If rights are truly fundamental then they should be permanent. The problem is only one of drawing them up properly in the first place. Ideally perhaps this view is correct but, as a practical matter, the need for periodic reconsideration is only slightly less strong for civil rights than for other aspects of the fundamental law. Evolving social, political and economic problems affect the entire constitution and the bill of rights is no exception. . . .

NEW PROBLEMS, NEW RIGHTS

We can expect continuing change. As society grows increasingly complex and interdependent, government will probably be called upon increasingly to play a bigger role in our lives. Individuals will seek additional guarantees and protections. Robert Hutchins states that "the principal reason why civil liberties as traditionally defined and defended do not interest the American is that they are inadequate to express the true dimensions of the problem of freedom and justice today."[1] He insists

---

* From *Bills of Rights.* (New York: National Municipal League, 1960), pp. 6–19. Reprinted with permission of publisher.

[1] *Bulletin,* The Fund for the Republic (May 1958), p. 4.

that the individual now needs protection from the possible dangers of a police state, for full freedom of communication, from the arbitrary character of the bureaucratic state and from the "remorseless tendency of the industrial system."

If rights are the outgrowth of historical circumstances, then future developments may be revealed through a close look at current problems.

PROBLEM OF DISCRIMINATION

Fourteen constitutions—in the southern and border states—still specify that the public school system be operated on a racially segregated basis. The constitutions of Georgia, North Carolina, Oklahoma, Texas and Louisiana direct that separate schools shall be provided for persons of the white and colored races. The constitutions of Florida, Kentucky, Mississippi, Tennessee, Virginia and West Virginia accomplish the same purpose by insisting that white and colored persons not be taught in the same school. Alabama, Arkansas and South Carolina provide for racial segregation in still other ways. These provisions have, of course, been nullified by the 1954 decision of the United States Supreme Court holding racial segregation in the public schools unconstitutional under the equal protection clause of the Fourteenth Amendment.

The controversy over desegregation has stimulated again a demand that "equal treatment" statements be included in state bills of rights. Despite that protection already available in the U.S. Constitution, eleven state constitutions now contain equal treatment clauses which apply generally or to specific problems. New York's sweeping statement demands that no person shall, because of race, color, creed or religion, be subjected to discrimination in his civil rights by person, firm, corporation, institution, nor by state, agency or any subdivision of the state. Colorado, New Jersey, Washington and Wyoming ban racial segregation in any form. The constitutions of both Alaska and Hawaii are eloquent examples of this type of guarantee. The Alaska document, in addition to an equal protection of the law provision, specifically states: "No person is to be denied the enjoyment of any civil or political right because of race, color, creed or national origin."[2] The constitution of the 50th state puts it this way: No person may "be denied the enjoyment of his civil rights or be discriminated against in the exercise thereof because of race, religion, sex or ancestry."[3] The strongest statement in an American constitution, however, comes not from a state but from the commonwealth of Puerto Rico:

---

[2] Art. I, sec. 3.
[3] Art. I, sec. 4.

The dignity of the human being is inviolable. All men are equal before the law. No discrimination shall be made on account of race, color, sex, birth, social origin or condition, or political or religious ideas. Both the laws and the system of public education shall embody these principles of essential human equality.[4] . . .

The elimination of discrimination based upon color or religion has received wide publicity, but there are other types equally important: discrimination in employment opportunities, in various organization memberships including labor unions, and in the giving of preferred treatment on whatever basis. These matters as well as racial discrimination will be of concern to constitution writers during the next few decades. Statements against discrimination will probably be added to more state constitutions. Some states will probably pass over the matter, leaving protection of the individual to the federal courts. . . .

PROBLEM OF BIG GOVERNMENT

American political leaders of the late eighteenth century accepted the principle that governmental powers should be separated into legislative, executive and judicial departments. One important corollary of the doctrine of separation of powers in the United States is that broad unlimited legislative powers should not be granted to executive officers. As many new functions have been placed upon the legislative branch, however, there has grown up a strong practice of delegating many of these functions to executive officers. This delegation must be kept within proper limits. One student of government writes with regret that the courts have ruled, in specific cases involving the delegation of powers at the federal level, that:

> At the pleasure of the bureaucracy one may not retain a radio broadcasting license, may not plant tobacco, may not raise sugar cane, must furnish demonstrators for his product to every outlet in an area regardless of circumstances, may be summarily ousted from the directorship of a bank, and may be put out of business for violation of a bureaucracy decree, after only a hearing by the prosecuting officials and decisions by them in their own premises.[5] . . .

The courts have served as watch dogs against arbitrary administrative procedure. Yet both the state and federal judiciary are reluctant to overrule decisions of administrative tribunals. The Supreme Court of Tennessee recently refused to interfere with administrative decisions unless the agency concerned exceeded its authority as granted by statute or violated

---

[4] Art. II, sec. 1.
[5] Spencer R. Girvan, *Rule by Executive Decree under Statutory Delegations, 1789-1950* (unpublished Ph.D. dissertation. Duke University, 1957), p. 400.

a fundamental rule of due process—failure to give adequate notice, conduct a fair hearing, or provide an opportunity for the aggrieved party to present evidence.[6]

These guarantees are important, but are they enough? Is there not a real danger that in an administrative state liberty may be lost by gradual erosion? Could not the desire for administrative efficiency and flexibility lead to practices which subvert freedom without ever being blatantly offensive "to the common and fundamental ideas of fairness and right"?[7]

An effective protection would result from the inclusion in a bill of rights of guarantees from arbitrary administrative action. Certainly a list of procedural and substantive rights specifically applicable to the administrative branch might be a fruitful beginning to effective checks on arbitrary administrative government. Little thought has been given to this problem by state constitutional conventions. Usually nothing more forceful is found in a state constitution than a statement lauding the separation of powers and stating that the three branches of government "ought to be forever separate and distinct from each other."[8] One can only regret that the new state constitutions of Alaska and Hawaii did not include provisions applicable to the administrative process. Certainly state constitutional conventions in the future might consider the possible inclusion in a bill of rights of guarantees like the following:

1. No person shall be bound by an administrative decision unless on a presentation of public notice; nor shall be be subject to the same official for both prosecution and adjudication, nor be deprived of liberty or property unless by a prescribed mode of procedure.
2. In all administrative proceedings, the accused shall have the right to a speedy and public hearing by an impartial arbiter and to be informed of the nature and cause of the accusation, to be confronted with the evidence against him, and to have the benefit of technical assistance in preparing a defense.
3. In administrative hearings, where the amount in controversy shall exceed twenty dollars, or when a fundamental right is involved, the right to a record of the proceedings shall be preserved. Proper appellate procedure must also be provided by legislative action.

The protection of substantive rights is as important as the maintenance of procedural guarantees in administrative actions. Professional licensing affords a striking illustration of this point. One professional group after

---

[6] *Hughes* v. *Board of Commissioners,* 319 S.W. (2d) 481 (1959).

[7] The American Civil Liberties Union has shown considerable interest in freedom from arbitrary action by administrative officials on the state as well as on the national level. See, for example, its report for 1951-53, *Freedom, Justice, Equality,* p. 84, and the 1957 report, *Justice for All,* pp. 21–23.

[8] See North Carolina constitution, Art. 1, sec. 8.

another has sought both legislative and administrative support for the establishment of educational and experience requirements, passage of an examination, and the issuance of a license as prior conditions for an individual to practice his profession.[9] Most of these regulations are proper and necessary, but all involve the delicate problem of balancing the general welfare with individual liberty.

The responsibility of the state to protect the health, morals and safety of its citizens must be weighed against the right of a person to select his own profession, the dangers of a potential monopoly or a return of the medieval guild system, and possible restrictions on consumer choice. The situation is complicated by the insistence of professional groups that regulations be administered by independent boards composed of members of the group concerned. Frequently these boards are not truly representative and employ vague standards in performing their duties, particularly with respect to the rules governing the revoking of licenses.[10] Constitution-makers might be justified in making an entry into a profession a right rather than a privilege, limited, of course, by a clear and present danger to the public welfare.

LABOR AND LABOR ORGANIZATIONS

An outgrowth of industrialization in the United States is a demand for constitutional recognition of the right to organize and bargain collectively. Similarly the successful development of large-scale labor organizations has stimulated a demand among some groups for recognition of a right to work without regard for union membership. So-called right to organize and right to work provisions have ardent partisans and in some states have set off bitter struggles over the question of recognizing, either constitutionally or legislatively, one or the other. These issues today constitute the most active questions involving labor management relations at the state level.

State constitutions, however, do contain references to other matters. The Wyoming constitution declares: "The rights of labor shall have just protection through laws calculated to secure to the laborer proper rewards

---

[9] There are at least 75 professions covered by regulatory provisions. They vary from the profession of a medical doctor to that of a guide-dog trainer. See "Occupational Licensing Legislation in the States," *State Government*, XXV (December 1952), 275.

[10] See Robert J. Frye, *Government Licensing—The Alabama Pattern* (University, University of Alabama, Bureau of Public Administration, 1958). See also *Schware* v. *Board of Bar Examiners of New Mexico*, 353 U. S. 232 (1957), and *Konigsburg* v. *State Bar of California*, 353 U. S. 252 (1957).

for his service and to promote the industrial welfare of the state."[11] The constitutions of Utah and Mississippi contain similar general statements of doubtful judicial enforceability. Six state constitutions—those of Kentucky, Louisiana, Missouri, Pennsylvania, Texas and Virginia—prohibit private local or special laws regulating labor. Arizona, North Dakota and Utah constitutionally ban the exchange of "black lists" by corporations. State constitutions refer to other matters lying on the periphery of "rights," such as those regulating the working conditions of women and children, guarantying helpful and safe working conditions and permitting establishment of minimum wages. None of these are presently controversial and few if any produce constitutional problems. The battle lines today are drawn around labor unions.

W. Brooke Graves writes that the right to organize "is one of the rights now in the process of establishment."[12] His evidence is substantial. New York in 1938, Missouri in 1945, New Jersey in 1947 and Florida in 1955 granted constitutional recognition of the right to organize and to bargain collectively. The fifth edition (1948) of the *Model State Constitution* of the National Municipal League contains the following provision, the language coming largely from the New Jersey constitution:

> Citizens shall have the right to organize, except in military or semi-military organizations not under the supervision of the state, and except for purposes of resisting the duly constituted authority of this state or of the United States. Public employees shall have the right, through representatives of their own choosing, to present to and make known to the state, or any of its political subdivisions or agencies, their grievances and proposals. Persons in private employment shall have the right to bargain collectively through representatives of their own choosing.[13]

Six state constitutions now contain "right to work" provisions which in effect prohibit the closed shop and union shop agreements between labor and management.[14] Over one-third of the states accomplish this through legislation. Nebraska's constitutional provision adopted in 1946 reads as follows:

> No person shall be denied employment because of membership in or affiliation with or resignation or expulsion from a labor organization or because of refusal to join or affiliate with a labor organization; nor shall any individual or corporation or association of any kind enter into any contract, written or oral, to exclude persons from employment because of membership in or nonmembership in a labor organization.[15]

---

[11] Art. I, sec. 22.
[12] *Op. cit.*, p. 239.
[13] Art. I, sec. 103.
[14] Arizona, Arkansas, Florida, Kansas, Nebraska and South Dakota.
[15] Art. XV, sec. 13.

Strong cases can be built for and against both right to work and right to organize provisions. From the constitutional point of view the question is whether a statement relating to either of these has a place in the fundamental law of the state. Are these matters truly fundamental? Is there overwhelming public support for one position or another? Or are the questions still so involved in controversy as to suggest that the people as yet have not developed sufficient agreement to warrant putting such matters in the constitution? Perhaps the wisest course is to follow the examples of our newest states, Hawaii and Alaska, which make no reference to these matters, leaving to the legislature the determination of the course of action which should be followed.

PROBLEM OF SUBVERSION

Constitution-makers, fully aware of the necessity and great value of the rights they place in a constitution, also recognize the possibility of the abuse of these rights. The great value of due process of law and of the protection from self-incrimination should not be forgotten, because undesirables and Communists take advantage of these provisions. Forty-four states now have laws which penalize those who advocate the violent overthrow of the federal or state governments. Potential conflict between these statutes and certain sections of a state bill of rights is immediately apparent. These conflicts have been left to the courts to determine.

Fortunately for the states the Supreme Court of the United States has made the control of subversion primarily a federal responsibility. In *Pennsylvania* v. *Nelson,* the Supreme Court approved the findings of a federal district court to the effect that: "Sedition against the United States is not a local offense. It is a crime against the nation. As such it should be prosecuted and punished in the federal courts. . . . It is not only important but vital that such prosecutions should be exclusively within the control of the federal government."[16]

Many state officials expressed the fear that this case opened the door for the federal government to invade a field of law occupied by the states and to supersede state law with federal law. The Supreme Court was quick to limit the possible application of *Pennsylvania* v. *Nelson* for, in the case of *Uphaus* v. *Wyman,* it held that the Nelson case was limited to the field of sedition and that federal law in the field of sedition superseded state law only when both proscribed the same conduct. Justice Clark, speaking for the court, said that it did not take away from the states the right to

---

[16] 350 U. S. 497, 505, (1956).

protect themselves for "all the opinion proscribed was a race between federal and state prosecutors to the courthouse door."[17]

States, therefore, can continue to prosecute for sedition against the state itself and can conduct investigations in this area. The control of sedition while primarily a responsibility of the federal government is also a matter for the states. Irrespective of the agency that exercises this power, control of suversion is a difficult assignment. Most citizens deplore the thoughts and deeds of the Communists but agree basically with Thomas Jefferson who wrote: "To suffer the civil magistrate to intrude his powers into the field of opinion, and to restrain the possession or propagation of principles on supposition of their ill tendency, is a dangerous fallacy."[18]

ONE PROBLEM OF LAW ENFORCEMENT

One result of the hearings conducted before the Kefauver Committee on Interstate Crime was to convince the people of America that crime is big business and that the criminal is using the best scientific equipment to expedite his work. To cope with this situation, law enforcement officials have also used to their advantage new means of securing information some of which, in the minds of many, violate the eighteenth century idea of private rights. Probably the best known of these methods is that of wiretapping. The police consider wiretapping an appropriate manner of coping with the criminal; others consider it a violation of the right of privacy. Shall a statement forbidding wiretapping and the admission of evidence gained in this manner be inserted in state constitutions? There is no clearcut answer to this question. Most state constitutions prohibit "unwarranted search and seizures" and leave to the courts the responsibility of determining what comes within this classification.

The New York constitution of 1938 prohibits wiretapping. The constitution of Puerto Rico has a similar section. Neither the Alaskan nor Hawaiian constitution mentions wiretapping. Doubt remains whether wiretapping is in some cases a violation of the right of privacy. Also it is possible there is sufficient protection in the constitutional bar against unwarranted search and seizure. Then, too, the Supreme Court has said that police methods offensive to human dignity are ruled out by the due process clause of the Fourteenth Amendment.[19] For these reasons there has been no strong concerted demand to include a provision of this nature in state constitutions.

---

[17] 27 Law Week 4394, p. 4395 (1959).

[18] An Act for Establishing Religious Freedom, W. W. Hening, ed., *Statutes at Large of Virginia*, XII (Richmond, R. W. and G. Barton, 1823), 85.

[19] *Rochin* v. *California*, 342 U. S. 165 (1952).

THE INDIVIDUAL AND THE COURTS

A basic element of each state bill of rights affords all citizens equal treatment in the courts. This is most often accomplished through inclusion of a broad guarantee of "due process of law." The courts are then left with the responsibility of defining and spelling out the exact meaning of this term. It is also common practice to list in a bill of rights individual steps and requirements considered necessary to give litigants and those accused of crime a fair trial. Matters such as methods of indictment, jury trial, double jeopardy, self-incrimination, excessive bail, cruel and unusual punishment and many other procedural requirements are the subject matter of these sections. . . .

Space does not permit a discussion of each procedural right, but one merits special consideration here—the right to counsel. Is this a basic right and should a statement to this effect be placed in a state constitution? An accused person can rely upon three possible constitutional bases for his request for legal counsel: the Fourteenth Amendment to the U.S. Constitution, the due process of law clause in his state constitution or a specific constitutional statement giving a right to counsel.

The Sixth Amendment to the U.S. Constitution states that in all criminal prosecutions the accused shall have the assistance of counsel for his defense. The Supreme Court of the United States has never held that the provisions of the Sixth Amendment are included in the Fourteenth. On the contrary, the Court in *Gallegos* v. *Nebraska* held: "The federal constitution does not command a state to furnish defendant's counsel as a matter of course. . . . Lack of counsel at state noncapital trials denies federal constitutional protection only when the absence results in a denial to accused of the essentials of justice."[20]

In many states legal counsel is essential to a fair trial and, therefore, is included in the meaning of due process, but courts in various states differ as to the essential character of the legal counsel requirement. Specific cases have required that the appointee must be competent and that he be given sufficient time to prepare his case.

Inclusion in state courts of the legal counsel requirement gains more and more favor. Quibbling by courts as to the necessity of counsel in each particular case is avoided. Also, if legal aid has value, it should afford protection to the poor and to the uninformed. In conclusion, there is real justification for the inclusion of particular guarantees as the one above

[20] 342 U. S. 55, 64 (1951).

in a bill of rights. Constitution-makers have not added too many stipulations. Particularly few additions and changes have been made to procedural requirements. This speaks well not only for the constitution-makers but also for the proper interpretation of due process by the courts.

part three

INTERGOVERNMENTAL RELATIONS

3

FEDERAL-STATE AND FEDERAL-LOCAL RELATIONS

The United States constitution, adopted in 1788, delegated substantial grants of power to the federal government, yet reserved a vast amount of power to the states. Both federal and state powers have expanded over the years. Although there have been occasional conflicts between the federal government and the states, relations generally have been cooperative and harmonious.

Throughout the history of the United States the question of the proper division of governmental powers between the national government and the states has been debated. The debate has grown stronger since the 1930s when the federal government embarked upon a major expansion of its activities.

Concern with the apparent trend towards centralization led to the creation by act of Congress in 1953 of the Commission on Intergovernmental Relations, a bipartisan commission of twenty-five members that reported in 1955. In 1959 the Advisory Commission on Intergovernmental Relations was established as a permanent bipartisan commission of twenty-six members to study continuously the relationships between the national, state, and local levels of government.

The excerpt from the 1955 report of the Commission on Intergovernmental Relations appraises the expansion of federal activities and discusses the question of the proper relationship that should exist between the federal government and the states. The Commission urged the federal government to scrutinize carefully the need for federal participation in present and proposed programs and to hold its participation to the minimum necessary to ensure the success of the programs.

The number and amount of federal grants-in-aid to states and localities has increased greatly since the 1930s to the point where they are a major source of state and local revenue.

The article by the Federal Reserve Bank of Boston describes the purposes of federal grants-in-aid, the basis of making grants, and examines the extent to which high income states contribute to low income states; the conclusion is reached that redistribution of income within states is more important than redistribution between states for certain federal grant programs.

The traditional short-changing of cities by state legislatures has induced city officials to look to Washington for assistance in solving their problems. The growth in federal aid to local governments has been phenomenal since the Federal Housing Act of 1949 was enacted; a reading of "New Tools for Housing and Community Development," prepared by the Housing and Home Finance Agency, reveals the magnitude of federal aid programs in the areas of low rent public housing, urban renewal, urban planning, community facilities, public housing for the elderly, conservation of open space, and urban mass transportation.

5. Introduction*

The United States has made a major contribution to the art of government by its successful operation of a federal system. This success has been especially noteworthy in view of the enormous strains on the system caused by military and economic emergencies of the sort that have occurred during the past quarter-century, and by the cumulative effect of the more gradual changes brought about by a dynamic and expanding economy.

In recent years, the almost continuous presence of a crisis, either economic or military, has accounted for vast expansions of National activities. Many of these programs have been of an emergency nature; a great many others, however, have lastingly influenced the division of governmental responsibilities between the National Government and the States.

Profound as their impact has been, war and economic crisis have not been the only major causes of the growing pressure for National action. Equally insistent pressures have been brought about by intensified industrialization and population shifts from rural to urban areas; new advances in transportation and communications; and, flowing from these developments, greatly accelerated mobility of people and interchange of ideas.

These changes have been reflected in part in a growing governmental concern with the economic and social welfare of the individual. And many individuals who once looked no further than their city hall or State capitol now turn toward Washington when problems arise. We are doing today as a Nation many things that we once did as individuals, as local communities, or as States.

The extensive readjustment of National and State responsibilities in recent decades was bound to stir questioning of the continued vitality of our federal system. Candor would probably compel many thoughtful Americans to admit having experienced some fear or occasional doubt on this score, at one stage or another of this momentous period.

To many, the expanding powers of the National Government seemed destined to reduce the States to mere administrative provinces. This prospect was sharpened by Supreme Court decisions which appeared to have the effect of removing almost all significant constitutional limitations on

* Commission on Intergovernmental Relations. From *A Report to the President for Transmittal to the Congress.* (Washington, D.C.: U.S. Government Printing Office, June 1955), pp. 1–6.

the expansion of National activities. It was often aggravated by the conviction that many of the newer activities constituted invasions of individual freedom and ought not to be undertaken by any level of government. Thus the fear of usurpation of State rights was frequently combined with the fear of undue paternalism.

On the other hand, many who had welcomed the expansion of National authority began to wonder if our system of federalism had become an obstacle to effective government. Their fear was that our form of government would prove too slow-moving and cumbersome to deal with the intricate social and economic problems of an increasingly interdependent society and to cope with authoritarian regimes of the Fascist, Nazi, and Communist varieties. Our governmental system must be remodeled, many thought, if it is to be adjusted properly to 20th-century conditions.

The Commission views both positions as extremes. The National Government and the States should be regarded not as competitors for authority but as two levels of government cooperating with or complementing each other in meeting the growing demands on both. Chiefly because of war and the recurring threat of war, the expenditures of the National Government have grown much larger than those of the States and localities. But State and local activities also continue to expand. Equally significant is the increased interest in and recognition of the importance of State and local governments as essential elements in an effective federal structure.

The continuing vitality of State and local government affords the most solid evidence that our federal system is still an asset and not a liability. To be sure, it is not a neat system, and not an easy one to operate. It makes large demands on our sense of responsibility, our patience, our self-restraint. It requires toleration of diversity with respect to taxes, roads, schools, law enforcement, and many other important matters. Those who have a passion for streamlining can easily point to awkward features.

Nevertheless, the federal principle, along with the principle of checks and balances, remains one of the great institutional embodiments of our traditional distrust of too much concentrated authority in government or, to state it positively, of our traditional belief in distribution of authority among relatively independent governing bodies. Experience has demonstrated the wisdom of the view of the Founding Fathers that individual freedom is best preserved in a system in which authority is divided and in which diverse opinions are reconciled through the processes of representative government. . . .

But experience amply justifies the view that our federal system, with the degree of flexibility that it permits, can be adapted to crises of the present and future as successfully as it has been to those of the past. As an instrument of positive government, it possesses—at least for a nation as large and diverse as ours—a clear advantage over a strongly centralized government. In helping to bolster the principle of consent; in facilitating wide participation in government; in furnishing training grounds for leaders; in maintaining the habit of local initative; in providing laboratories for research and experimentation in the art of government; in fostering competition among lower levels of government; in serving as outlets for local grievances and for political aspirations—in all these and many other ways, the existence of many relatively independent and responsible governments strengthens rather than weakens our capacity for government. . . . Our system of federal government can be in proper balance, therefore, only when each level is effective and responsible.

Responsibility implies restraint as well as action. The States have responsibilities not only to do efficiently what lies within their competence, but also to refrain from action injurious to the Nation; the National Government has responsibilities not only to perform, within the limits of its constitutional authority, those public functions the States cannot perform, but also to refrain from doing those things the States and their subdivisions are willing and able to do. . . .

Far from weakening the National Government, the strengthening of State and local government would increase its effectiveness. The responsibilities that unavoidably must fall on the National Government are formidable. The fullest possible utilization of the resources of the State and local governments is desirable both to supplement National action where National action is necessary, and to relieve the National Government of having to divert its resources and energies to activities that could be handled as well or better by the States and their subdivisions.

The National Government has therefore an interest, as well as a responsibility, in scrutinizing with the greatest care the degree of National participation in existing or proposed programs. . . . In addition to appraising carefully in each instance the need for National participation, the National Government should hold essential participation to the minimum required for attaining its objective. In all of its actions the National Government should be concerned with their effects on State and local governments.

The preservation and strengthening of our federal system depend in the last analysis on the self-restraint and responsibility, as well as the wisdom, of our actions as citizens. If we are not willing to leave some room for diversity of policy, to tolerate some lack of uniformity in standards, even in many matters which are of national concern and about which we may feel strongly, the essence of federalism, even if not the legal fiction, will have been lost. We must also realize that it can be lost, or its vitality sapped, by nonuse of State and local initiative as well as by over-use of National authority. We have therefore as citizens a responsibility to see to it that those legitimate needs of society that could be met by timely State and local action do not by default have to be met by the National Government.

Precise divisions of governmental activities need always to be con-sidered in the light of varied and shifting circumstances; they need also to be viewed in the light of principles rooted in our history. Assuming efficient and responsible government at all levels—National, State, and local—we should seek to divide our civic responsibilities so that we:

Leave to private initiative all the functions that citizens can perform privately; use the level of government closest to the community for all public functions it can handle; utilize cooperative intergovernmental arrangements where appropriate to attain economical performance and popular approval; reserve National action for residual participation where State and local governments are not fully adequate, and for the continuing responsibilities that only the National Government can undertake.

6. Income Redistribution in Federal Grants-in-aid*

Federal grants-in-aid to state and local governments last year amounted to $7 billion, or about 7 percent of total federal cash outgo. The growing importance of grants-in-aid is indicated by Administration estimates that such expenditures (including proposed new programs) will rise by about one-third from 1961 to 1963.

The payment of $7 billion to state and local governments and the collection of a corresponding amount of federal revenues necessarily involves some redistribution of income among the states. Largely because of the progressiveness of the federal tax system, interstate redistribution occurs even when such redistribution is not a significant objective of the programs involved. However, many grant-in-aid programs are designed to take account of differences in the needs of the states for various kinds of aid and of the capacity of the states to obtain revenues from their own sources.

* Federal Reserve Bank of Boston. From *New England Business Review*. June 1962, pp. 1–4. Reprinted with permission of publisher.

To what extent do the high-income states on balance contribute to the low-income states? To what extent do these programs result in aid funds returning to the same states which contributed the revenue to support these programs? How important is interstate redistribution in the determination of these programs?

Federal grant-in-aid programs serve a variety of purposes. One of these (the one most pertinent to this article) is to ensure greater equity in the state and local governmental services where national objectives are also involved. Some states have relatively large fiscal "needs." Thus sparsely populated states have a high per capita need for highway expenditure, but they may also be low-income states. Some states have high proportions of welfare recipients and may also have a relatively low "fiscal capacity" (as measured by per capita personal income).

Among the objectives of grant programs, perhaps the most important is to stimulate the states to provide new or greater services in which there is a substantial national interest. The interstate highway aid program is largely governed by national interests of interstate commerce and defense. This is reflected in the Federal assumption of 90 per cent of the cost of interstate highways. On the other hand, the Federal participation for primary, secondary and urban roads is in general 50 percent. At the same time differences in state needs are reflected in the allocation of funds by state on the basis of area, population and road mileage. Thus equalization of needs, stimulation of state activity, and provision for national interests are mixed in the federal road building program.

Another purpose of federal grants is to provide support for certain services through the federal rather than the state-local tax system. Local governments depend largely on the property tax and state governments largely on sales and excise taxes while the Federal government depends heavily on the individual income tax. Thus a large new burden on state-local governments may be more equitably supported through federal taxation. Public assistance grants in the 1930's represented an attempt to put a part of the burden on federal rather than state-local taxes. In recent years it has been argued that the scale of public education services is more than state-local financing alone can equitably provide.

Some grant-in-aid programs fill specific needs and their purposes bear little relation to differences in the fiscal positions of the states or of local government as a whole within the state. Education aid for federal "impact" areas (such as defense installations), though based on a specific local need, has little relation to the fiscal position of each state. Similarly, urban renewal grants are related to a specific local need which probably bears little relation to relative state fiscal positions.

Different objectives are mixed in various ways in different programs. Consequently, it is difficult to make any over-all judgment on the extent to which further "equalization" of state needs and resources is desirable. That would depend upon a case by case analysis of grant programs. Various public and private evaluations of grant-in-aid programs have suggested that greater weight should be given to differences both in state and fiscal needs and in fiscal resources or capacity.

EQUALIZATION IN GRANTS

Two major programs account for the greater part of federal grants-in-aid, namely highway aid and public assistance grants. The highway aid program has now become the largest single program. Public assistance grants account for more than half of all grant-in-aid expenditures financed through regular budget accounts, and half of public assistance grants are for old age assistance.

As noted above, highway grants are related to state needs as measured by area, population and road mileage. Grants for the interstate system are based on approved mileage and take account of the need for simultaneous completion of the system in all states. On the tax side, highway aid is financed by specified taxes on highway users, chiefly the 4¢ per gallon tax on gasoline. While state differences in needs are taken into account, differences in fiscal capacities are not taken into account except indirectly insofar as they are correlated with gasoline consumption.

Under public assistance programs each state determines its own eligibility requirements and standards of need subject to certain federal conditions. However, the Federal Government contributes a larger share of assistance payments where average state-local payments are small than where they are large. In 1958 for the first time the federal share of assistance payments was made to depend in part on the size of state per capita income in relation to the national average (within specified limits).

The formula for hospital construction grants used in the Hill-Burton Act is perhaps the best example of an equalization provision under which low-income states receive more federal dollars in relation to their population than high-income states and are also required to spend proportionately less for matching purposes. Needs are measured on the basis both of population and per capita personal income. Moreover, there is a sliding scale of matching requirements whereby the highest income states put up two dollars for every one dollar of federal aid received, while low-income states put up as little as one dollar for every two dollars of aid.

Similar provisions taking account of relative needs and fiscal capacities among the states are applied under the national school lunch program, the special school milk program, aids for vocational rehabilitation, waste treatment works and rural libraries. Such a provision has been included in proposed programs for aid for school construction and teachers' salaries.

Grants on the basis of state-wide indexes do not necessarily mean equitable treatment among localities. That depends on development of suitable methods of intrastate allocation of funds. In some cases federal law specifies the basis on which intrastate allocations are to be made.

REDISTRIBUTION BY STATE AND REGION

The extent of redistribution by state involved in federal grant-in-aid programs can be estimated by comparing the distribution of the federal tax burden by state with the distribution of grants-in-aid by state.

Actual grant payments (apportionments in the case of highway aid) to the state are taken as a good measure of the distribution of the benefits of these programs. However, the distribution of the *burden* of federal taxes by state must be estimated because official tax collection data reflect the place of payment or collection of taxes, not the location of persons who actually bear the tax burden. Thus over 90 percent of tobacco taxes are collected in Kentucky, Virginia and North Carolina, but the burden is borne by consumers in every state. Corporation income taxes generally reflect the location of head offices of firms, not the location of stockholders or customers. Consequently, the distribution of the tax burden by state must be estimated by allocating tax receipts on the basis of various economic series deemed to reflect the state distribution of the tax burden. The allocation used here is a Tax Foundation formula.

For purposes of comparison it can be assumed that in the aggregate for every dollar of federal aid one dollar must be raised in taxes. For grants-in-aid financed out of general fund taxes, the distribution by state of the tax burden required for grants-in-aid is the same as that for total general fund taxes. Highway aid can be compared with the burden of highway user taxes by state (those earmarked for the trust fund).

A comparison of the tax burden required for grants-in-aid with actual payments by state indicates which states on balance are the net gainers and which are the net losers from interstate redistribution.

Interstate redistribution has a distinct regional pattern: in general the northeastern states and those bordering the Great Lakes contribute a larger share of taxes than they receive in grants. On the other hand, the central, southern and mountain states are those receiving a larger share of grants than they contribute in the tax burden. California, Texas and Florida are the exceptions in the South and West, while Vermont, New Hampshire, Rhode Island and Maine are the exceptions in the Northeast.

The comparison in the table can also be used to estimate what proportion of grant-in-aid funds return to the same states which bore the burden of the required taxes. Such a calculation indicates that for budgetary grant-in-aid programs interstate redistribution amounts to about one-quarter of the total funds involved. The remaining three-quarters is the proportion of these funds making the "round trip" back to the same states to which a corresponding amount of revenues is attributable.

FEDERAL GRANTS-IN-AID COMPARED WITH TAX BURDEN
Fiscal Year 1961

	Budget Accounts		Budget Accounts Plus Highway Aid (Trust Fund)		
	$ Millions		$ Millions		
	Grants-in-Aid	Tax Burden for Grants*	Total Grants** in-Aid	Tax Burden for Grants	Tax Burden Per Dollar of Aid Received
TOTAL	3,931	3,931	6,571	6,571	$1.00
NEW ENGLAND	224	283	382	422	1.11
Maine	24	17	39	33	.83
New Hampshire	12	13	26	22	.85
Vermont	10	7	30	13	.43
Massachusetts	115	139	180	201	1.12
Rhode Island	19	20	32	31	.97
Connecticut	44	87	73	122	1.66
MIDEAST	624	1,097	1,035	1,564	1.51
GREAT LAKES	562	845	1,050	1,370	1.30
PLAINS	369	280	623	535	.86
SOUTHEAST	1,067	537	1,660	1,097	.66
SOUTHWEST	409	243	638	507	.79
ROCKY MOUNTAIN	131	82	263	163	.62
FAR WEST	546	564	920	914	.99

*Total grants as shown in the first column distributed by state on the basis of a Tax Foundation allocation of the burden of federal taxes (excluding trust fund taxes) by state. Table excludes shared revenues, loans and repayable advances, grants to territories, and grants for administration of unemployment compensation and employment services.

**Total highway aid distributed by state on the basis of a Bureau of Public Roads allocation of highway tax burdens.

Source: Grants-in-Aid — Treasury Department and Bureau of Public Roads; tax burden estimates — Tax Foundation.

Highway aid (trust fund program) involves less redistribution, although the interregional redistribution involved runs for the most part in the same directions as for other grant-in-aid programs. Only about 12 percent of highway aid funds represents interstate redistribution.

It is evident that the wealthier states in general contribute more in taxes than they get back in grants, while the poorest states get back considerably more in grants than they contribute in taxes for these programs.

INCOME RANK AND TAX BURDEN FOR AID

Ten States with Lowest per Capita Personal Income in 1960	Tax Burden per Dollar of Aid Received** Fiscal Year 1961
West Virginia	.45
Louisiana	.34
Georgia	.43
North Carolina	.57
Tennessee	.49
Kentucky	.46
Alabama	.35
South Carolina	.55
Arkansas	.27
Mississippi	.24

Ten States with Highest per Capita Personal Income in 1960*	Tax Burden per Dollar of Aid Received** Fiscal Year 1961
Delaware	2.49
Connecticut	2.01
Nevada	.89
New York	2.13
California	1.18
New Jersey	2.40
Illinois	1.62
Massachusetts	1.21
Maryland	1.43
Ohio	1.46

*Excludes District of Columbia and Alaska.
**Excludes highway aid program.

Historically, the extent of redistribution by state in programs other than highway aid has increased. However, the size and relative importance of the highway aid program over the last three years has reduced the extent of interstate redistribution for total grant-in-aid programs.

SIGNIFICANCE OF INTERSTATE REDISTRIBUTION

The allocation of the burden of taxation and the benefits of expenditure programs to particular geographical areas involves awkward statistical and conceptual problems. The benefits of highway construction, for example, are broadly diffused and a state allocation of benefits is necessarily somewhat artificial. Some would object to any specific allocation of benefits on grounds that with the mobility of our population, health, education and other aids may provide substantial indirect benefits to states other than the one receiving the funds.

Nevertheless, allocations of burdens and benefits by area (as well as by income class) continue to be of wide interest. Interstate redistribution reflects attempts to take account of differences in state fiscal needs and capacities and there is evidence that greater weight should be given in many programs to these differences. The problem of equitable treatment of different states in grant-in-aid programs remains even though equalization of fiscal needs and resources may not be a major policy objective.

Redistribution by state reflects only one aspect of these programs. For some programs redistribution *within* states is much more important than redistribution among states. Public assistance programs are designed to redistribute income from the "haves" to the "have-nots." Urban renewal and public housing projects serve to redistribute income from suburbs with high fiscal capacity to core cities with low fiscal capacity. In these cases financing through the federal tax system provides a more effective redistribution than financing at the state and local levels.

Finally, these programs cannot be evaluated by a consideration of redistributive effects alone. Their incentive effects, their impact on state-local finances, and their general objectives must also be considered.

7. New Tools for Housing and Community Development*

The Housing Act of 1961 . . . greatly increased the scope and effectiveness of the Federal Government's program of aids to housing and community development.

Existing programs designed for conditions of earlier days have been updated and in some cases expanded to accord with present needs. Gaps have been filled with new measures directed toward needs and market areas not previously covered. The old and the new have been blended into a comprehensive, up-to-date program supporting the national goal set by Congress in 1949, of a "decent home and a suitable living environment for every American family."

---

* Housing and Home Finance Agency. (Washington, D.C. 1961).

The program recognizes that accomplishments in housing and community development must depend on local initiative and responsibility. On the principle of help to those who help themselves, it offers a wide variety of aids to individuals and communities that are ready to put their own resources to work in solving their problems.

What has been done with the Federal assistance available in past years gives some indication of the accomplishments possible under the revised and enlarged program now authorized. Benefits of the aid programs administered by the Housing and Home Finance Agency, the arm of the Federal Government most concerned with housing and urban affairs, have reached into virtually every community of the country.

HOME FINANCE

By the end of 1960, more than 5.8 million homes had been financed with mortgages insured by the Federal Housing Administration, and FHA insurance had been used in providing almost 900,000 dwellings in multifamily developments. More than 24 million property improvement loans had been insured by FHA.

The Housing Act of 1961 not only continues and liberalizes basic FHA programs—it gives the Federal Housing Administration responsibility for pioneering attacks on such persistent problems as the deterioration of our existing housing supply and the chronic shortage of housing for families of moderate income. Through these new directions, the Act brings the tested techniques of FHA insurance programs into full participation in the over-all effort to supply good housing for all and to set cities on the course of sound future development. The new responsibilities of the FHA will be described in more detail later. Its basic mortgage insurance authorization is continued for the next four years without limit as to amount. The Act lowers downpayment requirements, raises maximum mortgage amounts, and increases maximum maturities from 30 to 35 years. Also, its rental housing program is broadened by making individuals or groups of individuals and partnerships eligible to borrow on FHA-insured mortgages.

LOW RENT PUBLIC HOUSING

By the end of 1960, approximately 1,400 communities had received aid from the Public Housing Administration on 3,351 low rent public housing projects which would provide homes for nearly 600,000 low-income families. Some 115,000 were still in planning or construction stages.

An additional 100,000 dwelling units are authorized by the Housing Act of 1961, the largest single authorization for the program since 1949.

With this help communities can go on with the job of rehousing their low-income families. Local authorities are given special help in housing elderly persons through higher Federal annual contributions for that purpose. Greater local discretion in setting admissions and continued occupancy policies is provided for also. And local agencies, public or private, can now receive grants from the Housing Administrator for development and demonstration of improved means of providing housing for low income persons.

URBAN RENEWAL

Federal grants totaling about $1.9 billion by the end of 1960 had been reserved by the Urban Renewal Administration to assist in meeting the costs of 870 slum clearance and urban renewal projects in 475 different communities.

The 1961 Act authorizes an additional $2 billion in capital grant funds, and makes it available until used. It raises the Federal share of urban renewal costs from two-thirds to three-fourths for smaller communities— those having a population of 50,000 or less (150,000 or less in economically distressed areas). It raises from 20 percent to 30 percent the proportion of Federal grant funds that can be used for nonresidential projects. Thus the new Act permits communities to proceed with their slum clearance and redevelopment programs with greater continuity and a broader choice of methods. Business firms displaced by urban renewal activities also benefit from greater Federal assistance. The dollar limit on Federal relocation payments to such firms is removed, and they are made eligible for Small Business Administration loans on special terms.

URBAN PLANNING

Nearly 1,500 small localities in 39 States were benefitting at the close of 1960 from URA grants for comprehensive urban planning. In addition, assistance had been given to 112 metropolitan and regional planning agencies in 34 States, including those having jurisdiction across State lines, and to 10 States for State-wide planning. There were in all 493 approved projects, most of which involved planning for areas including several localities.

The 1961 Act raises the Federal share of urban planning costs from one-half to two-thirds, and increases the grant authorization from $20 million to $75 million—more planning is made possible per local dollar expended.

COLLEGE HOUSING

By the end of 1960, the Community Facilities Administration had approved more than 1,200 loans totalling nearly $1.2 billion to help colleges finance construction of badly needed student and faculty housing. Also aided in this program, and included in these totals, are hospitals needing housing for student nurses and medical interns. More than 200,000 accommodations had been completed, and over 43,000 were under construction.

The revolving fund from which these loans are made is authorized by the 1961 Act to be increased by $300 million in July of each of the four years from 1961 to 1964. This $1,200 million increase will bring the total fund to $2 ⅞ billion. The Act also approves loans to nonprofit corporations which provide housing for more than one educational institution. With the availability of Federal loan funds over the next few years made sure, colleges can make longer-range plans for adding acutely needed housing.

COMMUNITY FACILITIES

By the end of 1960, loans from the Community Facilities Administration totalling almost $90 million had helped finance construction of 297 public facilities projects in 46 States, and 1,626 public works planning projects had been made possible by CFA advances totalling more than $37 million.

The 1961 Act more than quadruples the authorization for public facilities construction loans, raising the revolving fund from $150 million to $650 million, and concentrates the program on smaller communities. Eliminating States as eligible borrowers, it channels all aid to municipalities and other political subdivisions and such State instrumentalities as water and sewer districts. Loans are restricted to smaller communities —those having a population of less than 50,000, or less than 150,000 if located in an economically distressed area. The planning advance authorization is increased by $10 million, bringing the total to $58 million.

HOUSING FOR THE ELDERLY

Housing for elderly persons has been aided for several years through a special form of FHA mortgage insurance and through direct loans by the Community Facilities Administration, in addition to housing provided for low-income elderly persons in the public housing program. As of the end of 1960, financial assistance had been approved for 10,200 dwelling units through the mortgage insurance program and for 285 through the direct loan program. Provisions had been made for 25,200 units in low rent public housing.

The 1961 Act increases the authorization for the direct loan program from $50 million to $125 million, raises the maximum loan amount from 98 percent to 100 percent of development cost, and makes public agencies and consumer cooperatives, as well as other nonprofit sponsors, eligible as borrowers. The new Act also changes the method of calculating the maximum amount of an FHA-insured mortgage covering housing for the elderly, permitting insurance of larger amounts for projects with more rooms per unit.

THE NEW PROGRAMS

The Housing Act of 1961 has authorized new programs in which Federal aid is made available for the first time in several important areas of need, in addition to overhauling and up-dating the basic housing and community development programs with which most people are familiar.

Because these programs represent new and potentially very useful resources for individuals and communities in meeting some of the most pressing problems of our day, they are each described here in more detail.

One new program, for example, makes possible the first broad-scale attack on the deterioration of existing housing, one of the Nation's most important resources.

Another permits the Government to give effective aid in the provision of housing for families of moderate income—a field which has never before received major attention.

The conservation of permanent open space in areas of rapid urbanization is another problem for which aid is provided for the first time.

And urban areas can now receive, in limited amount, special assistance in solving the increasingly acute problems of mass transportation that many of them face.

REHABILITATION LOANS

As a result of the 1961 Act, the FHA can now insure loans for home improvements up to $10,000, with maturities up to 20 years or three-quarters of the remaining economic life of the property, whichever is the lesser. The interest rate will be as determined by the FHA Commissioner, but may not exceed 6 percent.

These loans are generally available for buildings containing from one to four family units; multifamily structures are eligible only if they are located in urban renewal project areas.

Improvements of structures less than 10 years old must involve major structural changes or correct defects which were not known at the time of completion of the structure or were caused by fire, flood or other casualty.

These loans must be adequately secured either by mortgages or by other types of security as required in each case. Where there is indebtedness outstanding against the property, the total debt, including the improvement loan, may not exceed the amount of a mortgage that could be insured by the FHA.

MIDDLE INCOME HOUSING

There has long been a pent-up demand for good housing among families of moderate income—income too high for low rent public housing, too low for decent housing on the private market. Only when dislodged from their homes by urban renewal or other public improvement activities could families in this group obtain special housing assistance. The Housing Act of 1961 attacks this problem by making the "Section 221" FHA mortgage insurance program for displaced families available on more liberal terms and broadening it to apply to moderate-income families generally.

SALES HOUSING. In the new program, for a two-year period, mortgage insurance for sales housing is made generally available on liberal terms for existing, newly constructed, or rehabilitated single-family dwellings in amounts ranging from $9,000 to $11,000. The downpayment, including closing costs, may be as little as 3 percent of acquisition cost. The term of the mortgage for a new or rehabilitated home may be as much as 35 years, and can be extended to 40 years if the FHA Commissioner determines that the purchaser can pay the monthly charges on a 40-year loan, but could not do so under a 35-year plan. The term is limited to 30 years for existing housing.

For displaced families, the downpayment, including closing costs, need be no more than $200, and the mortgage maturity can be 40 years.

RENTAL HOUSING. To help provide rental-type housing for moderate income families, the 1961 Act authorizes the FHA for a four-year period to insure low-interest-rate, 100 percent mortgages financing new or rehabilitated multifamily projects. Eligible borrowers are nonprofit organizations, limited-dividend corporations, cooperatives, and local public bodies.

The interest rate may be prescribed by the FHA Commissioner at a level below the market, but not lower than the average yield of all outstanding marketable obligations of the United States, currently $3\frac{1}{8}$ percent. The maximum maturity also is fixed by the FHA Commissioner. The usual FHA insurance premium may be reduced or waived if necessary to assure sufficiently low rentals. Mortgage amounts will vary according to the average number of rooms per dwelling unit and costs in different areas.

To assure capital for the program, the Federal National Mortgage Association is authorized to use its special assistance funds for purchase of the "below market" rental housing mortgages.

CONSERVATION OF OPEN SPACE LAND

The Housing Act of 1961 puts into the hands of localities a weapon to use in fighting one of the worst consequences of uncontrolled urban sprawl—the disappearance of open space. In areas where comprehensive planning is carried on, local public bodies may now receive grants from the Housing and Home Finance Agency to defray part of the cost of acquiring title to or controlling rights in permanent open space land that is important to execution of an area plan. Such open space reservations may be important not only as parks and recreation areas, but also as water sheds needing conservation, as protection against floods or water pollution, or to provide access for city dwellers to undisturbed natural areas.

An authorization of $50 million in grants is made for this new program. Grants may not exceed 20 percent of costs, except in cases of public bodies with broad area responsibilities, when they may be for as much as 30 percent. In extending this aid, the Housing Administrator is required to take action to assure that the local governing bodies are using existing public lands and other means that they have to preserve a maximum of open-space land with a minimum of cost.

URBAN MASS TRANSPORTATION

For urban areas where problems of mass transportation are a matter of concern, the Housing Act of 1961 makes three provisions—for planning assistance, demonstration grants, and transportation facility loans, on a limited or pilot basis.

Comprehensive planning for mass transportation is expressly made eligible for grants under HHFA's program of urban planning assistance. For this kind of planning, agencies appropriately chosen for the work involved, as well as official planning agencies, may be aided with grants.

Grants may now also be made to local public agencies for demonstration projects designed to contribute to the improvement of mass transportation or to the reduction of mass transportation needs. These grants, which come from the funds authorized for urban renewal projects, may not exceed two-thirds of project costs and may not be used for major capital improvements. They are limited to an aggregate amount of $25 million.

Loans may be made to public bodies or agencies to finance the acquisition, construction and improvement of transportation facilities and equipment, if (1) there is being developed for the urban or metropolitan area a program for a comprehensive mass transportation system, and (2) the proposed facilities can reasonably be expected to be required for such a system. The Act earmarks for this purpose $50 million of the funds authorized in the Agency's program of public facility loans.

4

INTERSTATE

RELATIONS

Inherent in a federal system is the problem of interstate relations. Since a vast residium of power is reserved to the states under a federal system, a lack of uniformity in governmental policies between the states naturally results. This lack of uniformity causes no problems in some fields but does create serious problems in other fields.

Businessmen operating across state lines encounter serious problems as Professor Walter F. Scheffer, a member of the Department of Government at the University of Oklahoma, points out in his article that examines reciprocity in the taxation of interstate trucks. Professor Scheffer concludes that bilateral reciprocity agreements have not produced equity for all parties concerned and calls for interstate cooperative action by states to adopt an "in-lieu-mileage" tax.

The interstate compact entered into by two or more states has been used with increasing frequency since 1900 and has proved to be a valuable method of solving common problems. The article by professors Frederick L. Zimmermann of Hunter College and Mitchell Wendell of American International College, staff members of the New York State Joint Legislative Committee on Interstate Cooperation, makes the interesting suggestion that local governments acting as agents of the state be allowed to negotiate and administer agreements across state lines to solve common problems. The importance of this suggestion is apparent when one considers the fact that ten of the twenty-five largest metropolitan areas encompass more than one state.

Interstate disputes are relatively frequent but usually not of a serious character. The most serious interstate dispute during the past few years has revolved around the distribution of the waters of the Colorado River. The importance of water cannot be understated in any part of the country, but its importance in the arid Southwest can be measured in terms of life and death; the future development of much of this area is dependent upon an adequate supply of water. Norman C. Miller, Jr., a staff reporter of the *Wall Street Journal,* presents a chronicle of the ten-year-old dispute between Arizona and California over the division of the water of the Colorado River. On June 3, 1963, the United States Supreme Court in general supported the claims of Arizona under conditions of normal river flow, but ruled that the Secretary of the Interior has complete power to allocate the water of the Colorado River when the flow drops below normal.

Walter F. Scheffer
8. *Reciprocity in the Taxation of Interstate Trucks**

Taxation of heavy motor vehicles operating in interstate commerce creates a complex problem. Every state employs the *theory* of the highway-user tax, such as the gasoline tax, in its attempt to make those who use the highways bear the principal burden of construction and maintenance. Each state, however, determines for itself the kind and amount of tax assessed its highway users. Consequently, considerable variations exist among the many states.

The interstate differences in highway-user taxes and regulatory policies create trade barriers and cause considerable loss of revenue to some states. If a state taxes highway use without considering the relative tax burdens in various states it can cause inequities for interstate operators of heavy motor vehicles. It is essential, therefore, that the states reconsider the problem of existing reciprocity agreements which are intended to provide relief to resident interstate truck operators from certain out-of-state highway user taxes.

Interstate tax reciprocity was originally based on a rather simple concept. The Committee on Highway Use Taxes of the National Association of Tax Administrators stated it in the following manner:

> It was felt that the imposition of certain taxes upon the same vehicle by more than one state created trade barriers "when multiple-state taxation of the equipment and service reaches the level where the cost is unreasonable when compared with the taxes on the same service wherein no state boundaries are crossed."[1]

In an effort to overcome multiple taxation of heavy vehicles operating in interstate commerce, a system of bilateral reciprocity agreements are worked out. At first there was no great problem involved because existing interstate travel was negligible in terms of both trips and cargo weights. By the early 1920's, however, the states already were faced with the problem of taxing interstate transports while seeking relief for the resident interstate truckers. Even then, it was not always easy to obtain agreement among the few states involved. Early attempts to arrive at uniform legislation affecting the licensing of motor trucks and buses among the

* From *National Tax Journal*. March 1956, pp. 75–83. Reprinted with permission of publisher.
[1] National Association of Tax Administrators, *A Practical Program to Improve Taxation of Interstate Highway Use*, 1952, p. 20, quoting Fred Meyers, *Highway Research Board Proceedings*, 1946, p. 8.

several states were generally to no great avail. Reciprocity agreements were easier to achieve, but, at most, they often proved to be temporary truce agreements in the truck-tax wars which have characterized the relations between states over the past thirty years.

FACTORS AFFECTING RECIPROCAL ARRANGEMENTS AMONG THE STATES

Provided all factors involved are equal, the practice among the states of entering into reciprocity agreements on truck taxes is an appropriate means for removing barriers on interstate commerce and giving relief to some truckers. In actual practice this is not the case. Each state is free to establish its own tax policy, regulatory measures, and enforcement procedures. These factors are very important in the making of successful agreements.

The National Association of Tax Administrators offers some examples which disclose certain salient facts that make many of the present reciprocity agreements untenable. A few of these instances are contained in the following:

> ... an operator may decide to register all of his trucks in State A (and he would probably do so if A's taxes were lower than B's), even though he used B's highways more extensively than A's. Bridge states may be greatly disadvantaged....
>
> Reciprocity may also be unfair to trucks within a state. For example, the truck traveling in two states may use State A's highways 25,000 miles a year. A truck of the same type which never leaves State A may travel only 10,000 miles. Under a reciprocal arrangement the interstate truck may pay nothing to A; even if fees are apportioned between A and B, the interstate truck will pay less to A than the intrastate truck although it uses the highways more.
>
> ... another example:
>
> a. State A has high annual weight taxes but no motor carrier taxes.
> b. State B has low weight taxes and also a mileage tax.
> c. State C has no weight taxes at all but has a mileage tax.

Under what circumstances should reciprocity be granted? Usually only the annual taxes are considered. The results are likely to be inconsistent. For example, A may collect as much from the average truck under its weight tax as B collects from its combined weight and mileage taxes. But B grants reciprocity on its weight tax so A gives B's trucks exemption from its weight taxes, even though B continues to collect mileage taxes from A's trucks. On the other hand, C has no annual tax to waive so A withholds reciprocity. C's trucks are taxed in A while B's are exempt although B may be collecting as much from A's trucks as C is.[2] ...

---

[2] *Ibid.*, pp. 22-23.

INTERSTATE CO-OPERATIVE ACTION AS A SOLUTION TO RECIPROCITY

It is undeniable that the states are faced with a dilemma. Where full reciprocity is realized, those states which impose the higher vehicle fees must give up the revenues which would be collected if out-of-state trucks were required to pay their share of the highway as do resident trucks. On the other hand, when a state withholds reciprocity, it imposes an inequitable burden on its domiciled vehicles operating in interstate commerce because they are inevitably forced to pay double or triple taxes, depending upon the number of states in which they travel. Some form of inequity appears inevitable under independent state action, regardless of the efforts made to mitigate the burdens on the affected interests. Basically, it is sound policy for a state to require all who use its facilities to pay according to the extent of that use. Therein rests the justification for the state to require nonresident payment of vehicle taxes. No foreign operator should have free use of the roads. But to tax such an operator doubly is not justified when the use which he makes of a state's highways is not double that of another whose operation is intrastate only. . . .

It is unlikely that the states, in the foreseeable future, will relinquish their power of taxation of interstate motor vehicles. From a practical standpoint, therefore, it is advisable to try to devise a new method of taxation which will allow the states to continue their tax programs but to adapt them to an equitable arrangement whereby both the state and the truck operators receive fair treatment. A plan of this nature was suggested in 1944 by the Board of Investigation and Research, which was established by Congress in 1940 to study transportation.[3] More recently, the plan has received support from the National Association of Tax Administrators[4] and the Council of State Governments.[5] These two organizations examined the workability of the original proposal and have prepared model legislation to implement the basic concept of the plan.

PROPOSED TAX LEGISLATION

The model legislation proposes that the states adopt an "in-lieu-mileage" tax to apply to certain weight groups of interstate trucks. This tax

---

[3] Board of Investigation and Research, *Interstate Trade Barriers Affecting Motor Vehicle Transportation,* Senate Committee on Interstate Commerce, Senate Doc. No. 81, 79th Cong., 1st sess., (Washington: Government Printing Office, 1945), pp. 75-76.

[4] National Association of Tax Administrators, *Taxation of Interstate Highway Use,* 1952.

[5] The Council of State Governments, *Suggested Interstate Highway Use Tax Law,* (Chicago, Illinois, 1952).

is designed to take the place of all other highway-user taxes, including gasoline taxes, registration fees, ton-mile or weight-mile taxes, and any other user tax imposed by the state and applicable to the particular vehicle within an established weight category. The intent is to calculate the "in-lieu-mileage" tax so that it is equivalent to the combined user taxes imposed on the intrastate operation of any particular truck classification. In other words, the plan contemplates the computation of a per-mile tax burden as though the entire operation of the vehicle was carried on within the state.[6]

After the state legislature establishes the various truck categories for mileage tax purposes, it would then fix a fair tax rate for each category. Operators of heavy interstate vehicles would be required to register them in their state of domicile in order to secure a license plate, preferably with an interstate designation. The license plate fee should be nominal to cover only the administrative costs. It would not be subject to annual renewals since its only use is to identify the trucker's acceptance of the plan and method of paying for road use. The operator would be free to travel in any other state adopting the plan. Payment of the mileage tax would be made periodically to the various states in which the truck traveled, according to the number of miles traveled in the state times the state rate per mile of operation for the specific vehicle.

The following example illustrates the manner in which the plan is intended to function. In 1950, state A's user taxes and fees assessed a three axle, tractor-semitrailer combination weighing 40,000 pounds gross and used as a for-hire contract truck a total of $1,190. Assuming this type vehicle travels an average of 45,000 miles per year, a mileage figure arrived at by the Bureau of Public Roads,[7] it would pay a tax equivalent to 2.64 cents per mile for all of its intrastate operations. Another truck with the identical characteristics to those of the first one is also registered in state A, but this second truck carries on interstate operations to the extent that only 15,000 of the 45,000 miles traveled are within the state's boundaries. A third truck, registered in a foreign state but bearing the same characteristics, also operates only 15,000 miles annually in State A. The taxes paid by each of the trucks would be accordingly: The first truck would, of course, pay $1,190 to State A; the second truck would pay 2.64 cents times 15,000 or about $396; the third truck would pay the same amount to State A as the second truck because it traveled the same distance over the state's highways. State A's trucks would pay mileage fees

---

[6] Council of State Governments, *op. cit.*, p. 4.

[7] E. M. Cope, "State Road-User and Personal Property Taxes on Selected Motor Vehicles," *Public Roads*, Vol. 26, No. 2, June, 1950.

to other states according to the extent of their travel in those states.[8]

If the suggested interstate highway-user tax went into effect, the rate per mile of operation would vary, and sometimes considerably, among the different states adopting the plan. Assuming that the vehicles in the different classes travel about the same mileage in the various states, one can arrive at the rate per mile for all the states.[9] If a single-unit truck weighing 18,500 pounds gross and traveling 25,000 miles a year is used as an example, the rate per mile based on the total taxes imposed would be equal to the following in the states indicated (*See* Table 1):

In each state there would be a deduction from the total mileage tax in an amount equal to the motor fuel tax paid by the operator, because that is included within the calculated mileage tax. Furthermore, the proposed plan provides for border zone traffic, resulting from residence near state borders, special trips in interstate commerce made by otherwise intrastate operators, and other clarifying items. . . .

TABLE 1

State	Total User Taxes (in Dollars)	User Taxes per Mile (in Cents)
Wisconsin	$528.84	$.0211
Iowa	313.84	.0125
Minnesota	279.80	.0112
Ohio	286.84	.0111
Indiana	273.36*	.0109
Michigan	264.13	.0105
Illinois	250.61*	.0100

*Includes property tax.

The proposed highway-user tax, however, is not free from defects. In the first place, there will inevitably be difficulties in administration. It assumes a degree of honesty among the units taxed which may not be present in fact. The total mileages traveled could be falsified so that the operator pays for the principal mileage in states with the lowest tax rate per mile. This is a problem for the high-rate states to check. A state whose taxes are considerably higher than those in neighboring states is susceptible to discrimination by those seeking to violate the intent of the proposed act.

8 For other examples refer to Council of State Governments, *op. cit.*, p. 4 and National Association of Tax Administrators, *op. cit.*, p. 26.

9 The Bureau of Public Roads, for example, listed the total taxes paid in 1950 by certain classes of commercial vehicles in all the states. E. M. Cope, *op. cit.*

In actual application it is doubtful that all states would agree to adopt this plan even within a general region. The proposed legislation provides for this contingency by allowing for reciprocal agreements with the non-conforming state, permitting, thereby, tax relief for the trucks of that state operating in conforming states, and vice versa. There are inherent, however, in this substitute reciprocity plan many of the difficulties present under the current arrangements. At some point it seems, though, that one is justified in assuming, where a reasonable plan is proposed, that the states will try to resolve these difficulties in good faith and that they will arrive at an agreement which is mutually satisfactory. None of the proposals regarding reciprocity is beyond criticism in respect to weaknesses, but some are more vulnerable than others and rely more upon rational application. The interstate highway-use tax is suggested as the least vulnerable under the method of attack—that is, co-operative interstate action.[10]

FEDERAL SOLUTION TO THE PROBLEM OF RECIPROCITY

The states *must* find an answer to their problem of taxing interstate trucks or the federal government may be urged to remove the obstruction to interstate commerce which the different state tax programs now impose. Proposals for federal intervention have received little or no real support, probably because of the recognized difficulties inherent in their solutions of the problem.

It is definitely established that the states have authority to tax non-resident interstate trucks.[11] It is suggested, however, that the states might agree to abandon this field of taxation by "the imposition of a federal tax distributed to the States on condition that the latter confine their direct taxation of motor vehicles to those of resident operators."[12] The difficulties which are likely to arise under federal solution are readily admitted by its proponents. It is believed that this solution would be cumbersome and difficult to implement, and that it would fail to remove

---

[10] See Bureau of Agricultural Economics, *Interstate Trade Barriers to Truck Transportation*, pp. 11–13, for some other recent regional approaches.

[11] *Hendrick* v. *Maryland*, 235 U. S. 610 (1915); *Kane* v. *New Jersey*, 242 U. S. 160 (1916); *Clark* v. *Poor*, 274 U. S. 554 (1927); *Clark* v. *Paul Gray Inc.*, 306 U. S. 583 (1938); *Capital Greyhound Lines* v. *Brice*, 70 S. Ct. 806 (1950).

[12] U. S. Congress, Senate, *Federal, State, and Local Government Fiscal Relations*, Sen. Doc. 69, 78th Cong., 1st sess., in pursuance to S. Res. 160, (Washington; Government Printing Office, 1943), p. 266.

all the inequities present in interstate movement.[13] On the other hand, if some action or threat of action is not taken at the federal level, the multiple tax burdens on interstate commerce are likely to increase, at least sporadically. Interstate commerce should not be subsidized, nor should it be burdened beyond its share.

Any federal attempt at taxation of interstate vehicles requires that a method of distribution or sharing be instituted which approximates closely the returns the individual states realize under present taxing arrangements. This is essential for practical reasons. The states must meet the condition peculiar to their areas, which include such factors as topography, soil and weather conditions as they affect the highways, economic ability or wealth, and miles of roads. These factors are important to the state in establishing its own rate of taxation. If the distribution of a federally-collected tax, imposed in place of the state tax, is made without consideration of the above-mentioned factors, the states may be subject to unnecessary financial loss. The problems apparent in a federal scheme of this nature appear to merit the conclusion drawn by Professor Maxwell when he surveyed the possibility of a federally-collected and shared gasoline tax as a substitute for state gasoline taxes. He said:

> The "fairest" plan that the mind of man could devise would not, moreover, remove the practical difficulty which arises from the fact that all the states must be treated alike when they are not alike in their present dependence upon taxation of motor fuel.[14]

Professor Maxwell's conclusion was cited with emphasis in the congressional study on intergovernmental fiscal relations.[15] The complexities of implementing a federal taxation scheme as considered in the above-mentioned studies may rule out a federally-collected gasoline tax plan as these studies conceived of such a tax. It does not, however, preclude the possibility of a different approach in the use of a federally-collected gasoline tax designed to replace state taxes. . . .

A federal program requires that there be, first, a definition of what is to be included as interstate operations subject to federal taxation. Only vehicles over a specified size and weight classification making more than a limited number of trips out of their state of domicile should, for instance, be subject to the federal law. After the truck categories are established, the problem is the taxation of the various classes. It appears logical that the entire tax program could be based upon a federal gasoline

---

[13] *Ibid.* Board of Investigation and Research, *op. cit.,* p. 74.

[14] James A. Maxwell, *Fiscal Impact of Federalism,* (Cambridge: Harvard University Press, 1946), p. 310.

[15] *Federal, State and Local Government Fiscal Relations,* Senate Doc. No. 69, 78th Cong., 1st sess., pp. 523 and 524.

tax, provided that the inequities inherent in this type of tax when used alone can be overcome. This seems possible in light of information and studies made in recent years on such items as:

1. Mileage traveled by certain weight trucks.
2. Total user taxes paid in the various states by trucks in the different weight and mileage categories.
3. The amount of user taxes paid per mile of operation.[16]

If a federal gasoline tax was imposed on various established categories of interstate operators according to a graduated scale based on their operations as determined, it would result in a reasonably equitable assessment for road use on all types of interstate commercial travel. For example, if it is found that the 18,500 pound gross weight single-unit truck travels approximately 25,000 miles annually, the rate of taxes per mile of operation can be determined for each state in the Union and the District of Columbia.[17] The amount of taxes to be paid to each state by this type vehicle can be determined by multiplying the total miles of travel made by all vehicles within this category by the user-tax rate per mile in each state. The total sum received from this truck category by the 49 taxing units could then be used to determine how much federal gasoline tax is required to bring into the federal treasury an equivalent to the sum now accruing to the states from this source. This federal gasoline tax would not be paid at the time of purchase, but rather at a later reporting date. The interstate operator would continue to pay existing state gasoline taxes and later would receive a refund because the federal tax is to replace all other user taxes.

To carry the example further, the amount of gasoline tax accruing to the federal government from the above truck category would be determined by dividing the distance traveled by trucks of this size by their average mileage per gallon of gasoline. For instance, if 6.5 miles was averaged on a gallon of gasoline and the truck traveled 20,000 miles in a year, it would have consumed approximately 3,077 gallons of fuel. The federal tax per gallon, especially arrived at for this truck category, times the consumption would be the tax payment required. If the federal tax is 10 cents per gallon of gasoline, the tax owed in this example is about $308.

The same factors and determination would be required for each size truck. A simplification in arriving at categories could be accomplished by agreements with manufacturers or, if that failed, by a period of arbitrary

---

[16] See footnote 7.

[17] See table above as an example in which the rate of taxes per mile of travel for one truck classification has been determined for a number of states.

classification of trucks. As time passed, more accurate and detailed information on operations and implementation of policy procedures in interstate commerce probably would provide a basis for ironing out inequities resulting from an initial lack of scientific information.

Each interstate operator would be required to keep a record of his operations in each state. There would be little incentive to falsify the extent of travel in each state because the federal tax would be the same regardless of where the miles were traveled.

After the federal government receives the periodic reports and payment of taxes from the interstate operators, it must provide for the distribution of funds to the states on a basis whereby each state will receive approximately the same amount as under present taxing arrangements. This can be accomplished by tabulating the total mileage of interstate truck operations carried on in every state in each of the categories established. This mileage times the user-tax rate per mile of travel imposed in each state for each classification of trucks will determine the share the respective states will receive.

A hypothetical example of the proposed distribution formula follows: Interstate truck operations in the 18,500 pounds gross weight classification reports a total of 5,000,000 miles of travel for a three-month period in State A. The rate per mile under the state tax program for this type of operation is 2.1 cents. To arrive at the state share from the interstate operation, multiply .021 times 5,000,000, which equals $105,000 received by the state for one-fourth of a year from one class of truck operation. It would cost the federal government no revenue, other than nominal administrative costs, because the graduated tax on gasoline would be calculated for each class of interstate vehicle so that the total collection by the federal government would equal the many unit-collections formerly made. All interstate trucks would pay a uniform tax to the federal government according to their classification, but two states having an equal interstate mileage credit would not necessarily receive an equal share of the federal distribution because of their different user tax rates per mile of travel. . . .

In spite of the obstacles inherent in this proposal, it seems to offer as much chance for implementation as the proposal requiring interstate co-operation. It is natural that the states should prefer an interstate co-operative proposal rather than an extension of federal participation. If the states fail, however, to solve their problem in a co-operative spirit, some form of federal action, along the lines suggested, appears justified. The record of state co-operation is replete with a willingness to take joint action through compacts, uniform legislation, conferences, and the like, on many subjects of mutual concern among the states. There is, however, as Professor Graves points out, an absence of co-operative agreements on current controversial issues.[18] And the problem of truck tax reciprocity stands prominently among these issues.

Frederick L. Zimmermann and Mitchell Wendell

9. Bridging State Lines*

Increasing attention must be given to the handicaps imposed on local government in the modern era by geographical limits. Ways must be found to bridge these boundaries. Methods of adaptation and integration are further complicated for communities along state boundaries. This problem of local government and state lines has attracted much consideration in its most spectacular manifestation, the major interstate metropolitan area. Some of the need for integration, however, applies, if on a lesser scale, to all local governments in state boundary areas.

The most far-reaching developments in the integration of multistate metropolitan areas have been the creation for particular regional purposes of joint state administrative bodies established by interstate compact. But the use of the compact to meet some of the problems of these areas has grown slowly since its first appearance in the Port of New York Authority. Moreover, a number of new applications have occurred in the same New York region, with creation of the Interstate Sanitation Commission in 1935, the Interstate Palisades Park Commission in 1936 and the Waterfront Commission in 1953.

Except for a limited early use in the Kansas City region, compacts have been employed in only two other major interstate metropolitan districts with the Missouri-Illinois creation in 1949 of the Bi-state Development Agency for the St. Louis area and the Pennsylvania-New Jersey establishment of the Philadelphia Port Authority and a broadened Delaware Bridge Commission in 1951.

The serious problem of the metropolitan area is the more critical because of the number and importance of our boundary cities. Of the 25 largest metropolitan districts, ten at least can be classified as in the boundary category: New York, Chicago, Philadelphia, St. Louis, Washington, Cincinnati, Kansas City, Providence, Portland (Oregon) and Louisville.

---

[18] W. Brooke Graves, *American State Government,* (Boston: D. C. Heath and Co., 1953), p. 840.

* From *National Municipal Review,* February 1957, pp. 71–76. Reprinted with permission of publisher.

Detroit and Buffalo are on the international boundary line. The problem is not limited to such giants. The Commission on Intergovernmental Relations reports that "of the 170 standard metropolitan areas, 23 extend across state boundaries and 28 others extend to a state line. Forty-three million persons—one out of every four—live in areas that are now or may soon become interstate." There are also innumerable smaller urban communities that straddle state lines or, if the growth of the country continues, bid fair to do so.

Methods of effecting integration across state lines, at least for some functions, must be developed. It seems increasingly evident that informal methods alone will not suffice and that more formal devices must be used to assure the necessary permanence and provide a sound legal basis for joint agencies and arrangements.

At least one such interstate community has sought integration of those functions that should be performed on an area-wide basis and that probably would have been undertaken in unified fashion if it had not been for the intervention of a state line. At least since 1920, the charters of Bristol, Virginia, and Bristol, Tennessee, have provided for the making of agreements for the operation and performance of certain services on a co-operative basis.

Both cities operate under special charters embodied in the statutes of their respective states. In consequence, the presently operative sewage disposal agreement is really an interstate compact entered into by the cities pursuant to authority delegated to them by state statute. It also can be said that, for the same reason, any other agreements that these two municipalities may conclude on the basis of relatively broad permission contained in provisions of their charters also will be compactual in character.

While the need may not be as great as in more densely settled communities, interstate arrangements between local jurisdictions can be useful also in rural areas. For example, Wisconsin and Virginia authorize interstate library agreements enabling communities along their respective boundaries to cooperate with communities in neighboring states in the operation of library facilities. Such contractual arrangements could be especially helpful in making possible the construction and maintenance of public works.

DELEGATION OF POWERS

Except for the Bristol arrangement, compacts relating to local activities have so far been negotiated and put into effect directly by the states concerned, even though their most obvious effects were on the local units.

Under the federal constitution interstate compacts are formal agreements between or among states given the status of law by legislative action of the participating states. Consequently, a more extensive use of compacts for local governmental purposes would be facilitated by the development of techniques for delegating compact-making authority to local governmental units so that they could negotiate and administer their own agreements.

There would seem to be no serious legal obstacles to such delegations of power by states to their political subdivisions. It is firmly established that local governmental units are agents of the states in which they are located. It is also fundamental that local governmental units have the capacity to make binding contracts. Consequently, localities could be delegated the authority to enter into formal agreements that would be binding upon them as contracts and upon the states in which they are located as interstate compacts.

Nevertheless, there are some practical decisions to be made if an interstate compacting power is given to political subdivisions. These relate to: (1) the degree of freedom to be accorded local governments in formulating and putting into effect the substantive provisions of a compact; (2) the harmonizing of divergent laws affecting state-local relations in the interested jurisdictions; and (3) the enforceability of interlocal agreements across state lines.

STATE'S LIABILITY

The first of these questions is important because a formal agreement between or among political subdivisions of two or more states, an agreement which has the force of statutory law, will of necessity be a compact between or among states. In consequence, the states will be guarantors of performance to which an aggrieved party may look for satisfaction in case of default by a local government. If a state is to have this liability, it probably should insist on safeguards. Accordingly, it would seem that at the very least state statutes authorizing localities to enter into compacts should describe the permissible subjects of such agreements in definite fashion: either by enumeration or by clear generic definition.

The question of local freedom of action has yet another aspect. How much state supervision should there be in the actual making and operation of the compact? The Wisconsin library project presents this question of supervision and control quite squarely.

One of the arrangements being considered would be for the Wisconsin Free Library Commission, a state agency, to make such compacts on behalf of the interested Wisconsin communities. It is probable that this body would be amenable to the making of the desired agreements at the request of the affected localities. But it is also true that since the Free Library Commission would itself enter into the agreement on behalf of the state, it would have to approve the actual contents of the compact; otherwise no agreement would be executed.

Whether this degree of control would be necessary in all cases is open to question. Depending on the circumstances, availability of an appropriate state official (perhaps the attorney general) for consultation, filing of the executed compact with the state, or embodiment of specific limitations in the statute conferring the compact-making power might be sufficient.

Further, it would seem that the purpose of state supervision and control would vary depending on the size of the localities involved. Larger municipalities normally have their own law departments and may be presumed to have the professional assistance necessary to the negotiation of equitable and legally satisfactory agreements. Smaller communities which cannot afford adequate counsel may require a greater degree of state help. No matter what the size of the locality, however, the state will always be interested in seeing that the compact does not subject it to unreasonable risks in its capacity of guarantor.

The harmonizing of divergent state laws is a problem that must be faced in the drafting of most interstate compacts. In the usual case, however, it is a problem easily solved. Since the compact is itself statutory law, it supersedes conflicting provisions of law. The recent Wisconsin-Illinois school district compact illustrates a possible solution to this type of problem. The operation of joint schools serving localities on both sides of the state border requires the harmonizing of applicable teacher certification, school attendance and similar state requirements which may differ from jurisdiction to jurisdiction. The compact contains specific provisions providing for the resolution of such divergencies.

The third problem relates to the enforceability of interlocal agreements across state lines. Attention should be given to the significant procedural phases of the recent litigation over apportionment of the waters of the Delaware River. In 1931 the United States Supreme Court rendered a decree allocating some 440 million gallons of water daily to New York City. Recently, the city sought to increase the allotment, thereby precipitating further litigation. Pennsylvania intervened to protect its interests in the Delaware Basin. Philadelphia also attempted to intervene but was denied the right to do so.

Philadelphia contended that home rule provisions of its charter gave it complete control of its own water system and consequently special interest in the suit. However, the court's opinion said that Philadelphia could not participate in the litigation because she had not shown an interest separate from that being presented by the state. A dissent maintained that it was obvious that New York City was participating in the suit in its own behalf and that the interests of Philadelphia were also substantial.

So long as interlocal compacts worked to the satisfaction of all concerned, no inquiry as to their enforceability would be necessary. Undoubtedly, many of the disputes which might arise could be settled by informal means. Before localities would risk important commitments, however, they probably would want to know whether they could obtain court settlement of any disputes over interpretation or performance of the agreements.

Particularly if the state statutes providing for such interlocal agreements were carefully drafted, there should be no difficulties in this regard. The local governments could secure enforcement in the same manner that they secure enforcement of their contracts. Also, the states could enforce because the interlocal agreement would be a compact.

MERITS OF THE COMPACT

States and localities wishing to consider the authorization of such interlocal agreements might receive considerable assistance from a draft of a suggested statute on the subject appearing in the *Suggested State Legislation Program for 1957*.[1]

The interstate compact is a potentially useful instrument for meeting the peculiar problems of integrating local interstate areas. Authorization by the United States constitution of this method of interstate agreement removes questions that might prove fatal for other approaches. Further, the compact because of its contractually binding character meets a basic need by providing the necessary stability. Not only is an interstate compact a statute in an enacting state but it is superior law in the sense that no later unilateral legislative action can conflict with the contractual obligations embodied in the interstate agreement. Because of these attributes the compact has been the accepted vehicle for the creation of joint administrative agencies of two or more states.

POWERS OF AGENCY

An interstate agency established by compact can be endowed with all the powers normally associated with local government. It can exercise eminent domain, finance, construct and operate public works and facilities, police these operations and collect fees therefrom to support revenue bonds. It can formulate and enforce regulations or ordinances. It can levy taxes in order to carry out and maintain a regional program. It can

---

[1] Council of State Governments, Chicago, 1956, 207 pages.

confer extraterritorial authority for specified purposes on courts and administrative officers. These powers can be delegated to an interstate agency on the same condition with respect to the establishment of standards and making of findings as would govern delegation of powers to the agency of a single state. The 1951 decision of the United States Supreme Court, in *West Virginia ex rel. Dyer* v. *Sims* (341 U.S. 22), embodying this important holding also has strengthened the position of the compact generally by emphatically reaffirming the enforceability of such agreements.

Compacts can be tailored to the particular needs of area and function. Since the effectiveness of the interstate compact approach does not require the fixing of any particular political boundary lines, it could be used to handle problems encountered in the large urban regions described by Charlton F. Chute,[2] in sub-areas of such regions or for rural problems, as well as for the more familiar metropolitan area.

Some students of the metropolitan problem have suggested that general integration of metropolitan areas is not necessary and that coordination may be limited to those problems which are peculiarly metropolitan in character. The compact method is adapted to such a particularistic approach. As the Incodel[3] proposal for a comprehensive water supply system in the Delaware Basin indicates, it is even possible to utilize a compact which would establish a joint enterprise to meet a problem common to two interstate metropolitan areas while also recognizing other legitimate needs of a region which far transcends the area of both metropolises.

It would be possible, of course, to formulate multi-purpose compacts and establish interlocal commissions of broad scope and powers, if desirable. The establishment of a single interstate municipality might be beyond the realm of present political feasibility. It would be possible, however, by providing for representation of the participating municipalities in the governing body of an interstate agency, to establish for particular purposes something of a league of municipalities bridging the state line. An interlocal agreement also could provide for the direct election of members of such a governing body by the electorate of the interstate area.

CONGRESSIONAL CONSENT

The compact clause of the constitution reads: "No state shall, without the consent of Congress, . . . enter into any agreement or compact with another state or with a foreign power." This wording has led some

---

[2] See the *Review,* June 1956, pages 274-280.
[3] Interstate Commission on the Delaware River Basin.

people to believe that the states can make no compacts of any kind without obtaining congressional consent. If this were a correct statement of the situation, it would apply to interstate compacts between local governmental units as a matter of course. The consequence might well be to discourage localities from attempting cooperation via compact. Not that Congress likely would oppose the joint or cooperative provision of municipal services across a state line where the local residents had indicated a desire for such an undertaking, but the extra effort and possible delay might seem too burdensome, especially for projects of relatively limited scope.

Fortunately, the vast majority of interlocal compacts would not need congressional consent at all. The courts have uniformly taken the position that a compact requires congressional consent only if it affects a power delegated to the national government or affects the "political balance" within the federal system. Moreover, the Southern Regional Education Compact, participated in by all the states from Oklahoma and Texas on the west to Maryland on the northeast, has been in full operation ever since 1949 despite the fact that it has never received congressional approval. In 1948, when consent legislation for this compact was on the floor of the Senate, the measure was sent back to committee after debate which indicated an interstate compact on education did not require consent.

Certainly an interlocal compact to maintain a park, establish cooperative library service, operate joint public school facilities, use common sewage disposal works or do most of the things that form the core of local governmental activity could hardly be said to affect the balance between nation and states or disturb a power delegated to the national government. Perhaps localities contemplating an interlocal compact might want to seek congressional consent for their agreement in very special cases. But the ordinary compact between localities in different states would not need consent and should come into operation without consent ever being sought.

Norman C. Miller, Jr.

10. Titanic Water Fight*

The average home uses 16,000 gallons of water a month, and to irrigate an acre of arid farm land for one growing season requires 1,600,000 gallons. It takes five barrels of water to refine one barrel of crude oil, and

* From the *Wall Street Journal.* April 30, 1962, pp. 1 and 10. Copyright 1962 Dow Jones & Company, Inc. All Rights Reserved. Reprinted with permission of publisher.

700 gallons to process a ton of oranges into canned juice. A brewer needs 13 gallons of water to make a gallon of beer.

Of such damp statistics, signifying the immense water requirements of modern society, are fights over water rights made. One of the most monumental of these fights is now approaching a final decision. The principal disputants are California and Arizona, and the water they are squabbling over is the Colorado River, to which both states have access. Sometime before recessing in June, the Supreme Court is expected to decide how the waters of the river are to be apportioned. In so doing, officials of the states involved believe, the court will also be deciding to a considerable extent the future course, for better or worse, of two of the nation's fastest growing areas.

The turbulent Colorado originates high in the Rocky Mountains north of Denver. It rushes southwest, cuts across a corner of Utah and then surges west through Arizona's Grand Canyon. After forming the Arizona-Nevada border, the river heads south and divides Arizona and California, 1,450 miles from its headwaters. For a region larger than France and covering portions of seven states—242,000 square miles of the most arid land in North America—water from the Colorado and its tributaries means the difference between prosperity and economic stagnation.

RISING WATER DEMANDS

Great as its flow is, the Colorado cannot meet the rising water demands of the parched Southwest. The growth of population, agriculture and industry has set the stage for what has been described as "the most important and complex water struggle in the history of the West." Fighting for water to sustain their rich farm lands, bustling industry and growing cities, Arizona and California for almost 10 years have waged a legal battle to justify their conflicting claims to the Colorado's flow. . . .

Southern California, including metropolitan Los Angeles and San Diego, currently uses more water from the river than the six other states with access to the Colorado River system combined. The river's water has nourished the Southern California boom, which since 1930 has seen population rise to 8 million from 1.6 million and assessed land values increase to $15 billion from $2.2 billion.

AN AQUEDUCT FOR ARIZONA?

But now Arizona, enjoying a boom of its own and worried about insufficient water supplies, claims it has the right to construct a $1 billion aqueduct to siphon off a vast quantity of Colorado River water presently used by California and carry it to the Phoenix-Tucson area. This thriving region in south central Arizona now receives no water from the Colorado, though it does draw some from a Colorado tributary.

Compounding the water problems of Arizona and California, which are in the Colorado's Lower Basin, are the plans of states farther upriver, such as Colorado and Utah. These Upper Colorado Basin states will almost double their use of the river's water within the next few years; a 40-year-old interstate agreement gives them the unchallenged right to do this. . . .

ONE GOVERNOR'S VIEW

Arizona, whose water claim was favored over California's in preliminary legal proceedings, contends it must have more Colorado water if it is to maintain its present rate of agricultural production and to continue urban and industrial growth. If Arizona wins the Colorado water case, "no new lands will be developed for irrigation," says Gov. Paul Fannin. "Our purpose is to decrease an existing long-range water supply deficiency for our presently irrigated lands and for our growing population and industry."

The growth of Arizona's cities and industry has been spectacular in recent years. Between 1950 and 1960 the population of Phoenix quadrupled to 439,000; Tucson's population increased fivefold to 213,000. Such companies as General Electric and Motorola have established facilities, creating the nucleus of an electronics industry. Federal and state authorities predict the Phoenix-Tucson area's population of 1,125,000 will double within the next 10 or 15 years. . . .

CALIFORNIA'S CASE

California's officials are firm in their insistence that retention of the present flow of Colorado water into the southern section of the state is essential. Today the river supplies, via an aqueduct system, the domestic and industrial water for 3 million out of 8 million people living in Los Angeles, San Diego and 93 other cities. Moreover, the river's water is the principal irrigation source for some 982,000 acres of farm land reclaimed from the desert.

If Arizona gets as much Colorado water as it demands, California authorities maintain, by 1970 or 1980 at the latest, depending on how fast the proposed Arizona aqueduct is built, Southern California's water supply from the Colorado would be cut by almost a third. Should this happen, existing intrastate water agreements would give agricultural areas in Southern California first claim to all the state's remaining supply of Colorado water. Thus, assert California officials, Los Angeles, San Diego, and other cities would be left without any water from the Colorado. The cities would lose almost half their total water supply.

California officials see two conceivable alternatives if part of their supply of Colorado water is shut off. But both pose costly problems for a state whose resources already are strained in absorbing new residents at a rate of some 1,600 persons a day.

One possibility is that cities faced with grave water shortages might be able to obtain water by paying a high enough price to the rural Southern California irrigation districts with priority water rights. This would keep the cities going, say California officials, but the resulting loss of water in rural areas would inevitably put a crimp in Southern California's agricultural output. The region is a major national supplier of avocados, dates, lemons, grapefruit, oranges and a variety of vegetables—crops with a total annual value of about $160 million.

NORTH-SOUTH AQUEDUCTS

The other possible way to replace Colorado water would probably keep both the cities and agriculture of Southern California running full tilt. But this alternative, which would entail the drastic acceleration of a program for construction of an aqueduct system running from the ample water sources in the north of the state to Southern California, would probably play havoc with state finances.

A 740-mile, $1,750,000 north-south aqueduct is already under construction, with completion scheduled by 1970. But state water authorities say this aqueduct would be of little help in alleviating a substantial loss of Colorado water; it is being built up to supplement the present Colorado water supply, not supplant it.

Construction of a second aqueduct had been planned for the 1990's, but officials fear a loss of Colorado water would make it necessary to advance this project by as much as 20 years. The second aqueduct would probably cost twice as much as the first because it would be necessary to tap water resources farther to the north, according to Raymond Matthew, who recently retired as chief engineer of the state's Colorado River Board. And if the construction timetable has to be speeded up, the second aqueduct would be built at a time when California will be paying off the huge debt incurred in putting up the first aqueduct, instead of after most of this debt was retired, as had been planned originally.

California authorities discount replacement of Colorado water by sea water conversion "barring a major and unforeseen breakthrough." The cost would exceed that of a second aqueduct, they say. . . .

HISTORY OF A LEGAL BATTLE

The legal battle over Colorado water began in 1952 when Arizona sued California over water rights. The Supreme Court is the trial court in suits between states, but the labyrinthine case reached the justices only last January 8. It is customary in complicated cases for the Supreme Court to appoint a "special master" to hold hearings and recommend a decision to the court. After exhaustive preliminaries, Special Master Simon H. Rifkind, a former U. S. District Court judge, started to take testimony in San Francisco early in 1956. When the hearings finally closed in August 1958, the transcript filled 23,000 pages. The special master delivered his 433-page report to the Supreme Court December 5, 1961. His recommendations, which the Supreme Court is free to modify or reject, were heavily weighted in favor of Arizona's claim.

Arizona, Judge Rifkind said, should get 2.8 million acre-feet of the first 7.5 million acre-feet available annually in the part of the Colorado below Hoover Dam, which spans the river between Nevada and Arizona. California should get 4.4 million acre-feet, and Nevada should get the remaining 300,000 acre-feet. An acre-foot of water is enough to cover an acre of land one foot deep, or 325,850 gallons.

If 7.5 million acre-feet of water is not available annually from the Colorado below Hoover Dam, Judge Rifkind recommended the supply be split this way: 58⅔% for California, 37⅓% for Arizona, and 4% for Nevada.

"DISASTROUS CONSEQUENCES"

Although the special master's formula would give more water to California than to Arizona, California officials argue that if the Supreme Court follows his recommendation, "disastrous consequences" would result for their state. They say Southern California now is using 5.1 million acre-feet a year from the Colorado; thus, if 7.5 million acre-feet of water were available, California would receive 700,000 acre-feet less than at present.

But California insists the actual loss would be much greater than this. They say Judge Rifkind's estimate that 7.5 million acre-feet of water would normally be available annually below the Hoover Dam fails to take into account several factors, including the prospect of more extensive water use in the Upper Basin. Though Judge Rifkind maintains California is overly pessimistic, the state insists its studies indicate the supply of water below Hoover Dam will amount to only 6 million acre-feet annually. This would mean California's annual share of Colorado water, under the special master's percentage formula, would drop to 3.5 million acre-feet—1.6 million acre-feet below current consumption.

Arizona was understandably pleased with Judge Rifkind's report. Under the apportionment he has proposed, Arizona believes it would have ample water to justify Congressional authorization of the proposed aqueduct. Even if the annual water supply available in the Lower Basin below the Hoover Dam totaled the 6 million acre-feet forecast by California, Arizona is confident it would have enough water to warrant the project.

5

STATE-LOCAL
RELATIONS

Dillon's Rule holds that cities are creatures of the state and may be abolished or modified by the state at will. Cities have long maintained that the state deprives them of sufficient power to adequately conduct their affairs. Until recently cities were supported in their contention by most political scientists. However, political scientists have begun to question the desirability of home rule in view of the growth of metropolitan areas and concomitant problems; political fragmentation hampers rather than expedites the solution of metropolitan problems.

The degree and types of desirable state controls of local government are debatable. The two excerpts from *State-Local Relations,* the comprehensive report of the Committee on State-Local Relations of The Council of State Governments, discuss the advantages of state administrative supervision of local governments and the most effective types of supervision. The Committee maintains that persuasion is preferable to the use of control devices such as absolute orders and substitute administration.

Senator Thomas C. Desmond of the New York State Senate throws interesting light upon the subject of state control of cities and the traditional explanation of state control as being due to rural domination of the legislature. Senator Desmond contends that rural representatives have little interest in city affairs and they are not responsible for the short-changing of cities. He cites the disadvantages of state control of cities, yet does not urge complete home rule for each city.

Although cities in attempting to solve their problems often feel restrained by the state, the latter does provide valuable assistance in many areas as Governor Nelson Rockefeller of New York makes clear in his description of six major municipal problems that the state of New York is helping to solve.

11. *Administrative Relations of States and Localities**

The growth of state and local functions has been accompanied by the growth of state administrative supervision over local activities. Reasons for this trend toward greater central regulation, which was rapidly accelerated by the depression of the last decade, are not difficult to find:[1]

1. Technological developments in transport and communications have pushed in the direction of centralization. Government must react quickly to meet changing situations. In the absence of rapid means of communication, decisions can be made and executed only by officials physically within local areas. Modern developments in ground and air transportation and in communication by phone, telegraph, and radio have greatly decreased the necessity of this local decision making. Frontiers have disappeared, local boundaries have been effaced, and basic decisions can be made from central points.

2. Experience has made clear that full efficiency and economy in certain governmental operations depend upon a large area of administration. In part, these economies result from reduced overhead costs and centralized purchasing; in part, they result from the planned integration of governmental functions. The demand for more adequate services and for their economical administration has thus resulted in the imposition of supervision and the actual transfer of some functions from local governments to the states.

3. There is an ever-growing awareness of a state-wide, and even a nation-wide, concern with respect to matters that were once considered purely local in character. A child of the most backward locality is a citizen of both the state and nation; his education and health, to take only the two most obvious examples, are therefore the concern of state and nation. Large numbers of people have developed the conviction that no justification exists for any part of the country to fall below a minimum standard of governmental service. If minimum services are not maintained, it is widely believed that some central agency must raise sub-standard conditions to an acceptable level of performance.

* Council of State Governments. From *State-Local Relations*. (Chicago: Council of State Governments, 1946), pp. 11–13. Reprinted with permission of publisher.
[1] Cf. Herman Finer, "The Case for Local Self-Government," *Public Administration Review*, Vol. III, No. 1 (Winter, 1943), pp. 51–58.

4. Finally and most immediately pertinent, the trend toward state centralization is due to the fact that there is no correlation between the tax-raising capacity of local governments and the cost of the services they must perform. Local governments have been called upon to assume a variety of new functions and to improve existing services. At the same time, localities have been compelled to rely principally on one source of revenue: the property tax. Diversification of the local tax base has occurred to some extent, but this process has been limited both by legal restrictions and by the difficulty of taxing mobile subjects within small areas.

As a consequence, localities have turned to the state governments for additional funds. In assuming increased responsibility for the support of services performed by local units, the states have imposed safeguards with respect to the use of these funds and have undertaken the supervision of activities for which the funds are expended.

ADVANTAGES OF STATE ADMINISTRATIVE SUPERVISION

The purposes of centralization are laudable. In a word, they are to raise the services of government to higher levels; to erase discrepancies in the quality of services; to increase the efficiency of their administration; and to distribute the costs so that no single area will be forced to carry a disproportionate share of the financial burden. The danger, however, is that centralization may reach the point where local freedom becomes substantially diminished and local self-government becomes an empty phrase.

The danger can be easily overemphasized. States now control local governments largely through "an amazing assortment of constitutional and statutory regulations which often minutely restrict communities when they should be free and omit regulation when administrative guidance would be helpful."[2] The manner in which these legal controls impede the freedom of local governments is described fully in Part Five of this report. A system of administrative supervision is a substitute for this type of detailed legislative control and is a greatly superior type of regulation from the viewpoint of both states and localities.

In the first place, administrative supervision has an element of flexibility that legislative control lacks. A legislative debt limit, for example, has no elasticity. Once the limit is reached, further loans must (1) await a special local act; (2) be made extra-legally; or (3) be arranged through

---

[2] Wylie Kilpatrick, *State Supervision of Local Finance,* Publication No. 79, Public Administration Service, Chicago, 1941, p. 47.

subterfuge, such as that of establishing a new unit of local government. Administrative overview, in contrast, can supply a rational test for local borrowing, based upon both need and the fiscal strength of the borrowing unit.

In the second place, legislative control usually becomes effective only when some individual becomes concerned enough to initiate legal action and to undergo the trouble and expense involved in court procedures. In the vast majority of cases, the issue is one with respect to property rights. As a result, local officials and local governments may not be supervised where supervision is needed unless some question of property is involved.

Thirdly, judicial action (the principal sanction of legislative control) is normally slow and expensive. Few individuals are willing to underwrite this expense when it must be personally borne in the event of an adverse decision.

Finally, the legislative control "is from its nature ineffective." Even under the most favorable circumstances, it operates only when the law has been violated. In such instances, its value cannot be questioned. But most local officials do not break the law deliberately, and their illegal action is almost invariably the result of uncertainty or ignorance with respect to what the law is. In actual practice, government and the public are less affected by violation of law than by its inexpert or inefficient administration. Legislative fiat and judicial sanctions are relatively ineffective in meeting this fact.[3]

On the other hand, the most effective type of administrative supervision is achieved through state bodies acting as service agencies, advisory and educational consultants, and cooperating units within the state-local framework. Administrative regulation is a continuous supervision. It depends upon a trained body of central officers rather than upon lawsuits of disgruntled taxpayers. It operates to improve the administration of local government from within, to increase citizen control over the affairs of local units, and to increase the effectiveness of the states' own programs.

In sum, administrative supervision is an improved, and not necessarily an additional, type of state regulation. In comparison with the traditional method of control by legislation, it offers states more certain means of achieving efficiency in the administration of state-wide programs; at the same time, it offers local governments a large amount of assistance and a greater measure of freedom in meeting their own day-to-day problems.

---

[3] Cf. R. K. Gooch, "England," *Local Government in Europe* (William Anderson, Ed.), D. Appleton-Century Co., New York, 1939, pp. 75-76.

12. The Most Effective Types of Supervision*

In a pioneer study of state administrative supervision, Schuyler Wallace listed supervisory devices "in the ascending order of their individual effectiveness" as follows: reports, inspection, advice, grants-in-aid, approval, review, orders, ordinances, removal, appointment, and substitute administration.[1] The progression in the stringency of the techniques in this list is obvious. Nevertheless, effectiveness should not be confused with heavy-handedness, and the history of state supervision indicates that day-to-day effectiveness is achieved through the persuasive devices rather than the more absolute ones.[2]

Supervision means more than control. Overlapping, but distinct from control, are other techniques whose use is both more frequent and more effective. Among these are services supplied by states to localities, including educational programs; technical advice given localities by state officials; and cooperative activities carried on by states with local units. The following principles are suggested in the erection of state supervisory programs:

1. CONTROL VS. PERSUASION

The control devices (e.g. absolute orders, appointment and removal of personnel, substitute administration) should be utilized only (a) to establish minimum standards of performance and (b) to meet emergency situations. The establishment of minimum standards insures adequate performance but frees localities from an undesirable rigid uniformity; and other supervisory methods can be utilized to encourage localities to exceed the minimum according to their own discretion. Control, as such, becomes an awkward and self-defeating device. It amounts to the absorption of local government by state authorities and can be justified only in extreme cases, i.e., when local officials cannot or will not adhere to state standards. Where control is chronic, the states' own standards may be at

* Council of State Governments. From *State-Local Relations*. (Chicago: Council of State Governments, 1946), pp. 41–46. Reprinted with permission of publisher.

[1] Schuyler Wallace, *State Administrative Supervision Over Cities in the United States*, Columbia University Press, New York, 1928, pp. 29-59.

[2] For Minnesota study coming to this conclusion and stressing effectiveness of grants-in-aid, cf. Edward Weidner, "State Supervision of Local Government in Minnesota," *Public Administration Review*, Vol. IV, No. 3 (Summer, 1944), pp. 226–34. For testimony of New York Commissioner of Social Welfare, cf. David Adie, *Responsibility of the State in the Supervision of Public Welfare Programs* (Reprint of speech), Albany, 1939.

fault. Or the function concerned might better be transferred to direct state administration.[3]

A state administrative agency might properly make it mandatory that localities utilize, as a minimum planning tool, certain budget forms setting forth basic elements in income and expenditure. Beyond this, however, state regulation of local budgets should be primarily persuasive in character. State officers should suggest and demonstrate more detailed methods of fiscal planning, encouraging local officers to exceed the legally required standards. The experiments in certain states by which state review bodies can set aside local budget items following the complaint of local citizens is a type of control that substitutes state for local opinions and should be avoided.

To take another example from the fiscal field: states can properly require that all local units of government keep suitable accounting records and that some uniformity be maintained with respect to larger classification and terminology. Beyond this diversity should be allowed and encouraged. No final best system of accounting can be achieved on a permanent basis, but experimentation and continuous consultation should produce ever-improving methods. This process of improvement cannot be achieved by flat mandate. It needs persuasion, consultation, and education.

2. CERTIFICATION: MINIMUM STANDARDS FOR PERSONNEL

The concept of minimum standards might be more generally transferred to the field of personnel. Teachers are the only large group of local employees whose competence must be certified by state agencies. But the teaching field is by no means the only area in which the technique is applicable. Standards of education, experience, and general competence can be established for workers in public welfare, police, fire, sanitation, and other activities. A plan for certifying such workers as a pre-requisite to employment might be a feasible method of state administrative supervision; it is no substitute, however, for a genuine competitive merit system. The latter aims at selecting the best available person for a given job; certification alone can only establish minimum standards.

3. INCREASED GENERAL SUPERVISION OF LOCAL PERSONNEL

It is unfortunate that local personnel systems are in a relatively low stage of development and that states give local governments relatively little aid in the selection and training of local officials. Good management

---

[3] Cf. *infra*, p. 53–55.

begins with qualified administrators: the simple fact is that no governmental program (rigidly regulated or not) can succeed without them. A further fact is that once personnel competence is assured other aspects of regulation can become more flexible.

States should increase their facilities for aiding local personnel administration. Every state, at least, should make technical advice and assistance available to all local units of government. Smaller localities should have the privilege of utilizing state facilities, while larger local units should be allowed to use state services or to establish their own civil service agencies under state supervision. States should discourage the establishment of separate agencies for localities of small size which cannot afford and do not have sufficient work to maintain necessary professional personnel workers. For these units of government, states should administer examinations, in-service training courses, and other personnel activities.

It is estimated that no more than 15 per cent of all county employees and no more than 65 per cent of all municipal employees are under merit systems.[4] As low as these percentages are, they do not reflect the fact that many local civil service systems are poorly administered and that principles of merit personnel work are frequently lax. States could serve their local units of government in no better way than by encouraging the installation and maintenance of high personnel standards. These standards would bring manifold benefits to both levels of government.

States could supply a valuable supplement to this program by maintaining a personnel exchange service for local governments. One of the greatest impediments to achieving a professional group of competent local officials results from the limited possibilities for advancement. Only the largest cities provide an adequate scale of increasing responsibility for high-caliber workers. Procedures to facilitate the promotion of efficient employees from smaller to larger localities would make employment in local government more attractive to persons of ability. The personnel exchange system would contribute to this type of advancement, would encourage proficient persons to enter the service of even small localities, and would make possible the recruitment of workers from wider areas.

4. EDUCATIONAL PROGRAMS FOR LOCAL WORKERS

As a part of their programs for fostering high local personnel standards, states should expand their present training facilities for local officials. Many state agencies, in cooperation with universities, local governments, municipal leagues, and professional associations, now offer training courses of one sort or another. The programs were stimulated in 1936 by

---

[4] Data supplied by the Civil Service Assembly of the United States and Canada.

the passage of the George-Deen Act which for the first time included "public and other service occupations" in the vocational education program financed jointly by national and state funds.[5]

The present training programs cover a wide field. In Michigan, California, New York, and other states, classes are conducted for local personnel officers. State departments in Louisiana, Connecticut, and many other states cooperate with the state universities in offering short courses for municipal finance officers. The New York State Department of Health, Department of Agriculture and Markets, and the New York State Conference of Mayors sponsor courses for city and village food inspectors. Training for local firemen and fire officers is given in many states, including Arkansas, California, Indiana, Iowa, Massachusetts, Michigan, Oklahoma, and Wisconsin. An equally large group of states sponsor police training. Schools for local assessors are operated in Kentucky, Pennsylvania, Maryland, New York, and other states. Courses are also given in some states for correctional and custodial officers; minor judicial officials; school board secretaries; unemployment compensation workers; business managers; lunchroom workers; public welfare, public health, sanitation and sewer employees; airport managers; and many others.

This list is by no means complete. As extensive as the programs are, states should take steps to enlarge them in three ways:

First, the programs should be extended to cover prospective municipal employees. Present courses, in almost every case, are aimed at those already employed. The importance of this in-service training can hardly be overemphasized; but pre-service training should be added so as to insure a constant influx of trained personnel to municipal positions. This can be accomplished simply through cooperative arrangements with state educational institutions.

Secondly, the training programs should be planned to cover a larger portion of the municipal field. Under the present system, courses are apt to grow haphazardly and without planning, new subjects being added at the request of individual groups. In many cases, a wider coverage of the field may be simply obtained by closer cooperation with university groups and professional organizations. A good example of how this may be achieved is furnished by the activity of the Public Service Institute in the Department of Public Instruction of Pennsylvania. Since 1938, the institute has had more than 23,000 employees enrolled in a wide series of courses; its work has been carried out in close cooperation with many professional organizations and has been materially aided by the University

---

[5] Cf. *Training for the Public Service Occupations* (Vocational Education Bulletin No. 192), U.S. Office of Education, Washington, 1937.

of Pennsylvania and Pennsylvania State College.[6] Various state departments in New York, the state municipal training institute, and State Conference of Mayors and Other Municipal Officials also offer an extensive program.

Thirdly, some unification in the direction of in-service training courses would be desirable. At least, this would mean some central office in each state to act as a clearing house of information and to aid in preventing duplications in programs. At most, such a central office would act to establish and devise curricula, prepare manuals, and bring some continuous, centralized planning to the present uncoordinated situation.

5. TECHNICAL ASSISTANCE AND COOPERATIVE UNDERTAKINGS

All the points thus far have stressed the importance of high personnel standards in local government. And this properly should be the main emphasis of a state program of administrative supervision. Once localities have facilities for recruiting and training efficient public servants, state supervision can be turned to supplying other types of assistance. These include the preparation of manuals of operation; administrative surveys and measurement studies[7] leading to suggestions for improved procedures; consultation to bring about reorganizations on the local level; technical advice from the states' specialized personnel; and conferences at which all may benefit from demonstration programs and the exchange of information. In every case possible, emphasis should be placed upon helping local offices to improve the efficiency of their performance. More direct services may also be of value to both levels of government, as when states market certain local bond issues, audit local accounts, establish demonstration programs in education and public welfare, and provide technical resources for testing materials to be used in local construction.

6. STATE-AID AND ADMINISTRATIVE SUPERVISION

An injudicious use of specifications attached to grants-in-aid can distort patterns of local expenditure and unduly restrict the scope of local discretion. There is some necessity for grants-in-aid without specifications as to

---

[6] Cf. "Pennsylvania's Public Service Institute—Activities Since 1938," *County Commissioner,* Pennsylvania State Association of County Commissioners, December, 1945, pp. 2–5, 23.

[7] The scientific measurement of administrative effectiveness is a rich, new field. State encouragement and financing of such studies would be highly desirable. For examples, cf. Clarence E. Ridley and Herbert A. Simon, *Measuring Municipal Activities,* International City Managers' Association, Chicago, 1943; Herbert A. Simon and others, *Determining Work Loads for Professional Staff in a Public Welfare Agency,* University of California, Berkeley, 1941.

the use or with broad specifications.[8] At the same time, the most effective means at the disposal of states to insure compliance with minimum standards and to increase the general level of performance by local governments is the grant-in-aid. In every case where a grant is given for a specific purpose, it should be formulated to insure an adequate standard of performance. At the same time, grants should be given with other larger purposes in mind, including those of erasing inequalities of service among local units and of enlarging the areas of local governments.[9]

Thomas C. Desmond
13. *The States Eclipse the Cities**

A perplexed Councilman of a city in upstate New York telephoned me not long ago to ask, "What kind of pipes will the state let us use for our city sewers?"

Although I am chairman of the New York State Senate Committee on Affairs of Cities, I was unaware that the state regulates sewer pipes. Since the question was solemnly put, I answered, just as solemnly, that I would look into it. Inquiries at several state agencies turned up a sanitary engineer who informed me that his bureau in the State Health Department most certainly does have the power to approve or veto the use of various types of pipes by cities.

This is one example—and not a far-fetched one—of how our states keep a tight, often choking rein on our cities in a variety of matters, from sewer pipes to tax rates, from bond issues to hiring a stenographer for the Fire Commissioner.

This year forty-six state Legislatures have held or are holding sessions, and headlines in newspapers across the country have echoed charges and countercharges of state and city officials on the issue of state control of municipal affairs. The clash between the city's desire—and need—for more self-government and the state's attempt to retain its dominant position over the city has once more been brought to the fore as a major problem of government. It is a major problem because although minor abuses by the states might be tolerated, when the states strangle local initiative, curb local responsibility, foist unnecessary expenses on local

8   Cf. *infra*, Part Four.
9   With respect to last part, cf. infra, Part Six.
*   From the *New York Times Magazine*. April 24, 1955, pp. 14, 42, and 44. Copyright by the New York Times. Reprinted by permission of publisher and author.

taxpayers and block new services needed in an age of urbanism, the cities have strong arguments for home rule.

What is the nature of the controls the states have over cities? How are they exercised? And what, specifically, are the results?

The controls are both legislative and administrative, and are applied and enforced in three ways. One is by passing laws that affect cities. Another is by judicial decisions. The third is by administrative curbs.

In theory the states can grant—or withhold—municipal home rule to any degree they wish. In practice they restrict home rule by enacting or not enacting laws—either special laws applying locally, or so-called general laws containing restrictive clauses aimed at certain cities. They can also do it by repealing or changing city charters. Like domineering mothers, the states refuse cities the right to run their own lives. Only twenty-one states make so much as a gesture toward granting some form of home rule to their cities, and even this is usually meaningless.

Thus, although cities have the right to elect their own officers and to carry out duties assigned to them by state Legislatures, in most states they do not have the authority to determine their own form of government or the powers they may exercise. Many do not even have the right to choose which revenue sources they can tap to support local services.

The judicial form of control stems from the fact that the courts have repeatedly ruled against cities and for Legislatures. Judges have denied cities any inherent right to self-government; cities are deemed the legal creatures of the state, with no powers except those granted by the state. Moreover, courts have ignored repeated evasions of constitutional prohibitions against laws applying to a single city.

As with legislative controls, so with administrative restrictions. States view the cities at best as irresponsible, unruly children capable of an amazing amount of mischief; therefore, they must be held to firm standards, if necessary by an occasional fiscal spanking. Today, nearly half the states force cities to follow state-prescribed budget systems and require periodic probes of city accounts, either by state agencies or state-approved accountants. The feeling is: spare the regulations and spoil the city.

States do aid cities in various ways. One is by providing technical assistance. For example, Joseph Watkins, a career personnel technician in the New York Civil Service Department, works in city halls throughout the state to help install modern personnel procedures. He also keeps a sharp eye out for violations of the merit system by job-hungry politicians. When such services are voluntarily accepted by the localities, neither local responsibility nor home rule is violated. But many states attempt to impose efficiency and virtue by restrictive state legislation which does more harm than good.

Another way states aid cities is by financial contributions. One out of every five dollars of the annual income of our cities comes from the states. But unfortunately the grants are usually hedged with many restrictions. Moreover, the cities must depend upon the real estate tax, a relic of the eighteenth century, for two out of every three tax dollars.

The states, viewing the cities as competitors for the taxpayer's dollar, not only force cities to rely on the property tax but also tightly limit the amount they can raise from this source. They have refused municipal pleas for the right to impose a payroll or an income tax, or to levy or increase taxes on local utilities—although the states themselves levy such taxes for state-wide use. This further shrinks the cities' tax base. In addition, Legislatures often yield to pressure groups and pass laws that force cities to raise the salaries of some categories of employes or to take on other fiscal burdens.

Thus, city officials, trapped between expensive demands for airports, roads, hospitals, schools or salary increases, and inadequate funds to pay the bills, are today walking a perilous economic tightrope. Yet in all the quarrels between cities and states, the cities usually have to battle with both hands tied behind their backs.

The net result of these methods of state control is that our cities must beseech legislators for their basic right to exist, to govern, to police their streets, to provide water for their people. Unless they obtain legislative authorization from the states, they cannot establish parking lots, regulate intracity buses, stop slaughterhouses from opening up in residential areas, or do any of a thousand things a modern city must do for its people.

The city dweller who is the victim of the system may wonder how state controls became so thoroughly clamped on municipal affairs. One reason was the powerful position which the states assumed at the beginning of our national history. After the Revolution the states inherited all the authority formerly held by royal Governors. At that time the Legislatures dominated both the executive and judicial branches of the state governments. The Constitution later confirmed many of the powers the states had assumed under the Confederation. But, in those early years, the efforts of state control were not too onerous, for cities were small.

The cities' real troubles began with the growth of urbanism. As cities increased in size, political power passed from the farm to the tenement. The "city vote" became a prime target for ambitious politicians. Lawmakers discovered that more votes were usually to be gained by sponsoring local bills than by campaigning for even the most desirable state-wide legislation. (In all State Capitols, local bills are passed or killed on the basis of "legislative courtesy." Customarily no bill affecting a city will be introduced or voted down without advance approval of the legislator representing that community).

This has led to a seeming paradox. The short-changing of cities by states is traditionally attributed to over-representation of rural areas in our Legislatures. Yet the rural representatives are by and large disinterested and do not mix in city affairs. The worst offenders in the strangulation of cities by states are legislatures from the cities. In New York State, for example, forty-five out of fifty-eight State Senators either live or work in cities.

In the course of time the growth of urban political power in Legislatures raised, in practice, the local legislative delegations to the position of superior governing bodies over the municipal officials. Without the approval of the local legislators the city authorities were unable to carry out needed programs. This proved especially troublesome when the legislative delegation was of one party and the municipal officials were of another, or when the delegation belonged to the minority party in the Legislature.

In the resulting stalemates the failures of cities to plan in advance to meet clearly emerging problems of traffic congestion, slum clearance and crime has created a recurring series of emergencies. Clutching at any straw, the cities have often turned to the states for what aid they can get. In addition, weak local officials have often evaded responsibility and passed on to the states the solution of sensitive issues. All of these factors have tended to put and keep the state in the driver's seat.

What, more specifically, is wrong with this system of state control over cities? In what ways does it harm the cities?

It has been argued in behalf of the system that the cities have brought some of their woes upon themselves. That is true. Corruption has been no stranger in city halls. To cite a minor but illuminating instance, one "H. Bell" was on Jersey City's payroll for years before someone discovered that he was a horse in the public works department and that a foreman had been collecting the "employe's" weekly pay check.

There have been many far-greater municipal scandals. Yet cities are not as corrupt as some believe. William Embler, former Deputy Controller of New York State, informs me that the state's audit of the books of 8,000 localities every two years has disclosed remarkable official probity. Sums misappropriated in a recent year have totaled no more than $7,800.

The main thing wrong with the state control system is that cities are now too big and too complicated to have their affairs handled by outsiders who may not be as familiar as they should be with city problems.

Half our people now live in cities with populations of 100,000 or more. Our cities have become giant diversified businesses, operating airports, hospitals and water plants. They are often the largest employers in their respective regions. They need freedom to regulate their growth and the increasing physical and social problems caused by their size.

Our cities have gained maturity. But instead of recognizing what they can and must do for themselves, the states continue to pass laws interfering with them, often for reasons of spite. Legislators can punish opposing cliques, grant concessions and act as benign overlords or petty tyrants.

Another evil of the system is its waste of time and effort. Before my committee recently were bills to permit Poughkeepsie to sell some land it had acquired for hospital purposes and no longer needs, to authorize Ogdensburg to spend $5,000 on publicity, to let Newburgh turn over a dead-end street to a factory that needs it to expand. In some Legislatures hundreds of local bills, of no concern to anyone except the single sponsor, must be considered and passed at each session.

Even when, states, out of the best of motives, substitute arbitrary regulations for local flexibility, the end result is often waste and sometimes danger. Because cities are required to accept "the lowest responsible bid" when buying material, they must often purchase machinery from a distant source which cannot service it, rather than from a nearby source which can. There is no leeway, no discretion. Thus, some fire trucks in one city today carry different sets of hose connections to every fire because the lowest bidder on hose connections did not have connections to fit the fire hydrants in that city.

Another thing wrong with such strong state control is that lobbies can often use the state's power over cities to enrich themselves. For example, a bill was passed at the recent session of the New York Legislature to require cities to equip each fire truck with two sets of gas masks of a type apparently made by only a few manufacturers. The bill amazingly, had been passed twice before but was vetoed by Governor Dewey. Now it has been passed a third time.

What can be done to improve the state-city relationship? How can the cities gain some independence?

I do not propose that cities be cut loose to operate on their own. Local affairs are too intermingled with those of other levels of government for cities to become wholly autonomous. Arterial highways, control over courts, wage and hour regulations, annexation of land, war against communicable diseases—these are things which transcend local interest and call for state action. But if the delineation of state and local problems is difficult at times, it is hardly insuperable.

The standard should be this: what the states can do better than the cities should be done by the states; what the states and cities can do best together should be done jointly; what the cities can do better than the states should be done by the cities.

There remains the problem of how to achieve this method of operation. Prof. Rodney Mott of Colgate University outlined for the American Municipal Association three conditions necessary to obtain home rule: (1) lively public support, (2) aggressive leadership by state leagues of municipalities, and (3) a change in the attitude of judges.

In Rotary Clubs and Chambers of Commerce, in women's clubs and welfare organizations, our people will have to voice demands that the states yield their authority over the cities. A rallying point could be a demand for the simple requirement that in every case where states force new expenses upon cities, the states would have to indicate how the expenses are to be met and authorize new tax levies if required. This would be a powerful influence in imposing a sense of responsibility on legislatures.

In states where the people have the right of initiative and referendum the voters can place freedom clauses in state constitutions which the lawmakers would not be able to skirt. In other states the campaign will have to be waged in constitutional conventions or by frontal attacks on the Legislatures.

At future sessions bills should be introduced to provide that cities shall have all powers that Legislatures are legally capable of granting to cities —subject to reasonable limitations. This would serve immediately to broaden the area of home rule. In addition, cities should be granted the power to draft and amend their own charters.

Not all public action, however, should be aimed at the states. The "buck-passers" on the local city councils who, when confronted with a politically hot issue, leave responsibility to the states, must be shown that the voters will not tolerate such supine behavior.

In the free association of cities the municipalities have opportunities to develop standards and employ experts without domination by the states. State leagues of municipalities need to be strengthened to bolster technical services available to cities to withstand state intrusion. There is no basic need for conflict. The well-being of the states and cities depends upon the vitality and integrity of both.

But the best argument of all for home rule is the well-run city. Home rule should be earned by demonstrated capacity to govern. As long as graft and incompetence are found in city halls the states will have an excuse to justify their tight control over cities.

The American Municipal Association's "Credo of the American Mayor" states: "We believe that the principle of municipal independence carries with it the obligation to face our own problems, to meet our responsibilities, to finance our own enterprises within the limit of local resources and consistent with practical economic and social factors." Here is expressed the spirit of responsibility which can win home rule and make it a means of progress.

Nelson Rockefeller
14. Intergovernment Cooperation*

Now let us look at some of the major problems of concern to municipal government in which the state has an important share of the responsibility —finances, education, housing, youth delinquency, commuter transportation, recreation, sewage disposal and highways. If you will forgive me for stressing the problems of one state, I shall deal with these problems on the basis of my personal experiences in New York because I would rather speak in terms of specific action rather than in theories or broad generalities.

First, *municipal finances*— The vital and increasingly important role of the state in its financial relationship to municipalities is underscored in New York by these facts:

1. New York State aid to localities has increased five hundred per cent in the past fifteen years—having increased from two hundred and fifty million dollars in 1946 to one billion and a quarter dollars in the current fiscal year—a billion dollar increase.

2. State aid to localities is six hundred per cent greater than federal aid to localities in New York State—contrary to popular impression.

3. State aid provides, on the average, about one-fourth of all municipal revenues.

In view of the important role that state aid plays in local government finances, the magnitude of its responsibilities to the municipalities is clearly evident. And it is basic to meeting this responsibility: that the state keep its own financial house in order so that it can meet its full responsibilities, and that the formulas by which state aid is distributed shall reflect changing local conditions. . . .

Second, *education*— The quarter-billion-dollar increase in state aid to local public school districts brings our total school aid to eight hundred

---

* From an address given at the 38th annual American Municipal Congress sponsored by American Municipal Association; Seattle, Washington; August 28, 1961. Printed with permission of author.

million dollars a year—more than the cost of the entire state government and its services.

New York State is now paying over forty-two per cent of the total local public school expenditures in the state. . . .

But there is another phase to the problem. The rise in elementary and secondary school enrollment in New York State is now moving on to the field of higher education and producing there a crisis in terms of adequate facilities. To meet this problem, we enacted this year a far-reaching plan for financial assistance to higher education which included: a new program of Scholar Incentive payments to approximately one hundred twenty thousand individual students annually; doubling the number of state scholarships to a total of seventeen thousand annually; providing increased student loans with no interest for the first five years; ten-year expansion program of the State University facilities; and a half-billion dollar lease-purchase plan for the Campus Building Construction Authority.

The state's goal is to double higher education facilities (public and private) in the next ten years, and to triple them in twenty-five years.

The resulting impact on the cities of this state assistance to higher education is well illustrated by the fact that the state now puts up almost forty-five per cent of the expenses of the University of the City of New York. . . .

And the state's role in education was further dramatically highlighted last Monday when we had to step in (with unprecedented action at a special session of the Legislature) to lift the public school system in the City of New York out of the clutches of local corruption and politics and assure fresh, high-calibre leadership.

I called the special session of the Legislature on behalf of the one million New York City public school children and their forty thousand dedicated teachers, upon the professional advice of the Commissioner of Education and the Board of Regents, in whose hands the State Constitution places responsibility for education in the state. This action was made necessary by a failure of local leadership to do anything of significance in response to repeated disclosures of maladministration, graft, inefficiency, favoritism and atrocious neglect of school repairs. The public had lost confidence in school leadership, and the quality of instruction was threatened. Therefore, the state had to act. . . .

Now let me turn to the third area, *housing*— The problems of housing and urban renewal are among the most urgent faced by all our municipalities.

In this field, middle-income housing is perhaps the most neglected area. Therefore, to help meet the financial aspect of this need head-on, the state created last year a new State Housing Finance Agency, with a bond of authority of over half a billion dollars as a start. To date, forty-one projects providing seventeen thousand four hundred apartments have been approved under the state's middle-income housing program. Mortgage commitments for these projects total one hundred ninety-five million dollars. And ten per cent of the apartments in each project are set aside to take care of our senior citizens. We are now developing some new ideas which we hope will greatly accelerate this middle income housing program.

In the field of urban renewal (a vital ingredient in the development of better housing) New York State now pays half the local share of project costs—and does so on a pay-as-you-go basis out of current revenues.

In addition, while most states depend on the Federal government entirely for loans and subsidies to provide low-income housing, New York State since 1939 has provided nine hundred sixty million dollars in loan funds and forty-two million dollars in annual subsidies for low-income housing, most of which has been used by the City of New York.

The state has an important obligation to help the localities in the housing field, and it is our feeling in New York that the state can act as a catalyst and coordinator in the realization of effective action in this field. The same is true for the urban renewal and low-rent housing programs. In my opinion, the Federal government should modify its programs to recognize state administration wherever the machinery exists to handle such a delegation of authority. It certainly would be in the interest of efficiency and coordination of effort.

Fourth, *youth delinquency*— Here, again, is a field of major concern to the administration and residents of our municipalities.

In New York State, to assist in meeting this problem, I requested and the Legislature established a Division for Youth, which has undertaken a program embracing advanced concepts which we believe to offer exciting new possibilities not only for the rehabilitation of delinquents but for the prevention of delinquency.

Under this Division for Youth we are setting up youth training camps to which youths in danger of becoming delinquent because of environment may be referred by appropriate social agencies with family consent, and other camps to which juveniles may be referred by the courts for rehabilitation in lieu of sentencing to reform school. This program also includes a large number of state-operated short-term adolescent retraining centers, and homes for youth needing an improved environment.

These new programs are in addition to the state's sharing in financial support of the care of juvenile delinquents in local facilities. The Division for Youth also provides state aid to localities for youth recreation and related projects.

Thus state expenditures to serve youth and combat juvenile delinquency have been stepped up sharply to twenty four million dollars this year. We believe this work is of major importance to the future as well as essential to meeting the state responsibility in assisting municipalities with their share of this serious problem of delinquency. Further expansion of this program is contemplated. . . .

Fifth, *commuter transportation*— Here is a critical field of municipal concern, a problem the magnitude of which has been growing by leaps and bounds.

In New York, the state has taken the leadership in effective inter-government cooperation both at the local and interstate levels:

1. At the 1959 session of the Legislature, the state worked out and shared with the localities a program of general tax relief for the railroads amounting to fifteen million dollars. Unfortunately, even this drastic action did not remove the threat of bankruptcy from two of our principal commuter roads.

2. Therefore, during the recent 1961 session, we had to take further action, working out cooperative steps with Massachusetts, Rhode Island, Connecticut, the City of New York and the County of Westchester to reduce further the local tax and other financial burdens on the New Haven Railroad. While unfortunately this did not prevent the railroad's ultimate bankruptcy, it did create improved conditions for continuation of its commuter service under the present trusteeship.

3. In addition, within New York, we worked out a plan whereby the state picks up half of certain additional tax concessions by the localities, and the additional tax relief was made contingent upon improved as well as continued commuter service. To assist the railroads in meeting this stipulation, the state is backing a one hundred million dollar Port of New York Authority bond issue to finance lease-purchase of new commuter cars by the railroads.

4. At the present time, I am working with the Governors of Connecticut and New Jersey to establish a tri-state agency to study the entire transportation picture in the New York metropolitan area—with the objective of regional action to achieve major improvement of the whole commuter situation. . . .

Sixth, *recreation*— In municipalities throughout the nation, parks and recreational facilities have become an essential ingredient for growth and development—not only for youth but for the entire community.

As in most states, the advance of urbanization is a major problem in New York with respect to assuring adequate park and outdoor recreation facilities for our rapidly growing population, now and for the future.

We came to the conclusion that we must act rapidly if we were to acquire and preserve for public use the necessary sites for camping, boat-landings, fishing, swimming, water sports, parks and other recreation facilities before they were swallowed up forever or could be obtained only at prohibitive costs.

Therefore, at my request last year, the Legislature authorized a seventy-five million dollar program to purchase such areas. The bill provides state aid to localities for this purpose at a ratio of three dollars in state money for every one dollar provided locally. This anticipation of the future's needs has met with enthusiastic response from local communities throughout the state, even beyond our expectations. All but fifteen per cent of the funds have already been committed.

This, again, illustrates the possibilities for far-sighted cooperative action on the part of the state in working with municipalities and other entities of local government to meet new and emerging problems.

There are two other areas of concern to municipalities which entail tremendous financial obligations and vitally affect the lives of their people, namely, *arterial highways* and *sewage disposal.*

For example, in New York State the local communities are already faced with the prospect of identified expenditures totaling $1.5 to $2 billion for sewage disposal plants—and the meeting of these expenditures would in many instances involve exceeding the total debt limit of the municipality. At the present time, the state's Office for Local Government is undertaking a major study as to the means of financing these requirements.

As far as arterial highways are concerned, the state is responsible for the engineering, construction, and a major portion of the financing of these roads—and these roads, probably more than any other single factor today, are shaping the future growth and development of most of our municipalities. The magnitude of these projects in terms of money can well be illustrated by the fact that the Legislature has authorized arterial highway changes in connection with the 1964 New York World's Fair alone, which will cost a total of ninety-seven million dollars, of which the state's share will be close to forty million dollars.

Therefore, whether we like it or not, the state finds itself right in the middle of municipal and metropolitan area planning in all its phases relating to transportation, housing, industrial development.

It became clear to me two years ago that New York State was neither adequately equipped to coordinate the plans and programs of the various state departments affecting local governments or to integrate these state's plans and programs with those of the local communities. Therefore, to meet this urgent need, I set up in 1959 an Office for Local Government and this year an Office for Regional Development.

The Office for Local Government has fostered joint action among local governments in solving mutual problems, served importantly as a clearinghouse for legislation affecting local government, and as a central point of information. It informs and assists the Governor as to local government problems and the formulation of policies to utilize and coordinate state resources for the benefit of local governments. It also conducts annual workshops on the problems of local government which have importantly stimulated thought and the interchange of information on solutions to these problems.

The new Office for Regional Development, with the guidance of its Planning Coordination Board made up of a Commissioner from within the executive branch of state government, has these major functions:

1. To bring about a conscious interrelation of the planning and development activities of the various state agencies;
2. To relate state planning and development to local planning and development and to Federal activities;
3. To spur all levels of government within the state to comprehensive planning and development on a regional basis;
4. To facilitate local planning and development activity by state action.

To my way of thinking, the real challenge of the future in meeting the problems of the metropolitan areas is not to set up some super-structure that would wipe out existing entities of local government. Rather the challenge is to develop a legislative framework and the means for effective cooperation between existing entities of government, with the state assuming its full responsibilities for coordination and leadership as well as financial support. . . .

I am convinced that state government must take a stronger leadership role and is the logical leader of intergovernmental cooperation in the solution of urban and regional problems. I support federal assistance programs based upon need and the equalization of opportunities for all Americans in pursuit of national objectives. The important consideration in the relationship between the three major levels of government is that each level shall fully meet its own responsibilities and not pass them on to another. . . .

part four

POLITICAL PARTIES
AND PRESSURE GROUPS

6
POLITICAL PARTIES AND PRESSURE GROUPS

The American political party has puzzled Europeans and even Americans. To many the sole purpose of a party appears to be to capture control of the government. The Chamber of Commerce of the United States in response to requests from its members for material designed to increase the political awareness and effectiveness of businessmen developed an *Action Course in Practical Politics* in 1959; a series of pamphlets and cases were prepared that present the inside story of politics.

"Political Party Organization" considers the development of parties in the United States, the influence of state election laws on parties, the functions of party committees, the role of the party leader, and party discipline. A careful reading of this selection will assist one to answer correctly the questions raised at the end of the two cases entitled "Running a Candidate" and "The Organization Viewpoint."

"The 'Engineering of Consent'—A Case Study" by Mr. Robert Bendimer, a free-lance contributor to major periodicals, is a remarkably complete account of the activities of two powerful interest groups in Pennsylvania, the railroads and the trucking industry, and deserves careful study by all serious students of the political process.

On the municipal scene the disappearance of the old-time political boss has been one of the most significant political developments in large cities in the twentieth century. The municipal political boss became so firmly entrenched during the nine-

teenth century that it appeared he had become a permanent
fixture, yet during the past thirty years the classic-type political
boss has disappeared. Leo Egan, a political reporter for *The
New York Times,* records the decline of the fortunes of Carmine
G. De Sapio, the leader of Tammany Hall in New York City, and
compares him with his predecessors.

15. Political Party Organization*

PARTIES ARE SHAPED BY STATE ELECTION LAWS

Development of our system of government has placed elections and politics largely in the hands of the states. The Constitution made no provision for political parties. The power to conduct elections was given to the states. In effect, this reservation of election power to the states also gave them the power to regulate the form and nature of the political parties. This has resulted—for all practical purposes—in 98 political parties, two in each of the 49 states. President Eisenhower recognized this when he referred to the Republican Party (prior to Alaska becoming a state) as not one party, but as "forty-eight state parties."

Even today, there is no provision in federal law for nominating candidates for president and vice president. In the early days of the Republic, the practice grew up of nominating candidates for president and vice president by a caucus of congressmen in each party. "King Caucus" was an unsatisfactory method since people of one party living in an area which was represented by a congressman of the other party had no voice in the choice of candidates. A movement developed to hold nominating conventions. The first national political convention was held by the Democratic Republicans in 1828 at Philadelphia to nominate John Quincy Adams for a second term. In 1832, all parties held national nominating conventions for the first time.

The conventions grew out of the need for a broader means of reflecting the wishes of the political organizations in the states in the selection of candidates. The national conventions have no sanction or authority under Federal law. They are effective only because individual states recognize their choices and put their nominees (or electors to the electoral college) on the state ballots.

State election laws shape the character of politics within the state by specifying how candidates shall be nominated and by setting up the conditions under which political parties operate.

Generally, state election laws cover:

1. *Size of the precinct or election district.* Ideally, this will be a geographic area containing from 600 to 1,000 voters.

* Chamber of Commerce of the United States. From "Political Party Organization." 1959. Condensed and reprinted with permission of publisher.

2. Establishment of a board of elections (terminology varies) to provide for polling places, man the polling places with clerks, establish the validity of candidates, provide ballots or election machines, and to canvass the ballots to ascertain election results. Usually there is one board of elections per county.

3. Method of nomination for office. Where there is a party primary election to select candidates, the law may govern the form of petitions and the number of names necessary to get a candidate's name on the primary ballot. The law will state filing dates, and the election day, the hours the polls will be open, etc. The law may provide that the board of elections will supervise and judge the party primary, or it may leave this to the political parties to supervise and judge.

The election law may state that nomination for public office or political party office shall be by convention or party caucus rather than a primary. It may then provide for the means of electing delegates to the conventions either by party primary or by caucus.

4. Methods of general election. The law will state the same kind of rules for the general election as are outlined above for the primary. General elections are never supervised by the political parties, however. They are always managed by the boards of elections, or similar governmental authority.

5. Eligibility of voters. State election laws require that voters in a general election shall be citizens, shall be of a certain age (generally 21, although it is 18 in Georgia and Kentucky, and 19 in Alaska). There are also residence requirements; there may or may not be a literacy test—and some states require payment of a poll tax. Most states require that voters register at some period before they vote. This is to allow time to make up the election rolls and judge the eligibility of the voters.

In addition to general eligibility requirements, there is usually a party membership requirement for voters in a primary election.

In states with *closed* primaries, voters are required to state formally their party affiliation, and may vote only for candidates of their own party. To change party affiliation they must make formal application no later than a specified date before the primary.

In states with *open* primaries, a voter can vote in either party primary.

In states with *"door ajar"* primaries, a voter may switch his allegiance at any time before the primary election.

In at least one state, candidates may file in both parties' primaries.

Where there is no party requirement for voting in a primary, and in caucuses or conventions where the state or party rules are easy to comply with, many people who are not really party members may participate in the election of party officials or in the nominating of party candidates.

Much has been written pro and con on the desirability of this practice.

6. *Structure of the parties.* The state law may provide for election in a party primary of one or two county committeemen, or precinct leaders, in each election district, and that these committeemen shall meet at stated intervals to elect a County Chairman and other party officers. It may provide for the election of state committeemen, and that they shall meet at stated intervals to elect state party officials.

GOVERNMENTAL	POLITICAL
FEDERAL GOVERNMENT	NATIONAL COMMITTEE
STATE GOVERNMENT	STATE COMMITTEE
COUNTY GOVERNMENT	COUNTY COMMITTEE
MUNICIPAL GOVERNMENT	TOWN OR CITY COMMITTEE
	WARD COMMITTEE
	ELECTION DISTRICT, PRECINCT OR NEIGHBORHOOD
CITIZENS	PARTY MEMBERS

Courtesy Public Affairs Counsellors, Inc., Management Consultants on Politics, 350 Lexington Avenue, New York, New York.

PARTY STRUCTURE

Political party structure tends to parallel government structure as this diagram illustrates.

A description and a diagram can only generally illustrate the structure of the political parties which vary greatly at the state and local level. In some states, the parties have almost no visible structure; in others, they have a clear definable structure which may then be virtually ignored because it is the local custom to do political business in the local political club.

Where the state election law specifically covers party structure, primaries and qualifications for primary voting, there is a formal party structure. In these cases, the members of a party have adequate avenues for taking part in the affairs of their party, if they wish.

Where the state election law is brief and general, party rules govern party structure, the nominating of candidates, and the election of party officials. These rules may be drawn to favor whatever party group is in power, can be changed at the discretion of this group and often are unavailable to the outsider. Where these conditions exist, insurgents in the party find it difficult to be effective.

In some areas there is little formal political organization. This is true of some Southern states where there is only one real political party. But whether formal or not, there is always some form of political organization. The organization is necessary to reach the voters, to persuade them, and to get them to the polls.

REPUBLICAN PARTY IN PENNSYLVANIA

Formal and Informal Organization

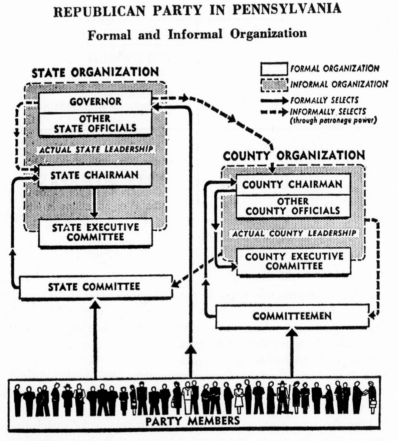

Courtesy Samuel Humes

MODEL STRUCTURE

Perhaps the best way to explain party structure is to analyze a more-or-less model system, with some of the variations in it.

PRECINCTS. The basic unit of a political party is generally the precinct, or election district. Terminology varies in different sections of the country, but the meaning is about the same. A precinct is a geographical voting unit with a certain number of voters residing in the area. The party leader in the precinct, called a committeeman, precinct leader, or similar name, gets out the vote of his party on election day. He develops a following in his precinct and if he is a capable person he can influence voters in party primaries and general elections.

WARD COMMITTEE. Large cities are often divided into wards consisting of several precincts. The committeemen or precinct leaders in the several precincts in a ward generally form a ward committee.

Ward committees may choose a nominee for a county supervisor, commissioner, or whatever the title may be in the particular area, as a representative to the county governing board. They may also name candidates for city councilman, alderman, trustee, or whatever this office is called in the area.

TOWN-CITY-COMMITTEE. All the precinct leaders in the town or city form a town or city committee. The town or city committee generally has an executive committee; the city executive committee is composed of ward leaders (chosen by the precinct leaders in their ward) and the officers of the city committee. The town executive committee is generally composed of its officers and a few other party members.

Town committees generally select nominees for mayor, councilmen, supervisors, police court judges, and town clerks.

City committees select nominees for mayor, city judges, city clerk, and other city officials. If members of the city council or county governing board are elected from wards, members of the city committee pass on ward committee choices for these spots. If members of the city council or county governing body are elected "at large," the city committee makes the decision, with the ward committee members participating only in their capacity as members of the city committee.

COUNTY COMMITTEE. Members of all the town and city committees or, in other words, all the precinct leaders in the county, form the county committee. The county committee will probably also have an executive committee chosen from town and city committee chairmen.

County committees choose the nominees for county executive if there is one. If not, the county governing board chooses its own chairman—

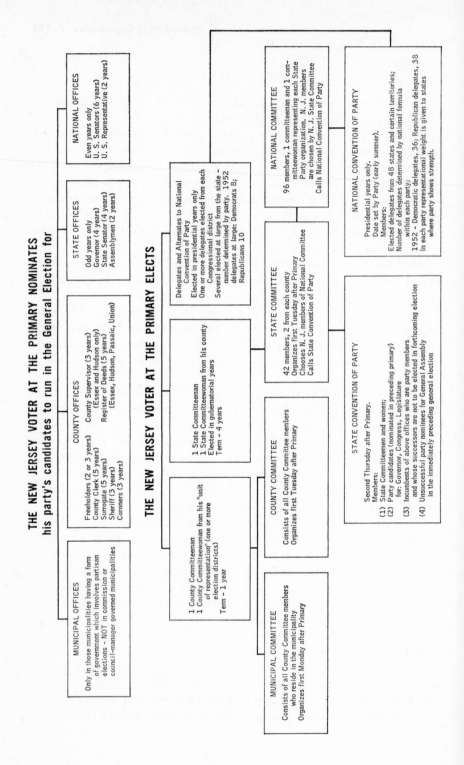

THE NEW JERSEY VOTER AT THE PRIMARY NOMINATES his party's candidates to run in the General Election for

MUNICIPAL OFFICES
Only in those municipalities having a form of government which involves partisan elections -- NOT in commission or council-manager governed municipalities

COUNTY OFFICES
Freeholders (2 or 3 years)
County Clerk (5 years)
Surrogate (5 years)
Sheriff (3 years)
Coroners (3 years)
County Supervisor (3 years) (Essex and Hudson only)
Register of Deeds (5 years) (Essex, Hudson, Passaic, Union)

STATE OFFICES
Odd years only
Governor (4 years)
State Senator (4 years)
Assemblymen (2 years)

NATIONAL OFFICES
Even years only
U. S. Senators (6 years)
U. S. Representative (2 years)

THE NEW JERSEY VOTER AT THE PRIMARY ELECTS

MUNICIPAL COMMITTEE
Consists of all County Committee members who reside in the municipality
Organizes first Monday after Primary

1 County Committeeman
1 County Committeewoman from his "unit of representation" (one or more election districts)
Term - 1 year

COUNTY COMMITTEE
Consists of all County Committee members
Organizes first Tuesday after Primary

1 State Committeeman
1 State Committeewoman from his county
Elected in gubernatorial years
Term - 4 years

Delegates and Alternates to National Convention of Party
Elected in presidential years only
One or more delegates elected from each Congressional district
Several elected at large from the state - number determined by party. 1952 delegates at large: Democrats 8; Republicans 10

STATE COMMITTEE
42 members, 2 from each county
Organizes first Tuesday after Primary
Chooses N. J. members of National Committee
Calls State Convention of Party

STATE CONVENTION OF PARTY
Second Thursday after Primary.
Members:
(1) State Committeemen and women;
(2) Party candidates (nominated in preceding primary) for: Governor, Congress, Legislature
(3) Incumbents of above offices who are party members and whose successors are not to be elected in forthcoming election
(4) Unsuccessful party nominees for General Assembly in the immediately preceding general election

NATIONAL COMMITTEE
96 members, 1 committeeman and 1 committeewoman representing each State Party organization. N. J. members are chosen by N. J. State Committee
Calls National Convention of Party

NATIONAL CONVENTION OF PARTY
Presidential years only.
Date set by Party (early summer).
Members:
Elected delegates from 48 states and certain territories;
Number of delegates determined by national formula within each party;
1952 - Democratic delegates, 36; Republican delegates, 38
In each party representational weight is given to states where party shows strength.

usually with the advice and consent of the county leader and his advisers
—county court judge, district or county or state attorney, depending on
what the chief county prosecuting officer is called. There may be other
offices to be filled also such as other judges, county clerk, sheriff, and so on.

Nominees may be chosen by caucuses, or in primaries, or even by
political clubs. Or they may be selected by a combination of these methods.
The executive committee of a city or county may do its choosing without
the formality of calling a meeting of the whole committee. The mechanics
of selecting candidates, in short, depend on the election laws, the party
rules and the customs of the area. . . .

It is the custom in some areas for the party organization not to take
sides or endorse candidates in the primary election, but rather to back
the winners of the primary in the general election. This may help minimize the seriousness of party splits, but it also may increase the possibility
of such splits.

STATE COMMITTEE. Each state has a state committee elected from different
parts of the state, generally a man and a woman from each of several stated
geographic areas—such as each county, senatorial district or other political
subdivision of the state. Almost invariably, the state committee will elect
a chairman who is the choice of either the governor or the candidate for
governor. A state chairman may be replaced after the campaign if his party
loses. If his party wins, he is usually retained but the party will replace
him if the governor wishes a change.

NATIONAL COMMITTEES. The national committees of both parties consist
of a committeeman and a committeewoman from each state. They serve
for four years and are formally elected at the national conventions.
Actually, of course, the party in each state picks its own committeeman
and committeewoman by methods established in that state, and the
national convention simply ratifies these choices.

In addition, the Republican National Committee rules call for in-
clusion of Republican state chairmen of those states which have voted
Republican in the last presidential election. The Democratic National
Committee does not have this rule.

The chairman of the national committee of the party in power is
selected unofficially by the president; the chairman of the other party's
committee is generally the holdover selection of the party's last presidential candidate.

At the primary in New Jersey, voters nominate party candidates for public office. They
also elect party organization officials. Note municipal, county, and state chairmen are not
elected at the primary. They are elected at a meeting of their constituent committee, the
members of which were elected at the primary. This system is typical of most states.
(Adapted from League of Women Voters of New Jersey chart.)

PARTY ORGANIZATION IN ARIZONA

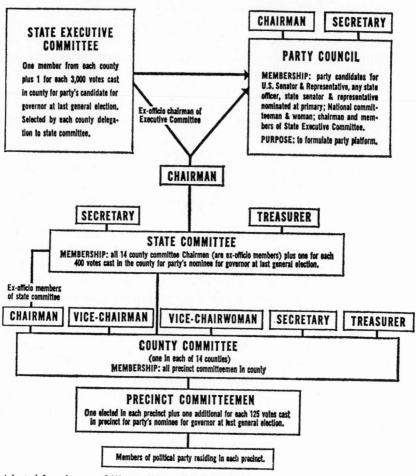

Adapted from League of Women Voters of Arizona chart.

These rules, of course, have exceptions. After Governor Dewey lost the presidential race in 1948, the Chairman of the Republican National Committee he had selected—Hugh Scott of Pennsylvania—resigned in 1949 after it became apparent he had lost the support of the majority of the committee members. Guy George Gabrielson of New Jersey was then elected to succeed Scott. . . .

FUNCTIONS OF PARTY COMMITTEES

An analysis of the different levels of party organization reveals these activities . . .

Town, city and county committees carry out these functions:

1. Organizing to get out the vote and win elections.
2. Nominating or endorsing candidates. (Exception: some organizations keep hands off in the primary, and back whoever wins.)
3. Providing services for the party and the voters, such as doing research, establishing a speakers bureau, holding social events, producing literature, publicity, etc.
4. Money-raising. Political organizations have year-round expenses as well as campaign expenses.
5. Managing patronage.

When state election law so specifies, the parties may also be in charge of primary election arrangements.

State committees and the two national committees are principally service organizations. In addition to the normal types of service, they also produce much "how-to-do-it" material for local use on organizing to win elections. In addition, the national committees arrange the national convention every four years. State committees arrange state conventions when they are called for by law or by party rules.

State and national committees have no nominating functions. They are active in campaigns, producing reams of literature and sponsoring radio and television broadcasts. They do not, however, directly organize to get out the party vote, since that must be done locally. They do hire field men to work in certain key areas with local organizations.

State and national committees also raise money and handle patronage.

THE POLITICAL ORGANIZATION

Few politicians will readily admit to the outsider that there is a political organization in their area because citizens generally feel the existence of a political "machine" is, in itself, an evil thing. Nevertheless, there is always an organization because people must organize to achieve any objective.

Ed Flynn, Democratic leader of Bronx County, New York, for over 25 years, put it this way:

> . . . The average voter did not realize that there were ten thousand political machines in the country, that government, particularly in our large urban centers, could not function without them, that there were both 'good' and 'bad' machines, and that the choice between 'good' and 'bad' lay always with the voters.
> . . . I know the facts of political life. I know that political machines, far from being anachronisms, are as modern as the combustion engine—and as indispensable. . . . I know that fighting 'bad' machines with hastily slapped together 'fusion' tickets is as futile as expecting civilian soldiers with only three months'

training to win a long war . . . as long as we have a two-party system of government, we will have machines.

Even where there is only one party, or the party organizations are weak, there are still organizations. They may be organizations dominated by individuals—as is the case in some of the one-party southern states—or they may be local third party "good government" groups, but there is always some kind of organization to help candidates get nominated and elected.

In the one-party southern states, in some areas of the West, and in places where local and county government is on a nonpartisan basis, the political organization may have less control over nominations than it has elsewhere. In these areas, the political organization tends to be weaker, less disciplined, and the elected official is more apt to be independent of his party organization.

Many people favor a weak party organization and strong candidate organizations in the belief that under this system candidates can be more independent, and that the "hidden government" of the party organization has less influence over the public office holders.

On the other hand, some authorities believe that weak parties and strong candidates lessen party responsibility, blur the issues and emphasize the candidates' personalities, encourage demagoguery and a self-serving attitude in the distribution of government perquisites. . . .

---

16. Running a Candidate*

John Schroeder has been unhappy with decisions of the Mapleville City Council. He finally decides the only remedy is to elect to the Council someone in whom people can have confidence. He wants to run Peter Hanson as an independent. Hanson is a civil engineer with an advanced degree in public administration who owns a small, successful engineering consulting firm in the city.

Inexperienced in politics, Schroeder wonders what it would take to carry out such a plan.

One afternoon, a salesman from out of town who had been calling on Schroeder for several years comes by. Schroeder knows he has been active in politics and sees an opportunity to get some answers. The salesman, Homer Cooper, is happy to oblige.

---

* Chamber of Commerce of the United States. From *Action Course in Practical Politics*. Workshop 2, Case Problem 1. 1959. Reprinted with permission of publisher.

Cooper mentions two steps. One is getting on the ball. The other is getting elected. And he makes these points:

1. A lawyer's services would be required. Cooper tells Schroeder he does not know what the law is in Mapleville but in his hometown Hanson would be required to have petitions signed by a number of eligible voters equal to 10% of the total vote cast in the last election for the office he is seeking.

2. Later (in the campaign) literature, posters, publicity releases, and advertising would be required. Skilled help would be necessary to prepare these.

3. The candidate would need to speak to important groups. For this, he would probably need some help with research and speech writing—and someone to arrange the speaking engagements.

4. A finance committee would be needed to raise funds. The campaign would require more money than any one person would want to contribute.

5. A precinct organization would be needed. By that, Cooper explains, he means somebody in each precinct to get signatures on petitions and then later, to get out Hanson's supporters to vote and to protect his interests at the precinct polling places.

6. Cooper says that while he is not familiar with Mapleville, if it is like his own town there is quite a bit to know about its political side. A man who knows local politics can save a candidate from many small mistakes that could hurt his chances of winning.

After Cooper leaves, Schroeder does some figuring. Mapleville has 18 precincts and the vote in the last state election was about 9,000. If Cooper is right about 10% of the vote being required on a petition, that would mean he needs an average of 50 signatures in each precinct to get Hanson on the ballot.

Schroeder reviews all the different jobs Cooper said must be done in a campaign. He remembers, too, Cooper's parting remark: "John, both parties have an organization already set up to do this kind of work. You ought to give some thought to getting a party to endorse Hanson and run him."

QUESTIONS

1. Cooper listed a number of things including legal advice, publicity and advertising, research, a planned schedule of speaking engagements, a finance committee, a precinct organization, and expert advice.

In Mapleville, how many of these things would Schroeder really need to get Hanson on the ballot and make him a serious contender in the campaign?

2. Explain which of these jobs would have to be done for a candidate to run for the Council—or similar office—in your community?
3. Which of these jobs, if any, would be most important in your community?
4. Cooper explained the problem of getting on the ballot in his town.
   A. In your community nominating is done by _____.
   B. Requirements for getting on the ballot are: _____.
   _____.
   C. How much of a problem would it be to get a candidate on the ballot in your community?
5. Cooper suggested getting Hanson endorsed by an existing political party.
   A. What are the disadvantages?
   B. What are the advantages?

17. The Organization Viewpoint*

Schroeder ponders Cooper's suggestions for getting Hanson endorsed by a political party and decides to explore the possibilities. Schroeder knows Frank White, chairman of one of the local parties. He makes an appointment with White.

All his friends agree Hanson is a good man for the City Council. Schroeder feels White would probably agree, too, and want to run him on the party ticket.

White receives Schroeder cordially but after hearing his story, shows no interest in running Hanson and gives his reasons:

1. As Mr. Cooper has explained, running for office is more than just getting your name on the ballot. To reach voters, interest them in the election, persuade them, and get them to vote, you need an organization to carry on a campaign.

2. We have such an organization in your political party here in Mapleville. With many years of hard work, we have built it into an effective organization with a good record for electing competent officials—some bad choices, perhaps, but by and large mostly good men. At any rate, it's the best means we have for getting good men elected.

---

* Chamber of Commerce of the United States. From *Action Course in Practical Politics*. Workshop 2, Case Problem 2. 1959. Reprinted with permission of publisher.

3. In order to be effective, we have to hold the organization together—
not always an easy task. To hold it together we have to:

A. Promote from within, when possible. Like business firms, we have
   found this a good policy. Bringing in an outsider, while occasionally
   necessary, causes resentment among the loyal party members.

B. We have to win. Workers lose confidence in an organization that
   loses elections—they drift away. To win, we have found that candidates must not only qualify for the job they are after, but they also
   must qualify as *good candidates*. It's better, too, if the candidate is
   politically experienced and knows how to handle himself when
   under attack by the opposition. Politically experienced men are also
   more effective public officials as a rule. They understand the system
   and how to work in it.

4. In concluding, White suggests that since Schroeder and Hanson are
interested in politics, he would like to have them help in the campaign
or with precinct work. He also suggests that if Hanson would become better known—join a variety of organizations and participate in civil activities—he might well develop into a strong candidate in some future
election.

Schroeder had never before realized that there was so much involved in
politics.

QUESTIONS

1. If you were Schroeder, how would you explain this interview to Hanson and his other supporters?
2. White emphasized the importance of holding a political organization
   together. What do you think he meant?
3. White mentioned "workers." Who do you think they are—what do
   they do?
4. White indicated there was a difference between being qualified to hold
   political office and being qualified as a candidate to run for the office.
   What did White mean?
5. What do you think White would judge to be important qualifications
   for a candidate?
6. Of all the reasons White gave, which do you think was his most important reason for not being interested in running Hanson on the
   party ticket?
7. After this interview what courses can Schroeder and Hanson take and
   what do you think of them?

8. To what extent are political party organizations in your community similar to those of White's party organization in Mapleville?

9. Do you think a political leader would really talk this frankly to a citizen about the "realities" of political party organization? Why?

18. The Newtown General Election Campaign*

CAST OF CHARACTERS

POLICY GROUP FOR CAMPAIGN

Clarence Barton	City Leader of a Political Party in Newtown
Wallace Kramer	Campaign Manager of Barton's Party for the general election
Ellis Low	Candidate for Mayor
Patrick Schmidt	Candidate for City Council
Bill Menefee	Candidate for City Council (incumbent seeking reelection)
Joe Ryan	Barton's party leader in Ward 2

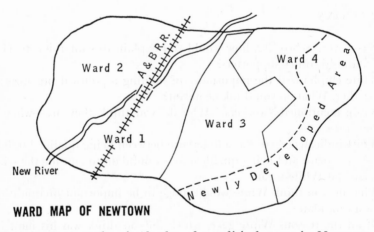

WARD MAP OF NEWTOWN

Clarence Barton, the city leader of a political party in Newtown appoints Wallace Kramer campaign manager on August 1 for the general

---

* Chamber of Commerce of the United States. From *Action Course in Practical Politics*. Workshop 4, Case Problem 1. 1959. Reprinted with permission of publisher.

election. Kramer has been a precinct leader for the party and has served on the finance committee. He has been active in politics for 4 years.

Councilmen are elected on a city-wide basis (as opposed to the practice in some cities of having the voters in each ward elect a councilman from that ward). Their term of 4 years is staggered, two running every two years.

Nevertheless, it has been the custom to select nominees for the council on the basis of one from each ward, so that each of the 4 wards would have at least one man representing it on the City Council.

The Mayor's term is two years.

Here is how the City Council now appears in terms of party representation:

NEWTOWN CITY COUNCIL

Office	Term	From	Party Affiliation	Up for Election
MAYOR	2 years	Ward 3	Opposition	This year
COUNCILMAN	4 years	Ward 1	Opposition	2 years hence
COUNCILMAN	4 years	Ward 2	Opposition	This year
COUNCILMAN	4 years	Ward 3	Opposition	2 years hence
COUNCILMAN	4 years	Ward 4	Barton's Party (Bill Menefee)	This year

VOTING STATISTICS

In the last election, the voting statistics in round numbers for each party, aside from variations between individual candidates, was about as follows:

Ward	Barton's Party	Opposition	Total Vote
WARD 1 (13 precincts)	2,000	3,700	5,700
WARD 2 (10 precincts)	1,100	3,400	4,500
WARD 3 (9 precincts)	2,400	2,100	4,500
WARD 4 (8 precincts)	3,300	2,000	5,300
	8,800	11,200	20,000

CANDIDATES

In the primary Barton's party organization backed Ellis Low for Mayor, Bill Menefee of Ward 4 for another Council term and Patrick Schmidt of Ward 3, also for the Council.

Ordinarily, the organization would have selected a Council candidate from Ward 2 instead of Ward 3, because of the custom of having one councilman from each Ward. However, the party leader in Ward 2, Joe

Ryan, had insisted on a completely unacceptable candidate. Since Barton had been unable to find a good man in Ward 2 who would "buck" Ryan, he put up Schmidt from Ward 3. Low and Menefee were unopposed in the primary, but Ryan contested Schmidt with his candidate. Their primary fight was bitter, but Schmidt won easily.

In addition to candidates for local office, there are county elections for District Attorney, Sheriff, and County Clerk. There are two state representatives, part of whose districts lie in the city; a State Senator whose district covers the county and two other counties; a Congressman whose district covers 15 surrounding counties; a U. S. Senator and a Governor. All of these are incumbents and of Barton's party. All are reasonably good candidates, except the Governor, who is unpopular because of his handling of certain matters affecting Newtown.

Low, Schmidt, and Menefee are generally conceded to be outstanding candidates: capable, successful, forceful, and appealing. They are all active in a number of civic groups. All three are vigorous and experienced campaigners.

This was no accident. Barton was out to win, had started preparation early, and saw to it that each man received a good publicity build-up well in advance of the primary. All three had been speaking at least once a week before various groups for almost nine months.

ORGANIZATION

Barton's political organization is in fine shape in Wards 3 and 4 where most of his party's votes come from. In Ward 2 he has the problem with Ryan. In Ward 1, the quality of the leadership is only average, and there are some precincts without leaders.

STRATEGY

The policy group, composed of Barton, Kramer, Low, Menefee, and Schmidt, sits down to thrash out strategy on August 10th. Kramer has already appointed and briefed his chairmen of publicity, finance, research, speakers, headquarters, volunteers, and others. Barton would handle coordination and supervision of precinct work himself.

They rapidly cover the following points, making decisions where they can:

1. Play down the Governor race, emphasize the local election since local candidates are strong, but the Governor is not popular.

2. Open main headquarters downtown in Ward 1 on the day after Labor Day and simultaneously begin the campaign. All ward and pre-

cinct leaders are to be gotten to the opening. The candidates would define the issues to the workers, then Kramer and Barton would brief and exhort the workers. Barton and Kramer would stay on after the meeting to meet with workers who had grievances, problems, or other things they wanted to be heard on. Asked whether he wanted publicity or not for the opening, Barton hesitates, then says, "No."

3. Concentrate on Wards 3 and 4. Work hardest on precinct organization there. Have each candidate spend some time in every precinct in those wards talking with the precinct leaders and voters at tea or coffee parties, neighborhood gatherings, super-market visits, etc.

4. Set up a working "Citizens for Low, Schmidt and Menefee" group. Kramer had found enough support among civic-minded citizens to assure this would be successful. It was decided to ask them to set up their headquarters in a store (with display window) in Ward 2, even though most members would come from Wards 3 and 4.

5. Set up letterhead groups of prominent doctors, lawyers, merchants, dentists, etc. Attempt to have at least one person in each group who is prominent in lay activities of a religious faith in town.

6. A rally is planned, though no date set. The governor's schedule calls for an appearance in Newtown on October 23. The governor's staff is pressing for a decision.

7. Kramer reports that the finance picture is good. Contributors have faith in the ticket and its chances. The finance chairman has a three-pronged drive going to get funds—through personal solicitations, a mailing, and a fund-raising dinner scheduled for September 15. Kramer is assigned to sit down with the "Citizens for Low, Schmidt and Menefee" to decide who that group should solicit for money and which regular contributors should be reserved for the standard party money-raising efforts. Barton is authorized to request a reduction in the finance quota for Newtown to go to the County Committee before the County Committee could call and ask them to raise the quota.

8. A tentative decision is made to buy a certain amount of newspaper space, radio and TV time, and billboards. Budgets are worked out for a paid staff, headquarters rent, literature and mailing costs, phone bill, funds for election day precinct workers, etc.

9. Kramer pushes through a proposal to set up two training schools for precinct workers and leaders: one evening school for registration-drive training, a second school four days before election on getting out the voters. The usual school for poll watchers and clerks is planned.

10. Plans are made for a central telephoning operation to cover selected precincts in Wards 1 and 3 that are known to be weak. A citizens group will be asked to set up a similar operation in Ward 2 to cover the whole ward.

ISSUES

On issues, the following breakdown is made:

Barton's Party		Opposition Party	
Strong	Vulnerable	Strong	Vulnerable

PROPOSED FLOOD CONTROL
 	
ROADS, SEWERS, AND SO ON
IN NEWLY DEVELOPED AREA
 	
ECONOMY IN GOVERNMENT
	Taxes to pay
	for roads
	and sewers.
		WELFARE,
		PARKS,
		SCHOOLS
			Flood during their
			   administration caused
			   deaths, property damage.
			Government inefficiency.
			Downtown traffic.
			Poor service in providing
			   pavements, sewers, and so on,
			   in newly developed areas.

Barton asserts that: "Our best issue is flood control. Wards 1 and 2 were hardest hit by the recent floods, and if we can't get the people down there to vote for us, at least it will discourage voting for the opposition. In the new housing developments in Wards 3 and 4 there is dissatisfaction over paving, sewers, garbage collection, street lights, etc. Hay can be made there. The only thing they can throw at us is taxes, and we can answer by pointing out their weakness in government economy and their inefficiency. Emphasize our strong points, hit their weak ones, never go on the defensive." Everyone agrees.

It is also agreed to stay away from national and state issues.

TIMING

As the campaign progresses, schedules are carried out well until the first week in October.

DAY AFTER LABOR DAY: Headquarters opens. Campaign officially begins. Precinct leaders are on notice to get moving.

SEPTEMBER 17: Finances are reassessed by policy group. A little short, even after the dinner. Finance chairman comes up with last-minute new solicitation gimmick. Citizens club is asked to contribute. No luck. Some resentment.

SEPTEMBER 30: Opposition accuses Schmidt of shady real estate deal in connection with property being sold for delinquent taxes. Charge he had bribed tax official. Barton advised: "Don't answer."

OCTOBER 5: Schmidt real-estate deal on front page every day. Everyone furious at Barton. Barton calls policy group meeting at Kramer's request. Barton says he originally thought it would blow over if they didn't answer.

Since it had grown to major proportions, they had better answer loudly, clearly, and quickly. The policy group decides to take time on radio and TV; ads in paper. Schmidt to appear on radio and TV. Barton warns Schmidt to answer clearly, summarize why he is innocent in not more than two main points, then go on to accuse opposition of delivering a low-blow, known to be trumped up. Further, accuse them of trying to cover up the real issues of flood control and services for newly developed areas. Day of broadcast, ad is scheduled saying "Schmidt on Trial—Tune in Tonight!" Next day's papers to carry ads on flood damage with pictures—copy to read "Stop danger to life and property! Vote for Low, Schmidt, Menefee."

OCTOBER 15: Club leaders called in. Women's club assigned responsibility for setting up and manning central phone operation on election day. Young people's club to start getting ready to man polling places in second ward if Ryan's people walk out. Ryan, still angry over primary, is now mad at citizens group activity in his ward. "Citizens for L S M are offending the voters in my ward, driving them over to the opposition," he says. "I may go with them." Ryan emotional. No peace terms possible.

OCTOBER 17: Governor's office delivers ultimatum on rally in Newtown. Either it is set for October 23 or it is cancelled. Barton has learned that the Governor is booked solid the week before election, so he tells Governor's secretary he would like to have him that week, on the 28th. Says his local campaign timing won't dovetail with a rally for the Governor on the 23rd. The Governor's secretary explodes, tells Barton—they can lose Newtown by no more than 300 votes if they are going to win the state. Barton says the governor will carry Newtown by 300 to 500. Conversation ends abruptly.

Barton calls in Kramer. They schedule a rally for Tuesday, the 28th, featuring local candidates. Kramer has already booked high school auditorium for 28th. They map out assignments for clubs, citizens groups, ward and precinct leaders, and campaign committee chairmen so that each person working on the campaign has a responsibility for bringing a certain number to the rally. Speakers chairman is made rally chairman. Kramer is to supervise generally. Publicity chairman assigned to promote rally. Barton is to supervise ticket distribution.

Barton issues orders to hold up all mailings, advertising, speaking engagements from Saturday until Wednesday and Thursday, the 29th and 30th.

OCTOBER 18: Opposition appears to be making headway with their record on schools and welfare. Candidates meet with Barton and Kramer, say that everything is going wrong, that they should shift and either find fault with the schools, say welfare spending is getting out of hand, or somehow cancel the opposition effect. Barton and Kramer soothe them; point out they are making headway on their own issues, more than they may realize. Say the opposition is definitely defensive on flood control. To shift the attack now would be to fight opposition on their own ground. Candidates reluctantly agree to continue original strategy.

OCTOBER 27: All city road equipment concentrated in 3rd and 4th wards. City has put on extra men. Pictures in paper. Barton says, "This is what we have been waiting for!"

OCTOBER 28: Rally. Low hits last-minute street paving in 3rd and 4th ward as obvious attempt to cover up in the week before election the sins of the past four years and an effort to buy the election by putting more men in the roads department. He calls this financing elections with tax-payers funds. The overflow crowd of party faithful cheer to the rafters. Rally on radio and TV.

OCTOBER 29 TO ELECTION DAY: Steady stream of ads and radio and TV spots as far as budget permits. Monday night radio-TV half-hour show at 10:30 P.M. Candidates and their families appear, issues summed up.

ELECTION DAY: Candidates shaking hands outside polls all day. Ryan jumps on bandwagon at last minute when he shows up to collect money to pay his election day workers. Club workers man many polls in Ward 2 where Ryan's people don't show up. Central telephone operations success-fully manned.

Low, Schmidt and Menefee win, with Schmidt trailing the others about 150 votes. The following chart indicates, in round numbers, the margin by which Low and Menefee won:

ELECTION RESULTS

	Barton's Party	Opposition	Total Vote
WARD 1	2100	3100	5200
WARD 2	850	2900	3750
WARD 3	3000	1600	4600
WARD 4	3950	1400	5350
TOTAL	9900	9000	18900

The governor ran well behind the local ticket, but carried the city by 250 votes. The U. S. Senator and other party candidates carried the city with margins of 500 to 800 votes.

QUESTIONS

1. Discuss the merits of the policy group's decision to "concentrate on Wards 3 and 4."

2. Barton and his policy group decide to stress local candidates and de-emphasize the Governor race.
   A. How did this affect campaign issues?
   B. How did it influence the rally?
   C. How might this decision influence the Newtown party organization's relations with the Governor?
3. How much importance do you attach to the public speeches, etc., planned for Low and Menefee before the campaign?
4. Experienced politicians named two reasons why Schmidt would be a weaker candidate (prior to the real-estate smear) than Menefee. What do you think they were?
5. In a way, Kramer and Barton by-passed Ryan, the leader of the 2nd ward, with the Citizens group.
   A. How do you feel about this?
   B. How else might they have handled the situation?
6. The campaign financing problem was not bad at all. What three factors influenced this result?
7. Barton advised Low and the other candidates not to debate the opposition's issues. Comment on his remarks in this regard.
8. At first, Barton insisted that Schmidt should not answer attacks on his real estate deal. Later they gained so much attention they became a major issue. What did you think were Barton's reasons for the original advice?
9. When Schmidt was required to answer, comment on Barton's advice before the TV appearance.
10. Barton held back the rally until one week before the election. He also insisted that no statements be made for four days before the rally, and he held up all mailings until Wednesday and all radio and TV appearances, spots and newspaper ads until Thursday.
    A. What effect was he trying to achieve?
    B. What are the advantages and disadvantages of this procedure?
11. Most decisions made in the campaign had to do with influencing the voters directly. Some others were made primarily to motivate the organization. Identify some of those primarily aimed at the organization.
12. Several actions were planned specifically to get out the "saints." Most of these were unspectacular and had to do with organization mechanics.
    A. Identify those you think fit this description.
    B. Identify the other actions of an issue or enthusiasm-raising nature directed at "saints."

13. A. What issue specifically was aimed at savables and sinners and was used to discredit the opposition?
    B. Why did Barton think it would be effective?
    C. Which issue was aimed at saints and savables?
    D. What was the dramatic result of pressing the issue?
14. Note that both Barton's party vote and the opposition vote in Ward 2 dropped off.
    A. What are the reasons for the drop in each party's votes?
    B. How can you account for the decrease in the opposition vote in Wards 3 and 4?
    C. How can you account for the increase in Barton's party vote in Wards 3 and 4?
15. It has been observed that Barton's party won not so much by getting out more votes than usual but by the fact that the opposition's vote was less than usual.
    A. Can you interpret how this happened?
    B. Would you consider Barton's campaign successful?
    C. In future elections, when issues are different, what changes in organization and strategy might be in order?

---

91. The Two-year Plan*

Arthur McCabe is the Chairman or leader of his political party in the town of Hackendale, population about 23,000. His party has just suffered a complete defeat at the polls in a municipal election. In the larger picture, his party also lost the incumbent Congressman, the State Senator, and the United States Senator. The Governor, also of McCabe's party, was not up for election or he might have gone down too.

Everybody had different explanations for the defeat. Conservatives said the party was too liberal and the liberals said it was too conservative. Some said the candidates were no good. Reasons ranged from Washington policies to Hackendale garbage collection.

Whatever the *real* reasons, McCabe was in danger of losing his party leadership unless he could demonstrate in the very near future some professional planning that would put his party back in office two years later. As a sincere and dedicated politician, he frankly wanted to keep leadership in the hands of an experienced "pro"—namely, Art McCabe.

Here are some of the problem areas in which McCabe thought it neces-

---

* Chamber of Commerce of the United States. From *Action Course in Practical Politics*. Workshop 6, Case Problem 1. 1959. Reprinted with permission of publisher.

sary to do something—and some of the facts in each problem area that McCabe took into consideration in his planning.

1. ELECTION STATISTICS*

	McCabe Party	Opposition	Total
Vote	3880	4743	8623
Percent of Vote	45	55	100
Eligible Voters (estimated)	5750	7140	14375
Registered Voters	4488	5374	11081
Percent of Registered Voters	40.5	48.5	89

*Reading horizontally, the top two columns total accurately, but the bottom three do not. The reason is that "eligible voters" and "registered voters" include unaffiliated voters, whereas in the election, only McCabe's party and the opposition were on the ballot, so these people had to vote for one or the other.

McCabe knows from experience that about 75% of registered voters in his area actually vote. Maximum effort is always put into the attempt to get 100%, but the percentage stays relatively constant. However, he figures that among the unregistered but eligible voters he might have about 1260 more voters of his party's persuasion.

2. ORGANIZATION

McCabe has 18 precincts in his town with 2 precinct leaders authorized in each. He classifies his precincts into 4 groups according to their section of town: 12 precincts are in relatively low income areas, 8 precincts are in newly built up sections occupied by middle income people, 12 precincts are in an older section of town which could be classed as a middle income area, and 2 precincts are populated by relatively high income families. He makes two tables according to this breakdown classifying his precinct leaders first according to performance, second as to whether he could rely on their support to keep his leadership of the town committee:

PRECINCT LEADER PERFORMANCE

Performance	Low Income	Middle Income New Section	Middle Income Older Section	High Income	Total
Good	4	4	9	1	18
Fair	6	2	2	—	10
Poor	2	—	—	2	4
Vacancy	—	2	1	1	(4)
TOTAL	12 (2 women)	6 (4 women)	11 (7 women)	3 (2 women)	32

PRECINCT LEADER LOYALTY TO McCABE

Reliability	Low Income	Middle Income New	Middle Income Old	High Income	Total
Reliable	9	2	4	1	16
Unreliable	3	4	6	1	14
Potential Rivals	—	—	1	1	2
TOTAL	12	6	11	3	32

McCabe has two potential rivals, both very able precinct leaders, both ambitious. Peter Moore from the "middle income old" area is a young lawyer who wants to get ahead. McCabe thinks he is apt to bite off more than he can chew. Moore would like to run for office or be appointed to a job where he could get valuable experience.

George Meighan, in the "high income" area, is in his 50's, successful, has turned over most of his business to his son, and would like to get into a political position where he could make his weight felt. He is very able, but not yet attuned to the ways of politics nor experienced in the field.

McCabe has one political club in his party organization, a women's club.

3. FINANCE

McCabe's town committee is in debt $1500.

His finance chairman of the campaign has been a poor choice—McCabe's fault. Fortunately, the chairman had indicated that one campaign was enough, and McCabe is free to recruit another without embarrassment.

He has two possible choices for finance work. A hustling, likeable, young salesman, Joe Clark, going up fast, but without good connections. McCabe thinks Joe has in mind contacting successful men through the finance work and using the assignment as a showcase to demonstrate his ability. If so, he would have strong motivation to do a really good job.

The other choice is a man in his 60's, highly successful, still active in his accounting firm and well established in the community. He has been a regular contributor and solicitor of funds for 10 years. He has never tried to use his ability to raise money as a wedge to obtain anything and has always been available to help out when needed. He has two drawbacks— he is not a politician and is not a good organizer or leader. As so many politicians do, McCabe wonders what this man, Harry Thompson, wants. He doubts that Thompson will work hard forever without some substantial recognition.

4. *CANDIDATES*

McCabe sees two problems in relation to choosing candidates. The first problem is the usual one of finding good men to run for local office. His second is to decide what higher office on a county, state or national level he might try to get for a Hackendale man.

A. *In the city,* McCabe has two possible candidates for a seat on the City Council.

Peter Moore is one. Moore is, among other things, a member of the Birdwatchers Society. He is also a good candidate type and capable of doing a good job in public office. Politically savvy. Conservative on most political issues.

The other possibility is Milton Santangelo. He is a successful hardware store owner, highly respected in his area. Although successful, he has not moved out of his old neighborhood near the railroad station. Santangelo is active in the Elks, his church, and the Garibaldi Club. Forty-five years old, Santangelo has an engineering degree from State College and played half-back on the local high school football team 28 years ago.

McCabe also has in mind two possible candidates for Mayor. Either would be acceptable for Councilman, too.

One is George Heath, past president of the Chamber of Commerce. While chairman of the civil affairs committee of the chamber, he was very effective in bringing about a complete property reassessment and also in finding a partial solution to the downtown parking problem. The first accomplishment left some scars, but the second was popular. The qualities that helped him become chamber president also make him a good candidate for Mayor. His record shows courage, ability, and effectiveness.

The other Mayor possibility is James Goldsmith. A lawyer, Goldsmith is somewhat liberal, and internationalist in his views. He has served on a state bar association committee and is well known for defending difficult and indigent cases. Several years before he formed a civic association which financed the erection of a public swimming pool with a combination of town funds and private subscriptions. A good trial lawyer, he could perform creditably on a speaking platform. Goldsmith served one term on the town council several years ago and acquitted himself very well. Popular almost everywhere in town.

McCabe would need one candidate for Mayor and one candidate for councilman.

B. *Higher Office.* McCabe decides that of all the possibilities, he would prefer to put a Hackendale man in the U. S. House of Representatives to replace the newly elected incumbent from the opposition party. The seat normally is held by a man of McCabe's party—the recent election was an upset. There is no chance that the beaten incumbent will be considered to run again.

The Congressional District covers 6 counties. This means McCabe must have the backing of his county leader and the leaders of two or three other counties to sew up the nomination for his man.

However, the Congressional seat is not considered a great plum by political leaders in McCabe's area, because a Congressman has very little patronage to dispense. Also, since unwritten rules preclude the defeated incumbent's county from running another man for the seat again, and since one other county has a man for the state senate seat, McCabe figures that these two counties are at least not contenders, at best, possible supporters for his man. The state senator spot was filled by one of McCabe's men from Hackendale before he was beaten. There are three counties in the state senatorial district, all of them within the Congressional District.

McCabe has two possible candidates, both of whom would be rated as conservatives on national issues.

One is the 32 year old secretary to the defeated incumbent. He is a natural candidate, and has a very compelling manner. He is an articulate expert on national issues and a formidable speaker. He has been active in civic affairs.

He is very well known in the district through his campaigning for his former boss and other party activities.

In addition to being a good candidate type, McCabe is drawn to him because:

1. He believes a strong candidate like this young man would pull the whole ticket along to some extent in a presidential year when national issues would be prominent in the campaign.
2. A young man could stay in Congress a long time and acquire valuable seniority. An older man would be likely to retire before assuming much seniority.

The other possible candidate is a successful man in his early 60's who would like to run. He has substantial friends in business, industry and the professions. As a candidate, the man lacks experience, and would have to be coached on issues. A passable speaker, good appearance, dignified. If McCabe gets this man the nomination he is certain his financial problems would be close to solved. He also feels, however, that the ticket would have to carry this man to some extent.

ISSUES

The Birdwatchers, a vocal and active civic group, are fighting the proposed plan to fill in some marshland on the edge of town because it would drive away certain unusual birds.

Public interest in "Business Climate" and the need for new industry in town are building up as a result of chamber of commerce work. The plan to fill in marshland proposes to use the new land for industrial sites.

Schools are quite adequate, but a look at long-term population growth, and physical depreciation, indicates that provision for expanding the schools in the near future is desirable.

Liberal-conservative split is a problem in both parties.

A women's civic group, a church group, and a local union are vocal on national and state welfare issues.

PATRONAGE

McCabe lines up some of the things he might want and assesses his bargaining position to get them as follows:

What He May Want	*What He Can Offer*
1. Congressional Nomination	1. Can give up claim to the State senate seat which has been held by a Hackendale man.
2. Delegate to National Convention	
3. County Clerk nomination (it is generally conceded at county head-quarters that Hackendale is entitled to name the man for this post, next election).	2. Can give up County Clerk spot he has a claim to.
	3. Has close relationship with Governor's new patronage man. This man can help him get some state jobs.

McCabe intensely dislikes using patronage to build his organization, preferring to rely on public recognition, participation, and a good program of work to develop his people and hold them together. However, he knows that somebody is going to get top positions and he would prefer, wherever possible, to bargain able men from Hackendale into these spots rather than concede them to other leaders who might be less exacting in their judgment on who can fill which jobs capably.

QUESTIONS

ELECTION STATISTICS
1. What interpretations can we make of McCabe's election statistics as background for discussing his problem areas?

ORGANIZATION
1. What problems do you think McCabe saw in the tables titled "Precinct Leader Performance" and "Precinct Leader Loyalty"?

FINANCE

1. What problems do you see in this information alone?
2. Thinking of McCabe's "two-year plan," what distinction do you make between his *immediate* and *long-range* money problems?

CANDIDATES

1. Congressional race

   What immediate advantages do you see in the younger man as a candidate for congress?

   What immediate advantages do you see in the older man as a candidate for congress?

   What possible disadvantages do you see in the younger man? Older man?

2. City Council and Mayor

   What are the advantages and disadvantages of each of the four candidates?

ISSUES To the extent that issues may help McCabe's party win the next election

1. What issue or issues can he stress to win the savables?
2. How can McCabe lessen the unfavorable impact of certain issues?
3. What issue or issues must he remain vulnerable on and take his chances?
4. What issue or issues can help in:
   A. Recruiting workers?
   B. Improving finances?

PATRONAGE

1. If McCabe can get the choice of delegate to the National Convention, what kind of man will he be likely to select in terms of:
   A. Party loyalty and service?
   B. Might he consider this a "recognition" post?
2. How might McCabe trade to get the choice of Congressman and delegate to the convention?

LOOKING BACK

1. What possible actions does it now appear McCabe might take in building up his organization and making his own leadership secure, avoiding a primary fight with one of his two rivals for town leadership?
2. McCabe and his town committee control the nomination for mayor, councilman, and county clerk. Assume that McCabe can, by trading, name the delegate to the National Convention and the candidate for Congress. Careful selection of the men for these nominations can be the key to solving or partly solving the problems of finance, issues, the leadership contest, balancing the ticket, appealing to different

income groups and the needs of the community. Considered in this light, whom might McCabe pick for:

Congress—why?

Delegate to National Convention—why?

Mayor—why?

Councilman—why?

County Clerk—why?

What problems are left unsolved by these choices of candidates? How might they be solved?

3. Explain how (in any way not yet covered) the facts in McCabe's election statistics and in the different "problem areas" are related.

4. A key factor in attracting money, workers, good candidates, and votes is making a party look as if it can win. In the next year and a half, what publicity actions can McCabe take other than making optimistic statements, to give the public the impression that his party would win?

Robert Bendimer

20. The "Engineering of Consent"—a Case Study*

Back in the days of Ralph Waldo Emerson it was thought, at least by Dr. Emerson, that if a man built a better mousetrap than his neighbor, the world would beat a path to his door. Today, thanks to public relations, we understand that the builder must first arrange for "the engineering of public consent" to mousetraps. Next he must acquire "earned recognition" for his particular model. And then, according to extreme practitioners, he must, if necessary, "create situations of reality" by setting up, for example, a National Citizens' Committee for the Urgent Capture of Mice. . . .

Edward L. Bernays, father of the "engineering" line and one of the most vociferously idealistic men in the business, undoubtedly had in mind only proper objectives for his approach, presumptuous as its phrasing may sound, but the case study we are about to make shows what can happen when "opinion engineers" are given their head. It is a short step, it turns out, from wangling public consent to kidding the public into imagining its consent has already been given—a thought that Carl Byoir & Associates, Inc., it would seem, daringly worked up to a whole creative system for manufacturing "situations of reality."

---

* From *Reporter*. August 11, 1955, pp. 14–23. Reprinted with permission of publisher and author.

(P.R.) MEN AT WORK

It is this system, with its overtones of modified Barnum, that under-lies, colors, and gives public meaning to the $250-million anti-trust suit formally titled *Noerr Motor Freight, Inc. et. al. v. Eastern Railroad Presidents Conference et al.*, but better known in the trade as the railroad-trucker brawl. Should this case ever come to trial in the United States District Court in Philadelphia, where it has long been at rest, it would doubtless sustain *Tide's* prediction of the "most hard-fought and bloody of the century's legal battles." But even in the event of a settlement, now strongly indicated, enough has spilled out in pre-trial skirmishes to afford a remarkably complete and lively panorama of public-relations men at work—at least one variety of the species.

There is no intent here to judge the case or to pass on the relative merits of hauling freight by rail or truck. Neither is it suggested that the "engineering" that went on in this celebrated battle is synonymous with public relations in general, though in varying degree its aspects are to be encountered elsewhere in the craft. To find them all together it was clearly necessary to pick an extreme case rather than describe a typical one.

Nonetheless, what gives the affair its special claim to attention is that the rival concerns—Byoir for the railroads and David Charnay's Allied Public Relations Associates for the truckers—are whirring dynamos in the business, that their clients are economic powers of the first rank, and that in their raucous clash not merely a public-relations firm is on trial but some of the commonly practiced techniques of public relations as well.

VICTORY AT HARRISBURG

On January 21, 1952, Pennsylvania's Governor John S. Fine faced a hard decision. Without his veto a measure called by its sponsors the "Fair Truck Bill" and by its opponents the "Big Truck Bill" would automat-ically become law. That outcome, the Governor knew, would not sit well with the railroads, traditionally a power in Pennsylvania politics roughly comparable to oil in Texas and sin in Nevada. On the other hand, both houses of the Legislature had passed the bill, which would have raised the weight limit for long-haul trucks allowed on the state's highways from forty-five thousand pounds to sixty thousand. Except for Kentucky, the Pennsylvania limit was the lowest in the country, far below that imposed by any of its neighboring states. The trucking business, smarting under the drastic curb, had itself become a force in the Pennsylvania capital, perhaps not as entrenched as exponents of the older form of transportation, but brasher, with considerable appeal to voters, and an ample supply of ready cash.

Caught in this crossfire of special interests, the Governor may well have acted on what he conceived to be the pure merits of the case when, six minutes before the deadline, he vetoed the weight-increase bill. If Governor Fine had been cross examined on the reasons for his action, he could certainly have made out an excellent case.

In the first place, the Maryland State Roads Commission was co-sponsoring a test of the relative damage done by various axle loads to concrete pavement, and with what appeared to be providential timing, an advance copy of an interim report had come to Governor Fine's attention. The tentative findings were hard on heavy trucks.

The Governor also understood that the Pennsylvania State Association of Township Supervisors, a quasi-official body, was all out against the "Big Truck" bill. Tens of thousands of postcards were pouring out under its imprimatur addressed to the car owners of the state, and it had produced a television program on the Maryland road test.

The Pennsylvania State Grange appeared to be equally aroused against the bill. Material had streamed out of its headquarters during the legislative battle, and the Governor must have known that the Grange had worked on state Senators, especially those from politically doubtful districts, to vote against the measure.

So insistent, in fact, was the opposition—even after passage of the bill— that the Governor felt obliged to hold public hearings two days before the deadline for his decision—and at those hearings the anti-big-truck witnesses had made an extremely impressive case.

HOW SPONTANEOUS CAN YOU GET?

The result of all this civic activity was the veto. *Vox populi* had been heard and heeded. Or so it seemed, for few persons outside the offices of Carl Byoir & Associates knew until much later:

1. That the public relations man of the Maryland State Roads Commission, which had co-sponsored the road test, had been advising the Byoir office, on an expense account, and was later to go on the payroll of Byoir's client, the Eastern Railroad Presidents Conference (E.R.P.C.), at $1,000 a month.

2. That those tens of thousands of postcards mailed out to motorists in the name of the Pennsylvania State Association of Township Supervisors had been prepared and mailed by the Byoir organization and billed to the E.R.P.C.

3. That during the fight for the bill, a Byoir lieutenant, according to his own subsequent testimony, made his headquarters in the Pennsylvania State Grange, whose literature was similarly drawn up by Byoir men and billed to the railroads.

4. Or, finally, that the impressive showing at the hearings was not the spontaneous plea of affected Pennsylvanians, but the carefully coached performance of Byoir-organized witnesses.

Allowing for a certain freedom from shyness essential to the profession, let Reynolds Girdler, then a Byoir executive, tell the story of the "CB&A team" in his own words:

> When January, 1951, opened, there seemed every reason to believe that the truckers would get their bill through, increasing the allowable weight to 60,000 pounds. The 17 railroads of Pennsylvania then started fighting. . . . They fought the bill for four months and then threw up the sponge. They reported to their superiors that they were licked. Even so the lobbyists in control of the railroad activity continued to oppose allowing the CB&A people to operate in Pennsylvania. Their superiors then thrust us down their throats.

Recommending a special award for C. Colburn Hardy, who commanded the Byoir forces in the Battle of Harrisburg, the interoffice memorandum continued:

> The team went to work in Pennsylvania beginning in June, 1951. Not only did they begin to generate publicity against the bill, but they were successful in getting a long list of organizations and individuals publicly to oppose the bill. Those organizations ranged from the CIO to the Pennsylvania State Grange. . . . Even after the bill was passed by both houses, clamor against the bill continued. . . . The CB&A team thereupon went out and organized twenty-one witnesses for twenty-one organizations against the bill. They prepared their statements and the publicity . . . Veto of this bill meant that some five million dollars worth of freight was retained on the Pennsylvania Railroad, because the trucking limit was not raised. This represented one of the most dramatic illustrations of the power of organized public opinion that anyone could hope to find. . . .

The opinion may have been more organized than public (Mr. Hardy, the award-nominee, modestly dismissed this description of his efforts as "over-enthusiastic"—"a sales pitch"), but the illustration was certainly dramatic enough. According to Edward Gogolin, general manager and first vice-president of the Pennsylvania Motor Truck Association, the veto "triggered the industry" into action.

While the truckers had never been a retiring sort, it was clear now that massive retaliation was in order. It was not surprising, then, that in May, 1952, they engaged the services of David Charnay and his Allied Public Relations Associates. As the Pennsylvania truckers' president, Floyd B.

Noerr, put it, "We were trying to find out who was stabbing us in the back, and then if we did find out, to pull out the dagger and bring suit."

The identity of the assailant could hardly have been as much of a mystery as all that. Certainly, Gogolin, Noerr's lieutenant, had a good notion since, as he was later to testify, "Practically every morning, to get to my office, I had to stumble over C. Colburn Hardy, the Byoir man, who was using the Grange office on the first floor of our building as his headquarters." Nevertheless, it was plain that Charnay's services were not being engaged merely to "engineer public consent" for the hauling of freight by truck. He was hired as well to do a detective job on a fellow publicist.

ENTER MISS SAROYAN

Long before the Governor's veto or Charnay's entry into the picture, the American Trucking Association was aware of the Byoir tactics against the long-haul truckers.

The reason for this was dramatic and simple. One day in July, 1951, a young lady named Sonya Saroyan, originally Sonya Jigarjian, walked into the American Trucking Association's Washington office to tell Walter Belson, its public-relations director, all about Life with Byoir.

After two years as secretary to the Byoir executive in charge of the Eastern Railroad account, Miss Saroyan—twenty-nine and variously described as "an attractive brunette" and "a very strange dish of tea"—had resigned or been fired, a point not easily determined. With her went a large packet of memos, reports, directives, letters, and releases, mostly carbons or copies she herself had made and which she therefore somewhat naïvely regarded as her "own property." All of it was intended to show how the art of public relations was practiced by her erstwhile employer. Belson accepted her offerings, along with two days of tape-recorded "testimony" at $50 a day, plus expenses. For nearly a year that seemed to be the end of Miss Saroyan's brush with adventure. . . .

At any rate, the truckers appear to have been extraordinarily slow to see the value of Sonya's contribution to their cause. At one point in the Battle of Harrisburg, Belson telephoned Gogolin to report that some pertinent material had been delivered to headquarters by an ex-employee of the enemy and to ask whether the trucking executive was aware of "certain things" going on in the state, more significant even than Gogolin's tripping over Hardy every morning on his way to work. Soon after, the Pennsylvania truckers dispatched an agent to examine the material in Washington and take notes. But it appears that if the Charnay organization had not taken over, the Saroyan dossier, in all its colorful detail, might have been left forever to gather dust.

THINGS GET GOING

It was in April, 1952, that three officials of the Pennsylvania Motor Truck Association called on David Charnay, an enterprising young man whose favorable impression on John L. Lewis had made him a major publicist, putting him in a position to ask the truckers, and to get, $36,000 a year, plus expenses, for his services. The sum was modest enough compared with the $150,000 a year the railroads were paying Byoir, plus expenses running up to $250,000, but still rather impressive for a man who only a few years earlier had been reporting nightclub doings for the New York *Daily News*. Besides the United Mine Workers of America account and a colorful and rewarding stint for the Nationalist Bank of China, Charnay had lined up such notable clients as Ballantine Beer and Eversharp. A man of versatile talents, he has managed to promote the fortunes of such diverse figures as Franklin D. Roosevelt, Jr., Richard Nixon, Robert F. Wagner, Vincent Impellitteri, and Louis E. Wolfson, the man who tried to take over Montgomery Ward.

In its preliminary phase the truckers' account was put in the hands of a former newspaper man named Henry Paynter, whose first order of business was to get a private detective on the track of Sonya Saroyan. She was located in New York, in May, and throughout the summer and fall, she says, Paynter and Charnay pressed her to release the material she had turned over to the American truckers office (which apparently would not yield it up to the Pennsylvania group otherwise), and to tell them more about the workings of the Byoir enterprise.

She was offered a job, according to her testimony, but turned it down. Eventually, as she tells the tale, she succumbed, on the understanding that the documents and her testimony—she had added an additional $1,050 worth—were to be turned over to a Congressional committee for investigation. Next thing she knew, she says, was the announcement in the papers of January 18, 1953, that the Pennsylvania Motor Truck Association and thirty-seven trucking companies were suing the Eastern Railroad Presidents Conference, thirty-one railroads, thirty-four individuals (mostly railroad presidents and ex-presidents) and the public-relations firm of Carl Byoir & Associates. . . .

Allowing for the natural exuberance of lawyers, especially in pre-trial procedures, it seems reasonably clear that in a public-relations war anything up to and including piracy may well be expected. In any event, what emerged from the Charnay firm's preliminary labors, as refined by the distinguished Philadelphia law firm of Dilworth, Paxson, Kalish & Green, amounted to the following charge:

That the defendant railroads had conspired, through vilification, slander, bribery, and assorted devices to drive the long-distance truckers out of business, with the objective of "carving out exclusive, monopolistic spheres of operation in the freight transportation business." To this end, the complaint ran, the Byoir firm had been hired and it "immediately initiated a vicious, corrupt and fraudulent campaign" to "obstruct, hamper and impede interstate transportation by motor vehicle," all in willful violation of the Sherman Antitrust Act. In its reply, the Byoir firm flatly denied these allegations.

Boiling down the charges as they related to Byoir, Dilworth at the pretrial hearings specified "misinformation . . . front organizations . . . distorted photographs . . . planting of stories . . . 'boilerplate' announcements . . . phony polls," and the like. To which Philip Price of the defense staff replied that much of the case seemed to be that the "defendants got together and called the plaintiff bad names."

Whether such activities as those alleged form a pattern that is vulnerable under the Sherman Antitrust Act may safely be left to the courts and the fullness of time, but the open discussion of these techniques, illegal or merely tricky, is of general interest to the public and of special interest throughout the whole hypersensitive realm of public relations.

LEAGUES AND FOUNDATIONS

If there is one obvious lesson to be derived from the railroad-trucker affair, it is that the fulsome interoffice memorandum is a luxury to be resisted. A specimen of the sort that prompted Dilworth to say he would guard with his life the collection of Byoir papers carted off by Miss Saroyan is this gem that Reynolds Girdler, the former Byoir executive, composed in 1949 to set the tactical line for promoting the firm's new railroad client:

> You can see from the foregoing that this account is utterly unlike the conventional one. *Here we do not have a client for attribution.* [Italics mine.] Of course we will release some stories under client attribution, but they will be of lesser propaganda importance than those we can generate from motorists, property owners, tax payers, farmers or women's groups. In sum, we not only have to create publicity ideas; we also have to go out in the field and create the groups and occasions so that those publicity ideas will become realities.

One of the groups they created, in the New York sector of the battle line, was the Empire State Transport League. When Girdler first testified about this organization, he modestly credited its formation to a small group of upstate New York businessmen. They were aided, he said, by Thomas Kiely, a Byoir man, but "only in the nicest kind of way," and besides the impetus was their own. Confronted, however, with a memorandum he had dashed off to his superior on the subject—another of the documents spirited out by the impulsive Miss Saroyan—Girdler freely admitted authorship. It read in part: "We formed the Empire State Transport League in New York because we needed an organization that could legitimately mail all types of propaganda on the general subject of trucks and highways."

The League had an address, of course—11 North Pearl Street, Albany, it said on the letterheads—but no office that a Dun & Bradstreet investigator could locate. A public stenographer took the mail and, presumably, relayed it on to the Byoir office. But the organization did have a constitution and bylaws, and for reproducing copies of these, along with membership-application forms, the Byoir firm duly billed the Eastern Railroad Presidents Conference on December 9 and 12, 1949.

The League was then all set to send out releases, reprints, and other such material, none of which would have been quite so persuasive if it had had to bear some such imprint as "Carl Byoir & Associates, Public Relations Counsel to the Eastern Railroad Presidents Conference" instead of "Empire State Transport League."

David I. Mackie, chairman of the E.R.P.C., has insisted that ". . . the real issue is not between the heavy truck operators and the railroads, but between an informed and militant public and the highway freighters." The League, it seems, was just a slice of that informed and militant public boiled down to a letterhead.

Another slice apparently was called the "New Jersey Citizens Tax Study Foundation," which was launched just as the Byoir office was warming up the campaign against the truckers. Among its original incorporators was one C. Colburn Hardy, then commanding the Byoir railroad campaign on the Jersey front. As Hardy later testified, "This was a personal matter that I did as a citizen, similar to a great many other civic projects in which I happened to be interested."

It was odd, though, that at the pretrial proceedings fifteen canceled checks amounting to $3,700.58 were produced from the Byoir files, made out to Fred W. Goodwin, executive director of the Foundation. The E.R.P.C. was also billed for the Foundation's envelopes, letterheads, and releases, as well as for "contributions" by the Byoir firm.

Still harder to square with Hardy's purely civic role in the Foundation was the directive he addressed to his staff with all the characteristic candor of Byoir executives: "We are also assisting in the formation of a new group: New Jersey Citizens Tax Study Foundation . . . ALL LITERA-TURE, ETC. from this group must be on plain paper and mailed from New Jersey."

Yet the Foundation solemnly turned out studies on highway finance and even conducted a poll that showed the public fairly panting for a mileage tax on heavy trucks. "As a fact-finding group," said the covering release, "the Foundation takes no position, merely reports the results." With equal solemnity the Foundation later released to the press a letter to the New Jersey Motor Truckers Association denying that it was a "front" for the railroads.

The New Jersey Automobile Owners, Inc., was clearly not started by Byoir, having been incorporated back in 1938. But, testified Hardy, "I helped in reactivating" it. The pattern was similar to the relationship between Byoir and the civic-minded tax students. Again checks were produced from the Byoir files. Again the E.R.P.C. was billed for material put out in the name of the do-good organization. And again there was the unfailing memorandum. This one, also from Hardy, said:

"We are cooperating with an autoist group, New Jersey Automobile Owners, Inc. . . . This group sends out considerable literature. It MUST be mailed in New Jersey."

There was a further injunction: "Whenever any letter goes from the N.J.A.O., a copy MUST be mailed to Robert A. Fox, New Jersey Automobile Owners, Inc., 155 Evergreen Place, East Orange, N. J. . . . ." A sensitive touch, perhaps, but it probably seemed only right and proper for Mr. Fox, as executive secretary, to be informed of what his organization was up to.

WHAT'S A 'FRONT'?

Practically every public-relations firm makes use of citizens' committees of one sort or another—and generally legitimate use. But as elsewhere in this business the area is cloudy, with only a shadowy line separating the relatively pure from the purely bogus. Thomas J. Deegan, chairman of the E.R.P.C.'s subcommittee on public relations, plays the ambiguity for all it is worth. Pressed by Dilworth, he expounded his views on fronts—"noble and ignoble":

" 'Front' can be the very evil one that we both talked about a moment ago, the Commy. 'Front' can be something as simple and genuine as Bing Crosby smoking a Chesterfield. 'Front' can be someone else with a co-interest saying the story that you are interested in, too, which, to my humble knowledge, is a perfectly genuine, proper thing to do. 'Front' has taken on even other connotations—Marilyn Monroe." . . .

GOING MY WAY?

While few public-relations men share Deegan's openly indulgent attitude toward the synthetic front, practically all of them endorse a close working relationship with what the trade calls "co-interest groups." In truth there would seem to be no reason why they shouldn't hitch a client's public-relations activities to the parallel program of another organization —as long as the thing is done openly. The rub is that it is not always, or even generally, done openly. Certainly not in this case.

The Grange, a good example of a co-interest group, was certainly operating in Pennsylvania before Carl Byoir & Associates were, and it continued to function there long after Messrs. Girdler and Hardy pulled out their "team." It was real and legitimate, but how independent it was in this particular campaign against the truckers is something else again. We have already indicated that a good quantity of the Grange's propaganda in that fight was created by Byoir men, though the Grange was not their client, and that printing, mailing, and other publicity charges were regularly paid for by their office. Weekly work reports from Hardy and his team, later cited at the hearings, indicate that the Grange's lobbying was supervised by, and even its letters written by, Byoir lieutenants:

> *June 28, 1951:* "With Grange, set up special program to contact Senators in doubtful counties. . . Wrote material for Grange News Letter."
> *July 29, 1951:* "Letters to editor from J. K. Mahood, Pennsylvania State Grange, to answer inaccurate charges of proponents of S 615 [the truck bill]."
> *May 9, 1952:* "Hardy wrote letter from Master, Pennsylvania Grange, to accompany reprint of National Grange Monthly reprint."
> *June 27, 1952:* "Mailing reprints over signature of Master of State Grange."

The Pennsylvania State Association of Township Supervisors similarly enjoyed the talents of the Byoir establishment, courtesy of the E.R.P.C., not to mention financial assistance. So, it appears, did the Citizens Tax League of Rochester, New York, and the Citizens Public Expenditure Survey of Albany.

It often happens that a potential co-interest group has to be subtly persuaded of its co-interest. In such cases, there is no substitute for the services of an eloquent member, and like all professional services these are not performed gratis. Such a "pro" par excellence is Mrs. Bessie Q. Mott, a veteran clubwoman, pamphleteer, and great-grandmother.

Questioning Swinehart at the pretrial hearings, Dilworth sardonically suggested that Mrs. Mott was "getting to be practically a regular" at profitable crusading. Yes, Swinehart agreed, "She works for a great many people. . . . She is a specialist in the field of reaching women's clubs, women's interests." Indeed she is, having given unstintingly not only to the railroads, but also to the Great Atlantic & Pacific Tea Company, when Byoir was fighting that chain's case in defense against the Justice Department, and, before that, to oleomargarine, which she served under the banner of Batten, Barton, Durstine & Osborne, Inc.

"But I don't take on a fight," says Mrs. Mott (Smith, '99), "unless it's something I believe in." However, the lines between her personal crusades and the interests of her organizations tend to get blurred. She is said to have allowed Byoir to pay for letterheads of the American Home Department of the New York State Federation of Women's Clubs which showed Bessie Q. Mott as vice-chairman and were used to invite ladies to a forum likewise paid for by the Byoir office. A pamphlet under her signature, called "Are We Being Railroaded into Socialism?" is alleged to have been printed and mailed at Byoir's expense, though the author was carefully identified only with the Public Affairs Department of the Federation. . . .

THE ROLE OF CLINTON JOHNSON

Inevitably, the spectacle of a Bessie Q. Mott manipulating women's clubs to the greater glory of a group of railroads has in it something of high comedy. Unhappily this element is lacking in the alleged working arrangements between the Byoir establishment and Clinton H. Johnson, public-relations agent for the Maryland State Roads Commission. The truckers' complaint uses harsh words and charges that Governor Fine's last-minute veto of the truck bill had been influenced by Johnson, who was in a position to have advance knowledge of the road test and who, at the same time, it said, had been receiving payments from Carl Byoir & Associates.

Johnson denied these allegations, but he conceded certain points that at least raise the question of propriety. Johnson's basic case is a simple one: He was not an employee of the State of Maryland but an independent contractor engaged to handle the public relations of the Roads Commission. His contract did not prevent him from engaging in other public-relations work as long as he did not let it interfere with his labors for the commission. Yes, he did make twenty to thirty trips to the New York offices of Carl Byoir & Associates, but his motive was to get their help in doing his job for the Maryland highway program.

At the same time, he gave the Byoir organization factual information about highway construction costs, overweight violations, and the like. At no time was he paid for services. Certainly he never took bribes nor did he misrepresent data or have any idea how the Byoir office got hold of the report on the road tests so far in advance of the general release. And, finally, he intended to bring suit against the truckers for libel and slander.

From Girdler's deposition we get a somewhat different perspective. Johnson did "interpretative and research work" for the Byoir office, he recalled, and was paid largely on the basis of the number of hours he put in. Girdler couldn't recall exactly the rate, and the arrangement does seem to have been pretty hazy all around. He recalled that amounts were given Johnson for expenses—Johnson confirmed this—without written statements, without itemizing, and often in cash. Girdler thought the expenses ran to $50 or $75 for an afternoon, night, and following day.

Hotel bills—Johnson usually stayed at the Biltmore—were often sent direct to Byoir. One of these, introduced as plaintiff's Exhibit P-65, covered a Labor Day weekend for Johnson and his wife, and must have been something of a bonus. Including theater tickets and meals, it came to $190.38. Johnson said it was for writing a free article for the Byoir firm— an article that, as it happens, never quite got finished.

In spite of Johnson's failure to remember payment for "services," several memos from Hardy to the bookkeeping department and at least one check bear the words "for research" or "services rendered." The sums were not high, but on January 1, 1953, Johnson went on a part-time basis with the Roads Commission and signed up as a consultant to the Eastern Railroad Presidents Conference for $1,000 a month. When plaintiff's counsel asked him, rhetorically enough, whether he considered this a "pay-off," his lawyer advised him not to answer. But he admitted that the Maryland Attorney General's office was investigating his relationship with Byoir while he worked for the Roads Commission and that as far as his state job was concerned, he was then on leave without pay. In a report later issued by the Attorney General's office Johnson was given a clean bill of health, but considered to have shown "poor judgment."

ACCENTUATING THE NEGATIVE

In the first of its many memoranda, in which it agreed to take on the railroad account, Carl Byoir & Associates laid down a few operating principles, to wit: The basic appeal must be directed not only to friends of the railroads but to motorists, conscious of hazards on the highway, and to taxpayers. Motorists are "ripe for action of some sort; but as yet they have not found a way to make themselves vocal or to express their resentment in legislation. . . . It is our task to accelerate these spontaneously generated currents."

Accordingly, the magazine department was ordered to start work "on the long process of researching and writing major magazine pieces." The radio department was "alerted to write scripts and create events acceptable to networks and local stations." It is a subject, wrote Girdler, that should "give us plenty of scope for the ingenuity that distinguishes CB & A departments . . ."

Excerpts from early work sheets show the turn that this ingenuity took almost from the start:

> Production Department: 10/4 . . . Selecting pictures . . . featuring worst truck tragedy within the past year. . . .
> 10/14 . . . Making layouts, selecting pictures, writing captions for Central States News Views featuring spectacular wreck near Gary, Ind., of large van-type truck. . .
> Radio Department: 10/21 . . . Securing radio script with mention of "nasty truck driver." . . .

Not all the railroad people took kindly to this sort of thing. Walter J. Tuohy, president of the Chesapeake & Ohio, was sharply critical of an inter-office Byoir memorandum that read in part:

> At belated last, this is confirmation of my understanding of our conversations concerning the desire of the account . . . to portray truckers as evil, sinister wrongdoers. Actually, the proposed program fell into three categories. . . 1. An effort by me to create and sell scripts to existing dramatic programs with the trucking theme as basic plot, picturing the trucker as a law-breaker, etc. As we discussed, invariably to conform with network requirements the "bad" truckers may have to be compensated for by "good" truckers but the poison will still be there and the damage done. 2. We will make all possible efforts to enlist the aid of regular and free-lance writers to utilize the truckers as a "heavy". . . .

William White, then president of the New York Central, testified that he had criticized some of these Byoir effusions as being in "an eager-beaver jargon that I didn't like."

On the other hand, Thomas J. Deegan, who besides being chairman of the E.R.P.C.'s public-relations subcommittee was vice-president in charge of the Chesapeake & Ohio's public relations, thought the stress on horror pictures perfectly proper because of the danger to the public from trucks carrying explosives. "Seeing the explosives truck photographed riding along the highway with nothing happening is interesting, perhaps, but certainly not striking," he remarked, "but seeing it exploded and children and mothers lying on the ground torn to bits brings one up short." . . .

RESORT TO LAW

Confronted with this feverish activity and broad assortment of stratagems, the truckers, on Charnay's advice, fell back on the law. It is not for the observer to contend, as the defendants have repeatedly contended, that the suit was brought as a counterattack in a publicity war. Assuming the plaintiff's perfect good faith in going to court, however, we can still appreciate the considerable tactical advantages that have accrued to them as a result.

By the very nature of the action, the enemy was put on the defensive. The plaintiffs also had an opportunity to strike an injured but gallant air and, through a "situation of reality" of their own making, get some pretty colorful publicity.

Two months after the intermittent pretrial sessions got under way, Robert McCay Green, co-counsel for the truck operators, filed an affidavit richly summarizing the testimony given up to that time and replete with stories of false fronts, weighted polls, and the doing of such persons as the remarkable Mrs. Mott. Five thousand copies went out to members of the Pennsylvania Motor Truck Association, the press, and interested outsiders. "Absolutely inexcusable," protested Byoir attorney R. Sturgis Ingersoll. But Dilworth blandly suggested that this was "obviously a protest inspired by your client, one of its happy ideas." Otherwise, he pointed out, the complaint would have been made to the court. Co-counsel Green added that by publicizing the document in this way, they had merely "kept the plaintiffs properly informed." And when Ingersoll sharply asked "Are the politicians in Ohio plaintiffs?" Dilworth settled for "This is too nice and too quiet a morning and we refuse to be needled."

It is true, of course that the doings of the truck operators and their publicists likewise became a matter of record, but because they had never put on anything like as intricate a campaign as their opponents and were not victimized by the disclosure of interoffice memoranda, there was much less for the railroad lawyers to work on. The latter were forced to make do with such scoops as the allegation that the truck operators had a war chest of $600,000, that they kept a hotel room in Harrisburg for "entertainment" (just as the other side did), and that even-handedly they doled out money to both parties shortly before elections. . . .

In perhaps needless detail, Dilworth dwelt on Byoir's medicineman period in the 1920's, when he collaborated with one X. La Motte Sage, A.M., Ph.D., LL.D., in the manufacture of Nuxated Iron. "The valuable blood, nerve force, and tissue-building properties of this preparation are due to organic iron . . . in combination with nux vomica," the label read. But the American Medical Association found less than four cents' worth of iron in a dollar bottle. Reminded of this finding by Dilworth, Byoir said, "That may be accurate," but it was still the best iron tonic on the market at the time. The trouble was with the distribution system, which he thought made such products too expensive. Another of his products was brought up—Seedol ("Natural Seed Bowel Tonic Works Wonders"). And furthermore, he had to defend his campaign in behalf of the A & P, which in 1946 cost him a conviction for conspiring to violate the Sherman Antitrust Act and a fine of $5,000.

Much of this line of questioning may have been irrelevant, as Byoir strenuously pointed out. "Ever since these depositions started to secure evidence," he complained, "that material has been used in many other ways by the Pennsylvania Truck Association to smear Carl Byoir." He added, rather wistfully it seemed, that to attract greater publicity the truckers had gone so far as to spread a rumor that a "Jelke girl" was to figure as a key witness at the trial.

But the grilling did serve to put Byoir on the defensive, and that evidently was the purpose. He felt obligated to disavow some of the phrases attributed to his subordinates in the railroad-trucker fight. Explaining that he had not been very active on the account, he said, "I am not taking the position that nobody ever did anything they shouldn't have done." But he was not for firing anyone. "If someone you tried to train gets a little too bright, a little too smart or too ambitious, his education needs working on." Let the truckers say what they would, the fact remained that "integrity is the cement of our business."

BLESSED ARE THE PEACEMAKERS

In the nature of things, the suit so far has aided the fortunes of Carl Byoir & Associates considerably less than those of David Charnay. But ironically, a settlement would prove still better for the latter than an eventual trial in open court, even one that resulted in a smashing victory for the truckers. Charnay is in this enviable heads-I-win-tails-you-lose position for the simple reason that in spite of the suit he has for some time been publicly and privately promoting the notion that the two branches of the transportation business "must decide to live together competitively and at peace."

Tide reported some months ago that in certain quarters "he is being touted as an 'industrial statesman' " for having brought railroad men and truckers together in a Council of Eastern Rail & Truck Common Carriers (C.E.R.T. for short) which seems to have found a potential meeting ground in the development of "piggyback"—the transport of truck trailers on railroad flatcars. . . .

Meanwhile, it is hardly possible to overlook the significance of what has been happening in Harrisburg in recent weeks. Once again, a bill to increase the weight limit for big trucks was put into the hopper. But instead of calling the Byoir men back into action again, the railroads almost immediately ran up the white flag. Associated Railroads of Pennsylvania, otherwise known as the railroad lobby, quickly announced that it would not oppose the measure. Its chairman, long one of the most trenchant foes of "big-truck" bills, did not exactly go all out for the measure, but it was plain that sweet reasonableness was the order of the day. "After a thorough study of the bill," he said, "we feel that it is reasonable in view of the laws of surrounding states." The bill was passed by the legislature and signed by Governor George M. Leader, Fine's successor. . . .

"WHAT'S OUR BUSINESS?"

Whatever impact the railroad-trucker affair may have had on the principals or on the public, the publicity seems to have sent tremors through a calling already jittery with self-doubt. For in spite of a surface brashness, the public-relations industry in general is surprisingly marked by self-searching, ambiguity as to function, and an almost pathetic yearning for recognition by the American public. . . .

Public-relations men are fond of viewing their function by analogy to other professions. Many see themselves as lawyers pleading before the bar of public opinion. A political member of the profession once spoke of promoting a major address by the President of the United States as "merchandising-in-depth." . . .

Actually this elaborate self-justification is a little bewildering to the layman who does not doubt that public relations has a legitimate and constructive role to play, one required by modern society. At its best it is a compiler and disseminator of useful information. More than that, it is increasingly a molder of policy in business and industry. . . .

Perhaps it is this impression of mounting importance that gives some of the best people in the business a feeling of uncertainty, a sense that considerably more responsibility is in order.

As *Tide* commented, "Understandably, the pre-trial deposition-taking in the truckers' suit . . . has quite a few PR men wondering about ethics and behavior of the business."

Leo Egan
21. The Political Boss: Going, Going—*

Five short years ago Carmine G. De Sapio was being described as a miracle man, one who was giving new life, new vitality and new power to urban Democratic political machines. Today his status is in jeopardy.

Ironically, it is the reputation he acquired as he was clawing his way to

* From the *New York Times Magazine*. January 8, 1961. pp. 13 and 21–22. Copyright by the New York Times. Reprinted by permission.

the top five years ago and his subsequent efforts to live up to it that are responsible for his present predicament. He was billed as a new type of political leader, a streamlined, modern, Madison Avenue version of the old-style machine boss, endowed with all the virtues and free of all the liabilities of the famous political leaders whose sun had set.

What Mr. De Sapio and those who hitched their wagons to his star overlooked was that the American electorate had had its fill of political bosses, old-style or new. Voters were looking for public officials who made their own decisions. They were fed up with the likes of John P. O'Brien, New York Mayor in 1933, who couldn't tell whom he was about to appoint because he hadn't gotten "the word."

A Tom Dewey or a Fiorello La Guardia or a Dick Daley (Mayor of Chicago), who are their own bosses, the electorate can respect and support, as it has proved time after time. But, given a choice between men they suspect of being controlled by others and men they regard as independent of such influence, their preference is for the independent, as they demonstrated with the election in 1950 of Vincent R. Impelliterri as Mayor of New York and in 1951 with the election of Rudolph Halley as President of the City Council.

Mr. De Sapio failed to appreciate this fundamental fact at Buffalo in 1958 when he forced the nomination of District Attorney Frank S. Hogan as the Democratic candidate for United States Senator, over the combined opposition of W. Averell Harriman, then Governor, Mayor Wagner and Herbert H. Lehman, then Senator. Now he is paying dearly for his mistake. Except that he flaunted his strength, he might still be the most powerful figure in the Democratic party in New York State today.

The mistake De Sapio made at Buffalo was one that Charles F. Murphy, his illustrious and wily predecessor as leader of Tammany and de facto boss of the Democratic party in New York State, carefully avoided. Unlike De Sapio, "Mister" Murphy (he was never called anything else by Tammany members) preferred to work in the background and was not above deception at his own expense to achieve his ends.

The late Senator Robert F. Wagner, father of New York's present Mayor, had a favorite political story dealing with "Mister" Murphy's talent for self-abasement. It concerned the selection of John F. (Red Mike) Hylan, then a County Judge in Brooklyn, as the Democratic candidate for Mayor in 1917, when Murphy was at the height of his power.

"Is Hylan a man we can trust and do business with?" Murphy asked John H. McCooey, his Brooklyn lieutenant, Senator Wagner recalled.

"He certainly is," Mr. McCooey attested. "Do you want to meet him?"

"No," replied Murphy. "I want you to ram him down my throat."

And that is what McCooey did. Civic groups were organized to demand

Hylan's nomination. Democratic clubs in Brooklyn passed resolutions commending the good Judge's independence of Tammany. Finally a "reluctant" Murphy threw in the sponge and accepted Hylan as the Democratic candidate for Mayor.

At Buffalo, De Sapio rammed District Attorney Hogan down the throats of elected Democratic officeholders instead of allowing them to ram Hogan down *his*.

The New York District Attorney is a widely known man of spotless reputation. By nominating him De Sapio hoped to induce voters of moderate views who had left the Democratic party over the prior fifteen years to return.

Nevertheless De Sapio's display of naked political power at Buffalo marked the apogee of his political career. It convinced a new generation of voters, without any experience under old-style political bosses, that there was no difference between old-style and new-style bosses.

This impression was heightened by De Sapio's physical resemblance to the motion picture and television stereotype of a sinister character. It is a resemblance attributable to his need for wearing tinted glasses because of an eye ailment (iritis), his taste in clothes (he likes the sharp kind) and his distinctive hair style (it usually looks as if he had just left the barber's chair after getting "the works").

Actually the resemblance between Carmine De Sapio and the more famous political bosses of the past is far more apparent than real. The meat on which this Tiger has fed since he came to power as leader of Tammany in 1950 has been so bland his predecessors would have spurned it in disgust.

During all his years as Tammany's boss, De Sapio has not had a single city franchise to sell. He hasn't licensed a single gambling establishment or brothel, so far as any records show. Nor have repeated investigations turned up a single instance in which he has shared the profits of a city or state construction or purchase contract.

In these respects his record presents a marked contrast to his better-known predecessors as political bosses in New York and elsewhere, most of whom amassed fortunes by engaging in just such activities.

William Marcy (Boss) Tweed, the classic example of a political boss, helped make the very name of Tammany a symbol of political corruption by the personal profits he obtained from politics.

A hulking 300-pounder, Tweed was one of the "Forty Thieves," as the city's Aldermen were known in his day. He supplemented a private profit from the sale of traction franchises with a share of the profits from contractors responsible for the building and furnishing of the famous Tweed courthouse which used to stand behind City Hall. He died in the old Ludlow Street jail.

Richard F. Croker, another of De Sapio's illustrious predecessors as the leader of Tammany, amassed enough money in nineteen years as the city's political overlord to retire to England and take up horse-breeding and the life of a country squire. One of his claims to fame was that he voted seventeen times on a single election day when he was 22 years old. At the age of 73 he married a Cherokee Indian girl who survived him.

"Mister" Murphy, a benign-looking gentleman who advanced the political careers of Senator Wagner, Alfred E. Smith and Jimmy Walker, likewise waxed rich as a political leader. It was frequently charged, but never proved, that a large part of his fortune was attributable to his success in obtaining a franchise for the Pennsylvania Railroad to build its tunnels under the Hudson and East Rivers. A relative had the general contract for the construction work.

The practice of licensing underworld characters to engage in illegal activities prevailed until relatively recent times. Jimmy Hines, an ex-blacksmith who carved out a tidy little political duchy for himself on the West Side, was sent to jail for licensing the late Arthur Flegenheimer, better known as Dutch Schultz, to run a policy bank.

In Murphy's day it was an open secret that some district leaders under him were granting extra-legal "licenses" for the operation of gambling establishments within their territories. Big Tim Sullivan was reputed to have granted the license for Arnold Rothstein's famous place, where many of the city's better-known theatrical and financial figures frequented the gaming tables.

The licensing arrangement was relatively simple. For a share of the profits, the licensor would see that the licensee was not unduly disturbed by the police. It was, of course, understood that a few token raids would have to be made on occasion and that certain small fry might have to go to jail from time to time. The inconvenience of such incidents was kept to a minimum.

Democratic and Republican political machines in other cities and in other states operated on substantially the same principles and in much the same fashion.

Among the better-known ones were the Boies Penrose and William H. Vare machine (Republican) in Philadelphia, the Frank ("I am the law") Hague machine in Jersey City, the Pendergast machine in Kansas City and the Crump machine in Memphis, Tenn.

In all instances the success and continued operations of these profitable organizations depended on remaining in control of the government. This was accomplished in a number of ways.

Arriving immigrants were helped to obtain jobs, then quickly naturalized and persuaded to vote for their benefactors. Needy families were given food, clothing and coal at Thanksgiving and Christmas and the breadwinner directed to employment. Those who ran afoul of the law found a friend in the machine's local representative who could persuade the judge to be lenient.

Thousands of voters were placed under obligation to the machine for minor favors. The advent of the automobile proved a bonanza. Ticket-fixing enabled the machines to put the drivers in their debt.

If the votes that could be coralled in this fashion were not enough, because of some outbreak of public indignation over the way a city was being run or the way taxes were mounting, there was always the possibility of stealing an election through use of repeaters, floaters, ballot-box stuffing and disorders that would dissuade anti-machine voters from casting their ballots.

The repeater method was probably the most widely used device for stealing an election, because a repeater could always be depended upon to vote right. Floaters, who were registered in colonies, were usually men of relatively low intelligence and often mismarked their ballots. The colonizing system, nevertheless, was frequently employed. There are many authenticated instances in which fourteen to twenty unrelated men were registered from a single room.

This is why rooming-house operators are still required by law to file lists of their tenants with the Police Department and boards of election well in advance of election day.

Ballot-box stuffing was used only in cases of dire emergency because, from the very nature of the operation, it became clear as the boxes were opened that fraud had been committed. In the case of repeaters and floaters this fact was not obvious; it took an investigation to establish that people who were not entitled to do so had been permitted to vote.

For most of a political machine's operations, control over the police force was essential. A license for gambling or vice could only be good as long as the police cooperated. This cooperation was achieved in two ways: through control of assignments and through a sharing of the "license" fees.

During the Seabury investigation, John F. Curry, then leader of Tammany and the dominant Democratic leader in the city, testified publicly that he regularly visited the Police Commissioner once a week and gave him "recommendations" for transfers and promotions within the department. A detective who interfered unduly with a mid-Manhattan license might find himself back in uniform patrolling the lonely beaches of Staten Island the following week.

Control over specification writing and inspection services in agencies responsible for construction contracts and municipal purchases was also essential. A former Borough President of Queens was convicted of conspiring with some subordinates to require the use of a particular make of pipe in all sewer construction. A supplier who was making short-weight deliveries had to have the cooperation of an inspector who would overlook the deficiency. Generally such an inspector would be one who owed his job to the dominant political machine.

The decline of city political machines started with women's suffrage and the curtailment of immigration in the early Nineteen Twenties.

Although slow to exercise their vote at first, women were more outraged than men at the alliance between political leaders and the underworld; they contributed heavily to reform movements designed to put an end to it. The Cable Act, setting up immigrant quotas, slowed the arrival of new candidates for naturalization to a trickle.

The effect of these two developments was greatly magnified by other events of the early Nineteen Thirties. The great depression called for measures beyond the financial resources of the machine, and so Government took over the functions of providing relief to the needy and of steering breadwinners to the jobs that were available.

The end of prohibition cut off a big source of underworld revenue and sharply reduced public toleration of law evasion. Municipal revenues were hard hit and city treasuries found themselves unable to satisfy the needs and desires of the machines. City charters were revised to reduce the opportunities for favoritism in the making of purchases and the award of construction contracts.

New York was harder hit by the cumulative force of these developments than many other cities. Fiorello La Guardia's reform administration was installed in City Hall to root out the evils disclosed by the Seabury investigation. Under direct orders from the White House, Tammany was placed on a starvation diet with respect to Federal patronage.

In other places like Jersey City, Memphis and Kansas City the anti-machine tide was slower in making itself felt, but its march was inexorable. As an institution the political machine was doomed and, in time, this fact became clear even to Frank Hague, Ed Crump and Boss Pendergast. Machines still persist in a few small cities, but even in these it is questionable whether they can outlive their present operators.

By their very nature, political machines run counter to what is fast becoming a fundamental American ethic: choices between candidates should be based on their merits or the merits of their programs. In the case of machine voters the merits of the candidates or their programs are the least of the considerations entering into a choice. Far more important is the desire to discharge an obligation or the lust for power and office.

Despite the setbacks he has received, De Sapio has continued to court the good opinion of the public. Even though the jobs are unsalaried, he obviously likes being leader of Tammany and Democratic National Committeeman for New York and won't surrender either place willingly.

The attraction of both offices is the power and position they give. John Adams once wrote that any man who can control more than his own vote is an aristocrat in a democracy. One who can control as many votes as the leader of Tammany becomes, by this definition, a first-flight aristocrat. By his control or influence over nominations and appointments he can advance or retard a political career. He is a man to be reckoned with, one whose goodwill is important. And De Sapio likes being important. It is a safe speculation that his political power is also an asset in the insurance business that provides his personal income.

In modern society, the political boss of old is being replaced by the expert in public relations, by the people who can create illusions and translate the intricacies of government into simple, understandable general principles, by those who know how to manipulate symbols.

Mr. De Sapio, on the basis of his record thus far, is not such a man. Rather he is a politician's politician. Other politicians respect and admire his handiwork. They welcome his counsel. In an earlier age, he would have been unbeatable. But this is the sixth decade of the twentieth century. Times have changed. That is why De Sapio's back is to the wall.

part five

STATE ORGANIZATION AND ADMINISTRATION

7

THE STATE LEGISLATURE

The principal policy-making body of a state government is the legislature. The drafters of the early state constitutions provided for the dominance of the government by the legislature. The state legislature, however abused its trust with the result the constitution was amended to place restrictions on the legislature. These restrictions today shackle many state legislatures and prevent them from fulfilling their responsibilities properly.

Reform of the state legislature long has been advocated. One of the most significant reports dealing with the state legislature was released in 1961 by the National Legislative Conference's Committee on Legislative Processes and Procedures. The Committee was greatly disturbed by the decline in the power and prestige of state legislatures and called upon legislators to put their houses in order. The report evaluates state legislatures and contains recommendations for strengthening them. It appears to be safe to conclude that most, if not all, problems associated with the typical state legislature and many problems of state government would be eliminated if the recommendations were adopted.

All state legislatures were bicameral from 1836—the year Vermont dropped the unicameral legislature—until 1937; in 1934 the voters of Nebraska approved a constitutional amendment providing for a unicameral legislature. Although Nebraska has operated successfully with a unicameral legislature since 1937, no other state has adopted it. The case for unicameralism has frequently been advanced in political literature, but seldom has the case for bicameralism been presented. The late Professor Frank E. Horack, Jr., of the University of Indiana, endeavored to counteract the views of the unicameralists by arguing that bicameral legislatures can be effective.

Dr. T. V. Smith, Professor Emeritus of Citizenship and Philosophy at Syracuse University, takes the reader behind the scenes of the Illinois senate in the 1930s and introduces him to the inner workings of a state legislature and the personal relationships that develop between the members by tracing the enactment of a bill from its origin in the legislator's mind to a period after its passage.

22. American State Legislatures in Mid-twentieth Century*

Laws must exist before they can be administered by the executive or construed by the judiciary. The special mission of the legislative branch in American government is to create the laws which then become the compass and concern of the other branches.

A review of the role of the legislature must commence with a recognition of the essential unity in the purposes for which government exists. Governments are instituted to secure to the people their "unalienable rights," the Declaration of Independence asserted. In establishing the means by which government should be carried on, the Founding Fathers developed and applied the concept of dividing the job among three co-ordinate and co-equal branches. The objective of this "separation of powers" was to safeguard the people's liberties, not to obstruct needed governmental accomplishments or to produce disharmony among the branches.

The task of the legislature was defined some fifteen years ago as ". . . essentially the determination of broad policies in a clear and decisive way; authorization of organization, personnel, powers, and finances adequate to administer its policies; and review of the effectiveness of those policies and their administration." (Committee on Legislative Processes and Procedures, the Council of State Governments, *Our State Legislatures,* revised edition, 1948, pp. 1-2). We concur in this definition.

The state governments in this century have experienced a tremendous expansion in their budgets, personnel and programs. They have been called on to face a widening spectrum of problems—social and economic affairs, education, institutional care and welfare, industrial expansion and resource development, transportation, metropolitan areas, relationships between persons in a changing society, and many others. These new and expanded activities have resulted in corresponding increases in the responsibilities of the legislatures.

In the evolution of our governmental institutions, the state legislatures have suffered a sorry decline in power and prestige during most of American history, a decline which has made serious inroads on the division

* Committee on Legislative Processes and Procedures of the National Legislative Conference. From *State Government.* Autumn 1961, pp. 245–52. Reprinted with permission of publisher.

of powers and coordinate character of the three branches of government. In recent years the people have come to realize, in increasing degree, that the capacity of state governments to meet the demands placed upon them —and thus to make possible the preservation of the federal system— requires the unshackling of the legislatures.

It is a fundamental thesis of this Committee that the Founding Fathers were wise in establishing the coordinateness of the legislative, executive, and judicial branches; and that the survival of responsible representative government in our country requires co-equality of the Legislative branch! Every sound effort to reemphasize the primacy of the legislature in evolving public policy should be encouraged, and restrictions which inhibit the achievement of that end should be eliminated.

The Committee recognizes that re-achievement of the traditional role and status of the legislative branch places an obligation on the legislature to put its own house in order. If the legislature is to do that, it must have the understanding and support of the electorate. This, in turn, requires a quantity and quality of news coverage of the legislative process that is often more hoped for than achieved.

The legislative process in most American states at mid-Twentieth Century is becoming a full-time function, in response to governmental expansion. Traditionally, the legislatures have been composed of "citizen legislators"—full-time citizens who are closely associated with their home communities, and who serve only part of their time in the state capitol. To a growing extent, at least in the more populous states, this tradition appears to conflict with the needs and requirements of the job, particularly if the legislature is to restore a greater degree of coordinateness with the full-time executive and judicial branches. There are undoubtedly real values in the tradition of the "citizen legislator." Its retention in the face of mounting legislative business will require continuing efforts in every state to provide the legislator with adequate staff and working conditions.

The problems dealt with in this brief report are by no means the only aspects of the legislative process deserving attention. One of the most basic problems of all is legislative apportionment. The Committee refrains from offering specific suggestions on this matter, but it is forced to the conclusion that the continued flouting of constitutional apportionment requirements will greatly prejudice the confidence of the people in the processes of state government. At the same time, it would appear that the reapportionment provisions in many state constitutions are unrelated to present political realities. The Committee earnestly suggests that each state which does not in practice reapportion at the intervals and in the manner constitutionally prescribed should make a thorough study of the problem and of possible methods for solving it, including the use of non-legislative reapportionment bodies such as those currently employed in a dozen states.

The Committee, similarly, has not devoted extended attention in this report to specific forms of professional staff services for the legislature. The silence of the Committee is not for lack of appreciation of the importance of this area, but because it has already been the subject of extended treatment by an earlier committee of the National Legislative Conference.

The Committee notes with pleasure the action of the National Legislative Conference in 1959 in creating a Committee on Legislative Rules. The existence of this group has made unnecessary development by this Committee of recommendations concerning rules.

The Committee draws attention to the everpresent and constantly changing problem of "conflict of interest." It suggests that states should give serious attention to this matter, including the possibility of developing codes of ethics for all state employees including legislators. Prior efforts in this field include studies by the legislatures in Minnesota, New Jersey, and Texas. Measures have been enacted in a number of states.

The Committee takes note of substantial progress by our state legislatures in the past generation, particularly since World War II, in equipping themselves for better performance of their tasks. These tasks are expanding, however; attention must continue to be directed to measures which will assure representative, responsible, and effective legislatures.

Local needs, requirements, and traditions will and should modify application of the suggestions that follow. To every extent possible, however, effort has been made to phrase the proposals flexibly, so that local accommodation can be made to the principles involved.

SUGGESTIONS FOR STRENGTHENING STATE LEGISLATURES

1. LEGISLATIVE-EXECUTIVE RELATIONS. *In all states, the leaders and the whole membership of the legislative bodies should exercise fully and imaginatively those powers inhering in the legislative branch, toward the goal of re-establishing the fuller measure of independence from the executive branch contemplated by the Founding Fathers. To this end, legislatures should establish improved procedures and staff facilities to assure effective legislative participation in such key areas as: pre-session evolution of public policy and preparation of legislative programs; appropriating public funds; auditing their expenditure; and reviewing the uses made by administrative agencies of the delegated power to issue and enforce rules and regulations.*

The drift of power from the legislative branch has slowed and to some extent reversed in recent years. Conscious, concerted, continuing effort will be required, however, before the balance is redressed. Opposition can be anticipated, as recent efforts in some states bear witness. The electorate is likely to be apathetic unless the purpose and objectives of change are made crystal clear.

A real beginning in restoring legislative powers can be made in most states within the framework of existing constitutions. To suggest that the legislature should become, in fact as well as in name, the law-enacting and appropriating body is not to deny the executive the proper scope for exercise of his legitimate powers.

The role and use of the executive veto is one phase which presents special problems for thoughtful consideration in many states. Changes in relevant constitutional provisions may be desirable as time goes on and as sustained efforts go forward to redefine roles and responsibilities. Immediately, however, the Committee suggests the following:

1. Legislatures should not rely on the executive veto to avoid responsible legislative action.
2. The executive should never veto bills sent to him during or after the session without declaring his reason therefor.
3. Wherever and whenever possible, legislatures should meet to review executive vetoes.

The Committee recognizes the need for delegating certain rule-making powers to agencies and departments in view of the increasing complexity of state government. There is need in many states for more systematic requirements concerning the publication, notice, and administration of such rules. The Committee also urges that newly-formulated rules should be subject to review by a committee of the legislature to determine whether legislative intent is being carried out.

In certain other respects the law-making branch should exercise forms of appropriate legislative oversight over administrative action. In a growing number of states, legislative post-audit agencies are helping to assure administrative adherence to legislative intent in spending appropriated money. Legislatures also might consider creating a committee to review agency practices in purchasing, personnel, and other respects, to assure that there is no evasion of statutory requirements.

2. LEGISLATIVE SESSIONS. *Undue limitations and restrictions upon the length and subject matter of legislative sessions should be removed.*

Restrictions on the length of regular sessions of legislatures exist in about two-thirds of the states. In most states the limitation is direct and the constitutions specify the number of days during which the sessions may continue, with sixty calendar days the most common. In several states the limitation is indirect, chiefly through cessation of legislative pay after a specified period.

Direct or indirect limitations on the length of special sessions exists in more than half of the state constitutions. About half of the states also limit the legislature in special sessions to subjects specified by the Governor.

Legislatures cannot properly fulfill their important functions without adequate time to consider and dispose of the questions before them. Undue restrictions defeat the deliberative character of legislatures, contribute to the so-called legislative "log-jam" at the close of sessions, and result in inadequate consideration of measures.

The Committee does not feel that any single solution will be equally applicable to all states, and therefore does not expressly recommend annual as against biennial sessions or the removal of specified restrictions on special sessions. The number of annual session states, however, has grown from four in the early 1940's to nineteen at present, and several more states are considering this move.

3. LEGISLATIVE TERMS. *The length of legislative terms should be established in such a way as (a) to assure effective responsibility to the voters, and (b) to provide desirable continuity in legislative experience. A term of four years in at least one house, with staggered terms, is consistent with this objective.*

Changes in the length of legislative terms have been infrequent indeed. In the recent past Ohio lengthened Senate terms from two to four years, and the new constitutions of Alaska and Hawaii have provided for two-year House and four-year Senate terms.

Two-year terms force legislators serving large constituencies to devote an undue amount of time to the business of running for office, with consequent reductions in time available for other legislative concerns.

In a number of states, the practice has grown up of using so-called "rotational agreements." These agreements are variously named in different jurisdictions but basically they designate the arrangement whereby one part (usually, one county) of a multi-part legislative district "elects" the legislator in the next session. Whatever historic jurisdiction there may be for such a practice, the Committee suggests that it be reviewed and if possible eliminated. Legislative districts rarely are so large and diverse as to preclude effective representation by an able, experienced legislator, and this conclusion is particularly true in sparsely settled areas which, characteristically, are the ones which employ the "rotational agreement." Such districts pay for this practice in loss of continuity of successive sessions by their legislative representatives, in loss of important committee assignments, and in other ways. Moreover the resultant weakening of the law-making role of the legislature is prejudicial to the achievement of co-equality of the branches of government.

4. LEGISLATIVE COMPENSATION. *From the viewpoint of good public service, and in light of the increasing amounts of time that legislators must devote to their duties both during and between sessions, their compensation in most states is now much too low. Likewise the pay of legislative leaders, faced with even greater demands on their time in most jurisdictions is notably out of line. Flat salaries rather than a per diem allowance should be paid. Salary and reimbursement of necessary expenses should be provided in amounts sufficient to permit and encourage competent persons to undertake growingly important and time-consuming legislative duties. Actual amounts of salary and expense money should be provided by statute rather than specified in the constitution.*

Adequate compensation permits legislators to devote as much time as necessary to legislative duties, both during and between sessions. These duties are not, in mid-Twentieth Century, such that they can be forgotten or ignored when the regular session adjourns. The contribution of the legislator must be measured more and more by this thoughtful participation in interim study activities which are essential preliminaries to the next session.

Relative to the same point, legislative compensation should not be such as to preclude able people who lack private means from serving because of financial sacrifice, or to force such people to find supplemental income from private interest groups or individuals. In light of the costs of running for and serving in the legislature, some financial sacrifice is inevitable for most people. The goal should be to reduce this sacrifice in order to assure ample numbers of qualified candidates and their independence from undesirable interests.

Provision also should be made for additional compensation of legislative leaders to cover costs incident to their added responsibilities. Reimbursement for travel, hotel and meals should be provided all legislators, both during sessions and on interim committees and research activities between sessions.

Some progress on these matters has been recorded during the past decade or so. In 1943 less than half of the states used the salary plan, whereas by 1960 some thirty-four were using it. Maximum salaries rose from $5,000 a biennium in 1947, in Illinois, Massachusetts, and New York to $15,000 by 1960 in New York, and $12,000 in California, Illinois and Pennsylvania. Salary levels were established by statute in only twenty states in 1947 as against twenty-five in 1960.

As to legislative leaders, a few states now make financial adjustment for the tremendous amount of time they must devote to the legislature's business. As an example, Massachusetts, an annual session state, doubles the regular annual legislative salary of $5,200 for the Senate President and House Speaker and pays an additional $2,600 per year to four other House and three other Senate leaders. New Jersey grants its House and Senate presiding officers $1,666 a year above the basic $5,000 salary; Ohio gives $2,500 over the basic $2,500; and Tennessee, which pays legislators on a session day basis, provides each presiding officer an additional $3,750 per year. Texas for over a decade has provided each of the two presiding officers a rent-free apartment in the capitol building.

The examples cited should not obscure the fact that most states have failed to keep pace with desirable change.

Most states have established retirement systems to cover their public employees. Only a few have extended such coverage to legislators. The Committee feels it is entirely within the bounds of fairness and propriety to grant legislators equitable retirement pensions which take into account length of service.

5. LEGISLATIVE EMPLOYEES. *Full-time legislative employees should be appointed on the basis of merit and competence. The tenure of technical and professional legislative personnel whose work does not involve partisan operations and activities should be determined by competence in the discharge of their duties, and not by changes in party or group control. As far as circumstances permit, the working conditions of legislative employees should not be less advantageous than those of employees in the executive and judicial departments.*

Major emphasis has been given during the past score of years to the establishment of permanent legislative services of a technical and professional nature. While this Committee has not reviewed these developments, it desires to record full approbation of this desirable movement—and further to express great satisfaction with the determination of most states to staff these agencies on the basis of merit, as mirrored by professional and technical qualifications. Consistent with the goal of legislative independence, however, it is suggested that career legislative employees should be independent of the recruiting, advancement, and disciplinary jurisdiction of the executive branch merit system.

On the housekeeping side of the legislative process, there has been a noticeable trend toward placing the office of legislative chief clerk or secretary on a full-time basis. About a third of the ninety-five such offices in the forty-eight states had been put on a full-time basis in 1957, most of them within the score of years just preceding.

Staffs serving standing committees have not, as a general rule, been supplied in the number or with the special knowledge which circumstances require. Most legislatures should devote much attention to this area.

6. LEGISLATIVE COMMITTEES: ORGANIZATION, PROCEDURE, PUBLIC HEARINGS, EXECUTIVE SESSIONS. *Committees should be reduced in number in many states. In any revision of the committee system, due regard should be given to organizing committees on the basis of related subject matter, equalization of workload, cooperation between legislative houses, and reduction in undue committee burdens on individual members.*

Provisions should be made for public hearings on major bills, with adequate facilities for such hearings. Advance notice of hearings should be published and made readily available.

The right of legislative committees to hold closed or executive sessions when necessary should be recognized, and its desirability emphasized.

There have been notable efforts since World War II to reduce the total number of committees in many states. Between 1946 and 1959, for example, the median number of House standing committees was lowered from thirty-nine to twenty-three, and of Senate committees from thirty-one to twenty. Nevertheless, in 1959 four state Houses of Representatives had fifty or more committees, and six Senates had thirty-six or more committees. Hence there is room for improvement.

Of perhaps even greater importance is the problem presented by multiplying unduly the number of committees on which the legislator serves. A survey in 1955 indicated that the average House member in seven states and the average Senate member in fifteen states served on seven or more committees; and in eight legislative bodies the average member served on ten or more committees. An average of sixteen committee assignments per member was reported in one case. This is a situation which places inordinate demands on the individual lawmaker. While no set standard appears achievable, the end objective should be to enable the individual legislator to do his constructive best in reviewing and perfecting bills in committee.

Another improvement in the committee process—increased use of joint committees—has been recommended much in recent years, but without notable response. Real economies in time, effort and money will result if joint hearings by committees of both houses are held on bills, especially on bills which hold high interest or are controversial. Several New England states, for example, provide ample evidence that widespread use of joint committees and hearings does not impose undesirable constraints or undue burdens on the legislators involved.

The Committee has addressed its attention to two additional aspects of legislative committee work, both involving legislative discretion and responsibility: (1) the power of committees to deny hearings and to kill bills; and (2) the power of committees to hold closed or executive sessions. This Committee asserts its belief that standing legislative committees normally do have and should have both of these powers. It is obvious that important bills deserve and must have public hearings. The legislature which denies that principle would learn the cost dearly. To require public hearings on all bills irrespective of nature, however, is to deny any legislative discretion, to dilute legislative time, and to increase unduly the length and cost of sessions, without commensurate gain.

The Committee is strongly of the view, also, that it is a misapplication of the slogan "freedom of information" and a positive mischief to the public weal to deny to legislative committees any opportunity at all for closed or executive session. Accommodation and compromise are inherent in all phases of the political process. Recognition of this fact does not imply impairment of legislative responsibility; it merely makes workable the legislative forum for the adjustment of public issues.

7. PREPARATION, INTRODUCTION, EDITORIAL REVIEW, AND PRINTING OF LEGIS-LATION. *Some states should consider limiting by rule the period when new bills may be introduced. States where bulk of bills has been a problem should consider authorizing and encouraging the drafting, filing, and printing of bills before the opening of the session.*

Where annual sessions are held unrestricted as to subject matter, consideration should be given to a system of carrying over bills on calendar from the first to subsequent sessions of the same legislature, both to expedite the legislative process and to reduce printing costs.

All bills and important amendments introduced should be printed prior to public hearings on them and before consideration by the legislature, and whenever possible they should be inspected before printing by bill drafters or revision clerks. Editorial review and appraisal of final enactments by competent staff should be provided much more widely than at present as a means of detecting errors and conflicts, prior to bill transmittal to the Governor.

Adequate provision should be made for printing new laws and making them generally available at the earliest possible time after final enactment and before they become effective. If the volume of session laws cannot be thus available, new laws, adequately indexed, should be reproduced in some alternate form such as "slip laws," "advance sheets," or some comparable method.

The introduction of bills late in the session frequently results in inadequate attention to their provisions, and in adding to the last minute "log-jam." Most legislatures have found it desirable to establish by rule some appropriate provision to ease this burden. In seeking a solution, however, it is suggested that the remedy take the form of a rule and not of a constitutional provision; and it is suggested also that a realistic date be selected in order that legislators may not feel forced to introduce "extra" bills (such as "skeleton" bills) in case they may need them after the introduction date has passed.

Many states in recent years have adopted various suggestions under this heading. Pre-session drafting by the official bill drafters is authorized in the vast majority of states, and pre-session filing occurs in some.

Carrying over bills still on calendar to subsequent sessions of the same legislature is practiced in Georgia, Puerto Rico, Rhode Island, and South Carolina, in addition to the Congress. The Committee suggests its consideration by other annual session states since time and money might be saved by its use.

With respect to printing or duplicating bills and laws, it should be borne in mind that the people affected by new legislation should have reasonable opportunity to know in advance the legal provisions with which they must comply.

8. USE OF MODERN TECHNIQUES AND EQUIPMENT. *Legislatures and legislative staff should explore the wide range and variety of electronic and other technological devices and processes now available with the view to adapting many of them to various aspects of the legislative process—roll-call voting, reproduction of legislative measures, preparation of the journals, recording of hearings and debates, and in other applications.*

Advances of technology have resulted in the availability of mechanical and electrical equipment which can be applied at many stages of the legislative process. These include dictating "jacks" at the desks of individual legislators, speedy methods for recording roll-call votes, automatic typewriters and teletypesetting devices which speed and render less costly and time-consuming the reproduction of legislative materials of various types, and other devices.

The electric roll-call machine is the oldest of these forms of electrical equipment. Since 1917, when the first such device was installed in the Wisconsin Assembly, thirty-four legislative houses have been thus equipped in twenty-eight states.

The application of these new devices can be very great. For example, this report recommends elsewhere that important amendments as well as bills be printed prior to consideration by the legislature. Reproduction devices now available and in widespread use make possible the duplication and distribution of material within a matter of minutes.

Legislative reporting is especially relevant in this connection. As a general proposition, it must be acknowledged that reports mirroring official action by the legislature and by its committees fall far short of the ideal. When the public lacks authoritative information as to the steps and the reasoning by which a legislative body has reached its conclusion, public regard for the body itself suffers.

9. LEGISLATIVE FINANCE AND FACILITIES. *The legislature should provide for a budget adequate to meet all probable expenditures during a fiscal period. It should have exclusive control over these finances and exercise that control with responsibility. Proper office space for the legislature should be provided to enable the members to carry out their duties efficiently as the law-making branch of state government.*

It is essential that the legislature have control over its finances and facilities. The glare of publicity which falls on legislative shortcomings in this area would assure continuing efforts to overcome such shortcomings.

Adequate facilities for the legislature would include, wherever possible, office space for all legislators and especially for the leadership, as well as reception rooms where legislators can confer with constituents, adequate gallery space for the public and press, facilities for legislative service agencies and other staff services, an adequate number of committee rooms, and adequate space for committee hearings.

10. ORIENTATION AIDS FOR LEGISLATORS. *It is suggested that all states arrange suitable opportunities and facilities for orienting new legislators with the legislative process and familiarizing all legislators with the tools with which they have to work.*

A recent survey showed that twenty-eight states held orientation conferences for members of the legislature during 1958-59. Generally, the conferences were held prior to the session but a few states scheduled them early in the session. They varied in length from a half-day to three days.

Arrangements for orientation conferences generally are made by legislative service agencies, legislative clerks, universities, institutes and bureaus of government, and law schools.

The Committee recommends that all states: (a) examine the various techniques available for orienting new legislators; (b) determine the best approach for informing the legislator of the processes and procedures of his legislature and the services available to him to enable him to do his job effectively; and (c) familiarize the legislator with the materials and facilities with which he must work.

11. LOCAL AND SPECIAL LEGISLATION. *In order that the legislature may devote its attention to formulating major public policy, general, optional, or home rule legislation should be enacted as substitutes for special legislation affecting cities, counties, and other political subdivisions of the states, particularly in matters of purely local concern. Consideration and settlement of claims against the state should be delegated to judicial or to administrative agencies.*

In spite of widespread constitutional prohibitions against local and special legislation, many legislatures consider large numbers of such measures. This places a heavy burden of purely local problems on the legislators. It also weakens local initiative and responsibility. With these factors in mind, the Committee recommends extension of the principle of local or home rule, consistent with minimum and uniform standards of statewide application.

Frank E. Horack, Jr.
23. Bicameral Legislatures Are Effective*

The proponents of unicameralism have catalogued its merits with a persuasive marshalling of virtues. They assert that the single bodied legislature:

1. Saves time and expense.
2. Guards against hastily enacted and ill considered legislation.
3. Eliminates the evils of the committee system and the dictatorship of the conference or steering committee.
4. Reduces total legislative costs and permits increases in legislators' salaries so that more qualified legislators may be procured.
5. Facilitates the non-partisan election of legislators.

The worth of these assertions can be measured only in terms of the function of a legislature in our modern society. The choices involved relate not to the form of a particular system of legislative organization but rather to the capacities of any system to realize the social and economic objectives of democracy.

In brief, society expects of a legislative body:

First. An adequate and accurate representation of the electorate in matters legislative.

Second. A capacity to enact accurate and effective legislation based on reliable research and reflecting practical experience.

Third. A facility for the expeditious enactment into law of the wishes of the community when the desires of the community are crystallized and the community is ready for action.

Fourth. The ability to retard legislative enactment when community policy is not yet crystallized and when inaction is more protective of

---

* From *State Government.* April 1941, pp. 79–80 and 96. Reprinted with permission of publisher and author's estate.

sound community growth than is premature legislative experimentation.

Bicameral assemblies have long been criticized for their "unrepresentative" character. It is true that the historic origins of bicameralism stem from a desire to give preference to propertied and titled classes. It is also true that this basis of representation has been discarded in American legislatures and legislators are selected by all electors without qualifications based upon economic status. The apparent irrational consequence of continuing a bicameral legislature with a unitary basis of representation is the foundation of the unicameralists' argument. But a system of representation founded on area will remain just as arbitrary in a unicameral legislature. And the practicability or desirability of formal interest group representation certainly is not now worthy of consideration.

ECONOMIC REPRESENTATION BY LOBBYISTS

Furthermore, the failure of the American legislature to secure adequate interest group representation is more apparent than real. Such representation, today, is informally achieved through lobbyists and representatives of farm bureaus, trade associations, labor unions, temperance organizations, and the multitude of interests that have found legislative representation desirable. The informality of this representation is its chief virtue. Within the framework of an orderly two party system, highly specialized interests may make their influences felt. And no matter what the popular superstition may be, legislators and lobbyists know that influence must come from integrity and ability.

With the growing formalization of legislative committee procedure, the lobbyist must work more and more, as the lawyer, in open court, relying on his special knowledge and skill. To be sure he represents his client —but that, indeed, is democracy.

In an ever increasing measure interest group representatives have demonstrated their capacity for these responsibilities. We have, in fact, today, a type of interest group representation which could be no more effectively achieved under the unicameral system.

The proponents of the unicameral system assert that it will attract more qualified men to the legislature. There is little assurance, however, that a change in legislative form will have more than temporary significance in improving the caliber of legislators. Nor indeed is there any certainty that the caliber of legislators should or need be improved. In spite of the over-emphasis on the deficiencies of legislative bodies the competence of legislators compares favorably with that of judicial and administrative officials. It is true that misfits find their way to legislatures as they do to positions of responsibility in other walks of life. But in a legislature these individuals seldom if ever have significant influence in the enactment or rejection of legislative proposals. Legislative leadership, in the main, is on a high level.

LEGISLATIVE PROCEDURE

Even with competent legislative personnel many critics assert that the bicameral procedure prevents fair and expeditious consideration of legislation. This argument is unconvincing. On the one hand unicameralists content that existing procedure clogs and delays the efficient consideration of legislation and on the other hand they assert that legislation may be rushed through the legislature and enacted without the safeguards of deliberation. Even if true these are not exclusively the consequence of the bicameral system. Procedure must rely on human integrity and judgment.

Criticisms directed at clumsy procedure frequently overlook the cause and justification for such procedure. Without desiring to defend some of the archaic constitutional limitations such as the three reading rules and certain voting procedures, justification of many deterrents to action may well be defended on the grounds of their deliberative effect. In other words when legislatures are unable to agree on proposals they frequently reflect the uncertainty of the society which they represent and the resulting inaction may best accord with the wishes of the electorate. On the other hand when controversies over policy have been settled in a given community the obstacles to rapid legislative enactment frequently are dissipated. Many informal devices promote this result.

With a single party in control of the legislature, the party caucus provides ready means for agreement on procedure and on enactment. The governor likewise in many instances provides the legislative leadership. He may sponsor specific legislation, submit administration bills, and through his office, insure their adoption. The legislature itself, by joint committees or by the joint meeting of the committees of the two houses, can and often does reduce the time for committee hearings and irons out the minor controversies so that final enactment is a speedy and formal process. Where solid public interest supports a particular legislative program, the bicameral system accomplishes the expedition of unicameral procedure so that *de facto* unicameralism is achieved.

The unicameralist will still respond that although the bicameral system can achieve the efficiency of the unicameral system its legislative product is still unconsidered, unsupported by reliable data, and poorly drafted. Often these charges are true; but the question remains whether the creation of a unicameral legislature will improve the product. Improvement can be achieved only through adequate legislative research and competent draftsmanship. These requirements are unaffected by the form of legislative organizational structure.

Within the framework of the bicameral system great improvement has already been made. The active and able research organizations maintained by the Kansas and Illinois Legislative Councils and the code revision commissions of several States have made outstanding contributions to the improvement of the content and form of legislation. The continuation of this improvement will depend, however, not so much on the change of legislative form as it will upon the increase in funds and personnel for those legislative agencies which have already demonstrated their capacity in improving the legislative process.

LEGISLATIVE COSTS INSIGNIFICANT

Perhaps the reader will feel that if the unicameral and bicameral systems are so similar in operation, that on the ground of expense alone the unicameral method should be adopted. An analysis of state budgets provides the answer. Legislators' salaries or even legislators' salaries plus the legislative perquisites are so small a proportion of the total state budget that an elimination of fifty per cent of the elected representatives would not change the proportion of state expenditures for the legislative department a single percentage point.

Though generally considered a controversy of form the unicameral-bicameral debate involves a fundamental issue of political philosophy. It raises a question of the flexibility of legislative action in terms of legislative responsibility to the electorate.

The streamlining of deliberation is obviously attractive in a world which places high value upon action. It is not accidental that the democratic influences of the early Greek civilization and the democratic movements of the later 18th and 19th centuries paralleled philosophical movements which found importance in idealism rather than in realism, which placed greater value in contemplation than in action. Conversely the pragmatic and realistic schools of the early 20th century consciously abandoned much of the moral and ethical nature of man for pure mechanism or Watsonian psychology.

THE CHALLENGE OF ACTIONISM

In the realm of politics, although the forms remain unchanged, innumerable straws in the wind indicate the effect of a machine age on the thinking and acting habits of the people. Even the bitterness of a political campaign has not produced great editorial writers or outstanding commentators; news print moves to larger type and shorter stories, from word to picture, and from printed word to radio voice. The forum fights an uphill battle to regain the position of the town meeting. Men have become accustomed to delegate tasks to others, to institutions, to machines. They want their answers ready made and so a philosophy of action challenges, in the realm of ethics and politics, the philosophy of deliberation. And it challenges a double-bodied legislature as an extravagance and a monstrosity. Indeed, the philosophies of those we consider not quite respectable challenge even the existence of any legislative or deliberative body. Action is the password. *Blitz* is the fashion.

The usefulness of joint legislative committees and the party caucus have already been elaborated as a means of unicameral action within the framework of the bicameral system. Unicameral action is necessarily the result of single leadership. It occurs in the American legislative scene only when there is a general unification of political and social objectives which have insured a political party a dominant position on the political scene. It seems to me that this is the outstanding advantage of a *de facto* unicameralism—it is not a permanent or fixed way of life for the State and its people. When there is uncertainty and doubt, the additional brakes that a second house of a legislature can provide is both necessary and desirable in order that legislative action does not run ahead of popular acceptance. When popular demand has unified on a particular social program so that whatever opposition develops cannot be described in terms of general uncertainty, machinery is then available in the framework of our present bicameral organization to speed the achievement of the objectives without an application of brakes by the second house. This ability to accelerate or brake the speed of government should not be abandoned quickly for a vehicle built on horsepower and without brakes.

T. V. Smith

24. The Human Factor in Legislative Halls*

Let us now approach, without undue disdain for small motives, our legislative subject, the Biography of a Bill. We are not to deal with the points of order nor with parliamentary obstetrics. That you can get in the manual of any given legislative body.

* From an address presented at Colgate University, March 2, 1948. Reprinted with permission of author.

THE GENESIS OF THE BILL

Now as a newly elected member of the Illinois Senate—1934, it was —I was the victim of my own ignorance over and over compounded. It seemed to me that I knew nothing of all the innumerable things that as a legislator I needed to know. I was, in the first place, not a lawyer. I quickly discovered, partly as a result of this, that there was no use in trying to read the thousand-odd bills introduced into the State Senate, for I did not understand what I read. Nor had I one-tenth enough time to master them even if I had been much more adequate in comprehension. The business of a modern state is wide, and there seemed to be bills about everything of which I was ignorant. Dimly I discerned that other new members were in the same boat, though not often as paralyzed at the rudder as was I.

Begotten of my personal need, therefore, my desperate, my pathetic need, was the initial thought of introducing this bill, a bill to create an institution that would relieve my distress and make lighter on other novices to come the load that was weighing me down. Thus was conceived the bill to provide a scientific body for the legislature staffed with the best social scientists to provide knowledge, the analogue of which both the executive and the judicial branches of government have long had in state and nation. There is a reason, of course, why the legislative branch has been slow to provide itself with scientific aid. And in that reason the politicians can be seen to be wiser than their scholarly critics; but, even so, not all-wise. The reason is that politics is not primarily a scientific matter; it is an enterprise of sportsmanship, a hazard in interpersonal relations. . . .

THE STRATEGY OF PATIENCE

I did not rush at once to feed the legislative hopper, however, nor indeed for many days, weeks and months. I thought it wise first to look around. I had to have votes for my bill if it were to become law; and I knew that anything that I, not only a professor but a professor of philoso- phy—"radical metaphysician," the hostile press had already lethally called me!—introduced, would be critically inspected. If my project was at all new—as this one was at the time—it would be called "radical" and worse; and so my first adventure into legislative relations for functional ends was to prove that I was a man before I was a professor, that I had sense under- neath sophistication, and most of all that I had sympathy for men as such before I got classed as I professionally was, "a highbrow."

A FRIENDLY ENEMY

The venture to establish oneself a right guy is too delicate for one honestly and fully to detail. Not all factors come to consciousness; and those that do, quickly fade with functional success or failure. If we fail, we must save face; and if we succeed, we must muffle pride. But at least two items come to mind that seem to me authentic and that appear important enough to mention in this serious connection.

The one was a friend that I had, the only Senator out of 50 that I knew to begin with. Clarence Darrow had introduced me to him in advance of my political debut—which introduction itself was an auspice as perilous as prestigeful, because of Darrow's dangerous heterodoxies. This Senator was at the time of my election the ablest and most respected member of the minority party. He had once been his party boss, with reputation strong but speckled. He had now, with the ebb and flow of party prestige, become to both parties "the grand old man" of the Senate, a symbol fairly above partisanship. Well, he was my first nugget on the way to my influence for any bill; and now I know, looking back, that I would never have got the Legislative Council bill enacted without his aid, nor could I have possibly prevented its early demise but for his strategic post-parturitional care. But that is to get ahead of my story.

HOW THE NIGHT SHIFT HELPED

... The first caucus of my party which I attended, without knowing a single soul, was already at the glasses, though not in its cups, when I arrived. The members seemed embarrassed at their reluctance to offer me a drink but not emboldened to overcome it. After a decent interval, I asked simply and naturally, if I might have a drink; and as somebody rushed to get me water for dilution, I poured a generous portion of somebody else's bourbon, and indulged myself neatly, as an exiled Texan might. I thought nothing more of this, being happily soon enough among the "haves." I was told the next morning, however, by a friendly informer, that the story was all over Capitol Hill before midnight and that I had made myself more friends by that simple act than many elected idealists made in months. Human relations in the legislature, as elsewhere, are indeed often composed of such flimsy, trivial, and sometimes unpraiseworthy stuff. No fellow politician, however, has ever, so far as I can recall, encouraged me to drink to excess, nor indeed do many of them do so.

Extrapolating this matter a little farther, an older friend, widely experienced in politics, had given me some good tips of a personal sort in regard to permitted vices. In advance he told me that I could certainly afford to drink with other legislators, if I carried it well; could play poker, if I did not lose my shirt; and indeed could do what was asked without losing face, only sexual promiscuity being of principle beyond the pale for a professor. Some, he said, might invite me to which we now know as the "kinsey" statistical curve parties; but not even scientific politicians could condone my acceptance of such invitations. This same distinction, not invidious to me, I found made in other premises. For instance, more than once when I went for explanation and advice to Senators sponsoring bills that seemed dubious if not downright "easy-dough" bills, I have been told, after getting a straight-face explanation of the bill in question, "but don't you get mixed up with this. It is all right for me, but not for you, Senator."

THE SUN SHINES ON THE DAY SHIFT

So much for a nocturnal glimpse or two into legislative life. I return now to the day shift. My lack of public reputation in the Senate was to be repaired sooner than I could have foreseen. I expected to bide my time, as new members should, to get a public hearing. Lincoln's birthday came in the second month of my initiation; and Springfield, Illinois, is sensitive, with the breath of celebrations, to the honor of being this civic hero's home and final resting place. A resolution was passed in the Senate setting the birthday aside for two commemorative speeches: one to be made by the sitting Lt. Governor, a more learned man than most, and the other speech by Senator Smith.

Now I was a Democrat, by courtesy a Southern Democrat—not long at least from Texas—representing what was largely a Negro constituency. The Resolution naming me to this Lincoln "honor" was introduced by a wily Republican. This curious fact led an amused reporter for the *Chicago Tribune* to remark that my enemies now certainly had me on the hot spot; that I would never get out of the predicament whole, whatever I said or did not say. It turned out better than the reporter thought, and worse, I suspect, than the wily opposition Senator intended. Learning that the Lt. Governor was to hold forth for an hour, and was to read his long speech at that, I arose, said my speciously extempore say in less words than Lincoln's own Gettysburg address, and before two minutes was over sat down to an ovation climaxed by my Republican Senator moving to print some thousands of the speech at state expense for distribution among the citizens. That was of course a lucky break for my reputation: for after that I felt myself, with a normal share of deference, to be a real member of the public body. Perhaps you will suffer the speech itself, as Exhibit J, in the Biography of the Bill.

No man made great by death offers more hope to lowly pride than does Abraham Lincoln; for while living he was himself so simple as often to be dubbed a fool. Foolish he was, they said, in losing his youthful heart to a grave, and living his life on married patience; foolish in pitting his homely ignorance against Douglas, brilliant, courtly and urbane; foolish in setting himself to do the right in a world where the days go mostly to the strong; foolish in dreaming of freedom for a long-suffering folk whom the North is as anxious to keep out as the South was to keep down; foolish in choosing the silent Grant to lead to victory the hesitant armies of the North; foolish, finally, in presuming that government for the people must be government of and by the people.

Foolish many said; foolish many, many more believed.

This Lincoln whom so many living friends and foes alike deemed foolish, hid his bitterness in laughter; fed his sympathy on solitude; and met recurring disaster with whimsicality to muffle the murmur of a bleeding heart. Out of the tragic sense of life he pitied where others blamed; bowed his own shoulders with the woes of the weak; endured humanely his little day of chance power; and won through death what life disdains to bestow upon such simple souls—lasting peace and everlasting glory.

How prudently we proud men compete for nameless graves, while now and then—to echo Wendell Phillips—some starveling of Fate forgets himself into immortality.

MAKING FRIENDS IN ORDER TO INFLUENCE LEGISLATION

Privately accepted as a friendly sort after the first night and publicly not disesteemed after the Lincoln speech, I held my oratorical breath for two years, "traded votes," as the saying invidiously goes, talked privately especially with fellow-new members about our joint predicament and how to cure or at least to make tolerable our ignorance, and made friends among members old and new wherever I could consistent with self-respect. Very little, believe me, goes on in trading votes or otherwise that trenches upon the self-respect of any robust member. But let me spell out somewhat more in detail the sort of things I did to help feather the nest of my fledgling before it was ever hatched.

Though a Democrat, I wrote speeches, especially radio speeches at which I was experienced, for a Republican Senator who was running for Governor. Though a member of the faculty of the University of Chicago, and being therefore investigated by the Senate Wallgreen Committee, I answered, behind the scenes, much of the mail received from the public by the Chairman of the Investigating Committee. He said that he did not know what to say, and trusted me to say the right thing. . . .

And what would you expect a certain Italian Senator to do after several friendly passes, such for instance as one which I well recall? I went to him one day, in a legislative lull, commented favorably on his tie and tailored suit. He looked glum and suspicious. I told him that I had a few months before been in Italy, his ancestral home. He said: "So what?" I laid on heavily how the Italians were lovers of beauty and how in that regard at least he was as good an Italian as I hoped he was American. "What the hell are you driving at?" he demanded to know. "Just this, Senator," I amusedly replied. "I have the most beautiful girl in the steno-graphic pool assigned to me, and she isn't worth a damn as a stenographer. You have assigned to you, I learn, the ugliest girl back there, but an excellent stenographer. I have much mail to answer," I went on, "and you I suspect have little." "None," he corrected. "Then," countered I, "What say—trade me your womanly brains for my feminine beauty." His hand was out, his face wreathed in smiles, and his words were happily in tune. "You're on, Senator; you're on." And so I was, not only *on the trade;* but for this and other reasons which I forget, I was on his list of friends. Embarrassingly so, in fact. He subsequently offered "to bump off" anybody who I would name for that honor.

But getting through him to the bill itself; when it had been introduced, two years later, and was being railroaded to a deadend committee by an unsympathetic presiding officer, my Italian colleague rushed up to me, whispering in my ear that I stall the speaker for a few minutes until he could corral the Republican votes. Quickly he returned and directed me to appeal from the decision of the Chair. Nobody was more surprised than the speaker, nor anybody more gratified than I, when the votes of the opposition party snatched my bill from the graveyard and sent it to a committee which later gave it a place on the calendar of the Senate—and a chance to be born.

COMPENSATORY ALLIES AND STRATEGIC RETREATS

But other things happened to my baby while it was still a bill. To lift it from partisan suspicion, I asked two Republican Senators, who had become my friends, to join their names with mine in sponsoring the bill and piloting it up the calendar Calvary as that ascent proves to many a poor savior. Moreover, to strengthen its support on my own side of the chamber, I asked a downstate Democrat (I being from Chicago) to make a fourth to sponsor it. And upon advice of my old Republican friend's legacy from Darrow's solemn injunction that the Senator was to watch over me when Darrow couldn't, I cut the appropriation required—it should have been $40,000—down to the token figure of $10,000, to win economy votes; and I sacrificed, on the same advice but with even greater pain to my ideological part, a philosophic preamble, lest Benthamite verbiage scare less literate votes away.

MAKING THE FIRST HURDLE ONLY TO SPRAWL

Well, to make a long story too short for anything but highlights on the human factors that conditioned the bill, after some three years of single minded fixation upon it the bill passed, was engrossed and became a law. Let only radicals, and very young liberals, rush to celebrate, they who do not know the price of legal progress. My bill had been badly damaged at the birth, as are all idealistic measures on the way to collective fulfillment. Moreover, it had lost its patrimony. The appropriation achieved was hardly enough to organize the Council provided, certainly not more than a beginning for the staff of social scientists which the statute contemplated for continuous study and report upon pressing legislative problems. And worse than all this, if it could seem worse to you than lack of money, was this: The Lieutenant Governor, outwitted in strategy, had the last word. It was he who had the appointment of the Senate members of the House and Senate Council. Of course he appointed enough bad material, he thought, to guarantee a failure.

IT COULD HAVE BEEN WORSE, BUT NOT MUCH WORSE

I can say this for the Lieutenant Governor, however; he did *not* appoint Senator K., whom I had once inadvertently called a "rat" and who, rising to the full width of his 340 pounds, advanced upon me to the accompaniment of his first public utterance in thirty years of tenure: "Nobody can call me a rat and live—nobody!" I assuaged him somewhat, while other Senators held him off me, by declaring to the presiding officer that I accepted his challenge, permitted him to choose the weapons, but with one stipulation which I wished to make in the presence of the whole Senate: that I be given three hundred yards to start! This, I say, somewhat assuaged him, though it had all to be done over more slowly and indirectly after a downstate newspaper chain carried both our pictures undergirded with some such caption as this: "Senator K., listening to the flow of professional language from Senator Smith at last heard one word which he understood—and rose vehemently to deny that he was a rat!"

Senator K was not appointed to help oversee this scientific body, but he would have been more promising of success than some who were appointed; for as I say, Senator K and I became fair friends after our fracas.

John, the saloon-keeper, *was* appointed, good old inarticulate John who in a quarter century had never made a public speech, and very likely merely because he had nothing to say. Joe, the vendor of I-know-not-what behind the front of a flower-shop Joe, too was put on the Council. Some of the House members were a little better in promise. I say advisedly "in promise!" for, truth to tell, even John and Joe turned out much better in performance than the Lt. Governor intended or than I could have hoped. Thereby hangs a tale in the implementation of the statute more dramatic than anything I have remembered to tell in connection with its enactment. And back of the performance is, again, my wily Republican friend from Darrow's bequest, a professional politician whose experienced advice I had the good luck initially to take, as long since I have learned to seek it out and to treasure it as full of reliance.

UP AND AT 'EM AGAIN!

This human thing of fraternization across the party line is the glory of our two-party system. I never made an important political decision, as touching even my own promotion in the Democratic Party, that I did not first listen intently to whatever advice this Republican would give me. I complained to him, in my initial inexperience, about the appropriation slashed by me at his prompting. He replied sagely, "Better a live statute with little money than a dead bill with too much." No gainsaying that. But, as I put it to him later: "How do we operate for biennium so to justify our continuation, without financial support? Social scientists do not work for nothing." "We'll manage the money," he cautioned me, "as time goes on. Let us go ahead as though we had money."

That was well and good, save only when I suggested to him that we bring to Chicago the Research Director of the Council of the Kansas Legislature (after whose success we were trying to pattern): to help us organize, recruit a staff, and get off to a likely start, my Republican friend countered with the outrageous alternative suggestion that we take our whole Illinois Council (some twenty-five members) on a junket to Kansas, a junket, mark you, that would practically squander the whole appropriation of $10,000: Seeing how shocked I was at such improvidence, he said quietly that he thought the boys would like to have a trip out of the State, that they'd learn something if they went to see, whereas they would not listen if we brought somebody up to speechify to them. How right he was, I was soon to learn; for I took his advice.

THE HIGHER STRATEGY

Not only the advice to go, but more audacious advice as we went. But note how he figured the matter and how right he was. Why even John, the saloon-keeper was impressed with seeing a seating chart with his name printed on it by the Kansas Council within thirty minutes of our arrival at their Council meeting, that John remarked on it to me as an example of efficiency which he lacked in Illinois; and I noticed that he folded the chart with his name on it to take home, as he confided to me, to show his grandson.

The further cooperative attitude on the part of John came about largely because of the advice which my Republican friend had given to me on the Pullman car which I had chartered for the junket. My friend suggested that in the committee assignments, an honorable place be found for John, the saloon-keeper, and even for Joe, the ambiguous vulgarian. When I told my friend not to try to kid me, that I had been kidded by experts, he countered with very wise words. "You know," he said, "that the real weakness of our Council is the fear on the part of the rank-and-file of the legislature that the Council will become a little assembly and rob them of what small function and honor they have. Whatever we can do to keep our Council from appearing to be a highbrow thing will strengthen it in public esteem. That esteem will become its strength and the hand that feeds it money whereon to succeed. John's recommendation of the Council, or even Joe's, would do it more good in the long run, he concluded, "than your or my support; for we are high-brows."

OUT OF THE MOUTHS OF SALOON-KEEPERS . . .

I could see how shrewd and humane was that advice. Of course I took it; and John blossomed like a green bay tree even before the trip was over, and that gnarled trunk bore faithful fruit ever afterwards. . . .

The Council was "made" when word got around that John was sold on it (and Joe, too, for that matter, but it is another story). To the best of my memory John never knew his limitations. But he watched how I voted or discerned what I wanted; and he never deviated from his articulate loyalty that night in Kansas. They also served who only know their betters —and keep their word. (We're all betters to somebody, and debtors, in turn, to most.)

ANOTHER HURDLE SURMOUNTED

The hurdle of poor material surmounted and money found to continue, you might think that we could not celebrate success. Not of the legislative variety of success, not yet. A decade is a normal time to get any worthwhile bill passed, constituted, corrected, implemented, and grounded in the affections of people enough to keep it alive and growing. The Council was bi-partisan in organization, but would it prove non-partisan in performance? That had been a fear. and it still remained a question. My Republican friend and I picked the Research Director by hand, from our own State University. We stood by him as he built an able staff of young researchers to serve our legislative needs. Then I moved on to Congress, knowing, that my baby, though born and growing, had hazards, not only without but also from within. I kept in touch. Within a biennium, there befell what had disclosed the Achilles heel to more than one such would-be-bi-partisan committees. The State of Illinois, normally Republican but heavily Democrat when I became Chairman of the Council, reverted to type and went overwhelmingly Republican. This was the opportunity to lop off, in the name of economy or honest conservatism, all the newfangled Democratic luxuries that had been thrust upon the State. But when the axeman came to my child, the Legislative Council, he found, noiselessly enthroned and sitting there stolidly, though not as innocently as Buddha—whom do you guess he found there in the Chair? Right you are: he found our old wily Republican friend, the Elder Statesman of the victorious party! When my wily ally asked the axeman what he wanted, the axeman replied graciously and not untruly, that he wanted to inquire of the Chairman's health—and how, too, was his wife and children! Another victory, but not yet time to celebrate!

DARKEST JUST BEFORE DAWN

It is *always* a little too early heedlessly to celebrate legislative achievements. Eternal vigilance is the price of liberty institutionalization. Nothing is secure until it is institutionalized, and it is not secure then until it has become tradition. Years are required for this osmosis political. It was about a decade, after I got interested in this idea of the bill, when I heaved my greatest sigh of relief, and decided that my child was able to fight its own battles. But that sigh of relief was qualified by coming after the closest shave the Legislative Council ever had in Illinois.

Long absent from the scene, frequently from the State, I had lost more and more contact, nursing only a citizen's interest in the institution. Suddenly I was called long-distance and told by a friend in Illinois that my all-but-grown child was doomed that very day unless I could intervene with the majority leader in the Senate to spare the axe falling upon the total appropriation, long undisputed by either party. Now it happened that the leader in question had long been a political enemy but longer still a personal friend. The hardest working man I ever knew, he never swore, he never gambled, he never drank. It was he who earned the reputation I got undeservedly: the reputation of reading every bill ever introduced in the Senate.

THE DAWN, THE SUN, THE DAY!

I called him. After an exchange of greetings, I complained to him in my most pathetic voice of my latest bereavement. He was all sympathy, asking whether it was my father? my mother? my wife? No, no, I told him, in anguish—not any of them. Was there anything he could do? "Take that axe off the neck of my legislative child, I fairly shouted at him." "How would you like, after all your legislative years, to be shorn at a blow of all your triumphs? I have only one, one only child, the Legislative Council, and now I am reliably informed that you expect to kill it before the setting of the sun." "You win," he genially replied. "I had meant to kill it but I will honor our old relationship, and let it live. How much appropriation do you think it should really have?"

8
THE STATE GOVERNOR

From a position of dependence upon the legislature the governorship has evolved into the most important state office. However, with the exception of a few states with new constitutions, the governor is the chief executive in name only; executive power is diffused among a number of independently elected officials, boards, and commissions. All early state constitutions reflected a distrust of a strong executive; they limited the governor's powers and provided for a strong legislature. It was not until the early part of the twentieth century that a movement began to strengthen the executive powers of the governor, provide him with staff assistance, lengthen his term, and increase his salary.

Professor Byron R. Abernethy in a study prepared for the Governmental Research Center of the University of Kansas attempts to resolve the questions of what removal powers the governor should possess and whether these powers should be constitutionally granted.

Senator Thomas C. Desmond, a member of the New York State Senate, describes the magnitude of the typical governor's duties and responsibilities and finds him generally ill-equipped to carry out these duties and responsibilities. Senator Desmond offers a prescription designed to increase the governor's ability to play a more effective role as the chief executive of the state government.

Frank Bane, chairman of the Advisory Commission on Intergovernmental Relations and formerly executive director of The Council of State Governments, draws upon thirty-five years of experience with 414 governors to describe the job of being a governor.

Byron R. Abernethy
25. *The Governor's Removal Power**

The questions posed here are: "What should be the extent of the governor's removal power?" and "Should this power be constitutionally protected?" But before attempting to resolve the questions of what the power *should be,* it would perhaps be well to determine what it *is.*

The appointment and removal power of the President of the United States has now been pretty well clarified by the Constitution, by statute and by Supreme Court decisions. His power to appoint was given broad constitutional recognition. It has been recognized and legislated by the Congress. But the Constitution has from the beginning remained silent on the matter of the President's power to remove federal appointive officials. This has led to some difficulty as the Congress somewhat belatedly sought to impair removal power long exercised by American presidents when it passed the Tenure of Office Act. That attempt failed. A subsequent law passed in 1876 sought to restrict the president's power to remove postmasters, and laws creating independent boards and commissions, such as the Federal Trade Commission, and the civil service laws, have likewise imposed some limitations on the President's power of removal. The authority of Congress to thus restrain the presidential power of removal has been tested in and resolved by the courts to the end that the rule has become rather firmly established in the Federal Government that the chief executive has unlimited removal power over agents of the executive power. In the instance of agents of the constitutional powers of Congress, specifically the independent regulatory commissions, Congress may limit the exercise of the President's removal power to removal for causes named by Congress.

States and state courts have been by no means so generous in recognizing an inherent executive power of removal over the agents of state executive power. Early state constitutions, establishing governments characterized by legislative supremacy and fear of a strong executive, granted rather narrow appointive power to the governor, and naturally were not sympathetic with an extensive executive power of removal. In some, New York for example, the power to remove was at first made coextensive with the limited power to appoint under the scheme of a council of appointment. But even where such power existed originally, it could not

* From *Some Persisting Questions Concerning the Constitutional State Executive.* (Lawrence, Kansas: Governmental Research Center of the University of Kansas, 1960). pp. 50–58. Footnotes in original omitted. Reprinted with permission of publisher.

survive the influence of Jacksonian Democracy. The idea that the governor might remove executive and administrative officials was not to be reconciled with a growing sentiment for their popular election, and the new democracy could not tolerate the idea that public officials chosen by the sovereign people should be subject to removal by another official, also popularly elected by the same "sovereign." Hence the legal principle took root in states that the governor, unlike the President, has only such power to remove public officials, regardless of how they may have been selected in the first instance, as the state constitution or statutes expressly confer upon him. In other words, the prevailing constitutional rule in states is that the governor has no inherent power to remove agents of the executive power, even where he has the authority to appoint them in the first instance, and that he can do so only if the state constitution or state law expressly says that he may, or where the appointment is not for a fixed term.

Hence, in seeking to define the removal power of the governor, one finds no automatic inherent or implied executive power to remove subordinates (except in Indiana), but must look for positive constitutional or statutory authorizations for the the governor to remove public officials. Here one finds that states have been reluctant to confer upon their governors extensive removal power. The constitutions of fifteen states, including that of Alaska, expressly recognize some removal power for the governor. Those of Alaska, New Jersey, and Missouri provide the most extensive grants of such power. The Alaskan Constitution provides that the heads of all departments, except the secretary of state, who is popularly elected and serves in the capacity of a first successor to the governor, "shall serve at the pleasure of the governor." The revised Missouri Constitution provides that "all appointive officers may be removed by the governor." In spite of this wording, the power of the Missouri governor to remove executive department heads is not as extensive as is that of the governor of the State of Alaska, however. Missouri's Constitution provides for the popular election of the secretary of state, state treasurer, and auditor in addition to the lieutenant governor. These naturally are not included in the offices subject to the governor's removal power.

The revised New Jersey Constitution provides that single heads of the principal departments shall "serve at the pleasure of the Governor," except of course in the case of the attorney general and the secretary of state. It also authorizes the governor to remove for cause any officer who receives his compensation from the state except a member, officer, or employee of the legislature, an officer elected by the legislature, or a judicial official. Such removal may be made, however, only after the serving of charges and an opportunity for public hearing. The removed official also is entitled to judicial review of both the law and the facts.

In Colorado, Illinois, Maryland, Nebraska, New Mexico and West Virginia, the appointees of the governor may be removed "for cause." The Pennsylvania governor may remove the secretary of the commonwealth and the attorney general at his pleasure. In Delaware, the secretary of state serves "at the pleasure" of the governor.

The Constitutions of Alaska, Missouri, and New Jersey represent a marked increase in state constitutional recognition of the power of removal for governors, and go far toward establishing by positive declaration a power of removal comparable to that which the courts have held is an inherent executive power of the President. The state constitutions of course do not tell the entire story. Statutory enactments also affect materially the power of the governor to remove statutory officials, and there is some evidence to suggest that as the governor's power to appoint has grown, legislatures have been somewhat inclined to enhance correspondingly his power of removal over persons appointed by him. No comprehensive study of such statutory authority in American states appears to have been made, however, and what evidence there is suggests that while there has been some enhancement of the statutory removal power, it is likely still to be hedged in with numerous restrictions in many states, such as requiring Senate confirmation of removal, where such confirmation has been required for appointment, or insisting that removal be "for cause" with guarantees for the filing of charges, a public hearing, and so forth, which is far removed from providing that subordinates serve at the governor's pleasure.

Also, any extension in the governor's power of removal, whether constitutional or statutory in origin, has naturally not extended to elected state administrative or executive officials. Members of regulatory boards and commissions in states also tend to be exempt from any general removal power enjoyed by the chief executive, just as they are in the national government.

One state alone represents an exception to the general pattern of state policy regarding the legal removal power of the governor. That is Indiana, and constitutional policy declared by the courts of that state seems to have been produced by unfortunate experiences growing out of the attempt to make use of the lieutenant governor as the head of one of the major executive departments. The Supreme Court of that state in 1941 adopted for all practical purposes the policy of the federal courts with regard to the removal power of the state's chief executive. It held that the power to appoint and remove officers in the executive and administrative department of the state was a part of the executive power, of which the governor, being vested with the executive power could not be divested, inferring that the power of appointment and removal were inherent in the executive power of the state.

Thus, in Indiana, the governor would appear to be endowed constitutionally with extensive removal power, even in the absence of affirmative grant by either the constitution or by statute, a power which in fact may not be taken from him by the legislature under the court's theory of separation of powers. It appears that in deference to political considerations, however, governors of Indiana since 1941 have made very moderate use of this somewhat unconventional judicial recognition of their power of removal.

The governor's power to remove local officials is even more limited. In general, he has not been given that power, although in three states, New York, Michigan, and Wisconsin, the governor may remove certain local law enforcement officers such as the sheriff and district attorney. Three factors appear to have been influential in denying the governor power to remove local government officials. First, they are popularly elected and therefore responsible to the people of the communities or districts which elected them. Second, local government, rightly or wrongly, has often been considered an agent of the legislative rather than of the executive power of state government, and therefore not properly subject to executive control. And third, the persisting demand for local self-government and opposition to the trend toward centralization of political power has been a barrier to giving the governor this power to interfere in the "local" affairs of a community.

What then should be the extent of the governor's removal power? To dispose first of the matter of the governor's power to remove local government officials discussed immediately above, as long as the theory persists that the people of a community should be free to govern themselves in all matters of local concern, through their own locally chosen public officials, it does not seem proper that the governor should be authorized to interfere with that local government by removing locally chosen public officials unless they are clearly obstructing state government activity or policy, or are clearly guilty of official misconduct. It is true that local governments are constitutionally creatures of, and agents of, the state. But as long as the state in creating those local governments and in providing for their functions and powers, continues to leave important state functions, such as law enforcement, in their hands for administration at their will, the basic premise for interference by the governor is denied.

Serious question may exist as to the wisdom of leaving important state functions, such as tax collection and the apprehension and the prosecution of criminals, in the hands of local governments and of locally elected officials. But as long as the state legislature or the state constitution places those responsibilities there, it is difficult to see how removal of locally elected officials by the governor can be justified. If it is desired that local government officials, such as tax assessors and collectors, sheriffs, and prosecuting attorneys, be made subject to the removal power of the governor, it would seem that their offices should first be integrated into the state administrative structure under the governor's control; that county and district sheriffs and prosecuting attorneys should first be made officials in a state department of justice, for example, no longer elected by and responsible to local electorates, but appointed by and responsible to the head of a state-wide executive department of justice, under the control of the governor, with its head appointed by and removable by the governor. In such an administrative arrangement, there could be no question about the propriety of the governor's power to remove local agents of a state executive department. But until such an integration of offices and responsibilities has taken place, the basic assumptions of the relationships between agencies of local self-government and the governor would be violated by the latter removing from office a popularly elected local governmental official. In so doing, he would not only be removing an unsatisfactory official, he would be challenging local majority will, and the very capacity of the local community to govern itself. No governor should be placed in a position where he is forced to make such a challenge, even as an implicit one.

This is not to suggest either that all local government offices should be integrated into a state administrative hierarchy of command culminating in the governor. Many local government officials are occupied primarily with local affairs, and should conduct them as the local majority wants them conducted. The governor's removal power should not extend to such officials. Their removal for wrongdoing should be at the hands of the local community. But there are some local officials, especially those responsible for the enforcement of state law, whose functional responsibilities are primarily to the state, not the local community. The state should not be required to accept either unsatisfactory performance in those offices, or the use of those offices to obstruct state purposes. These officials are in fact state officials, not local officials, and probably should be made that in fact and in effective responsibility. When that is done, and only then, satisfactory lines of responsibility to the governor, who is charged by the constitution with seeing that the laws are faithfully executed, can be established, including the power to remove the local agents of the state when their performance is not satisfactory.

In the meantime, the governor's power to remove officials at pleasure certainly should not be extended to include such local government officials. If he is given any power of removal over them, it should be limited to removing only for the most serious causes, these to be proved after charges and a public hearing. Such is, of course, so limited a removal power as not to be tremendously significant, but it is the only kind of removal power which can be satisfactorily reconciled with the basic assumptions of the governmental order within which it is to function.

Turning next to the governor's removal power over state executive and administrative officials, it seems rather obvious that the governor's power of removal should not be expected to extend to independently elected state officials. Where the constitutional system is keyed to decentralization and division and diffusion of responsibility, with the people the ones to demand and secure responsibility of each elected official, the removal power of the governor cannot consistently be extended to apply to other popularly elected state officials. It should apply only to his own staff, to officials which are appointed by and responsible to him. This is not to say that such a decentralized administrative structure is desirable. But it is to say that an extensive removal power for the governor, extending to all the principal state officials is completely inconsistent with the basic assumptions of a decentralized administration, and that it would be unwise, to say the least, to mix the two. As in the case of local officials, the most that might be called for would be removal only for the most serious causes, after filing of charges to be proved in an open hearing. Even this is probably not desirable because of the position in which it places the governor. It would seem desirable to leave removal of such officials to the usual procedures of impeachment, address, or recall, and not involve the governor's removal power in such independently elected administrative offices at all.

Similarly, in so far as the legislature is free under the constitution to do so, and does, create "independent," regulatory and quasi-judicial boards and commissions, to exercise what is essentially legislative as opposed to executive and administrative authority, those agencies probably should not be subject to the governor's removal power except on such bases as the legislature determines. Again, this is not to say that such independent agencies should be created in state government. Indeed, there is much reason to question the wisdom of creating such agencies at all. But it is to say that where such agencies do exist, extending the governor's removal power to embrace the removing of such officials at his pleasure, or for reasons of public policy, would be inconsistent with the assumptions upon which such agencies were created in the first instance. And if the members of such boards or commission are directly elected by the people as they are in many states, then the difficulties of the situation are doubly compounded.

Here again the most that can be said for extending the removal power of the governor to such officials is that it should extend to authorizing the governor to remove them for causes clearly indicated in the statute or constitutional provision creating them, and then only after the filing of charges to be proved in a public hearing.

Contrasted with these limitations on the governor's removal power, however, if the people of the state have determined to have a centralized and responsible executive department and state administration, the governor's removal power must be extensive. He should have authority to remove at his pleasure all members of his staff, and the responsible heads of all the principal executive departments, and to remove for cause all other administrative personnel in the pay of the state, after the pattern set by the Alaska and New Jersey state constitutions.

The central theme of the centralized state administration is that the governor is placed in full command of the executive and administrative work of the state government, as the managing president is placed in command of administering the affairs of a private corporation, and is then held accountable for the way in which all the state's business is handled. If this scheme is to function efficiently, the executive in command must not only have the authority to appoint his subordinates upon whom he must depend for getting the state's business attended to, but he must be free to control those subordinates after they have been selected. That control can be effective only if he has the power to supervise their conduct in office, and to remove them from office when that conduct is not pleasing to him. His control, moreover, must not be limited to seeing that they do their work and do it efficiently, but to seeing that their policies and their conduct are in harmony with the policies of his administration as a whole. If the governor is to be held responsible for the work of his administration, as it is contemplated he will be under a centralized state executive, then his authority must be commensurate with that responsibility, and that means, either directly or indirectly, an appointive and removal power as extensive as the administration for which he is to be held accountable.

Cause should not have to be established for the removal of key officers occupying positions vital to the success of the governor's administration. Those officials can affect significantly the smooth operations and the success of his administration without in any way committing an illegal act, or neglecting their administrative duties. Mere personality clashes between key administrative personnel may reach the point where replacement of one or both parties concerned may become necessary to restore harmony within the administration. In such a case, the governor must have authority to restore and maintain that harmony.

Personnel less vital to the success of the governor's administration may well be protected by the usual civil service requirements of cause, notice, and possibly hearing, after a probationary period has been served. But the

200 / The State Governor

power to remove must extend to these employees where cause exists. If the governor is to be really held accountable for all state administration, then this power to remove for cause, protected by the necessity for charges and hearing, should extend as it does in New Jersey to "any officer or employee who receives his compensation from the state." This will include officers and employees of boards and commissions too. But it does fix responsibility upon the governor to correct wrongdoing anywhere in the state government outside the legislature and the courts.

This is an extensive power of removal which these suggestions place in the hands of the governor, but it is tremendously important to responsible government, and is vital to the success of a centralized state administration. But how is it to be established? Should the legislature be left free to fix the removal power of the governor in the public interest, or should it be protected in the state constitution?

Flexibility in administrative matters is provided by legislative control over those matters. But it is difficult to see why flexibility is to be desired here. The general appointment and removal power of the governor, the broad outlines of constitutional policy governing those powers, are fundamental and timeless. They determine in part the basic nature of the government being established. They belong in the constitution. Certainly it would be improper to attempt to enumerate the administrative positions embraced by the governor's removal power. Those change. And the creating, abolishing and changing of particular agencies is a legislative function. It should remain with the legislature, and this should not be done by constitutional provision. But establishing the broad framework of executive responsibility within which, and consistently with which, the legislature is to create and change administrative agencies is a proper constitutional task. A part of that framework, and a part vital in determining the nature of the entire state executive and administrative organization, is the extent of the governor's removal power. It has a place in the state constitution. It can be embodied in the constitution, as it has been in the constitutions of New Jersey, Alaska, and Missouri, for example, without in any way encroaching upon the proper legislative function of establishing state administrative machinery.

Not only is it appropriate to embody such provisions in the state constitution, it is probably highly desirable to do so. Given the strong tradition which exists in state government, both in legislative practice and in judicial precedent, against an extensive removal power for the governor, it would seem wise, if a responsible, centralized state administration is what the people of a state want, to protect the governor's removal power in the constitution.

Thomas C. Desmond
26. *To Help Governors Govern**

The rise of a growing crop of able young Governors across the country
has been a striking political phenomenon of recent years. They are in
some cases ambitious, independent and better equipped for their offices
than their predecessors—and a good thing, for their problems are bigger,
too. Depression, wars and zooming population have combined to multiply
the responsibilities of state governments.

Lord Bryce found in the Eighteen Eighties that our Governors had
little money to spend, little dignity, little power and little to do. Today,
however, Governors preside over a middle layer of government that spends
nearly $20 billion a year, helps support more than a million indigent
elderly, operates huge mental hospitals, a vast system of prisons and
bulging universities, employs a million persons, including armies of inspectors and state troopers, minutely regulates big utilities and the corner
grocer, constructs thousands of miles of highways, tollways and speedways,
and pokes a well-meaning if often heavy hand into most social, economic
and psychological dislocations in the country.

The Governor is expected to be a court of last resort for anyone
wronged in his state, referee between conflicting economic forces and chief
social worker. He must be (or at least appear to be) a sage financial expert,
and at the same time a kind of Roy Rogers chasing "the bad guys,"
whether they be "the insurance lobby" or "the public utilities" or "the
corrupt opposition" or any other convenient scapegoat of the moment.

He is the symbol and conscience of the state. As such he must fulfill a
role that calls upon him to visit the sick, the lonely, the aged, and to pat
on the back an underpaid mental hospital attendant. He must be the
state's chief tub-thumper, a one-man chamber of commerce, heralding the
glories of his state's valleys, mountains, rivers, farmers, laborers, women,
manufactures and agricultural products. The Governor of Oregon, for
example, last fall bet a native salmon against a hog wagered by the Governor of Iowa as to whose state university would win a football game. It's all
in a Chief Executive's workday.

The heart of a Governor's job lies in legislation. "More than half of my

* From the *New York Times Magazine.* June 2, 1957. pp. 14–20, and 22. Copyright by the New York Times. Reprinted by permission of publisher and author.

work as Governor," said Theodore Roosevelt, "was in the direction of getting needed and important legislation." Governors, through their power to approve or veto legislation and to call special sessions to deal with specific problems, are an integral part of the lawmaking process.

A Governor must understand our check-and-balance system of government. A study has shown that one Governor was able to get only 17 per cent of his bills through a hostile Legislature, while in another state the Governor was able to get 75 per cent of his program enacted by a friendly Legislature.

Even for politically shrewd, veteran Chief Executives the task of dealing with traditionally balky, unpredictable, and sensitive Legislatures and their politically wise legislative leaders is a critical challenge that can plunge a Governor into political oblivion—or, sometimes, propel him into the national spotlight.

The Governor also finds he must serve as party fund-raiser and patronage dispenser. He must buoy the morale of party committeemen in Squidunk and bring peace to warring intraparty factions in Squeedunk. More fundamentally, he learns that if he is truly to be effective as Governor it is not enough to be Governor. He must capture his own party's political machine, as Governor Dewey and as Governor Knight of California did, or else be forced to dicker, scrap or submit to a party boss who is the real source of power and leadership.

While, up to recent times, many Governors were boss-selected, boss-elected and boss-run, today more of them are running their parties and either openly or covertly are the "bosses." At national conventions the Governors increasingly are elbowing aside U. S. Senators and state party chairmen in determining Presidential nominees. For example, the announcement by Senate Minority Leader William Knowland that he will not seek re-election in 1958, but return to California, is commonly taken to mean he has deemed it wise to try to touch the Governorship bag en route to home plate, the Presidency. One reason for this development is that increasingly the Governorship is a stepping-stone toward higher office.

All this would seem to make the office of Governor a potent—and, in some respects, a pleasurable—one. Certainly there is never any dearth of candidates for election and re-election. But once in office the winner quickly finds that our outdated state structure is perversely designed to make it harder, not easier, for him to play his many roles.

The problem is as acute for the people of each state as for their Governor. Their first concern clearly is that he serve them well while he is in the State House. And they must ask themselves whether the office itself is equipped to handle the massive problems that confront our commonwealths today—problems like segregation, air and river pollution, port development, water shortages and the need for huge school and hospital outlays.

At the eighth American Assembly, meeting at Harriman, N. Y., in 1955, outstanding students of state government agreed that we need Governors "empowered to lead." Today, as the Kestenbaum Commission on Intergovernmental Relations, appointed by President Eisenhower and Congressional leaders, has said: "Few states have an adequate Executive branch headed by a Governor who can be held accountable generally for executing and administering the laws of the states." Our Chief Executives are shackled with ancient but effective managerial handcuffs that would be intolerable in most private businesses.

For example, the typical Governor is confronted with hordes of state commissions, boards and departments, although modern management principles decree that no executive should have more than eight to ten officials reporting directly to him. The Council of State Government found in 1950 that the Governor's "span of control" in Texas covered 124 agencies; in Ohio, 122; in Colorado, 140. The result is that most Governors cannot keep a controlling finger on what is going on in their own state. The Council of State Government concluded: "Most Governors have a more difficult job than that of the President of the United States in giving effective managerial direction from the top."

The typical Governor, however, receives for this massive task a take-home pay that would be sneered at by a Madison Avenue account executive—or even by some of the school superintendents in his own state. Salaries scale down sharply from the $50,000 a year, plus tax-free expense, paid New York's Governor to a median take-home pay of about $10,000 for other Chief Executives. One recent Governor, blessed with five children, complained to his fellow Chief Executives that his wife, in addition to her duties as First Lady, had to do the family cooking and washing.

To add to the Chief Executive's difficulties, many state agencies are headed by boards appointed to terms overlapping his own, or are designated by the Legislature and are, therefore, quite independent of him. Thomas E. Dewey, when Governor, summed up the feeling of many of his fellow Governors, when he frankly said, "I get ten to twenty letters a day complaining about state boards and commissions over which I have no authority. I don't mind writing back that I have no control over them, but what galls me is that people don't believe me."

Al Smith, one of the really great practicing political scientists of the twentieth century, said in an age when problems were far simpler than those which confront our modern Governors: "The man doesn't live who can understand the job in his first two years." Yet twenty-two states today restrict the Governor to a two-year term and in many states he cannot succeed himself. What stockholder would invest in a private concern that limited its chief executive to a two-year, or even a four-year, hitch?

In some states, the people still elect not only their Governor and Lieutenant Governor, but also the Secretary of State, the Attorney General, Treasurer, Auditor, Tax Commissioner, Highway Commissioner—and even the State Printer in Kansas and Nevada and Collector of Oyster Revenues in Delaware! Many such elective officials, although nominally on the Governor's "team," spend most of their time plotting to unseat him. "Seventy per cent of the Governor's time," one Chief Executive has candidly confessed, "is spent picking the daggers out of his back each morning thrust there overnight by other ambitious elected state officials."

In many states the rivalry between the Governor and Lieutenant Governor has become notorious. One Governor in recent years did not dare leave his own state because he could not trust his Lieutenant Governor not to pardon a corps of prisoners; another was a virtual prisoner within his own state lines because he feared, if he took a trip outside, the Acting Governor would raid the Treasury.

State Constitutions commonly affirm that the "executive power" shall be vested in the Governor, and then proceed to strip him of effective executive power over state agencies. Some measure of the frail powers of the Governor is seen in the complaint of Frank Lausche, until recently Governor of Ohio, about the inadequate power of Governors to remove local officials. "The tragic situation exists," he says, "where lawless people in the community, working in consort with duly elected local officials, are able to laugh at the Governor in his helplessness."

At the same time laggard laws give our Governors petty pen-pushing jobs and clerical assignments. Governor Harriman, for example, cannot change a job title or add a position without himself signing a request that has to be sent to two different agencies, nor can officers of the National Guard in many states be appointed without the Governors themselves signing the papers of appointment.

The modern Governor is by no means helpless. He has three powerful tools with which he can sometimes overcome the handicaps thrust in the way of being a real Chief Executive: the force of public opinion, the executive budget and political patronage. He can go over the heads of opposing officials and reach the public through press, radio and TV; by marshaling public opinion he may be able to lead state agencies. He can use the power of assembling the state budget to keep warring departments in line. He can use his political patronage and influence to build up support.

But the need to resort to such methods merely emphasizes the central fact: election to a Governorship does not earn a man the right to govern, only the right to struggle to govern.

Today we need to meet the challenges of our times with sufficient authority vested in our Chief Executives to enable them to serve us effectively. And we can do this without losing our liberties. We need to give our Governors a sufficient administrative staff to relieve them of many of their minor duties. We need to finish the "short-ballot" campaign, begun so valiantly years ago, by chopping down the list of statewide elective offices to two or three at most. The term of office should be long enough to enable the Governor to learn his job well and serve the public expertly and earn the right to re-election. All boards and commissions need to be consolidated into a dozen agencies headed by appointees of the Chief Executive. We cannot rid the Governors of all their problems, nor should we. But at least we can mold the office into a post better suited to the ever-increasing demands of modern times.

Frank Bane

27. The Job of Being a Governor*

Among the ablest and most devoted politicians in the country are the Governors of the states. I think I know. I have worked individually, directly and personally with 414 Governors over a period of thirty-five years. And how the job of being Governor has grown during this period!

The most spectacular and important change that has taken place with respect to the office of Governor has been the great expansion of its duties and responsibilities. They have grown because state government has grown. Today state government is the largest, most pressing and most important business in practically every state. And that, of course, was not always the case.

---

* From *State Government.* Summer 1958. pp. 184–189. Reprinted by permission of publisher and author.

WHEN CEREMONY WAS IN FLOWER

Prior to World War I in Virginia, as in most other states, the Governor was the social and ceremonial head of the state. Most department heads were elected in one way or another, by the people or by especially constituted boards—finance, agriculture, education, welfare, etc. There were few, if any, highway departments in those days. Highways were the responsibility of the localities. To a much more exclusive extent than now, so were other public functions in which state governments now carry a heavy share of the job. Moreover, government at all levels—local, state, federal—had far less to do than now. The Governor of the state ran his office, it is true. But a large part of his time was spent attending meetings, presiding at ceremonials and leading parades. . . .

THE QUALIFICATIONS ARE BROAD

How does the Governor go about his work? What are his qualifications? What does he have to have to do his job?

Gubernatorial methods may vary immensely, and they do. So may individual characteristics. But one thing is certain: the Governor needs to be a man of breadth. He must be ambidextrous, and then some. An individual might be a wonder, a genius, and a great public benefactor in any one of numerous professions, and still be a flop as Governor.

For every Governor should have—and if he is to be an outstandingly successful Governor he must have—the gifts of popular leadership, executive ability, decisiveness, studious inquiry, and the skill of political competence in the broadest and most constructive sense.

Popular leadership in itself requires many things—personal warmth, ability to persuade, knowledge of the public business, the art of working with people. But even these personal qualifications aren't enough. In order to lead, a Governor must have definite policies and he must have a dynamic program. His policies and his program are the keystones of his administration and everything else is built around them.

LEADERSHIP AND THE LEGISLATURE

Throughout his term of office, from beginning to end, the Governor will give most of his time and attention, inevitably, to the development of these policies—and to seeing to it that the legislature enacts the program he bases upon them. This requires of him initiative, imagination, understanding of the legislative process, and the ability to lead the major officials associated with his administration into a cooperative endeavor to seek legislative enactment of the essential measures. Above all, it calls for effective liaison and relations with legislators and legislative leaders.

Here the methods may vary indeed. I have known Governors, for example, who sometimes were accused of "clobbering" their legislatures. If their legislative programs were in danger, they took to the airways and told the people on the radio or on television things that brought a barrage of remonstrances to the legislators from the home folks—with the result that the legislation passed. That's one way. For most Governors who use it it's a last resort way. To produce steady year-in-year-out success, the Governors who've been most successful with their legislators have relied on close knowledge of the top legislative leaders, and repeated contact with them. In some states, Governors themselves have possessed a degree of broad political control throughout the state which, at times, has enabled the slightest word from them to win the needed legislative support. In other states much more persuasion has had to be practiced with the legislative leaders. Whether the persuasion is entirely intellectual, or based on personal loyalty, or the result of charm, or a combination of these and other factors—the Governor has to practice it most of the time.

A TOP BRACKET EXECUTIVE

The Governor also must be a top bracket executive. For, let me repeat, he is in charge of the day to day operation of what usually is the largest and most important business in the state.

The ways of Governors in executive action, like their methods in legislative liaison, are cut in no rigid mold. I'll cite three examples. One recent Governor—one of the most successful in the country—operated his office with almost mathematical neatness and dispatch. Everything was always in order when I visited him there. His channels of command were clear and precise. His desk was "clean." Another, equally successful Governor, had an almost equally orderly office. But his lines of command—to outsiders—often were a puzzle. If he didn't get what he wanted done, as he wanted it, along one channel, he had the knack of shifting the assignment to someone else. Sometimes his cabinet officers might not know "just where they stood." But the Governor, with extraordinary traits of personal warmth, had an administration that functioned effectively indeed. A third Governor whose offices I used to visit had the same kind of success despite the fact that his administrative organization had the appearance of sprawling all over the state house; he was not, perhaps, an expert in "channeling"—but he personally knew the major business of his state so well, and he personally led his subordinates so well—that the jobs got done, with enthusiasm and effectively.

But, again, a Governor today needs a great deal more than the personal skills and characteristics of the good executive leader. And increasingly our Governors are securing these extra necessities. To perform their executive functions successfully, most Governors have three major tools directly under their supervision and immediately at their service.

ARMS FOR MANAGEMENT

First, there is the planning bureau, division or service. Planning agencies, as such and so named, are comparatively new in state government—largely a postwar product. But Governors have always had some type of planning organization, agency or conference. They have had to. The planning agency helps develop policies, outlines programs and presents them to the Governor for his consideration. Perhaps most important, the planning agency looks ahead and appraises developments in advance—to help the Governor meet his problems, sometimes crises, as they develop. . . .

Secondly, the Governors have relied, increasingly, upon budget bureaus or agencies. These are the units through which they exercise their most immediate and direct supervision and control over operations. The "executive budget" is comparatively new in state government—about thirty years old. It is also new in the federal government, the U. S. Bureau of the Budget having been established in 1922.

Before the budget bureaus and the executive budget were established, all departments and units of the states, as well as at Washington, were on their own to get what they could from the legislative bodies. Now that has changed, and much to the good. Under the executive budget system, now prevalent in almost all the states, the Governor makes up the budget for the entire state government. He does so after extensive consultation with all departments and agencies, and after analysis by his budget bureau of the departmental requests on the one hand and available financial resources on the other. Thus the Governor is familiar with the fiscal problems of the state, at their inception, and with the proposed expenditures. He submits the budget as a whole to his legislature, and usually it is Bill Number One.

The budget bureau has enabled him to do that. Thereafter, the appropriations having been made, a competent budget bureau is the right hand of the Governor in seeing to it that all funds are expended for the purposes for which they were appropriated, and that the business of the state in its many ramifications is conducted efficiently and economically. It is not too much to say that a good state administration, an outstanding Governor, always has an effective, smoothly operating budget facility.

But even if he plans well and budgets scientifically, the Governor needs still more for his executive job. As Alexander Pope said:

> For forms of government let fools contest;
> Whate'er is best administer'd is best.

Others have put the same sound idea more directly: first-class, top bracket officials can make any system work, but incompetent hacks can ruin the best system ever devised by man. In government, as in business and almost everything else, the major problem is personnel.

The last decade has brought a rapid extension of personnel agencies in state government. Many of them are attached directly to the Governor's office. Through the recent extension of personnel units, through the development and expansion of merit systems, and through the promotion of governmental services as a career, state governments have been staffed increasingly with competent, well trained—in many cases highly technical—officials and employees. These are the kinds and types of men and women a Governor needs to administer his complex duties and responsibilities. . . .

A SCHOLAR AND A POLITICIAN

But—however good his agencies are—the Governor himself must be a student of government. Otherwise, he is lost. The old Jacksonian concept that anybody is competent to operate government is gone, and the Governor has to answer all sorts of questions that no bureau can decide for him.

What to do about the complex realms of state-local and federal-state relations? What to do about a tax program to provide adequate revenue and yet not place the state at a competitive disadvantage? To what extent should the state provide for elementary and secondary education through state revenue? How should institutions of higher education be organized and operated to provide adequate training and avoid duplication? What parts of available revenue should be spent, respectively, for public welfare, health, conservation, etc.? What effect will the enormously expanded birth rate have upon the state next year and five years hence, and what shall the Governor do about it now?

These are some of the questions a Governor must answer. His agencies can advise and counsel him. They can't decide. No one can speak for him. The Governor must be a student of government himself. If his decisions are to be good decisions, and stand up, he must have thought them through.

Finally, a successful Governor is a successful politician. Whether you define "politician" as one skilled in the science of government or as one skilled in the art of acquiring and holding office, the top bracket Governor meets your definition.

At bottom, this means that he knows how to get along with people. He knows how to sense their interests, their needs, their wants. That applies to his relationships with the individuals he faces across his desk. It applies to his relationship with the people as a whole. The superior Governor must always be a little, but not too far, ahead of public opinion. As one of our present-day Governors put it, he must "raise a standard out front, but not so far that it is beyond the horizon of the people." The Governor must have a great and abiding interest in and concern about the individual citizen, and he must *radiate* this concern. One who does not possess this qualification is not a politician, and hence not a Governor, for long.

THE GOVERNOR "HIS OWN MAN"

So the successful Governor's capacities and ways cover a wide gamut. And over and above them all something else is involved in almost everything he does. The good Governor has to be what Lincoln Steffens called "a principal." He has to be his own man. He must be able to bear the weight of single, personal, and sometimes very lonely responsibility.

Before he came to office the Governor may have been—in many cases was—a subordinate, in politics and government. Now he's Number One. He has to stand on his own. He is responsible before the whole state for his administration. When things go wrong in it, he can't pass the buck.

It isn't easy to carry this kind of responsibility. Governors may make it *look* easy. But a Governor feels the weight of the burden just the same.

I have known many Governors who, after lonely personal deliberation, have stood up to be counted and give a Governor's lead to their people on issues which their advisors said were "too dangerous" to deal with. These Governors knew that *somebody* had to deal with them—and they were elected as that somebody. I have known Governors who have parted with old and long trusted friends—dismissed them from service—when the old friends went wrong. They have done it firmly, but with private grief. . . .

GROWTH IN OFFICE

How do you know, before he's elected, that a Governor will have all the qualifications he needs—including the courage? The answer is, you don't. The fact is, good Governors are to a considerable extent made on the job. They grow with it.

And they grow not only in strength but in breadth. It does things to a first-rate human being to make him the representative of all the people of his state. When the erstwhile "city politician" becomes Governor, he is likely soon to see that rural problems aren't as simple as he'd thought. When the former rural politician becomes Governor he develops a new attitude to the cities of his state, whose representative he has now become. The Governor is the Governor of all the people—wherever they live, whatever their creeds, and whatever their politics. Few jobs anywhere are so broadening in their challenge. The good Governors rise to that challenge. . . .

9

STATE ADMINISTRATIVE
ORGANIZATION
AND REORGANIZATION

Industrialization and concomitant urbanization subsequent to the Civil War were responsible for a proliferation
of state activities. New activities were undertaken without any
consideration being given to integrating and coordinating them
with existing state activities. This haphazard growth of state government reached the point early in the twentieth century where
it became apparent to many that reorganization was essential
and that the central theme of any reorganization must be the
strengthening of the executive powers of the governor.

Article IV, Section 6 of the constitution of Hawaii contains
organizational principles recommended by organizational experts and merits careful study by states contemplating administrative reorganization.

The Report of the Secretary to the Governor of New York sets
forth recommendations for the reorganization of the executive
branch of the state government and the reasons for the recommendations. This report contrasts the existing organization with
the proposed organization. In reading such a report one should
critically analyze the logic of each recommendation and attempt
to anticipate the opposition, if any, it will engender.

28. *Executive and Administrative Offices and Departments**

Section 6. All executive and administrative offices, departments and instrumentalities of the state government and their respective functions, powers and duties shall be allocated by law among and within not more than twenty principal departments in such manner as to group the same according to major purposes so far as practicable. Temporary commissions or agencies for special purposes may be established by law and need not be allocated within a principal department.

Each principal department shall be under the supervision of the governor and, unless otherwise provided in this constitution or by law, shall be headed by a single executive. Such single executive shall be nominated and, by and with the advice and consent of the senate, appointed by the governor and he shall hold office for a term to expire at the end of the term for which the governor was elected. The governor may, by and with the advice and consent of the senate, remove such single executive.

Whenever a board, commission or other body shall be the head of a principal department of the state government, the members thereof shall be nominated and, by and with the advice and consent of the senate, appointed by the governor. The term of office and removal of such members shall be as prescribed by law. Such board, commission or other body may appoint a principal executive officer, who, when authorized by law, may be ex officio a voting member thereof, and who may be removed by a majority vote of the members appointed by the governor.

The governor shall nominate and, by and with the advice and consent of the senate, appoint all officers for whose election or appointment provision is not otherwise made by this constitution or by law. The legislature may provide for the suspension or removal for cause, by the governor, of any officer for whose removal the consent of the senate is required by this constitution.

When the senate is not in session and a vacancy occurs in any office, appointment to which requires the confirmation of the senate, the governor may fill the office by granting a commission which shall, unless such appointment is confirmed, expire at the end of the next session of the senate; but the person so appointed shall not be eligible for another interim appointment to such office if the appointment shall have failed of confirmation by the senate.

---

* *The Constitution of the State of Hawaii.* Article IV, Section 6.

No person who has been nominated for appointment to any office and whose appointment has not received the consent of the senate shall be eligible to an interim appointment thereafter to such office.

All officers appointed under the provisions of this section shall be citizens of this State and shall have been residents of the State for at least three years next preceding their appointment.

---

29. Proposed Reorganization of the Executive Branch of New York State Government*

EXECUTIVE OFFICES OF THE GOVERNOR

The Constitution vests the Governor with "the executive power" and holds him responsible "that the laws are faithfully executed." It also establishes an Executive Department which he heads. This Department was intended to provide the Governor with the staff assistance he needs to plan and direct most effectively and efficiently the various activities of the Executive Branch of State government.

Under the 1927 reorganization plan only the Divisions of the Budget, Standards and Purchase, State Police and Military and Naval Affairs were assigned to the Executive Department.

Instead of developing according to the original concept by the incorporation only of additional staff services, the Executive Department has been expanded to include a number of line agencies. It has become a catch-all for 13 practically independent agencies ranging from the Division of Housing to the Lottery Control Commission. Of the 18 units within the Department, only the Civil Defense Commission and the four originally named units can really be considered as appropriate staff agencies.

RECOMMENDATION 1. *The Executive Department should be discontinued as a department and the work of the line operating agencies within it transferred to other departments appropriate for the assignment of these functions. The Constitution should be amended to authorize the creation of the Executive Offices of the Governor which would comprise the following units:*

---

* From *Report of the Secretary to the Governor.* (Albany, N.Y.: December 29, 1959), pp. 18–27.

Executive Chamber
Office of the Budget
Office of Civil Service
Office of General Services
Office of Civil Defense
Office of Military Affairs
Office of State Police

The six offices, in addition to his personal staff in the Executive Chamber, will provide the Governor with the staff units he needs to manage Executive Branch activities and to carry out his law enforcement functions and his duties as head of the State's military and civil defense establishments. Their designation as "offices" is intended to differentiate them from line departments and to describe their relationship to the Governor.

Having the Governor serve as head of a department, as in the case of the existing Executive Department, is inconsistent with his position as head of the entire Executive Branch of State government. Nor is it realistic to prescribe by law that the Governor designate a single administrative officer as head of all staff services for the Governor. Each Governor should be given the flexibility to arrange within his immediate staff for the assignment of responsibilities best suited to his needs and wishes.

RECOMMENDATION 2. *The Executive Chamber should be continued as the Office of the Governor to meet his immediate staff needs, particularly in program planning, evaluation, coordination and development.*

The complexity and scope of responsibilities faced by State government places a great burden upon the Governor in his exercise of program leadership. He has as his immediate staff for this purpose the Secretary to the Governor who advises and assists in the development and review of State policies and programs; the Counsel to the Governor who advises and assists on legislative and legal matters; the Press Secretary who advises on public relations and acts as liaison between the Governor's Office and all news media; the Appointments Officer who assists in the selection of persons for appointment to key positions and executive assignments; and Special Assistants who perform duties specifically assigned.

These staff members and their aides inventory existing and emerging problems, evaluate plans proposed by departments to meet these problems, and recommend State policies. The staff members accumulate for the Governor information and research findings, evaluate the relative urgencies of competing services and functions, and help determine immediate and long-range objectives. They must be in constant communication with the departments relative to programs and policies, and help coordinate departmental activities to assure the achievement of program objectives.

All these functions can best be performed by a staff closely associated with the Governor, and selected on the basis of competence to meet his special needs, and help handle the types of problems pressing for his attention.

OFFICE OF CIVIL SERVICE

RECOMMENDATION 3. *The present Department of Civil Service should be designated as an Executive Office and renamed the Office of Civil Service. The Civil Service Commission should be continued for its present purposes. The functions of the Classification and Compensation Appeals Board and of the Merit Award Board should be assumed by the Civil Service Commission. The functions of the Health Insurance Board and the Public Administration Sponsoring Committee should be undertaken by the Office of Civil Service with the aid of appropriate advisory committees.*

Personnel administration is a necessary managerial arm of the Chief Executive. The personnel agency should, therefore, have a relationship to the Governor comparable to that of other staff agencies like the Office of the Budget and the proposed Office of General Services. This is given emphasis by the increasing need for competence in the public service and the shortage of trained manpower to carry out the necessary program activities. The current State personnel program is being directed toward raising the level of employee competence and performance rather than merely "policing" the merit system. But to put this concept into full operation requires that the personnel functions be organized into a closer working relationship with the other staff agencies and the Governor.

A significant step in this direction was taken when, in 1953, the President of the State Civil Service Commission was established as head of the Civil Service Department. State administration can be further enhanced, and personnel management improved and strengthened by including the President of the Civil Service Commission as a member of the "management team."

The State Civil Service Commission should remain as presently constituted, to make rules for the administration of the Civil Service system in accordance with the principles of merit and fitness, subject, as at present, to the Governor's approval; to hear appeals from administrative determinations; to adjudicate cases; and to provide advice and assistance to the President of the Commission and to the Governor on matters of personnel policy. It should also, as discussed later in Recommendation 60, take over the Pension Commission's function of acting on requests for extension in service of employees past 70 years of age, and absorb the functions now performed by the Classification and Compensation Appeals Board and the Merit Award Board.

OFFICE OF CIVIL SERVICE

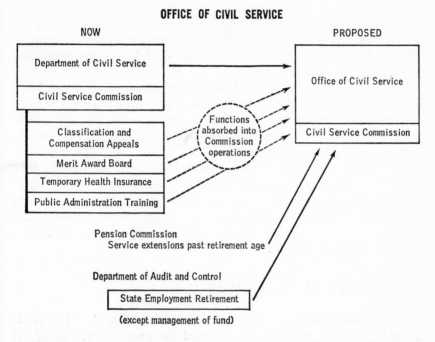

The Temporary Health Insurance Board was established to develop a health insurance program covering State and local government employees and to negotiate a contract with private insurance carriers. The contractual relationships have been established and the processing of employees' claims is being carried on by the staff of the Department of Civil Service.

The Sponsoring Committee on Public Administration Training oversees the program of internships and in-service training in public administration conducted by the Department of Civil Service and a graduate program supported by the State University.

The functions of the Temporary Health Insurance Board and the Sponsoring Committee on Public Administration Training should be more closely integrated into State personnel operations, using advisory bodies where appropriate.

RECOMMENDATION 4. *The administration of the State Employees' Retirement System should be transferred from the Department of Audit and Control to the Office of Civil Service. Responsibility for the management of Retirement System funds should be transferred to the proposed De-partment of Finance with the requirement that there be an advisory com-mittee and an outside post-audit.*

The Retirement System provides a major employee benefit which has substantial influence on the recruitment and retention of employees. The administration of the System should be integrated into the State's person-nel program and made a responsibility of the Office of Civil Service, rather than the Department of Audit and Control, which is basically an auditing and accounting agency.

The investment of the funds of the Retirement System, however, is not related functionally to the day-to-day operations of the System. The func-tion should be delegated to the proposed Department of Finance, which, as recommended later, would be responsible for the management and dis-bursement of State funds generally.

This arrangement should be accompanied by the requirement of a peri-odic post-audit of the trust funds by the Comptroller or by a State Auditor appointed by the Legislature. In addition there should be an advisory committee composed of the Director of the Budget, head of the Office of Civil Service and public members to review annually the operations of the fund and to report thereon.

OFFICE OF GENERAL SERVICES

RECOMMENDATION 5. *A new Office of General Services should be estab-lished. To this Office should be assigned the present functions of the Division of Standards and Purchase, together with additional responsibili-ties as described in the recommendations below.*

The Office of General Services should be a central staff agency to pro-vide essential central "housekeeping" services. It would continuously re-view such services and recommend economies and improvements that may be accomplished through centralized services. To this agency should be assigned such responsibilities as centralized purchasing; standardiza-tion of equipment and supplies; the management of office space; the maintenance of State buildings and non-institutional properties; the man-agement of the State's automobile fleet; the inventory, rehabilitation and distribution of equipment and furniture; the management and disposi-tion of records; printing and duplicating; and the distribution of supplies and other materials.

RECOMMENDATION 6. *The Office of General Services should be assigned the responsibility now in the Department of Public Works, for the main-tenance and operation of public buildings.*

The Division of Standards and Purchase and the Department of Public Works currently share responsibility for the State's building management program.

The Division of Standards and Purchase is in charge of renting office space for State agencies, allocating office space on the basis of requirements established for unit operations, and supervising the rehabilitation of office space in certain State-owned office buildings.

The State agencies whose administrative expenses are paid or reimbursed from sources other than State funds are charged by the Division of Standards and purchase whenever they are allocated space in a State-owned office building.

The Department of Public Works is responsible for the rehabilitation of most office buildings and for the day-to-day activities involved in cleaning, maintaining and operating all State office buildings except the State Education Building and the State Office Building at 270 Broadway in New York City. The Education Building is maintained by the Education Department and the building at 270 Broadway is maintained by a building management corporation under contract with the Division of Standards and Purchase.

The Department of Public Works is basically responsible for carrying out a program of designing, engineering and constructing State facilities such as highways, bridges and buildings. It is also responsible for maintaining and operating many of these facilities in addition to canals and flood control projects. Its maintenance and operation work on highways, bridges, flood control projects and canals is sufficiently technical in nature to require substantial professional direction and make desirable a close relationship with the engineering aspects of the Department's program. This is not true of the work required to maintain and operate office buildings.

The managerial functions of allocating space, negotiating rentals and maintaining State office buildings should be assigned to a single agency. They would properly belong in the proposed Office of General Services.

RECOMMENDATION 7. *The Office of General Services should be assigned the functions and responsibilities of the Board of Commissioners of the Land Office presently in the Department of State.*

The Board of Commissioners of the Land Office has custody of, sells, leases and transfers among State agencies all State-owned lands not devoted to any specific purpose such as highways, forests, canals, and parks. The lands under the jurisdiction of this agency include lands under water, abandoned canal lands and lands acquired for taxes and through the foreclosure of United States loan mortgages. The Board exercises control over the entry upon and use of such lands, inspects lands granted by the State to determine compliance with conditions and restrictions, and receives payment for the grants of State-owned lands. The Board has custody of the original land records of the State and maintains the necessary records and files concerning its own operations.

Placing custody and responsibility for State lands in the Office of General Services would integrate the land program into the general real estate management program, and would facilitate positive and energetic action to put as much unused lands as possible into productive use, either through sale or rental, or for other State purposes.

OFFICE OF GENERAL SERVICES

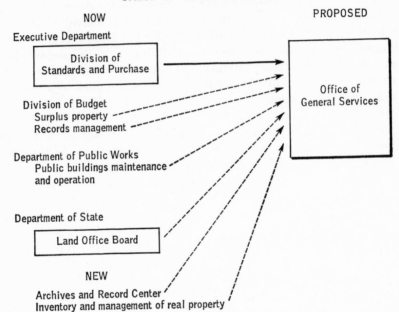

Land transactions are now authorized by an ex-officio board consisting of the Secretary of State, the Attorney General and the Superintendent of Public Works. The Board would not be needed for this operation if there were substituted a system whereby land transactions would be the responsibility of the head of the Office of General Services, subject to approval by the Attorney General and the Comptroller.

RECOMMENDATION 8. *The Office of General Services should be given responsibility for establishing and maintaining an inventory of the real property of the State and of records of the transfer and sale of such property.*

The records concerning land owned by the State and used for State purposes are scattered among several State departments including Audit and Control, Public Works and State.

Assigning to the Office of General Services the additional responsibility for establishing and maintaining an inventory of the real property holdings of the State would provide a central point for maintaining all necessary information regarding the lands of the State.

RECOMMENDATION 9. *The functions of the present Division of the Budget regarding the disposition of surplus property and the management of State records should be transferred to the Office of General Services.*

Under present practices, when a State agency no longer has use for certain equipment, it declares it surplus. The Division of the Budget then takes steps to transfer it to other agencies or to sell it on the open market. In many cases, it is difficult if not impossible to realize from this equipment a monetary return equal to its potential use value. There is a reluctance on the part of State agencies to accept surplus equipment which needs refinishing or repair because they have no facilities to put it in proper shape.

Significant economies could be realized if equipment that is declared surplus were to be properly examined, evaluated in terms of its usefulness to the State, rehabilitated, and stored and distributed as needed.

The inventory control, repair and disposal of surplus property are functions closely associated with procurement and supply. Accordingly, the surplus property responsibilities of the Division of the Budget should be transferred to the new Office of General Services.

The Division of the Budget carries on certain functions in relation to the management of State records which also more properly would belong in the Office of General Services.

RECOMMENDATION 10. *An archives and records center should be established and responsibility for its operations assigned to the Office of General Services.*

The State has instituted records management controls and procedures covering the disposition and transfer of its records. Studies have shown that such procedures, if supplemented by the establishment of an archives and records center, would effect substantial economies through the release of valuable office space and equipment used to house records with no immediate reference value, and through the release of large quantities of storage space now rented for the housing of records that must be maintained for a period of time prior to their disposition. The use of warehouse type storage areas and modern methods of records storage provide the best means for storing retained records at a minimum cost per square foot of area.

Assigning the operation of the State's archives and records center to the Office of General Services would properly provide for its integration within the total State records management program, as part of the general housekeeping activities of the State.

OTHER STAFF UNITS

RECOMMENDATION 11. *The Divisions of the Budget, Military and Naval Affairs, and State Police, and the Civil Defense Commission should be continued and their names changed to reflect their designation as executive offices of the Governor.*

Since these units have relatively well defined responsibilities and specific functions, there appears to be no valid reason for recommending any basic changes in their organization. Their designation as executive "offices" is in accordance with the earlier recommendation that such offices be established to provide staff services for the Governor.

DEPARTMENTAL REORGANIZATION PROPOSALS

One of the principal methods by which the 1927 reforms sought to assure a rational and effective organizational structure for State government was the Constitutional limitation on the number of civil departments. In the 32 years since that time, however, the State has entered new fields of activity and many traditional areas of State service have expanded or changed in significant ways.

In a number of instances, new agencies have been created to meet emergent needs and changed conditions instead of meeting these situations by reorganizing or assigning new duties to existing departments. The reasons for this action appear to have been diverse—to focus executive attention on a new function, to dramatize the inauguration of an activity, to satisfy a pressure group, to meet what appears to be a temporary situation, to avoid a hard decision in placing a new function that has interdepartmental aspects, or to by-pass the procedure of Constitutional amendment.

The result has been the creation of a large number of State agencies which are not integrated into the departmental framework and a consequent increase in the number of units reporting directly to the Governor. The potpourri of agencies lumped into the Executive Department furnishes a prime example.

BOARDS AS HEADS OF AGENCIES

The reorganization of 1927 also sought to improve State administration by abolishing many multi-member boards and commissions and substituting single executives as the heads of agencies.

It is a generally accepted principle of management that multi-member boards are not effective for the day-to-day direction of administration. They can, and do, have an important role as quasi-judicial bodies to protect individual rights in appeals from administrative decisions. Boards are also useful in providing advice and counsel to departmental executives and the Governor.

A board which has both the day-to-day administrative responsibility and the appellate functions, however, cannot achieve the full objective of insuring independent review of appeals when it acts on what are basically its own determinations. Moreover, since no one member of an administrative board can be held responsible for the board's action, the fixing of accountability for results is difficult, if not impossible.

The overlapping terms of members of boards heading executive agencies tend also to diminish the responsiveness of such agencies to the program of the elected Governor and the Legislature.

Despite the 1927 objective of reducing the number of administrative boards, many boards have since been created to head new agencies and autonomous or semi-autonomous units within existing departments. The over-all effect has been to diminish the degree of gubernatorial control over these agencies and responsibility for performance and results.

While boards can play a useful role within the organization structure, they should be employed with due consideration of their weaknesses as well as their strengths.

Most of the day-to-day administrative functions performed by multi-member boards and commissions would be better carried out under the direction of a single administrator within departments engaged in related functions. Boards having adjudicative or appellate functions should be retained where there is demonstrated need to protect individual rights.

TEMPORARY COMMISSIONS

Temporary Commissions are uniquely suited to the investigation of special problems, the development of solutions and the drafting of legislation.

There has been a tendency, however, to assign administrative functions to commissions, partly because of the constitutional limitation on the number of departments, and partly because of the experience certain commissions have accumulated in the course of their research activities. Some have been operating as administrative bodies for years and there is no evidence to indicate that their discontinuance is planned.

Independent temporary commissions performing regular administrative functions that are likely to continue should be divested of them, and these functions transferred to appropriate executive departments.

INDEPENDENT INTERDEPARTMENTAL COMMITTEES

There are a number of continuing interdepartmental committees formally established by executive order and reporting to the Governor. There are also departments and agencies of State government which have responsibility for the major concerns of these committees. In order that these committees may have continued executive interest and leadership, as well as staff services, each should be attached to the department of major concern with the head of the department designated as chairman.

Certain of these committees have been dormant for some time and consideration should be given to their dissolution.

DEPARTMENTAL STRUCTURE

As heretofore noted, there are today too many units in State government reporting to the Governor. No well-run business would burden its chief executive with such a span of control. The 1927 reorganization plan to limit the number of departments and to incorporate all executive functions within them, so far as practicable, was sound then and is sound today.

The orderly arrangement of the functions of State government within a limited number of departments and the clarification of lines of authority and communication should improve State management, facilitate the legislative review of administrative performance, and make State administration more accountable to the people.

RECOMMENDATION 12. *The Constitution should be amended to provide that there should be no more than 20 civil departments of State government. The specification of department names and the assignment of functions should be reserved for statutory enactment.*

RECOMMENDATION 13. *The following departments should be continued or established:*

Agriculture & Markets	Economic Development
Audit and Control	Education
Banking	Finance
Conservation	Health
Correction	Highway Safety

Housing & Community Development   Municipal Affairs
Industrial & Labor Relations   Public Service
Insurance   Public Works
Law   Social Services
Mental Hygiene   State

The 20 departments recommended include 18 existing departments. There would also be integrated into these 20 departments 12 of the agencies now located within the Executive Department and a number of independent Boards and Commissions.

The reduction in the number of independent agencies reporting to the Governor, and their integration into departmental operations, will strengthen executive direction and control and help to achieve more efficient, economical and effective service to the people. More order and simplicity in departmental organization will also help to coordinate the activities of State government, to eliminate jurisdictional differences and friction, and to decrease overlapping and duplication of services.

10

THE STATE JUDICIARY

The state judicial system has been subjected to strong criticism and many reforms have been recommended over the years. Dr. John H. Romani, assistant dean of the School of Public Health of the University of Michigan, presents an overview of the state judicial system with its shortcomings and recommends corrective action.

The best method of selecting judges is frequently debated. Should all judges be appointed by the governor as they are in five states or should judges be popularly elected? If they are to be popularly elected, should they run against an opponent in the election or simply against their record, a negative majority removing them from office? Adolph A. Berle, Jr., a prominent lawyer who is also a professor of law at Columbia University and a former assistant secretary of state, explores the question whether judges should be elected or appointed and reaches the conclusion based upon the New York experience that it does not make much difference which method is utilized.

Congestion has been plaguing many state courts in the post World War II period. Some have placed the blame for court congestion squarely on the jury system and urge that it be modified or abolished except in serious criminal cases. David W. Peck, a justice of the New York Supreme Court from 1943 to 1957, renders a ringing indictment of the jury system as the culprit responsible for court congestion and prescribes in civil cases trial by judges under a rule of comparative negligence.

John H. Romani
30. The Courts*

Revision of the judicial article in a state constitution has as its objective the establishment and maintenance of an effectively functioning state judiciary. Achievement of this end requires that the judicial article, like other sections of the constitution, be written as simply and as concisely as possible. Simplicity and conciseness are desired not for their own sakes but because the constitutional document should contain materials dealing only with matters of fundamental importance. The filling in of administrative and other details—whenever and wherever necessary—is more appropriately the task of the legislature or the judicial department itself. In these terms, the judicial article should contain only those provisions necessary to create the state court system, assure its independence and provide for its effective and efficient operation.

The indictment against the existing system of state courts is not new. In a speech before the American Bar Association in St. Paul in 1906, Dean Roscoe Pound stated it thus:

> Our system of courts is archaic in three respects: (1) In its multiplicity of courts, (2) in preserving concurrent jurisdictions, (3) in the waste of judicial power it involves . . . by rigid districts or courts or jurisdictions, so that business may be congested in one court while judges in another are idle.[1]

Similarly, the reforms required to correct these deficiencies have been known for many years. Arthur T. Vanderbilt, the late chief justice of New Jersey and a leading student of judicial administration, outlined the prescription in these terms:

> The first essential of a sound judicial establishment is a simple system of courts . . . three are all that are needed in a modern judicial establishment: (1) A local court of limited civil and criminal jurisdiction, (2) a trial court of general statewide jurisdiction, and (3) an appellate court or courts, depending on the needs of the particular state.[2]

At issue are two matters: To what degree are the difficulties noted by Dean Pound and others the direct result of constitutional provisions? To

---

* From Salient Issues of Constitutional Revision. (New York: National Municipal League, 1961), pp. 115–130. Reprinted with permission of publisher.
[1] Quoted in Shelden D. Elliott, Improving Our Courts (New York, Oceana Publications, Inc., 1959), pp. 15–16.
[2] "The Essentials of a Sound Judicial System," Northwestern University Law Review (March-April 1953), as reproduced in Robert L. Morlan, Capitol, Courthouse and City Hall (2nd ed., New York, Houghton Mifflin Company, 1960), p. 169.

what degree can the necessary reforms be achieved by constitutional revision?

At the outset it is perhaps desirable to distinguish between two terms that are sometimes confused in the literature and to explain the relationship of these concepts to the problem of constitutional revision. The terms in point are: the administration of justice and judicial administration. Administration of justice refers to the operation of the courts in accordance with law and in such a manner that equitable decisions are rendered in as many instances as possible. Judicial administration refers to the operation of the machinery of the courts and is primarily concerned with questions of organizational and administrative efficiency and effectiveness.

The two ideas are separable in the sense that it may be possible to run the courts efficiently and still not have justice done, a possible example being court systems in totalitarian societies. Poor or bad judicial administration, however, can contribute directly to the denial of justice, as illustrated by administrative procedures that lead to extended delays in getting cases heard in court. Organizational shortcomings that result in overlapping or conflicting jurisdictions among the courts, and thereby create uncertainty and confusion for the layman and lawyer alike, are another example. Revision of the judicial article in state constitutions seeks, primarily, the elimination of provisions that inhibit the adoption of sound judicial organization and administrative procedures as a means of improving the administration of justice.

The salient issues involved arise directly from the differences between what is now found in state constitutions governing the establishment and administration of state courts and what is needed to enable these courts to function effectively under today's conditions. There are three basic problem areas: court structure and organization, selection and tenure of judicial personnel and judicial administration.

COURT ORGANIZATION

The question of court structure and organization concerns two separate but closely related matters. First is the structure of the court system. By this is meant the different levels of courts, the particular types of courts within the system, and the relationships among these levels and types. Second is the problem of jurisdiction. Jurisdiction may be simply defined as the competence of a court to consider a case. This power may be general, covering all kinds of disputes, or it may be restricted to specific classes of controversy—traffic, juveniles, domestic relations, probate, etc. A court may have authority to hear cases when they are first tried, original jurisdiction; or its competence may be limited to reviewing cases on appeal, appellate jurisdiction. Some courts may possess both original and appellate jurisdiction—original in certain cases and appellate in others.[3]

Jurisdiction of the courts is also territorially defined. Some state courts may consider cases that arise in any part of the state. Municipal and county courts, by contrast, are generally competent to hear only those cases that arise within the boundaries of these particular subdivisions.[4]

At issue is how these questions of court structure and jurisdiction are dealt with in state constitutions and the problems which flow from the constitutional determination of judicial structure and organization.

THE STRUCTURE OF THE COURT SYSTEM

A problem arises from the practice of establishing specific courts by constitutional provision. The local courts in New Orleans, the juvenile courts in Cadoo, East Baton Rouge and Orleans Parishes, and the domestic relations court in East Baton Rouge Parish are all created by the constitution of Louisiana (Art. VII, secs. 52, 53, 83 *et seq.*). The Florida constitution sets up a special criminal court of record for Escambia County and also authorizes the legislature to establish similar courts in each county of the state (Art. V, secs. 9, 10). All seven courts serving Baltimore, Maryland, are defined in the constitution of that state (Art. IV, secs. 1, 27-39, 41A). Even a most cursory examination of the *Index Digest of State Constitutions* reveals similar provisions in other state constitutions.[5]

Beyond this, the territorial and substantive jurisdictions of many courts are outlined in great detail in present judicial articles. The boundaries of the districts of the eight circuit (general trial) courts in Maryland are specifically described in the Maryland constitution (Art. IV, sec. 19). The substantive jurisdiction of county courts in Oklahoma is carefully spelled out in the Oklahoma constitution (Art. VII, secs. 12, 13, 17, schedule 18). Circuit (general trial) and justice courts in Mississippi have, by virtue of constitutional provision, concurrent jurisdiction in criminal cases where punishment does not exceed a fine or imprisonment in a county jail (Art. VI, sec. 171). Other illustrations can be provided almost without end.[6]

---

[3] The Supreme Court of the United States, for example, has original jurisdiction "In all cases affecting ambassadors, other public ministers and consuls, and those in which a state shall be party" and appellate jurisdiction in other cases arising under the constitution and laws of the United States. (U.S. Constitution, Art. III, sec. 2).

[4] The qualification here has reference to the right of parties in a case, under certain circumstances, to have the trial conducted in a court outside the area where the case arose.

[5] Legislative Drafting Research Fund of Columbia University (2nd ed., New York, Oceana Press, Inc., 1959).

[6] *Ibid.*, pp. 210–212, 239–244, 302–306.

Constitutional creation of a number of different courts, along with the definition of their jurisdictions, leads to a variety of difficulties. Of first importance are the resultant rigidities in the court system. Modifications in court structure can be accomplished only by the cumbersome process of constitutional amendment. Consequently, changes which may be needed are frequently never made because of the obstacles involved. As new demands have arisen, it has been much easier for state legislatures, when authorized to do so, to add on to the court system the level and type of courts required. For the most part these additions have not been made with any idea of unifying the basic structure of the courts in the states. As one commentator has observed:

> It seems generally perceived that ephemeral changes in population, in case load and in the aggressiveness and skill of court personnel have brought about haphazard piecemeal shift and redistribution of court structure until most present systems are mere conglomerations.[7]

A second and equally important consideration is the jurisdictional inadequacy that has developed. This is particularly true with regard to disputes involving the family. The Home Term Court in New York City, established specifically to work with the parties concerned to alleviate the underlying causes for the difficulties, cannot provide many of the remedies —divorce, separation, removal of children from the home—that may be required. All it can do is to persuade the persons to accept their obligations and, failing this, resort to fines and jail sentences.[8] The lack of procedures to deal with known sex offenders and to enforce a mother's responsibility to support her children are examples of other inadequacies noted by one observer.[9]

THE SPECIAL PROBLEM OF THE MINOR JUDICIARY

Almost all studies of court organization agree that the minor judiciary —specifically the justice of peace courts—constitutes the weakest link in the present system of state courts and urge that this type of court be abolished.[10] The justice courts, generally staffed by part-time persons with

[7] Maxine Boord Virtue, "Improving the Structure of Courts," *The Annals of the American Academy of Political and Social Science,* 287 (May 1953), 143.

[8] Morris Ploscowe, "The Inferior Criminal Courts in Action," *The Annals of the American Academy of Political and Social Science,* 287 (May 1953), 9. See also Earl Lomon Koos, "Family Problems and the Court," *ibid.,* pp. 27–33.

[9] Virtue, *op. cit.,* p. 143.

[10] The literature concerning the inadequacies of the justice of peace system is considerable. A classic is Edson R. Sunderland, "The Efficiency of Justices' Courts in Michigan," *Fourth Report of the Judicial Council of Michigan* (Ann Arbor, the Council, 1934). See also any standard work in American state and local governments, particularly the chapters dealing with the courts and rural government.

little or no legal training, have been notorious for fee splitting, an inordinate number of judgments for the plaintiff, independence from supervision by other courts in the system and lack of knowledge of the law.[11] The existence of these courts—particularly in and around large urban centers—contributes greatly to the multiplicity of courts with concurrent and sometimes conflicting jurisdictions. In an age when most people can easily travel to courts in neighboring population centers, it is difficult to understand the need for continuing justice courts in each and every locality. An even more fundamental consideration is that the jurisdiction of these courts is generally so limited that—save for certain traffic violations and minor civil disputes—parties involved must turn to other courts.

Justice of peace courts are discussed here as a constitutional issue because they are constitutional courts in about half the states. Not only are these tribunals given constitutional status but also their jurisdiction, the manner of appointment of the justices, and other details of their operation are frequently outlined in the judicial article.[12] The attention given in state constitutions to justice courts accounts for no small part of the length of these documents. Much would be gained by eliminating the justice courts as well as the references to them in state constitutions. California, Connecticut, Missouri and Tennessee are among the states which in recent years have done away with this level of the judicial system and replaced it with a more adequate set of inferior courts generally staffed by full-time, salaried judges. The gains in the quality of justice in these and other states which have followed this practice have been substantial.[13]

THE CONSTITUTION AND THE COURTS

Except for the justice of peace courts, the basic issue is not whether the various special courts and levels of courts are needed, but whether these different courts should be specifically created by constitutional provision. Actually all that is needed is a statement similar to that found in the constitution of Hawaii (Art. V, sec. 1):

> The judicial power of the state shall be vested in one supreme court, circuit courts and in such inferior courts as the legislature may from time to time establish. The several courts shall have original and appellate jurisdiction as provided by law.

---

[11] See Gail M. Morris, *Justice of Peace Courts in Indiana* (Bloomington, Bureau of Government Research, Indiana University, 1942).

[12] Several examples may be found by noting the entries in Legislative Drafting Research Fund, *op. cit.*, pp. 303–310.

[13] A brief discussion of these developments may be found in Clyde F. Snider, *American State and Local Government* (New York, Appleton-Century-Crofts, Inc., 1950), pp. 270–273, 280–281. See also Charles W. Pettengill, "Court Reorganization: Success in Connecticut," *American Bar Association Journal*, 46 (January 1960), 58-61.

Here, in the compass of less than 50 words, the outlines of a unified state judicial system are clearly set forth, with authority granted the legislature to modify the system as needed. Specialized courts are not prohibited but may be created or abolished as the times may require; jurisdictions of the courts may be adjusted to take account of population and other movements in the state. A truly ideal statement would provide for a single court of justice with subdivisions for special purposes.

The capacity of the Hawaii legislature to adapt the structure of the court system in that state may be contrasted to the incapacity of the Kentucky legislature. The Kentucky constitution enjoins the legislature from creating any courts other than those set up in the constitution (sec. 135). In addition, the constitution spells out in great detail the number of courts for each area, the jurisdiction of these courts and other matters concerning their organization. At least by implication, the legislature has little or no discretion in dealing with the problem of judicial organization and students of the Kentucky court system note this lack of legislative authority as a prime barrier in securing more effective and efficient judicial administration in that state.[14]

Proof of the validity of the principles suggested here is found in the experience in New Jersey under its revised constitution. The 1947 New Jersey constitution did away with an archaic and rather complex system of state courts and replaced it with a unified system under the direction of the chief justice of the Supreme Court of that state. Observers of the new system in operation have all agreed that it has led to substantial improvements in the administration of justice in New Jersey. Delays in getting cases heard have been greatly reduced; decisions are rendered much more rapidly; rules and procedures in the courts have been simplified and improved.[15] What has been accomplished in this state stands as a model for other states as they undertake revision of the judicial article.

SELECTION AND TENURE OF JUDICIAL PERSONNEL

A second requirement for a sound judicial system is the recruitment as well as retention of outstanding men and women to staff the courts. That people with this quality are now found in state court systems is more a

---

[14] Legislative Research Commission, Commonwealth of Kentucky, *Kentucky Circuit Courts* (Frankfort, the Commission, 1957), p. 2.

[15] See William J. Brennan, Jr., "After Eight Years: New Jersey Judicial Reform," *American Bar Association Journal*, 43 (June 1957), 499–502; Shelden D. Elliott, "Arthur T. Vanderbilt: Administrator of Justice," *State Government*, XXXI (Autumn 1958). 224; and the section on Judicial Administration in the *Annual Survey of American Law* (New York: New York University School of Law).

tribute to the individuals themselves than to the systems under which they were selected. State constitutional provisions governing selection and tenure of judicial personnel are among the more severely criticized sections of state constitutions, not only for the excessive detail that is found but also for the kinds of procedures outlined.

QUALIFICATIONS OF JUDICIAL PERSONNEL

Much of the unnecessary detail in the present judicial articles is the result of writing into the constitution specifics concerning clerks of courts and other court personnel. The election or appointment of clerks of the general trial courts is constitutionally prescribed in twenty states; the number of such clerks for each county or district is set forth in the constitutions of eighteen states; duties imposed on these officers are described in the constitutions of Delaware and Louisiana.[16] Moreover, the Kentucky constitution provides that clerks of county courts meet certain constitutional qualifications (sec. 100). And in Delaware the constitution provides for the election of clerks of the justices' courts (Art. III, secs. 22, 23).

Placement of this kind of provision in a state constitution violates directly the precept that a constitution should contain only materials that deal with questions of fundamental importance. It is akin to writing into the constitution qualifications and selection procedures for the governor's secretary. This is not to suggest that clerks of courts should not be provided for; rather it is to note that establishment of these offices is more appropriately a function of statutory law.

Beyond this is the consideration that many state constitutions set forth a long list of special qualifications for holding judicial office. While these formal requirements vary from state to state, many of the constitutionally stated qualifications border on the superfluous. The Maryland constitution states that, among other things, judges shall be selected from those admitted to the "practice of law . . . who are most distinguished for integrity, wisdom and sound legal knowledge" (Art. IV, sec. 2); Arkansas requires that county judges be of "upright character" and that its Supreme Court judges be of good "moral character" (Art. VII, secs. 29, 6). No one would suggest that judges should not have these qualities but spelling them out in the constitution is no guarantee of securing judges with these exemplary characteristics. In a negative sense there is added to the state constitutions words and sections that, to say the least, contribute little to the effective functioning of government.

---

[16] See Legislative Drafting Research Fund, *op. cit.*, pp. 219–220.

THE SELECTION OF JUDGES

A more basic and fundamental question concerns the provisions governing the selection and tenure of judges in the state courts. Most severely criticized are those which provide for the direct, partisan election of judges. In the words of Dean Pound: "Putting courts into politics and compelling judges to become politicians . . . has almost destroyed the traditional respect for the bench."[17]

The practice of electing judges is a product of the "Jacksonian Era" in American history, during which time pressures were exerted to elect more and more officers of government as a means of further "democratizing" the system. States which prepared constitutions under this influence abandoned the traditional procedure of executive appointment, defending the move on the grounds that election would mean judges more responsive to the public and a higher quality of judge, since election substituted judgment of the population as a whole for that of the executive and a confirming body—one or both houses of the legislature or the executive council.[18]

There is nothing in the experience with judicial elections to demonstrate that judges more responsive to the public have been elected or that the quality of the bench has been improved. That able persons have been placed in the courts is fortuitous and in spite of the system.[19] On the other hand, the partisan election of judges has put the judges themselves into the mainstream of party politics. In the selection of candidates emphasis tends to be placed on the individual's capacity to win an election; this particular talent is hardly a valid test of one's ability to serve effectively as a judge.[20] Moreover, campaigns for available judgeships have been known to take on the appearance of circuses, bearing no relevance to the substantive questions involved or the qualifications of the candidates for the offices.[21] It must also be noted that, with the large number of offices and issues to be decided upon in any election, voters are hard pressed to exercise any real discretion in choosing judges. Conse-

---

[17] Quoted in Elliott, *Improving Our Courts,* p. 16.

[18] This practice of executive appointment and council approval is still used in Massachusetts and New Hampshire.

[19] See Stuart H. Perry, "Shall We Appoint Our Judges?" *The Annals of the American Academy of Political and Social Science,* 181 (September 1935), 97–108; and Rodney L. Mott, "The Judiciary," *Model State Constitution* (5th ed., New York, National Municipal League, 1948), p. 36.

[20] See Daniel S. McHargue and Eleanor Tabor Linenthal, "Should the Judicial Article Be Revised?" in *The Voter and the Michigan Constitution in 1958,* Robert H. Pealy (ed.) (Ann Arbor, Bureau of Government, University of Michigan, 1958), pp. 54–55.

[21] See Perry, *op. cit.*

quently, most voters accept the judgment of their party, fail to vote, or more or less blindly mark their judicial ballots.[22]

Two considerations have made the direct election of judges somewhat more palatable than might appear on the surface. First is the movement away from partisan to nonpartisan elections. But even here there are serious questions about the effectiveness of this system. In Michigan, for example, candidates for the highest court in the state are nominated in partisan conventions but run on a nonpartisan ballot (Art. VII, sec. 23).[23] To be sure the final election is nonpartisan, but it is interesting to note that the partisan composition of this court has changed from a Republican majority to a Democratic majority in the last ten years during which time the Democrats have assumed control of all statewide elective officers. Second is the fact that many judges die, retire or resign in midterm, allowing opportunity for the executive to fill the vacancy for the remainder of the term.[24] When the term is completed, the appointee runs as an incumbent and, in most states, under normal circumstances, he will not be opposed for re-election. However, there are cases where incumbent judges have been defeated not because of poor judicial performance but primarily because their party, as a whole, did poorly in that election and the judicial candidates, like candidates for other offices, were turned out by members of the opposite party.[25]

Despite the almost universal opposition of both the bar and the bench to the direct election of judges, the practice persists in one form or another in a majority of states today. Partisan election of at least some judges is constitutionally prescribed in 22 states; nonpartisan election obtains in several others. In five states—Connecticut, Rhode Island, South Carolina, Vermont and Virginia—the legislature selects some or all of the judges; executive appointment holds in Delaware, Maine, Massachusetts, New Hampshire and New Jersey.[26]

Executive appointment of judges is the pattern at the federal level as well as the states listed above. The argument usually raised concerns the influence of patronage considerations upon appointments. Regardless of this influence—to the extent that it does exist—effective and respected

---

[22] A popular discussion of this problem is found in Morton Sontheimer, "Our Reeking Halls of Justice," *Collier's* (April 2 and 9, 1949) reproduced in Morlan, *op. cit.*, pp. 137–144. See also Snider, *op. cit.*, pp. 275–278.

[23] See McHargue and Linenthal, *op. cit.*, pp. 55–56.

[24] See Vanderbilt, *op. cit.*, p. 170.

[25] A case in point is the defeat of an incumbent Republican judge by his Democratic opponent in 1960 in Pennsylvania. The Democratic candidate was clearly the beneficiary of his party's sweep of that state in 1960 inasmuch as he ran without the endorsement of several segments of the Pennsylvania Bar.

[26] A summary of election and other data about state courts may be found in the *Book of the States*, published biennially (Chicago, Council of State Governments).

judiciaries have been maintained where this system is used. After all, the governor is the only official really held responsible on a statewide basis; considerable support can be mustered for vesting the appointing power in him.

The Citizens Union of New York City has for many years supported a proposal, first sponsored by Henry L. Stimson before the 1915 New York State Constitutional Convention. It provides that:

1. The election of judges be nonpartisan;
2. The governor (or in the case of metropolitan lower court judges, the mayor) file his recommendation of a nominee for each vacancy, leaving time for opposing nominations to be offered by petition;
3. The executive nominees be identified on the ballot with the words "nominated by the governor (mayor)."[27]

An alternative to both executive appointment and the direct election of judges is found in the proposal advanced by the American Bar Association in 1937 and the plans adopted in California in 1934 and Missouri in 1940. The essential features of these procedures are for initial appointment by the executive from a panel of nominees made by a group of citizens representing the bar, the judiciary and the public. After service for a specified time, the judge's name is placed on a separate ballot with the question, "Shall Judge Blank be retained in office?" If he is approved by the voters he serves to the end of his term. He may seek re-election by indicating, within a certain time period, his desires to the election officials. If defeated, the process begins anew with the nomination and gubernatorial appointment.[28]

Among the advantages of this procedure is that the judge is not required to conduct an exhaustive campaign; nor is he required to run against a specific candidate, only on his record in office. Further, the initial screening of candidates by an outside commission gives some assurance that the governor will be restricted to qualified persons who have demonstrated a capacity for judicial work.

The record in those states where this method has been adopted has been

---

[27] "Who Picks Our Judges?" *The Searchlight*, XLIII (New York, Citizens Union of New York City, December 1953).

[28] A brief review of the California and Missouri plans may be found in Snider, *op. cit.*, pp. 276–277. The Missouri plan is examined in some length in Jack W. Peltason, *The Missouri Plan for the Selection of Judges* (University of Missouri Studies. Vol. XX, No. 2, Columbia, University of Missouri, 1945). See also Harold J. Gallagher, "The American Bar Association Program," *The Annals of the American Academy of Political and Social Science*, 287 (May 1953), 167.

good.[29] Fears that the courts would be dominated by one or another of the political parties as a consequence of executive appointment have been largely unfounded. In the twenty years that the plan has been in operation in Missouri, nearly as many Republicans as Democrats have been appointed, despite the fact that there have been many more Democrats in the governor's office than Republicans. Similarly, the voters have not in a single instance discriminated on the judicial ballot in terms of partisan considerations, although the state has been swept by both parties during this time. An equally important point is the general improvement in the quality of the court system and the general satisfaction with the plan as expressed in reapproval of the basic ideas by the people and the legislature on two separate occasions.[30] In recent years modifications of this plan have been adopted in other states. It is the method approved by the voters of the new state of Alaska. It is under consideration in still other places. A potential danger lies in the development of undue influence on judicial selections by the organized bar. A real philosophical question exists as to whether the public should subdelegate to any private organization this much power in the selection of public officials.

Revision of the judicial article should, at a minimum, eliminate election as the means of selecting judges. Experience with the combination appointment and election procedure has been good. So has been the experience with executive appointment at both the federal level and in those states where it still holds.

THE TENURE OF JUDGES

The problem of tenure depends in part on the manner in which judges are selected. Life during good behavior is employed at the federal level with generally good results. In New Jersey judges of the Supreme Court and Superior Courts (general trial courts) are appointed initially for seven years and upon reappointment to serve during good behavior until the age of 70 (Art. VI, sec. VI, par. 3). Alaska requires approval at the first general election held three years after the initial appointment and at every tenth year thereafter for Supreme Court justices and at every sixth year for Superior Court justices (Art. IV, sec. 6).

A final matter concerns the retirement of judges. There is some debate as to whether this needs to be a part of the constitution. The newer constitutions—Alaska, Hawaii, New Jersey—all require retirement at age 70.

---

[30] Elliott, *Improving Our Courts*, pp. 177–179.

[29] Several articles have been written evaluating the results in various states. See Laurance M. Hyde, "Choosing Judges in Missouri," *National Municipal Review*, XXXVIII (November 1949), 491–493, 503; Elliott, *Improving Our Courts*, pp. 177–179.

Alaska, however, provides that retired judges may be used on special assignments. The important consideration is that the constitution provisions do not preclude continuance of service of an individual judge when such is in the best interests of the state. Pensions and the like are matters which should be left for the legislature to determine but nothing should be placed in the judicial article that would exclude judges from any general system for all state employees.

ADMINISTRATION OF THE COURT SYSTEM

Good organization and competent personnel cannot, by themselves, guarantee the effective and efficient administration of justice in a state. The manner in which the court system is managed and directed, and carries forward the handling of cases and other daily business, is also important. While these are largely questions of detail, their significance in the operations of the courts requires some consideration in the revision of the judicial article.

THE RULE-MAKING FUNCTION

Of first concern are the rules of practice and procedure under which the courts function. Most of these rules have developed over the years and, to the layman at least, appear to hinder rather than expedite justice. Some of this feeling arises from the fact that rules of procedure have not been kept up to date in many states. The constitutional issue is where authority to make rules should be vested so that, in so far as possible, there is continuous review and, where necessary, modification.

Historically, state constitutions have not dealt with this question and by implication the authority to make and promulgate rules has been left to the legislature. This practice has not been satisfactory for it has meant in some states the development of highly detailed and inflexible codes which have tended to create delays and place undue attention on the procedures as ends in themselves. As one observer has noted:

> Legislated rules are largely formulated *a priori* by a body which is distant from the scene, presumably concerned with questions of more public import and often, unfortunately, subject to political pressures. Little wonder, then, that legislative rule-making . . . has inevitably led to an inflexible procedure on which haphazard tinkering has merely developed an overparticularized, complicated, cumbersome machinery.[31]

---

[31] Herbert Peterfreund, "The Essentials of Modern Reform in the Litigative Process," *The Annals of the American Academy of Political and Social Science*, 287 (May 1953), 155.

In other states, the legislature has delegated this power to the courts but has not provided the courts with sufficient assistance to accomplish the task.[32]

The experience of both the bench and the bar with the *Federal Rules of Civil Procedure* adopted in 1938 and the manner in which these rules were constructed and subsequently revised have led many to suggest that a similar approach be tried at the state level.[33] In essence, Congress gave the Supreme Court authority to promulgate rules of procedure for the federal court system. An advisory committee, composed of leading jurists and lawyers, drafted the rules under the supervision of the court. These rules were then reviewed by others throughout the country and amended. The end result has been a simplified and highly workable code that has expedited the business of the federal courts. Several states have adopted substantial portions of the code for use in their state systems.[34] The important consideration is that the rules were developed in light of the actual needs of the courts and by persons best able to understand these needs.

Among the newer state constitutions the practice has been to vest this authority in the Supreme Court of the state. Both the New Jersey and Hawaii constitutions give this power to the courts without reservation; the Alaska and Puerto Rico constitutions provide that such rules may be altered, under certain circumstances, by the legislatures.[35] What should be done in an individual state is dependent in part on past practice. If the constitution is silent it may be advisable specifically to vest this right in the highest court by constitutional provision so as to be certain as to the responsibility for carrying out this important function.

To give the courts the right to make rules and procedures is not, in itself, sufficient. At some point adequate provision must be made for assistance in developing these procedures. For this reason it is sometimes urged that the constitution establish a judicial council or conference with the major function of advising and helping the courts in the discharge of their responsibilities.

---

[32] See McHargue and Linenthal, *op. cit.,* pp. 64–65.

[33] Vanderbilt, *op. cit.,* pp. 172–173.

[34] Peterfreund, *op. cit.,* pp. 160–161.

[35] See Constitution of Alaska, Art. IV, sec. 15. Rules may be changed by a two-thirds vote of the members elected to each house of the legislature. See also Constitution of Puerto Rico, Art. V, sec. 6. Rules adopted by the court must be submitted to the legislature at the beginning of a session and do not go into effect until 60 days after the close of the session, unless disapproved by the legislature. The legislature also has the power to amend or repeal these rules at any subsequent time.

ADMINISTRATIVE ORGANIZATION OF THE COURTS

Existing judicial councils or conferences vary from state to state. In some they are official agencies charged with specific duties relating to the study of the court system and recommending improvements in the administration of justice.[36] They are constitutional bodies in only Alaska and California. The utility of such organizations has been demonstrated,[37] but they need not be established by constitutional provision.

Last, but hardly least, is the problem of managing and directing the court system. It is astounding but true that not until 1939 was there any real system of administrative supervision and control of the various court systems in this country. The establishment of the Administrative Office of the United States Courts in that year constituted a major advance in the field of judicial administration. States have followed this precedent slowly; New Jersey in 1947 became the first state to make constitutional provision for the management and administration of its court system (Art. VI, sec. VII, par. 1).

The importance of adequate administration of the court system cannot be minimized. The judicial establishment in any state is a large organization. It has hundreds, sometimes thousands, of employees; it must establish and maintain property ranging from court buildings to law libraries; it is involved in handling and processing quantities of paper; in brief, it must carry forward a great number of activities that are necessary for the courts to function in an effective manner. To assume that this could be done efficiently without any real measure of direction or control over the various parts of the organization would be foolhardy. Yet for all practical purposes this is what was, and still is, the case in several states.

In terms of revising the judicial article, two items stand out as being of prime importance. First is the desirability of designating the chief justice of the highest court in the state the responsible administrative head of the system. He should have the right to supervise and control employees of the court system, transfer and reassign judges as case loads and court dockets require, and develop administrative and other procedures for handling the nonjudicial business of the courts efficiently and effectively. For him to discharge the various tasks he must have the assistance of an administrative officer and staff. The job of these people is to prepare materials and gather information required by the chief justice in his capacity as administrative chief, including the formulation of the budget

---

[36] See Snider, *op. cit.*, p. 283.

[37] Glenn R. Winters, "Silver Anniversary of the Judicial Council Movement," *Journal of the American Judicature Society*, 33 (August, October 1949), 43–49, 79–84.

for the over-all system, collection of statistics, development of common personnel standards and the like.[38]

It is argued that provisions of this sort are not needed in a modern state constitution. The importance, however, of defining responsibility for administration of the courts strongly suggests the need to indicate this in the basic law of the state. It is the practice that was recommended and followed in Alaska, Hawaii and New Jersey. Much of the improvement in the New Jersey court system is directly attributed to the fact that this designation of an administrative head was set forth in the constitution.

SECURING JUDICIAL REFORM

None of the suggestions offered in the foregoing discussion is new. All of them have been known to students of the problem for at least a half-century. Failure to adopt them or to revise judicial articles in accordance with these principles strongly indicates the need for vigorous action in support of change. Opponents to judicial reform are numerous. Members of the minor judiciary will fight to preserve their status, members of special groups will resist removing certain courts from the constitution, political parties may oppose selection of judges other than by direct election. Success requires the united support of an enlightened bar, judiciary and citizenry. Only where there has been this combination of forces has reform been achieved.

Adolf A. Berle, Jr.
31. *Elected Judges—or Appointed?**

How should judges be chosen? The only honest answer is that the method is less important than the true source of the appointment. Here is one method now in use:

> Dwight D. Eisenhower, President of the United States of America, to all to whom these presents shall come, GREETINGS:
> KNOW YE that, reposing special trust and confidence in the integrity, prudence and ability of John Doe, I . . . do appoint him a Judge of the District Court of the Federal District Court for the Southern District of New York. . . .

---

[38] See Vanderbilt, *op. cit.*, p. 171, 174–175, for a review of the tasks involved as administrator of a court system.

* From the *New York Times Magazine*. December 11, 1955, pp. 26, 34, 37–38, and 40. Copyright by the New York Times. Reprinted by permission of publisher and author.

John Doe, being fully confirmed by the Senate, thereupon holds his judgeship for life. This is the appointive system; the Federal Government has it, and also a number of states, notably, Massachusetts.

Here is the second method:

> We, the undersigned, the members of the Board of Election in The City of New York, having canvassed the whole number of votes cast at the Election on [such-and-such a date] according to the original statements of said votes filed with us in the manner directed by law, do hereby *certify* that Richard Roe, of 10 West 76th Street, New York, N. Y., was duly elected a Justice of the Supreme Court. . . .

This is a judgeship obtained by election in an open campaign. A majority of states uses this system for some, and New York uses it for all, of its higher court judges. In New York the term is commonly for fourteen years. The judge was nominated by a political party or group, he financed and carried on a campaign for election, and so got the job.

Both methods have had their advocates in a long-standing public debate, and both are now being considered by the Temporary Commission on the Courts which is preparing a report on judicial reform for submission to the 1956 Legislature.

Offhand, you might assume that the two systems are as different as possible. You would be wrong. The two systems are in ultimate analysis almost the same.

Factually, both the appointive and elective methods really mean that judges are chosen by the chieftains of the political parties involved. Your judge will be just as good as the political leadership of the area involved —state, judicial district, county, as the case may be. There seems to be no escape from this. Let us look behind the formal procedure and see what really happens.

Take the appointive system, prescribed by the Constitution of the United States with regard to all Federal judges. The idea was that judges should be as far removed from political pressure as possible; so they are appointed by the President (in state systems like Massachusetts, by the Governor). Once appointed, they cannot be removed except by impeachment. Their salary cannot be cut; neither Legislature nor Executive can do anything to them. But behind the certificate of appointment, a quite different drama goes on.

A federal judge is to be appointed, let us say, for the Southern District of New York. The President (unless he happens to come from that area) cannot possibly know the men who should hold judicial office. His principal law officer is the Attorney General of the United States. It is a recognized part of the Attorney General's job to recommend judicial appointments. Except in the case of his own district, he does not know the men either. So he expects, and the fact is, that the Republican state chairman of New York (assuming a Republican Administration) will make a recommendation, commonly in conjunction with the Republican Senator or Senators, if any, from the state. The Attorney General knows perfectly well that none of these men will recommend except after consultation with the county Republican leader who handles patronage in the district. That county leader has a group of hungry district leaders; they want credit for giving out the job (if they do not want the job themselves); indeed, they have been eying the particular vacancy for a good while. Probably several contesting leaders urge their pet candidates. The county leader has to resolve the question.

When, as in the case of the Federal judicial districts, the district covers more than one county, and even crosses state lines, he has to work it out with other leaders. Quite likely there has been a considerable ruckus— probably the continuation of ruckuses of previous years—resulting in a prior understanding about whose turn it is to get the next vacancy. The individuals who want the job have been busy as beavers lining up political support all the time.

County leaders, if they are any good, weed out the obviously impossible candidates. They finally arrive at an understanding that John Doe has the background necessary to be a judge, and decide that his appointment will satisfy the district leader who is entitled to it. All hands having been squared, a recommendation goes up. The local United States Attorney has probably been in on the discussions; he is likely to be asked by the Attorney General whether the man is all right. Not, you understand, whether he is the best possible man for judge, but whether his character, standing and so forth, are such that his appointment will not excite controversy.

The views of the state chairman have been ascertained. Consultation with the party United States Senator is usually essential; he is a political power himself; if the man is obnoxious to him, he can block confirmation by the Senate. (The most cruel Congressional prerogative is that of "courtesy of the Senate"—a polite way of saying that if a Senator objects to a Presidential appointment from his party in his state, all other Senators will vote against confirmation.)

By now, the "way is cleared," as politicians say. The recommendation goes forward to the Attorney General. He gets reports. The F.B.I. has investigated and discovers the man never joined the Communist party or murdered his mother-in-law. The local bar associations have reported him "qualified" for the job. The United States Attorney's Office has indicated that the man will do (not infrequently the United States Attorney is himself a candidate for the job). The party National Committee agrees because the party state chairman has agreed.

The Attorney General thereon takes or sends the whole dossier with favorable recommendation to the President, who sends up the name of the prospective judge to the United States Senate. The appointment goes promptly to the Committee on Judiciary; unless the man has made important enemies, this body after reviewing the file reports recommending confirmation; the Senate confirms; the Presidential certificate of appointment is issued; a new judge mounts the bench in the United States Courthouse in Foley Square.

On analysis, the real choice was made by the party leader or leaders in the unimpressive setting in which political parties act.

How about elective judges?

The power of choice is in the same hands, though the stages are somewhat different. The Constitution of the State of New York says that the justices of the Supreme Court (which in New York is not "supreme" but is a trial court) and the county judges shall be elected for a term of fourteen years. But, if an elective judge serves out his term with even moderate competence, the salutary and unbreakable custom in New York is that he shall have renomination by *all* parties, thus guaranteeing re-election.

For practical purposes, therefore, election is for life or until retirement age. He can only be displaced by a two-thirds vote of both houses of the Legislature on charges of misconduct. True, judges are nominated not by ordinary party convention, but by special judicial district conventions which are naively supposed to mean that the ugly hand of politics is somewhat removed from their choice. In practice, a judicial convention consists of a slate of delegates put up by the district leaders. Invariably they nominate the candidates arrived at by the county leader and his district leaders in the same way as are candidates recommended for appointment by the President.

But, at least, isn't there an election? A Republican does run against a Democrat, so that the people have something to say? No. Or at least, frequently not. There are few "doubtful" judicial districts in most states —very few, indeed, in New York. The Democrats know absolutely that they have control in most districts in the city; the Republicans have exactly the same control upstate. In the "safe" districts, the county leader's nod is equivalent to nomination and election.

When the election is in doubt, the practice increasingly has been for the leaders of both parties involved to get together. Not infrequently when three judges are to be elected, you find two Democrats and one Republican, or two Republicans and one Democrat, all nominated by *both* parties.

The rival party leaders have sat down together, figured out the relative possibilities of the situation, agreed that one should nominate two judges and the other should have the third, canvassed their district leaders, decided on the deal and put through the nominations.

For practical purposes in that case, one of the judges has been picked by the Republican county leader; two have been picked by the Democratic county leader; as there is no contest, the election is a form. From time to time, of course, there are real contests. They are relatively rare.

So for practical purposes, ultimate power to choose every judge, elected or appointed, rests in the hands of the county machines of the two major political parties. There are exceptions, but so few that they rather prove the rule.

At this point one conjures up visions of a crooked, politically influenced bench. Has this been the fact? No, it has not. Surprisingly, the results in this strange and unpredictable working of the American political system have been good. The level of the New York elective bench rates as "good"; the level of the Federal appointive bench falls just short of continuous excellence.

If you examine the grimy surrounding circumstances, you would swear that it could not happen. Politics fairly burgeons in the selective process, frequently of the least savory kind. In nominating a man for the bench, a county leader frequently considers what kind of campaign contribution the candidate will make to the party war chest. At one time in New York City no one could expect a Democratic judicial nomination unless he was prepared to lay down $20,000 as a "contribution" to the campaign fund; frequently the quotation has been higher. When several men want the job (this is usually the case), they may even bid against each other.

One justice of the New York Supreme Court was widely know as the "$100,000 Judge" because he or his friends reportedly laid that contribution on the line. He got the job—and, having got it, did a remarkable piece of work. He was assigned to resolve the endless chaos resulting from the failure of the guaranteed mortgage companies in 1933; and he succeeded.

Powerful party figures often want judgeships for their relatives. The late Samuel Untermeyer had amassed a legal fortune. He was a thumping power in Tammany councils. He arranged to have two of his sons, Alvin Untermeyer and Irwin Untermeyer, named to the bench. Both turned in outstanding records.

The old Brooklyn boss, John McCooey, had his son put on the New York Supreme Court; a relative of the late Ed Flynn of the Bronx has quite recently got similar recognition. The old Manhattan Republican county leader, Sam Koenig, was represented on the Supreme Court bench by his brother, Morris Koenig.

Occasionally the nomination can be useful for other reasons: a party stalwart may have aspirations to be Mayor, and the organization can conveniently remove him from the situation by putting him on the bench. Yet the fact is that most of these men, once there, do an honest and effective job.

Politics does not quite end with appointment or election. A judge does have a considerable amount of patronage to distribute. In the Federal courts he can appoint trustees in bankruptcy, receivers, referees, and so forth. In the state courts he can appoint special guardians and other court officers. Both sets of judges have at least one very important appointment, namely, a law clerk or law secretary. It surprises almost no one to find that a Democrat invariably appoints Democrats to these jobs—not infrequently lists of suggestions are given him by the party which nominated him. His secretary is quite usually an aspiring lawyer with a good record for party fidelity.

But by now our judge is on, not off the bench, and he is thinking of his own reputation. If there is anything conspicuously wrong with the party follower he is asked to appoint as receiver, special guardian, referee, or the like, he knows the onus falls on him, and will find a way of appointing someone else. His law clerk on whom he must rely for continuous legal research has to be pretty competent, else the judge is in trouble.

Everything considered, the results have been paradoxically satisfactory. I have seen a Tammany judge, under the heaviest political pressure, decide squarely against his party organization in a proceeding to invalidate a nomination, the case involving construction of the election law. It did not hurt his career.

There have been scandals occasionally. They have been rare. One judge whose appointment was at least partly forwarded by the famous underworld character, Frank Costello (at all events, the judge thought so), has turned in an unexceptionable record of judicial probity.

Still, one asks, is this rational? When choosing a judge we ought to be looking for the highest level of character and legal ability; we ought not to be dredging the party machines. Cannot better ways be found? Unquestionably, while the system has worked reasonably well, many men who should be on the bench never get there. Really first-rate lawyers rarely reach the bench. It looks like tempting Providence to expect figs from political thistles.

A number of possibilities have been suggested. One has been that all appointments to the state courts should be made by the Governor for life.

This merely makes the Federal method of appointments general through-out the country. As we have seen, this merely means a political recommendation to him, instead of a political nomination for election.

A much discussed Western proposal has been that the bar association in each area shall make up a panel of names from which appointments or nominations for election, as the case may be, shall be drawn. In theory this is splendid: a bar association should be arbiter of legal ability, guardian of professional ethics, setting standards for the bench as well as for the bar.

In practice it is not so simple. Bar associations fulfill all these functions as long as, and only so long as, they stay out of politics. If at any time bar associations obtain power to name candidates for judgeships, would politics stay out of bar associations? Not probably. Most politicians are lawyers, and politics is one of the standard ways by which lawyers become known in their community. (On one occasion, even the Association of the Bar of the City of New York—blue ribbon organization of the country—was pressured into endorsing an individual for election. Its president, Harrison Tweed, a friend of the man in question, delivered a smashing rebuke, and in New York such an incident is not likely to be repeated.) What a bar association can do is to invite consultation with it before candidates are nominated for election or proposed for appointment, but only on a single issue: is the candidate of good character and professionally fit for the job?

Bar associations can—and do—issue reports to their members and to the public, stating that all of the candidates are of good character and are professionally fit to be judges—or the contrary, if any of them are not. Such verdicts have influence only. They may help to guide voters. In New York City, they frequently do not. Possibly such reports would have more influence on a Governor urged to appoint an unfit man.

But if the bar association ever is endowed with power to choose judges, or to make the panel from which judges are chosen, you can bet your last dollar that every political machine will suddenly take an enormous interest in seeing the bar association has the right president and picks the right committee on judiciary.

Political influence will be present in practically any system which can be devised. It will be there if judges are chosen by the Legislature instead of by the Governor, or by the Congress instead of the President. It will be there if they are chosen by a non-political council. It will get out of hand in every case where public opinion does not demand that judges be of good quality.

American public opinion is the reason why, in the main, American judges, Federal and state, have been good; it is the controlling reason; and it is the only safeguard. The American public unquestionably reveres its bench. A Governor or President who has appointed a bad judge hears from it in the newspapers, from his political opponents, and at the next election. He transmits his annoyance at once to the Attorney General and through him to the district leader who urged the appointment.

Next time around, recommendations from that source get bad treatment. Even county and district leaders dislike a bad reputation. Their other activities are likely to come in for more careful and wholly unwanted scrutiny if they have produced men who affront the desire of practically everyone for incorruptible and capable courts.

The crookedest politician knows that; and he can estimate very closely the extent of public interest. Public opinion, as a rule, has little interest in choosing who should be judges. But it is wholly clear that it wants good judges and someone's scalp if they are not. If that public opinion ever flags, the standards of acceptability used by political leaders and the quality of judges, however chosen, will promptly drop. Whenever the public and the press show interest in the subject, politicians will move up their standards and even "bosses" will request that the men proposed be top quality.

David W. Peck
32. Do Juries Delay Justice?*

Old as the phrase "the law's delay" may be, there is a new awareness of the seriousness of it, a final determination to do something about it. People are concerned about the condition and consequences. They want to know the cause and cure. They are beginning to suspect that the operation of the jury system has a close connection with the matter and they want to understand it.

The condition is clear and stark enough—delay in reaching cases for trial of two, three and even five years in city courts across the country. The consequences are missing witnesses and failing memories at the time of trial, miscarriages of justice and a denial of timely justice which is the essence of true justice.

* From the *New York Times Magazine*. December 25, 1955, pp. 8 and 30–31. Copyright by the New York Times. Reprinted by permission of publisher and author.

The cause of delay *is* the jury system. It is the inherent slowness of trial by jury, a pace which cannot keep up with the flood of cases coming into court, which creates a bottleneck and prevents timely dispositions. Why is a jury trial so slow? Compare it with a trial before a judge without a jury and the answer will be apparent.

Although the process of taking evidence by questions of lawyers and answers of witnesses is naturally slow, a trained and disciplined judge, if left alone to hear and decide a case, can conserve time by keeping a case on the track and keeping it moving. Before a jury, however, lawyers feel that many more questions, simple steps and explanatory excursions are required for the jury's benefit. They also think that a case can be colored, effects heightened, or a jury moved by some embellishment or side line. Frequent objections from the opposing attorney, either as a legitimate protection of his client's rights or to create some diversion of his own, stall the case. Any jury trial is so interrupted, slowed down and stretched out.

If a case is tried before a judge, the judge ascends the bench and the trial begins with the taking of testimony. He has familiarized himself with the case in advance by reading the pleadings. He does not need any preliminary education in the form of oral statements by counsel. The lawyers try the case strictly according to the rules, directly to the point and without interruptions.

When the evidence is finished the case is finished. The judge has followed the case closely, made his notes, and is ready at the end of the trial to render a decision. Summation or argument by counsel is seldom necessary. If the case is a difficult one, and time is required to render a decision, the judge can take the case to his chambers or home for study and dispose of it without taking more time out of a court day. The judicial process can thus be expeditious.

The same case before a jury has a long beginning before a word of testimony is taken. The preliminary process of selecting a jury is protracted with the personal questioning of prospective jurors by lawyers endeavoring to ascertain their attitudes toward the case and likely reactions to the evidence. When the trial begins, it is not with the taking of testimony but with opening statements in which the lawyers tell the jury what the case is all about. The evidence is then taken. But the conclusion of the evidence is not the end of the case.

The lawyers must sum up, tell the jurors all over again what the case is about, hash and rehash the evidence in an endeavor to persuade the jury. Then the judge must charge the jury as to the applicable law and give them the directions which are to guide their deliberations and govern their determination of the case. Finally, the jury retires to undertake its own decisional process.

It may readily be seen why the average jury trial takes between three and four days—three times as long as a trial before a judge without a jury. That simple statistic is the measure of court delay. The time which a jury trial takes in excess of a judge trial is the delay factor. The present complement of judges working without juries could keep the courts up to date. Three times the present number of judges and juries together would be required to do the same.

The multiple of three does not tell the whole story, however, of the time lost and multiple time expended in the process of jury trials. The fact is—as amazing as it appears upon analysis—that it takes 108 jurors over any period of time to do what one judge could do in the same time. That is the ratio or coefficient of jurors' time to a judge's time in any case.

The mathematics of the matter have been proved by records kept. First, there is the base of twelve jurors to one judge. Then there are two additional multiples of three which much enter into the equation. As observed, it takes three times as long to try a case with a jury as without a jury, meaning that in the actual trial process the time of thirty-six jurors is taken to do what a single judge could do.

But, preliminarily, in the process of assembling jurors, keeping them available in sufficient numbers for possible need, and in examining them and accepting or rejecting them for actual service, two-thirds of a jury panel's time is lost, or, to put it another way, only a third of a panel's time is actually employed in the trial of cases.

The cost of jury trials, in dollars as well as in delay, is much higher than anyone would think. The cost for court facilities, clerks, attendants, judge and jury in the Supreme Court of New York County is $750 a court-room a day. The average jury trial of four days thus costs the taxpayers $3,000—more than the amount involved in many cases. The dollar figures in other cities may be less, but the costs are relatively as high.

Lawyers must be paid for the long time spent in court and in waiting for trials to come up. The plaintiff's lawyer will receive from one-third to one-half of any amount won by verdict. A huge bill is paid in insurance premiums for the defense of lawsuits as well as for the payment of judgments. Altogether the cost of a jury trial to everyone is likely to be several times the amount the plaintiff retains out of any recovery.

A jury trial is thus not only slow and expensive in itself, but the accumulative delay, increasing the lawyers' burden and the risk of a miscarriage of justice and postponing realization on just claims, is undoubtedly reflected in excessive contingent fee arrangements, inflated verdicts, excessive insurance premiums and the public expense of maintaining the court system.

I do not share the feelings which some lawyers and judges have that jury verdicts are not trustworthy on the merits. Jurors are extremely conscientious and seldom can it be said that their verdict falls outside of the bounds of fairness and reason. Undoubtedly, the caliber of juries would be improved if the judges of some courts were less indulgent in excusing jurors and tolerating the avoidance of jury service, and if all courts followed the example of the Supreme Court of New York County, requiring all to serve although consulting their convenience as to the time of service.

But it is not in the make-up of juries that our trouble primarily lies. I would never advocate the elimination of jury trials on the ground that the quality of justice thus obtained is bad. It is the quantity of justice obtainable by jury trials, with the resulting delay and cost, that is the problem.

The plain fact is that the trial process designed for and inherited from the rural society of several centuries ago is not suited to handling the enormous volume of litigation resulting from the high speed, complexity and congestion of modern city living and the automobile age. Indeed, we have been saved from a complete break-down of court services only by the fact that 95 per cent of the cases eventually get settled. But because settlements often are not made until the eve of trial, settlements as well as trials are delayed by the length of time it takes to reach a case for trial.

There are three alternatives to suffering a continuance of present conditions. One is to eliminate or substantially qualify the right to a jury trial in civil cases. A second is to multiply courthouse facilities, the number of judges and other court personnel, and the call upon the citizenry for jury duty, in order that enough courtrooms with a full complement of jurors will be available to keep abreast of the intake of cases.

A third is to take the automobile cases, which constitute about 50 per cent of the cases and clog the courts, out of the courts and place them in an administrative agency which would award damages, regardless of fault, on a compensation basis as in Workmen's Compensation.

The points made by the advocates of this last plan—"compensate instead of litigate," they say—are (1) automobile accidents are the inevitable incident of the day in which we live and the economic consequences should be borne by society as a whole rather than by the individuals involved; (2) it is difficult to determine fault at best, and impossible to determine fault after long delay which allows witnesses either to fabricate or to forget; (3) the present rule, that an award of damages may be made to an injured party only upon his satisfying a jury that he was wholly free from fault and that the accident was entirely the fault of the other party, is unrealistic and unfair.

Considering the injustice inherent in the present system, the inevitable delay and the enormous cost of maintaining it, they urge that the system be abandoned and be replaced by a compensation system which is swift, sure and economic, in providing limited but fixed awards for injured persons in accordance with the injuries sustained and resulting financial loss.

There are strong objections to a compensation system. It is not altogether fair to disregard fault as a consideration in fixing liability or to limit the compensation of an injured party to something less than full damages. It is rough justice rather than fine justice.

In between the jury system and a compensation system is another possibility which would provide both fine justice and swift justice in personal injury actions. It is a system of trial by judges, without juries, under a rule of comparative negligence rather than under the present rule of contributory negligence.

Now, if an injured party has been negligent, even in the slightest degree, and his negligence has contributed in any way to causing the accident, the law says that he may not recover anything, although the defendant was principally to blame.

Under a rule of comparative negligence, the court would weigh comparatively the negligence of the parties and apportion liability accordingly. A plaintiff would not be barred from compensation if he was negligent, so long as he was not principally at fault, but his compensation would be reduced from an amount of full damages by the percentage by which he was found to have been responsible for his own injury. An able, experienced and conscientious judge could thus determine liability and calculate damages quite accurately and fairly. And he could do it in a third of the time a jury would take, cut costs all around correspondingly, and keep the courts up to date.

Said G. K. Chesterton, "I would trust twelve ordinary men, but I cannot trust one ordinary man." Perhaps this is a practical expression of the philosophy of the jury system. We certainly want to hold to jury trials in serious criminal cases, but should we slavishly adhere to jury trials in all civil cases? We can maintain the system for civil cases, and perhaps it is worth while, but we must understand the consequences, count the cost, note the alternatives and then deliberately decide what is in the public interest.

The constitutional guarantee that a man may not be deprived of his life or long deprived of liberty without a judgment of a representative body of the community is a safety factor of first importance.

The same considerations do not apply, however, or at least not to the same extent, to civil cases—ordinary commercial disputes or personal injury cases. Indeed, ours is the only country in the world which any longer attempts to handle civil litigation within the jury frame, and coincidentally it is the only country which has court delay. England, the cradle of the common law and of the jury system, abandoned juries in most civil cases long ago.

Jury trials in civil cases are only a matter of habit and history. The most important civil cases, although the least numerous, are tried without a jury. Cases for an injunction or to compel the performance of a contract, cases for a marital separation or involving the custody of children—in fact nearly all cases except claims for damages—are tried without a jury because those actions happened to grow up in a compartment of the law, known as "equity," outside of the jury sphere.

There is no reason for jury trials in the one area and not in the other. The same reasons for or against jury trials apply equally to both. We are thus controlled by tradition rather than by reason in the division of cases which may or may not be tried before a jury. In many places, as in New York, a person may even be tried and sentenced on a criminal charge involving up to a year's imprisonment without a jury trial.

Despite a certain affinity for the jury system, born of tradition, the American people are not, I suspect, as enamored of the system in civil cases as are the lawyers. It is the lawyers who are the sticklers for the jury system—some because they feel that it gives them a wider scope for their talents, or that they may fare better with a less impressive case before a jury than before a judge, or that a jury may take a greater liberty with the rule of contributory negligence than a judge would take—but mostly because they are accustomed to jury trials and are resistant to change.

Delays do not bother lawyers. A busy lawyer with a lot of cases does not care whether the case he is trying today is yesterday's case or yesteryear's case. The Bar will not be moved to change the jury system until it is pricked by a strong public sentiment.

It is the public which pays the price and suffers the ills of congested courts and delayed justice. Every citizen shares in the cost and burden of an inefficient court system—and runs the risk that he may be the next victim.

Justice will be delayed until the people are moved to action—either by a vast new investment in court plant and personnel and by a far larger participation in jury service, or by a change in the trial process.

part six

LOCAL ORGANIZATION AND ADMINISTRATION

11
RURAL GOVERNMENT

Outside of New England the county is the basic unit of rural government. It must be pointed out, however, a number of counties are urban. In New England the basic unit of rural government is the town, an increasing number of which are urban.

The county for years has been subjected to strong criticism and many political scientists have advocated its abolition. Until recently it appeared that the county as a unit of government was growing weaker; Connecticut abolished counties in 1960 and Alaska entered the Union without counties in 1959. However, the defeat of attempts to form a "super" government in metropolitan areas and the initial success of the reformed Dade County in Florida have spurred interest in the reform of county government to meet the challenges of metropolitan areas. Bernard F. Hillenbrand, executive director of the National Association of County Officials, writes of the recent growth of counties and the growth of interest in counties and paints a bright future for them.

The township, found in fourteen mid-Atlantic and Midwestern states, has been losing its vigor. Many of its functions have been transferred to the county and/or state. Dr. Paul W. Wager, professor of government at the University of North Carolina, records the decline in the number of townships and township functions and maintains that in densely populated areas townships should be transformed into a government comparable to the New England town and should be abolished elsewhere.

Special districts have mushroomed in recent years. Although usually established to perform one function, a number of special districts engage in a variety of activities. Mr. Norman C. Miller, Jr., a staff reporter of the *Wall Street Journal,* details the reasons why special districts are formed, how they are formed, and the problems associated with them. Of special interest is the formation of special districts in California by land developers to obtain funds to develop the land.

Bernard F. Hillenbrand
33. County Government Is Reborn*

Many people have mistaken ideas about county government. They have a mental picture of fat politicians sitting around a pot bellied stove, spraying tobacco juice into a copper spittoon, and plotting how to grease the political machine. Actually, have you been in a courthouse lately? One is more likely to find that it is a modern, air-conditioned building with automatic data-processing machines in the basement; an ultra efficient, two-way sheriff's radio on the roof; and everything in between just as modern—symbols of 20th Century progress.

County government will be the dominant unit of local government in the United States in the next decade. The following facts offer support for this belief:

1. In the six-year period from October 1951–October 1957, county government (as reflected by the number of full-time employees) increased an incredible 36 percent—an average increase of 6 percent per year, while municipal government and the general population increased only 3 percent per year.

2. Virtually every state in the union reports that its county governments have been authorized to undertake a host of new governmental responsibilities.

3. Our 3,047 county governments now employ 668,000 full-time people and spend about $6.5 billion per year.

4. One county (Los Angeles County), for example, employs 37,000 persons and has a payroll larger than 41 of the states. In these terms, many counties are larger than one or more states.

5. Some 133,360,000 Americans are served by county governments.

These facts seem to indicate that counties are growing like adolescents. A portion of the increase in the importance of county government is reflected in the expansion of traditional county government services, due both to the population increase and the traditional American demand for improvement and expansion of existing services. These demands have brought spectacular county improvements in election administration (automatic ballot-counting); penal administration (honor farms); admin-

* From *Public Administration Survey*. May 1960 (University, Miss.: Bureau of Public Administration, University of Mississippi), pp. 1–8. Reprinted with permission of publisher.

istration of justice (streamlined court procedure and use of special service personnel, psychiatrists, etc.); roads and highways (use of modern earth-moving equipment); record keeping (up-to-the-minute machines and techniques); education (student aptitude testing, special counseling, etc.); health and welfare (out-patient clinics for the mentally ill and spotless hospitals).

The really tremendous growth of county government, however, has come in urban areas where the existing units of government have demonstrated that they are not capable of solving area-wide problems. Here one finds counties assuming responsibility for police and fire protection, planning and zoning, water supply, sewage disposal, civil defense, industrial development, air pollution control, airports, traffic control, parks and recreation, urban renewal, and finance administration.

RURAL AND URBAN COUNTIES TODAY

Today, the life and needs of the rural citizen have changed. He drives an automobile and probably shops as often in the downtown area of the city as does the suburbanite. He sees the same programs on television and his general standard of living is not in any way inferior to that of his city cousin.

From the county government, this rural citizen demands very high and efficient levels of services. He wants good roads, the best of educational and recreational facilities, modern fire and police protection, public health and welfare facilities, and a host of other services.

County governments, moreover, have expanded to provide these services but this expansion has caused many problems, particularly the problem of how these services are to be financed. Counties to a very large extent depend upon the property tax for revenue. The inadequacy of property taxes in our present economy is well known and, as a result, our counties have been experimenting with sales taxes and state-collected, locally-shared taxes to augment the property tax. As long as counties are dependent upon the property tax as their principal source of revenue, county officials must appeal to both state and national governments for financial assistance, even though there is strong resistance on the part of these officials to increased state and Federal control.

The population shift from rural to urban areas is compounding rural problems. A county road, for example, is just about as expensive to maintain as a city road, even though there are fewer citizens to use it. In fact, most services increase greatly in cost per-citizen-serviced when there is a decrease in population. Many counties in Mississippi and in other parts of the South are struggling with areas that are depopulating, which has stimulated these counties to pursue vigorously new industry. Those familiar with the property tax know that in most cases residential property alone cannot support a high level of education and other services. A community, therefore, must have new or expanded business and industry. In a county that is depopulating, the need to attract new industry is more urgent than ever.

Here again we see the particular value of the county as a unit of government. A municipality usually cannot serve effectively as a unit to promote new industry. It is a costly activity; and after a great deal of effort, the industry sought may locate in the vicinity but outside the very municipality which attracted it in the first place. Since the industry is outside the municipal taxing jurisdiction, it would derive no immediate tax advantage. A county, by contrast, serves the entire area; and the business is taxable by the county no matter where it locates in its boundaries. Since all citizens in the area bear the cost of county government, a new industry eventually helps reduce the total tax liability of all the individual citizens of the county.

County government in the rural areas, by and large, seems to have satisfied its constituents. That the county is the most promising and virile unit of rural government is attested to by the tendency of rural citizens to dissolve their township governments, where they exist, and transfer their functions to the county.

In the urban areas, on the other hand, "the fat is in the fire." Substantially, there are two different arguments advocated as solutions to urban problems: one group argues that the only real solution is the creation of more municipalities or independent authorities while an opposing group argues that all existing units of government are ineffective and should be abolished, giving way to new "super governments." But county officials find that neither position is a realistic solution to immediate problems. Instead, the county is being called upon to assume those responsibilities (one by one) that are of an area-wide nature, such functions as transportation, civil defense, water and sewerage, planning and zoning, and others.

In a typical urban area we find these conditions. The central city is declining in population and the more well-to-do are moving to the suburbs. The central city is being populated by the less well-to-do; gradually it contains more older people and fewer business and professional people and those whom college professors like to call the "leader group." The tax base no longer is able to provide sufficiently high levels of services because new business and industry continues to locate outside the city. Traffic congestion and deterioration of the downtown business district set in.

The core city tries annexation as a means of increasing its tax base.

Surrounding the core city are a host of smaller cities that do not want to lose their identity. In unincorporated areas there is equal resistance to annexation because the suburbanites would be required to pay city taxes but could not, in most cases, obtain the same level of services as those in the core city. Often when the core city taxpayer realizes how much it is going to cost initially to provide city services to annexed areas, he balks too!

The crisis usually comes in a single functional area. The airport, for example, needs to expand its runways to provide jet service, but airports are (contrary to fancy bookkeeping) usually money losing propositions. Usually this airport is located physically outside the city. Always it serves the people of an entire area but is supported usually by city taxpayers only. The city fathers realize this fact, and the county is asked to take over their responsibility. Thus one finds that two of the most modern airports in the nation—Miami in Dade County, Florida, and Detroit, in Wayne County, Michigan—draw upon the total resources of the county area.

Here it is important to burst the bubble of a popular fairy tale. County officials are not trying to take over anything. The reverse is true. Most county officials have plenty of problems to occupy their minds and are reluctant to seek new ones. Usually the idea starts with some study group or with municipal officials themselves. County officials have, of course, urged legislation to allow them to provide municipal-type services (at a fair price) to county residents not in incorporated areas, which is something quite different.

It might be well to dispel another fiction. The day of rip-roaring city-county fights is just about over. Cooperation is the new watchword. For every case of real or imagined city-county tension, there are a dozen cases of city-county cooperation. These range from something as simple as informal exchanges of equipment or services to something as complex as formal contracts for services. Sometimes the city provides services to the county and sometimes the county provides services to the city. In either event both sets of officials are working together far better than most people realize.

ADVANTAGES OF COUNTY GOVERNMENT

As a solution to local problems, county governments offer many innate advantages that theoreticians sometimes overlook. In the first place, counties have a long and honorable history of service, dating from the earliest times in America and before that in Great Britain. Henrico County, Virginia, for example, was established in 1611. It will not be until 1967 that this county will have served the United States of America as long as it served as a unit of local government of the Virginia Colony. This county is, today, one of the most progressive in the nation; its advance in the area of automation is the envy of many larger communities.

Second, counties provide the territorial limits for the organization of many non-governmental as well as governmental activities. Medical Societies are nearly always county-wide, as are Bar Associations. Nearly all of the nation's agricultural and rural service programs are based upon the county as the primary unit. A large part of our educational systems are county-oriented. The national census uses the county as the basic accounting unit. Virtually all of the country's systems of courts and administration of justice are county-oriented. Conservation and soil conservation districts are usually coterminous with a single county.

Perhaps the greatest advantage of a county is that everyone in the state is served by a county government. Whether a voter lives in a city or in the rural portion of the county, he is represented on the county governing body. The notion that county functions are beyond the control of the city resident is, of course, false since the city resident is required to contribute to the financial support of the county since he participates in the election of representatives to the county governing body just as the rural resident does. It is true, however, that very often a rural resident has a stronger voice in county affairs because he has only one unit of government to keep an eye upon and therefore is more vigilant in county affairs. The city person has both his city and county governments to watch; and because his attention is divided, he may be less knowledgeable about his county government. This problem, however, can be remedied. In a democracy every citizen has the positive obligation to participate fully and intelligently in the affairs of his governments no matter how many there are. We certainly concede that actual participation in local affairs is increasingly difficult—particularly for that poor citizen who is served by a city, school district, multiple-service-district or authority, and by his state and Federal governments as well.

Finally, the county serves as the political base upon which our two-party system is built. The county is the fundamental organizational unit of both major parties and is their basic strength both state-wide and nationally. Because the parties are based on the county, they are controllable by the electorate. This political arena is the one place where all of the interests of the community are represented. Many decisions about local affairs are and should be made at this level because all interests are represented. The decision as to whether limited community funds are to be used to build a school or a bridge is, in this sense, political; and typically it is debated (or mutually endorsed) by the two parties in two-party areas and by opposing factions of the same party in one-party areas.

COUNTY PROBLEMS

To say that counties have a bright present and an even brighter future is not to say that they do not have problems. Chief among these is the absence of home rule (the right of local people to decide local affairs for themselves). Originally (and presently, for that matter) counties were established as local administrative districts of the state. Their responsibilities were quite simple in the beginning, enabling the state to establish a uniform system of county organization and to spell out in precise detail, in statute or constitution, exactly how the counties were to discharge these responsibilities. Most counties, however, are still forced to operate under these same rules in spite of changed circumstances which have brought on new responsibilities. As a result, counties now find themselves in a veritable strait jacket of state control.

The problems created by this rigid control are numerous. Most county officials are severely restricted in establishing local salary scales for county employees. In Massachusetts, for example, the state legislature has complete control over local county budgets, personnel and all. In order for a county official to purchase a typewriter, the item and the specific cost must be included in the county's budget and approved by the state legislature.

Increasingly the functions that counties are called upon to assume require endless special state statutes, and yet all but a handful of state legislatures meet only once every two years to consider substantive legislation. Many of the restrictions that are most disruptive of orderly, sensible local determination, moreover, are spelled out in the state constitution—an extremely difficult document to amend.

THE NEED FOR EXECUTIVE LEADERSHIP

Of all the difficulties facing counties, perhaps the most complicated is the absence of an executive comparable to a municipal mayor, a state governor, or the President of the United States. As a matter of fact, in some states there is no real separation of legislative, judicial, and executive functions at the county level. Instead, we find single, elected officials discharging all three functions.

Opposition to a single chief executive runs very strong at the county level and apparently lies deep in the American concept of government—stemming from a fear of placing too much power in the hands of a single individual.

Two trends in the practices of American counties appear to be running contrary to this attitude, however. In some states—California, for example

—the elected county supervisors (composing the county governing body) are turning to the professionally-trained, appointed county executive to discharge the mountains of detail incident to conducting the public business. Approximately 36 of the 57 counties in California have reported the creation of a position of this nature (under various names). Once adopted, the elected supervisors appear to have become the strongest supporters of the concept.

The other trend is in the direction of an elected county executive, undistinguishable from a strong mayor at the municipal level. The city and county of San Francisco and the city and county of Denver both have an elected mayor who also is, in varying degrees, responsible for county affairs. This is also true of the mayors of New Orleans and Baton Rouge and their parishes (counties) in Louisiana. Baltimore County in Maryland; Westchester, Erie, Nassau and Suffolk Counties, all in New York; and Milwaukee County in Wisconsin also have recently adopted the county-wide elected chief executive plan.

One of the most strenuous criticisms of county government has come from those who argue that there are too many elected executive positions at the county level, and indeed the list is long. Some 68,000 county positions are filled today by election. Chief among those attacked is the position of coroner. Lately, many statistics have indicated that there is a trend away from the election of many of these officials, but the National Association of County Officials has always taken the position that every community, in accord with home rule standards, should have the right to elect or appoint their officials as they see fit. If they want to elect the coroner, then they should have that right. It could very well be, as many of the defenders of the long ballot argue, that most of the officials who are elected to these positions now would probably be the ones who would hold them as appointees if the system were changed. Compared to the county problems caused by the crippling effect of almost exclusive reliance on the property tax, the election-appointment controversy pales into insignificance. This is not the problem over which to draw the battleline.

RELATIONS BETWEEN GOVERNMENTS

Nowhere is the philosophy that "no man is an isle unto himself" more true than in county government. At no time in history have the relationships between the Federal, state, and local governments been more complex; and, to quote an old infantry maxim, "they are bound to get worse before they get better." Take a single function—highways. The Federal government imposes a tax upon gasoline and other highway-user products and uses a portion of these funds to help finance certain highways that have been determined according to national defense or national economic need. The states in turn build and maintain all Federal-aid roads (with minor exceptions) and in addition levy gasoline and other highway-user taxes to finance a portion of the Federal-aid roads and all state highways. Counties, in turn, do not generally have access to highway-user fees (unless shared with them by the states) but do build and maintain an overwhelming proportion of the roads in the United States—largely with property taxes.

Why not, then, give one level of government the responsibility for all roads? Could the Federal government abandon the roads and the Federal gasoline taxes to the states and leave it to them to build all roads? No! States are all in competition one with the other for business and industry. Some would not levy the gasoline tax; many roads of national import would not be built in individual states. The same arguments would apply if the county were to build all roads. The opposition to having the Federal government build them is obvious.

This one case, therefore, illustrates why, for the forseeable future, most governmental functions must be on a partnership basis (including private enterprise) and why these interrelationships are so complex.

COUNTY AND METROPOLITAN PROBLEMS

Metropolitan problems of today have grown so numerous and important to the welfare of our society that a whole new profession dedicated to their study has sprung up; but from the nearly 200 major studies produced by these professionals, less than half a dozen have realized the adoption of a substantial number of their recommendations. Because metropolitan problems often spill over the bounds of a single county, these studies have neglected the county as the potential core around which their solutions might have been built. But those studies which have shunted aside the county have done so in the face of evidence in practice of the adaptability of this unit of government to new conditions.

Counties have met metropolitan problems through the use of multi-county arrangements. Since 1924, Montgomery and Prince George's Counties in Maryland have had a bi-county Suburban Sanitary Commission (controlled by the counties) to provide water, sewage and refuse collection for hundreds of thousands of county residents in the area (there are few cities). Franklin County, Massachusetts, is the headquarters of a multi-county fire protection setup that brings fire protection to rural areas in Massachusetts, Vermont, and New Hampshire. And, there are literally hundreds of similar examples of two, three, or more counties joining to provide these or other area-wide services.

More recently the multi-county (and city, too) arrangements have flourished in great counties and their cities in Connecticut, New Jersey, and New York have banded together to start an area-wide approach to some of their metropolitan problems. The Supervisors' Inter-County Committee, composed of six counties in the Detroit-Wayne County numbers. In the New York area, some 22 areas are banding together voluntarily to solve their area-wide problems. The same is true of the four counties, two in Virginia and two in Maryland, who are banding together with the District of Columbia in the Washington area, and of the multi-county-city approach also being tried in the San Francisco Bay area.

If the county is proving that it can be placed in combination like building blocks, it is also showing that it is divisible, too! Counties everywhere are reporting great success in creating special districts to provide special services to selected parts of the county. All residents of the county pay a basic tax for county-wide services such as welfare, education and administration of justice. In addition any area that wants water and sewerage, for example, can have it provided by the county and can pay separately for the service. Thus the special service district under the control of the county governing body can provide municipal services to those that need them and who will pay for them without interfering with the farm resident who does not need them. Thus we have the farmer and the city dweller living happily side by side and serviced by the same county, and once again the county has shown its adaptability to the needs of its residents and their circumstances.

IS THE COUNTY OBSOLETE?

Critics of county government have taken heart from the fact that the Connecticut Legislature, under Governor Abraham Ribicoff's leadership, has voted to abolish the state's eight counties on October 1, 1960. Does not this refute much of what has been said here? No. County government in Connecticut was not typical of county government in other parts of the United States. The county commissioners were not elected; they were appointed by the state legislature upon recommendation of the county representatives and senators elected to the General Assembly. Through years of centralization of power at the state level in Connecticut, the counties had been gradually stripped of all important functions and were left pretty much with the single major function of maintaining jails. This and the remaining minor functions performed by the counties, therefore, will not now be given to another unit of local government but will be taken over by the state.

How serious is the loss of Connecticut's counties to the county movement in the United States? While the nearly 300 county employees will now be absorbed by the State of Connecticut, the loss is insignificant in the stream of expanding county government. When this loss is weighed against an average daily increase of over 150 employees per working day, the loss of Connecticut's counties will stem the national tide of county progress by approximately two days.[1]

In only a few other areas of the United States are there no counties to be found. Rhode Island is so small that it has never needed county political subdivisions and Alaska has created local units called Boroughs. There is now some consideration being given to creating counties. Hawaii, of course, has no separately organized cities. Honolulu is a city-county like San Francisco. With these few exceptions, therefore, county government can rightly claim to be the one universal and all-encompassing unit of local government. County government is not dead. Instead, it has just begun to live. It has proved that it is flexible, adjustable, resilient, and full of potential for meeting the needs of a new America. County government is, indeed, reborn.

Paul W. Wager
34. Townships on Way Out*

Political institutions, particularly at the grass roots, change slowly. In 1934 the Committee on County Government of the National Municipal League issued a report, *Recommendations on Township Government*. It was written by Arthur W. Bromage, chairman of a subcommittee set up to look into the need and effectiveness of this unit of local government then existent in 22 states. The recommendation was that, except in New England, the unit be gradually abolished.

At that time there were 18,725 organized townships (or towns) outside New England. They existed in sixteen states excluding Washington, which had townships in only two counties. Now, in 1957, according to the U.S. Bureau of the Census, the number has decreased to 15,692 in fourteen states, again excluding Washington and also South Carolina, which has two organized townships. In two states, Oklahoma and Iowa, township

---

[1] Since there were 668,000 employees (in 1957) and an average annual increase of 6 percent, there will be an average daily increase of employees (based on a five-day week) of 150 persons (excluding holidays).

* From *National Municipal Review*. October 1957, pp. 456–460 and 475. Footnotes in original omitted. Reprinted with permission of publisher.

government either has been completely liquidated or has been reduced to such a shadowy existence as to warrant exclusion from the enumeration.

In Oklahoma townships were abolished, for all practical purposes, by a constitutional amendment of 1933 which deprived them of the power to levy taxes. The Oklahoma legislature then transferred to the county those functions which had been performed by the township, the most important of which was highway construction and maintenance.

In Iowa, the townships lost jurisdiction over local roads by act of the legislature in 1929. They continued for some years to enjoy a few other functions—oversight of the poor, provision of minimal health services, control of noxious weeds, care of cemeteries and the assessment of property. A few years ago the county was given jurisdiction over the assessment function and also the appointment of the weed commissioner. While townships there still have a certain amount of vestigial status, Iowa townships are now treated in census statistics as adjuncts of the county governments and are no longer counted as governmental units.

The net reduction in the other states is only 389 units. This reduction has been due to the liquidation of township government in individual counties, notably in Minnesota and the two Dakotas. The change in two decades is shown in the following tabulation:

	1933	1957
Illinois	1481	1433
Indiana	1016	1008
Iowa	1602	——
Kansas	1550	1540
Michigan	1268	1262
Minnesota	1973	1828
Missouri	345	328
Nebraska	506	478
New Jersey	236	233
New York	932	934
North Dakota	1470	1392
Ohio	1337	1335
Oklahoma	969	——
Pennsylvania	1574	1565
South Dakota	1177	1080
Wisconsin	1289	1276
	18,725	15,692

The decline in the importance of township government may be measured also in the loss of functions by those still in business.

FUNCTIONS LOST TO TOWNSHIPS

ADMINISTRATION OF JUSTICE. Justices of the peace and constables are still elected in a majority of the states but in steadily declining numbers. Also from all over the country there comes the report that in few townships are there any candidates, and some who are elected do not bother to qualify. The explanation for the rapid disappearance of the ancient office of justice of the peace is, of course, the absence of a need for a neighborhood magistrate in these days of automobiles and good roads and the widespread establishment of county or district courts with a somewhat broader jurisdiction.

The constable is even more of an anachronism in a modern high speed age and has almost disappeared from the scene. The evidence multiplies that the township is no longer needed or much used either for law enforcement or the administration of justice.

WELFARE AND HEALTH. The many faceted social security program, supported in large part from federal and state funds, has pretty generally relieved the townships of such residual welfare functions as they had twenty years ago. In New York State the last vestiges of poor relief were transferred to the county in 1947. Today only in Illinois, Indiana, Ohio and in some counties in Minnesota do the townships play any role in welfare administration and only in Illinois is their contribution to its support more than nominal.

Twenty-five years ago the township was still being utilized quite widely as an area for a rudimentary health service. As of 1952, there were 1,333 full-time local health departments of one sort or another serving 1,637 counties, including 279 cities and covering areas with a combined population of approximately 120 million people. The picture throughout the nation is by no means uniform, however. In 1950 there were only two county units in South Dakota and one in Pennsylvania; on the other hand, New York had 100 per cent county-wide coverage and Michigan 89 per cent.

The availability of federal funds under the Hill-Burton Act to assist with the cost of hospital construction has given further stimulus to the adoption of the county as the unit of support of hospitals and the hospitalization of indigents.

ASSESSMENT AND COLLECTION OF TAXES. The property tax has always been the mainstay of local government, and in earlier days the practice developed of having real and personal property assessed or listed by assessors representing jurisdictions smaller than the county. In the states which had townships, these were used as assessment districts with the assessor almost always popularly elected as a township officer. The values placed on property by these local assessors were used not only as the basis for township levies but for county and state levies as well. To overcome competitive undervaluation, it was usually necessary to provide some method of equalization at the county level.

TOWNSHIP FUNCTIONS REMAINING

This system has been perpetuated and assessment of property remains one of the two most common functions of township government. It is a township function in all or many of the counties in twelve of the fourteen states covered in this report. It is a county function in Ohio and, since 1950, has been in Nebraska. In Indiana it is a township function in townships with 5,000 or more population but in South Dakota in the rural areas only. It was the loss of this function to the county that completed the liquidation of township government in Iowa and in several other states there is now a county assessor who gives general supervision to the work. This is true in Indiana, Missouri, Kansas, Nebraska and in a number of counties in Minnesota. The trend is unmistakably in the direction of county assumption of the assessment function, usually over the vigorous protest of the state associations of township officials.

The collection of taxes has not so generally been a township function though it is, at least prior to delinquency, in New York, Pennsylvania, Michigan and in a few populous counties in Illinois.

HIGHWAY ADMINISTRATION. The principal function of township government, far outweighing all others combined, is the maintenance of local roads. Though all township roads were transferred to the counties over twenty years ago in three states—Iowa in 1930, Indiana in 1932 and in Michigan gradually from 1931 to 1936—the movement thereafter slowed down. There have been additional shifts from the township to the county-unit plan but only county by county and by local option rather than by legislative fiat.

Under such a county option plan, more than half the Kansas counties have abandoned township highway management. As of January 1955, there were 53 counties which had adopted the county unit plan and 52 which cling to the township system. The townships which have lost the road function have little to do and this is reflected in the fact that in these townships 40 per cent of their budgeted expenditures are for administrative overhead.

A similar optional law for the transfer of township roads to county-wide road districts is in effect in Illinois, but little advantage has been taken of it.

Still another method is being used to overcome the handicaps inherent in the conduct of road work on the township scale. This is for the officials of a township, of their own volition, to enter into an agreement to have the township's road work done with county forces and equipment. Widespread use is made of this contract plan in Minnesota and Wisconsin. A study made of 545 Wisconsin towns in 1952 showed that county forces were maintaining town roads in more than half the towns.

Pennsylvania has no county roads in rural areas—only state roads and township roads. In the 1930s the State Department of Highways absorbed into the state system a large mileage of township roads, but the effort some years later to transfer responsibility for the rest of the local roads to the counties was defeated. Today Pennsylvania has many small and poorly managed township highway units. It has been estimated that only 263 of the state's 1,513 second class townships could meet the minimum qualifications for an effective highway unit.

In Illinois in 1953 local rural roads were administered by 1,408 townships in 85 counties which have organized townships and 107 road units in non-township counties. In four of the latter counties the road unit was the entire county. The average road unit was comprised of 48 miles of rural roads. The State Division of Highways, in a detailed study to determine the effect of size of road unit on cost per mile of road concluded, "there appears to be ample justification for the belief that costs per mile decrease as the miles maintained by the administering unit increase."

In New York, as of 1950, the town highway system accounted for more than 52 per cent of the total mileage of rural highways and urban streets. The bulk of the mileage had a traffic count of less than 50 vehicles a day and some of the town mileage had fewer than five vehicles. About 36 per cent of it did not even have a gravel surface. One-third of the town highway mileage was serving land abandoned or unlikely to remain permanently in agriculture.

The state legislature of 1950 set up a ten-year town highway program which called for the improvement of about one-half of the town highway mileage, or more than 26,000 miles, at a total cost of $146,400,000, with the state providing about half the over-all cost. The act was designed (1) to limit improvement to those roads that would serve communities of economic stability and (2) to require each township to contribute to the cost in proportion to its ability.

A DECREASING ROLE

These illustrations of the decreasing role played by the townships in the four fields in which they once played important roles are evidence enough that in the rural areas they have outlived their usefulness. Further evidence is the lack of interest in township meetings in states providing for such meetings, and the dearth of qualified candidates for township office in the township states generally. Every argument advanced twenty-odd years ago for their elimination has become even more cogent with the passage of time.

Tradition, the alleged values of local self-government, and political advantage are the main reasons why townships remain. The last of these factors is probably the principal one. Threatened with the loss of their jobs and political influence, township officials have united into powerful state associations—as, for example, in New York, Pennsylvania, Michigan and Ohio.

Township government has shown greater signs of weakening in those states that do not use the township as the basis of representation on the county governing body. For example, Minnesota and Missouri both reduced the number of townships during the 1940s, but Wisconsin, Michigan, New York and Illinois townships remain relatively powerful because they are units for representation on the county board of supervisors and thus can offer another reason for continuing their existence. But this is an insufficient reason for retaining an outmoded unit. Town government is no more needed in the rural parts of New York State than it is in North Dakota for the very good reason that it has nothing particular to do.

COSTS GO UP

Surprisingly, despite shrinking functions, the cost of township government does not show a decline. Township revenues in the fourteen township states increased from $197 million in 1942 to $422 million in 1953, 114 per cent. Expenditure figures for these two years are not available but presumably they do not differ greatly from the revenue figures. The comparative figures for the two years by states is shown on page 274.

It will be noted that the only state which showed an actual decrease in township revenue was Indiana and this appears to have been due to a reduction in township taxes for schools. The state which showed the sharpest increase was Michigan due no doubt to the generous allocations to the townships from the proceeds of the state sales tax. Indeed in the township states as a whole the upsurge in spending has been stimulated by aid from other governments. In the eleven-year period revenues from local sources increased 104 per cent, whereas grants from other governments increased 163 per cent. Increased spending does not necessarily signify rejuvenation if somebody else is furnishing the money.

A closer analysis of contemporary township government would almost certainly show that most of the increased activity is in a relatively few

TOWNSHIP REVENUE
(in thousands of dollars)

	1942	1953
New York	$53,487	$132,615
New Jersey	20,027	58,174
Pennsylvania	23,408	43,125
Ohio	8,305	24,492
Indiana	30,696	10,790
Illinois	22,928	32,780
Michigan	4,138	26,670
Wisconsin	19,500	59,613
Missouri	1,658	3,836
Kansas	4,687	9,083
Nebraska	722	2,937
South Dakota	1,204	3,616
North Dakota	1,268	4,364
Minnesota	5,257	10,138
TOTAL	197,285	422,233

populous townships which are providing a number of urban-type services. This suggests that in recommending the dissolution of townships a distinction needs to be made between townships in rural areas and densely populated townships, often but not necessarily within metropolitan areas. Here there is often a demand for services not demanded or needed on a county-wide basis and which cannot always be supplied by a nearby city.

Several states have already recognized the need for some diversity in township organization and powers. New York distinguishes between first and second class townships—those with a population of 10,000 or more being designated first class and vested with somewhat greater police power.

Townships in Pennsylvania are likewise divided into two classes. Townships of the first class are those having a population density of 300 or more per square mile; all others are townships of the second class. However, change from second to first class is subject to referendum. First class townships are urban in nature and frequently perform functions similar to cities and boroughs.

Townships in New Jersey are given a wide range of power and frequently perform functions associated elsewhere with municipal governments.

TERMINATION OVERDUE

There is no threat to local self-government when the enlargement of the service area is no greater than the new modes of transportation and communication warrant. The radius of a county is no greater in travel time today than was the radius of a township in 1900. The average citizen in his business and social activities is offering testimony every day to this fact, yet he will often let himself be persuaded that a larger political unit is a denial of local self-government.

Local government needs to be preserved and strengthened but it needs to be defined in twentieth century terms. It has been amply demonstrated that in most areas there is no longer a need for township government. There may be a need to develop in the densely populated townships a kind of township government that approximates the town government of New England. Where town government can evolve into a useful vehicle of community service it certainly has a place in contemporary America; elsewhere its termination is already overdue.

Norman C. Miller, Jr.
35. *Tax-free Enterprise**

San Francisco — You have acquired some raw land which you would like to sub-divide and sell for home sites. Your problem: You can't afford to put in the necessary water lines, sewers, roads and other basic facilities.

The solution: Hold an election in the area you own and your lone ballot will turn your property into a political body known as a "special district." Then you can sell municipal bonds, on which the interest is exempt from taxes, and use the proceeds to develop the land. Buyers of the home sites will be obligated to pay off the bonds.

Fantastic as it may seem, this is precisely what has been done on more than one occasion here in the Golden State. It is an unusual but perfectly legal procedure and illustrates merely one of the growing variety of pur·poses for which special districts are rapidly being created.

Special districts are political subdivisions usually established either by a vote of property owners in the proposed district or by a routinely·passed special act of a state legislature. Usually they are created for a single purpose, such as to provide sewage service or water facilities, but sometimes they are empowered to carry out several different types of functions. In size, districts range from massive to minute. The Metro-politan Water District of Southern California has issued more than $229 million in bonds to finance a water supply system for Los Angeles and other cities. On the other hand, one Texas water district recently annexed to Houston covered only three-tenths of a square mile and in its last election had a turnout of only four voters.

A "NOTABLE PHENOMENON"

The proliferation of special districts throughout the states adds up to a "notable phenomenon of the past decade," according to a recent report by the Congressional Advisory Commission on Intergovernmental Relation; this group was established by Congress in 1959 to study the problems involved in coordinating the activities of the various levels of government in meeting common problems. The last time the U. S. Census Bureau counted, in 1957, there were 14,405 special districts in all the states, up from 12,319 in 1952. These figures don't include school districts, which are considered a separate category of local government. No one is sure how many special districts there are today, but there undoubtedly has been a sizeable increase since the Census Bureau's last tally. In California alone, about 230 special districts have come into being since 1957.

Despite this multiplicity of special districts, hardly anyone has an accurate idea of what all these agencies do in the name of the public. "Special districts are the least known, least understood and least cared about class of government in the United States," declares a report by the University of Texas Institute of Public Affairs.

The little-noticed spread of special districts is beginning to cause concern among many specialists in local government affairs. Critics give these general objections: Creation of special districts splinters local government and thus diffuses official responsibility; voter confusion and apathy about district affairs often results; and district governing boards often wield important power without many, if any, effective restraints.

"These districts too often become a sort of kingdom unto themselves," contends Lynn F. Anderson, assistant director of the University of Texas Institute of Public Affairs. "What we need to do is to integrate our local governments. But these districts represent a further fragmentation."

FOR PRIVATE GAIN

In a few cases, some critics charge, special districts are being created for the gain of private individuals. And if the number of small, thinly-populated special districts continues to grow, some authorities fear a few may default on their bonds, damaging the credit rating of many sound districts—perhaps even the credit of states and neighboring cities.

As with bonds issued by other governments, special district bonds aren't subject to Federal and state taxes. The largely unregulated growth of special districts is beginning to worry a number of specialists in tax-exempt bonds. Declares one such bond man in New York: "There are so many sparsely-settled districts incurring debt in anticipation of a sharp rise in population that you wonder how they are all going to make out in the long run."

To be sure, most special districts are created to perform legitimate functions needed and demanded by the public, and conduct their affairs in an efficient and businesslike way. The great advantage of special districts is that they are not hamstrung by existing boundaries such as might be the case with cities and counties. By taking in all of an area that needs a particular service, special districts can operate unencumbered by political conflicts that often impede cooperation among local governments.

Formation of special districts provides a way to circumvent constitutional debt limitations which curb the expansion of services by cities in many states. For instance, Indiana cities can issue general obligation bonds, usually secured by property taxes, totaling no more than 2% of their assessed property values; but the debts of special districts are not charged against cities.

For an idea of how some of the newer special districts are organized, take a look at one here in California, which has spawned more of these agencies than any other state except Illinois.

A few miles south of San Francisco, the Estero Municipal Improvement District rules 2,606 acres of raw land, some of it marshy, adjacent to San Francisco Bay. The district was created with hardly any discussion by a special act of the 1960 California legislature. Nobody lives within its boundaries. The land is 95% owned by T. Jack Foster & Sons, a real estate development firm which, by virtue of its property ownership, has the voting power to elect the district's three-man governing board. The firm paid $12.9 million for its property.

Shortly after the Estero district was organized in September 1960, it authorized $55.5 million in bonds. These funds will be used by the district to reclaim land, install streets and provide utilities for "Foster City," a community for 35,000 people which the Foster firm says it plans to develop.

Seated in offices shared by the Foster firm and the Estero district, the developers and district officers predict Foster City will be worth $550 million when completed about eight years from now. As the district's land-filling operations proceed, the Foster firm intends to sell most of the lots to builders who, in turn, will put up and sell houses. The bonded debt of the district will be a first lien on the home owners' properties.

So far, $4.5 million of Estero district general obligation bonds, secured by the district's tax-levying power, have been offered to investors. The Foster firm obtained a mortgage loan of about $9 million when it bought the district land, but the bonds are senior to this obligation. Grande & Co., Inc., of Seattle, Wash., is the underwriter for the bonds. The sales literature for the bonds states that the estimated 1962-1963 true valuation of the Estero land is $23,206,000 based on a private appraisal. This appraisal, the sales literature says, "provides a comprehensive view of the security of these general obligation bonds."

VALUATIONS DIFFER

However, San Mateo County assesses the same land at $761,350. Since assessed valuation in the county generally represents about 21% of actual value, this indicates an actual valuation on the Estero land by the county of $3,805,000, or $19.4 million less than the valuation arrived at by the independent appraiser.

T. Jack Foster, Jr., vice president of the development firm, dismisses this as a "picky" difference; the county has not taken into account the development firm's elaborate plan for the land, he says. The Foster firm pays taxes to the county on the basis of the county valuation.

Also in its sales literature, Grande & Co. emphasizes the relatively high annual interest rates of up to 5.6% available on the Estero bonds. In addition, the bond house stresses its conviction that the Estero bonds represent an opportunity to "invest with safety." In answer to an inquiry from a prospective bond buyer, a Grande & Co. representative offers the assurance that "we cannot regard this (Estero) development as a speculative venture."

Most state officials, while questioning whether tax-exempt bonds should be used to raise funds for such purposes, believe the real estate development by the Estero district will prove successful, thanks to a rapid growth in population in the surrounding area.

Some special districts aren't looked upon as favorably by state and local officials.

One is the Embarcadero Municipal Improvement District, near Santa Barbara. This district was formed under a special state law by two developers, H. Roy Steele and Irwin W. Harris, to transform 1,320 acres of range land into a residential community. Through the district the developers authorized issuance of $8,874,000 of general obligation bonds and in January 1961 sold $1,207,000 of bonds as a first issue.

DEVELOPERS INDICTED

When a Los Angeles mortgage firm that had loaned money to the Embarcadero developers went into bankruptcy last year, state officials had an occasion to inspect the operations of this special district. In October 1961 a Los Angeles County grand jury indicted Messrs. Steele and Harris on 35 counts of grand theft, misuse of public funds and conspiracy. Among other things, the indictment alleges the developers received $90,000 in kickbacks from individuals doing work within the district for companies controlled by the developers.

In addition, it is charged that district funds were spent for such things as box seats to the Los Angeles Dodgers' baseball games, and to pay for Diners' Club bills, car rentals and bar tabs. Messrs. Steele and Harris have pleaded innocent to the charges and are scheduled to go on trial March 26. In the meantime, officials are trying to sort out the tangled affairs of the district.

Ambitious development projects by special districts in California are by no means limited to real estate ventures. Near the desert resort of Palm Springs, the Mount San Jacinto Winter Park Authority is busily constructing a two-mile aerial cable on the side of a mountain. When the project is completed next year, two 80-passenger cars dangling from the cable will whip skiers and sightseers out of the desert heat to the snows high atop San Jacinto Mountain. At both ends of the cable line, the San Jacinto district is building restaurants. It is hoped that 500,000 persons a year will use these facilities; if so, ample revenue would be provided to pay off the $7.7 million of bonds sold to pay for the project.

There is a strong possibility, however, that it will be more difficult in the future for California special districts to undertake promotional ventures. For one thing, the Embarcadero case prompted the state to reactivate the State Board of Investment to consider regulation of some or all of California's special districts.

But there is not likely to be any attempt to impose sweeping regulatory measures on special districts. Says one state official: "With so many districts that pride themselves on their independence, you would get into quite a political hassle if you proposed to make them all subject to some sort of central control."

12

URBAN GOVERNMENT

Urban governments in seeking to improve their efficiency have been turning to the council-manager plan that is patterned after the corporate form of business organization. The manager plan has been accepted by forty-nine percent of the cities with a population of over 25,000 and thirty-nine percent of the cities with a population of between 10,000 and 25,000, yet it has not been adopted by the largest cities, which prefer the mayor-council plan.

Dr. Wallace S. Sayre, Eaton professor of public administration at Columbia University, describes a new managerial idea in large cities: the establishment under the elected mayor of a general manager. He predicts that the council-manager plan is unlikely to be adopted by large cities. His prediction merits close examination and such an examination is provided by Mr. John E. Bebout, director of the Urban Studies Center at Rutgers University, who takes issue with Professor Sayre's contention that the strong mayor-manager plan is more in accord with American tradition than the council-manager plan. Mr. Bebout concludes that most of the largest cities will operate in the future under the mayor-council plan and that these cities should continue to experiment with the use of a professional staff.

A number of attempts have been made to classify the types of leadership roles played by various city managers. Mr. Steve Matthews, city manager of San Antonio, Texas, places managers in three categories and concludes that the successful manager is one who develops leadership in other people.

A considerable amount of literature has dealt with the future of cities and much of it has been pessimistic. Mr. Robert Moses, a man who has held many top positions in state and municipal governmental agencies concerned with New York City, attacks strongly what he calls the "Jeremiahs" who maintain that cities are doomed. Mr. Moses says their reports of the death of cities are greatly exaggerated and sums up his article by asking a few pointed questions that merit serious consideration.

Wallace S. Sayre
36. The General Manager Idea for Large Cities*

A new managerial idea is taking hold in the large cities of the United States. This idea is that the administration of large city governments requires general managerial direction and that this requirement can best be met by establishing under the mayor a general manager who will, in greater or less degree, be the city government's second in administrative command. The general manager plan thus builds upon the strong-mayor tradition as the most widespread form of city government in the United States. By marrying the manager idea with the idea of the elected chief executive, the general manager plan preserves the office of mayor as the center of political leadership and responsibility. In large cities this center is widely regarded as indispensable to effective government.

The general manager plan may be regarded either as a competitor of the council manager idea or as a more mature form of the manager idea, reflecting the judgment in the larger cities that the council manager plan represents an unnecessary surrender of the values of leadership and accountability found in the institution of the elected chief executive. The general manager or mayor manager plan, its proponents emphasize, captures the advantages of the council manager plan without the risks of abandoning the elected chief executive. An effective manager, they believe, is no less likely to be chosen by a mayor than by a city council.

The council manager plan has not found acceptance in the large cities of the United States. Cincinnati, the largest city using the plan, has a population of a half million. Of the seventeen other cities having a population of a half million or more, only one city—Cleveland—has ever adopted the plan, and it was abandoned there more than twenty years ago. In the last decade (perhaps even longer), no large city has given serious consideration to the adoption of the council manager plan.

The literature of the council manager movement does not provide an answer to the question: why has the plan failed to find support in large cities? In fact, the literature does not tell us much about the ecology of the council manager plan in adoptions and operations. Why, for example, are half of all the council manager cities to be found in six states (California, Florida, Maine, Michigan, Texas, and Virginia)? Does the council

* From *Public Administration Review.* Autumn 1954, pp. 253–258. Reprinted from *Public Administration Review* by permission of the American Society for Public Administration.

manager plan find acceptance primarily in particular social, economic, and political environments? Does it, for example, find greatest acceptance and operate most successfully in one-party or in "non-partisan" constituencies? Is the affinity between the council manager plan and small and middle-sized cities the result of the plan's suitability for the management of the particular governmental problems to be found in cities of such size? Is the council manager plan particularly attractive to cities which are growing rapidly in size or to those which are declining in population and resources? To these and other questions about the council manager plan we do not yet have the answers.[1]

THE LARGE CITIES TURN TOWARD
THE MAYOR MANAGER PLAN

Eight large cities (Boston, Los Angeles, Louisville, Newark, New Orleans, New York City, Philadelphia, and San Francisco) have now established some kind of general managerial assistance for the mayor. In two others (Chicago and Detroit) proposals for such general managerial arrangements have been made.

This new managerial trend in large cities has not resulted from an organized effort by municipal reformers with a symmetrical design for the improvement of city government. In fact, this new form of the manager idea in city government has not yet acquired a distinctive label. Some observers call it the mayor manager plan, to emphasize its contrast with the council manager plan; others call it the mayor administrator plan; and still others name it the general manager plan.

The general manager idea for cities began its governmental history in San Francisco in 1932, when charter revision movement established the office of chief administrative officer. This office represented a compromise solution between those who urged a council manager form and those who supported the retention of the strong mayor form. The plan was not widely noticed, but it has prevailed to the general satisfaction of the electorate. In 1938 New York City's new charter established the office of deputy mayor, an office which developed more as a center of legislative and political assistance to the mayor than as a center of managerial aid. In 1941, Lent D. Upson proposed a general manager under the mayor for the city of Detroit, but the proposal was not accepted. In 1948, Louisville

---

[1] For a program of research in this field, see "Party and Administrative Responsibility: Council-Manager Government," in Interuniversity Summer Seminar on Political Behavior, Social Science Research Council, "Research in Political Behavior," 46 *American Political Science Review* 1009–15 (December, 1952).

began a related experiment with the appointment of a city consultant-administrator who serves as general managerial assistant to the mayor. In 1951, Los Angeles established a city administrative officer. In the same year, Philadelphia's new charter took a long step forward in developing the general manager idea by establishing the office of managing director with substantial powers. In 1953, New Orleans adopted a new charter which established the office of chief administrative officer, with powers similar to but greater than those of Philadelphia's managing director. In the same year, Boston established a director of administrative services and Newark adopted a new charter which established the office of business administrator under the mayor, the option under the New Jersey statutes closest to the general manager idea. In 1954, New York City established the office of city administrator, with Luther Gulick the first incumbent. And in September, 1954, the staff report to the Chicago Charter Revision Commission recommended the adoption of the general manager plan for that city.[2]

Thus the experiment begun in San Francisco over twenty years ago has captured civic interest and has led to official action in an impressive portion of the large cities. Why has this happened? Several explanations may be suggested:

1. The council manager plan had proved to be unacceptable in large city environments, but the values of the managerial idea were still sought in some more attractive structural form.

2. The office of mayor—an elected chief executive who is the center of energy and of public leadership and the focus of responsibility for policy and performance—had become too important an asset in large cities to be exchanged for the speculative values of legislative supremacy and a city manager as represented in the council manager plan.

3. The mayor manager plan fits comfortably and easily into the Amer-

---

[2] Accounts of these developments are scattered and fragmentary. In addition to the charters of the several cities, see Richard S. Childs, *Appointive Municipal Administrators under Mayors; A Review of the Precedents* (Citizens Union Research Foundation, Inc., 5 Beekman St., New York City 38, 1953), 10 pp.; Boston Municipal Research Bureau, *Highlights of the Reorganization Ordinance* (Bulletin No. 180, Dec. 29, 1953); Charles P. Farnsley, "Louisville's Mayor-Administrator Plan," 68 *American City* 116–17 (Jan., 1953); Bert W. Levit, "San Francisco's Unique Charter," 34 *National Municipal Review* 273–77, 286 (June, 1945); Los Angeles Commission for Reorganization of the City Government, *Final Report* (April, 1953), 21 pp.; Temporary State Commission to Study the Organizational Structure of the Government of the City of New York, *Four Steps to Better Government of New York City: A Plan for Action*, Part 1 (Sept. 28, 1953), 136 pp.; Part 2 (Feb. 1, 1954), 102 pp. Charlton F. Chute prepared a useful survey of these developments, "Modern Ideas on Administrative Assistants for the Mayor in Large American Cities," for the Chicago Charter Revision Commission which will be summarized in a forthcoming report of that commission.

ican political system: it preserves the elected chief executive; it keeps the mayoralty as the focus of the party battle; it emphasizes the values of integration, hierarchy, and professional management, all made familiar doctrine by a half-century of administrative reorganizations in national, state, and municipal governments and by the doctrine of the council manager movement itself.

EMERGING ELEMENTS OF THE GENERAL MANAGER IDEA

The idea of a general manager serving under the mayor has not been a pre-packaged solution developed as finished doctrine by municipal reformers. Rather, its evolution has been experimental, each application being worked out in relation to local experience and governmental conditions, and varying with the boldness or caution of local leadership. There are several discernible trends in the successive adoptions, however. These can be briefly stated as follows:

1. The general manager is increasingly made more clearly the managerial agent of the mayor, "The mayor's man." In San Francisco in 1932 the manager was made virtually irremovable, but under 1953-54 provisions in New Orleans and New York City the manager holds office at the pleasure of the mayor.

2. As the manager is made more responsible to the mayor, he tends to be given more power—to approach more nearly the status of second in administrative command. In New Orleans and Philadelphia, the cities which represent the most full-bodied application of the general manager idea, the manager is given, for example, the power to appoint and remove the heads of most of the city departments with the approval of the mayor.

3. There is a continued ambivalence in deciding whether the general manager's authority and responsibility should center upon the "staff" or upon the "line" agencies and activities of the city government.

In almost every instance the manager is given primary responsibility for administrative planning and for other organization and methods work. In Los Angeles and New Orleans he has responsibility for budget preparation and execution; in Philadelphia and New York these activities are not under the manager's jurisdiction. In no city does the manager directly supervise the personnel agency. In New Orleans, New York, and Philadelphia the "line" agencies are the manager's major responsibility. The two extremes are represented by Los Angeles, where the manager's responsibilities are focused upon the management functions (except personnel), and by Philadelphia, where the manager's powers are centered upon the "line" agencies.

4. There is some tendency to create a new and smaller cabinet institution under the mayor, consisting of the general manager and the heads of the "staff" agencies. This is particularly the case in Philadelphia and New York. The heads of the "line" agencies, when they function as a cabinet (as they do in Philadelphia), do so in a meeting presided over by the manager.

VARIATIONS IN THE OFFICE AND POWERS OF THE GENERAL MANAGER IN FIVE LARGE CITIES

The variety as well as the trends in the development of the general manager idea in the large cities of the United States may perhaps best be seen through a more specific description of the office and the powers conferred upon it in Los Angeles, New Orleans, New York City, Philadelphia, and San Francisco.

TITLE: In San Francisco and New Orleans the manager is called chief administrative officer; in Los Angeles, city administrative officer; in Philadelphia, managing director; in New York, city administrator.

APPOINTMENT: In every instance, the manager is appointed by the mayor. Only in Los Angeles is council approval required.

TERM: In San Francisco, Los Angeles, New Orleans, and New York, no term is specified. In Philadelphia the term of the manager is four years, corresponding to the term of the mayor appointing him.

REMOVAL: In New Orleans and New York the mayor may remove the manager. In Los Angeles, the mayor may remove the manager, but the approval of the council is required. In Philadelphia the mayor must prefer charges; the manager may appeal his removal to the Civil Service Commission which may award him compensation but may not restore him. In San Francisco the mayor may not remove; the manager is subject to recall in an election, or the legislative body may remove him by a two-thirds vote. In Los Angeles and New Orleans the council may also remove the manager—in Los Angeles by a two-thirds vote and in New Orleans by a majority vote of all members.

POWERS OF THE MANAGER: The powers of the managers may be described in three categories: (1) the power to appoint and remove heads of city agencies; (2) the power to supervise city administrative operations; (3) the power to provide general advice and assistance to the mayor.

1. *To appoint and remove heads of agencies:* In Philadelphia, New Orleans, and San Francisco, the managers appoint and remove the heads of specified city departments and agencies. In San Francisco the manager does not need the mayor's approval for such appointments or removals; in Philadelphia and New Orleans the mayor's approval is required. In New Orleans the manager's power to appoint and remove extends to the

heads of all but two city departments (law and civil service); in Philadelphia it includes all but finance, law, and personnel. In neither of these two cities does the power to appoint and remove include members of boards or commissions. In San Francisco, the power extends to departments specified by name in the charter; such departments constitute about half of the city agencies.

In neither Los Angeles nor New York does the manager have the power to appoint or remove heads of departments.

2. *To supervise city administrative operations:* In San Francisco the power of the manager to supervise is confined to the departments specifically assigned to him by the charter. In Los Angeles the manager's opportunities for supervision flow solely from his role as city budget officer. In Philadelphia the manager's power to supervise is largely confined to the departments whose heads he appoints, but some more general supervision flows from his powers to perform the administrative analysis function in all city agencies.

In New Orleans the manager has more general supervisory authority. He supervises not only his own subordinate agencies (which include most of the city agencies), but he also gives "general oversight" to law, civil service, and the City Planning Commission (which are outside his appointing and removal authority), prescribes standards of administrative practice to be followed by all agencies and boards, prepares and supervises the operating and capital budgets, surveys the organization and procedures of all agencies and boards, and may require reports from any or all of them.

In New York City the city administrator, although lacking any power to appoint or remove, has a broad supervisory assignment. Under the direction of the mayor, he "shall supervise and coordinate the work of all agencies under the jurisdiction of the mayor" except law, investigation, budget, the construction coordinator, and boards, commissions (which include personnel), and authorities. He may convene heads of agencies singly or collectively, procure information and reports, require the keeping of management records, conduct work studies, and establish management standards for most, if not all, city agencies.

3. *The power to provide general advice and assistance to the mayor:* In Philadelphia and New York the manager is under a special obligation to serve as general management adviser to the mayor. In Philadelphia the managing director is required to report periodically to the mayor concerning the affairs of the city government (not merely the affairs of his own departments), and he is authorized to make recommendations on matters concerning the affairs of the whole city government. In New York the city administrator is required to "prepare annual and all such other reports as the mayor shall require," and to "analyze and report to the

mayor concerning impending policy decisions affecting the management of the city and the agencies." He is also directed to "maintain liason with civic and community groups on matters of governmental management."

In both Philadelphia and New York the manager derives special status from cabinet arrangements, established by the charter in Philadelphia and by the mayor's action in New York. In each city there is a small top-level cabinet group meeting weekly with the mayor, in which the manager plays a central role.

The managers in the other three cities have no explicit responsibility to serve as the general adviser to the mayor on management matters. In these cities, the manager's role in this respect is implicit, if it exists at all. In San Francisco it would seem difficult to join such a role with that of an almost autonomous manager. In New Orleans it would seem to be a logical and natural development. In Los Angeles, it would appear to be a more confined but possible development.

THE FUTURE COURSE OF THE MAYOR MANAGER PLAN

The invention and recent growth of the general manager idea in large cities is a product of many influences. Some of these influences would seem to be of reasonably permanent rather than transient character. The larger cities of the United States have developed complex administrative establishments which require strengthened central managerial leadership, direction, and coordination. These cities have also, almost without exception, developed an increasing reliance upon the elected chief executive —a mayor with extensive powers to appoint, to remove, and to direct the heads of administrative agencies—as the main institution of governmental leadership and accountability. The electoral contest for this office has become the primary instrument of popular control of the city government and the main occasion for public education and participation in city affairs. The office of mayor in large cities has, in addition, become more important as a prize in the party battle, its possession one of the significant keys to state and even national party power. It would seem unlikely that any large city would abandon such a governmental and political asset.

But if the institution of the "strong" mayor in large cities has come to stay, then it would also seem that such mayors, no less than the President, need managerial help. The mayor manager idea is a response to this felt need in the large cities. In this sense, the mayor manager plan is in the mainstream of the administrative doctrine heralded by the President's Committee on Administrative Management in 1937, and reaffirmed by the Hoover Commission's later studies of the national government. The central idea of these studies, and dozens of their counterparts in the states, has been to strengthen the position of the elected chief executive in his political and administrative leadership.

The mayor manager plan is likely to dominate the course of large city administrative reorganizations for the next several years. The council manager plan is not likely to break into the large city league, because this plan does not represent an accommodation to either the political or the managerial requirements of the large cities. The emergence of the mayor manager plan has breached the monopolistic claim of the council manager plan to the managerial virtues by presenting the new and strong competition of an alternative manager plan.

Not only is the mayor manager plan likely to hold its own and to extend its scope to most of the largest cities, but it is also probable that it will become an attractive solution for many (perhaps most) of the one hundred and five cities with 100,000 population or more. In contrast with the council manager plan, the mayor manager plan is elastic in its formal arrangements, and it can thus respond more easily to local priorities, customs, and personalities. To the strong mayor cities, it offers an evolutionary transition, buttressing rather than discarding the values which have been built up around the leadership of the elected chief executive. To these cities, the mayor manager plan offers the same managerial gains as does the council manager plan, but at much less risk. The strategic and tactical advantages of such an offer in the political world can hardly be exaggerated.

The mayor manager plan will, as it evolves toward its own institutionalization, be confronted with dilemmas which can now be only partially anticipated. The plan may ultimately acquire its own protective guild of practitioners and advocates, transforming it into an inelastic plan unresponsive to the changing needs of the cities. It may be drowned in a few dramatic "failures."

The mayor manager idea will probably encounter its severest test in the effort to give the manager sufficient power to provide him with adequate leverage to infuse the values of professional management into the administration of a large city government. Philadelphia and New Orleans have made the clearest and strongest effort to insure this result. The Devereux Josephs Commission, in the most complete formulation of the mayor manager plan *(Four Steps to Better Government of New York City,* 1953-54), proposed still greater strength for the manager while making him also more clearly the mayor's administrative agent. The range of variation in managerial power is wide among the cities using the mayor manager idea. The trend in official action and civic opinion—particularly on the manager's appointing power—is not conclusive, but it seems to run toward the grant of greater managerial leverage.

The mayor manager plan will also encounter, perhaps early in its development, the politics-administration dilemma which increasingly be-devils the council manager plan in operation. Can the general manager be at once both a professional administrator and the mayor's second in administrative command? That is, can he be (with the mayor) the effective maker and protagonist of policy proposals which are certain to be con-troversial without sacrificing his professional managerial status? This dilemma plagues the council manager plan even more deeply (because council manager doctrine emphasizes council monopoly over policy while practice underscores the necessity for policy leadership by the manager), but this fact provides merely an advantage rather than a solution for the mayor manager advocates. The trend in mayor manager cities is not yet clear, but the general manager in a large city seems at this stage no more likely to become a career manager in that city than has the city manager in his.

Some observers profess to see in the mayor manager plan merely a compromise step toward the council manager plan. The reverse would seem to be the more likely development, if any such transference is to occur. The essential ingredient of the mayor manager plan is the appoint-ment and removal of the manager by the mayor as the elected chief executive. The distinctive contrasting feature of the council manager plan—the selection of the chief administrator by the city council—was not only something of an historical accident in the United States; it was also a striking anomaly in a country in which the most distinctive political institution is the elected chief executive as the keystone of political, gov-ernmental, and managerial progress. The mayor manager idea has the great and lasting value that it brings the reorganization of our city gov-ernments back into a familiar focus, consistent with our efforts in the national and state governments. In this respect it is an indigenous political idea.

John E. Bebout
37. *Management for Large Cities**

In the Autumn, 1954, number of *Public Administration Review* Pro-fessor Wallace S. Sayre announced that "a new managerial idea is taking hold in the large cities of the United States."[1] The idea, as Mr. Sayre

* From *Public Administration Review.* Summer 1955, pp. 188–195. Reprinted by permission of the American Society for Public Administration.
[1] "The General Manager Idea for Large Cities," 14 *Public Administration Review* 253–258.

explains it, is the double-barreled proposition that the administration of large cities "requires general managerial direction and that this requirement can best be met by establishing under the mayor a general manager who will, in greater or less degree, be the city government's second in administrative command."

The article concentrates on the second part of the proposition, namely, the idea that the best way to achieve over-all management in large cities is through the strong mayor-administrator plan rather than the council-manager plan. In the course of his argument the author makes certain observations about the history, theory, and practice of council-manager government that are virtually an invitation if not a command to further exploration and rejoinder.

I

While Mr. Sayre's article purports to deal simply with the problem of management in "large cities," whatever they are, many of the author's reflections on the council-manager plan raise serious questions about the validity and permanence of the place it has already won in the American municipal scene. Consequently, the article amounts to an oblique attack on the foundations of a system that has been generally hailed both here and abroad as one of the most important American contributions to the science and art of government. It is, therefore, necessary to review the Sayre thesis in a somewhat broader context than would be called for if it actually applied only to the few giant cities.

In developing the case for the "new managerial idea" Mr. Sayre asserts that it is built "upon the strong-mayor tradition as the most widespread form of city government in the United States." He puts great stress upon the office of the elected chief executive "as the center of political leadership and responsibility." An underlying idea running through the article is that the mayor-manager or mayor-administrator plan is more consistent with the history and tradition of the American political system than the council-manager plan with its reliance upon legislative supremacy. The plan, he asserts, "is in the mainstream of the administrative doctrine heralded by the President's Committee on Administrative Management in 1937, and reaffirmed by the Hoover Commission's later studies of the national government. The central idea of these studies, and dozens of their counterparts in the states, has been to strengthen the position of the elected chief executive in his political and administrative leadership."

This is an interesting interpretation of American political and administrative history as it relates to city government. It fits neatly the theory that government, like all Gaul, is or should be divided into three parts, executive, legislative, and judicial. It also accords with the popular notion that, despite the fact that local and state government came first, the pattern hammered out in the Constitutional Convention of 1787 should be the inspiration and guide for all our governments. Unfortunately, it strikes the present writer as about as historical as Parson Weems' story of the cherry tree.

There are no statistics that support the notion that the strong mayor plan is or ever has been "the most widespread form of city government in the United States." On the contrary, the tradition of American city government is one of government by commissions and committees. To be sure, there are more so-called mayor-council cities than there are commission or manager cities. According to the 1955 *Municipal Year Book,* 52 per cent of all cities over 5,000 have the mayor-council plan, whereas 14.1 per cent have the commission, 30.3 per cent have the council-manager plan, and 3.6 per cent operate with town meeting or representative town meeting.[2] However, a substantial majority of the mayor-council cities have what any textbook would rate as the weak mayor rather than the strong mayor plan. Since one of the common characteristics of weak mayor governments is supervision of departments by council committees, which often means the chairmen thereof, many so-called weak mayor governments are much closer in operation to the commission than to the strong mayor plan.

If we go back some years we discover that since 1917 the mayor-council plan has lost a good deal of ground percentagewise, especially in larger cities. Of cities over 30,000, the percentage with the mayor-council plan (weak and strong) dropped from 59 in 1917 to 43 in 1952. During the same period the percentage of council-manager places rose from 5 to 36.[3]

Cincinnati, with council-manager government, is the only city over 500,000 that does not have some variation of the mayor-council plan. It is certainly not without significance, however, that the council-manager plan is the most popular in the next lower population group—250,000 to 500,000—[4] as well as in the 50,000 to 100,000 and 25,000 to 50,000 populations groups. Except for the small group of very large cities, it is in the distinctly small-city class—5,000 to 10,000—that the mayor-council plan has a wide margin over all others. Of these 1,181 cities, 62.2 per cent have the mayor-council plan, 23.7 per cent the council-manager plan.

To say the least, these trends cast doubt on the thesis that the strong

---

[2] *The Municipal Year Book, 1955* (International City Managers' Association, 1955), p. 57.

[3] *Forms of Municipal Government* (National Municipal League, 1953), p. 2.

[4] 39.1 per cent of the cities have the council-manager plan, 34.8 per cent the mayor-council plan, and 26.1 per cent the commission plan. *The Municipal Year Book, 1955,* p. 57.

mayor-administrator plan is better tuned to American tradition than the council-manager plan.

At the end of his article Mr. Sayre complains that a "distinctive . . . feature of the council-manager plan—the selection of the chief administrator by the city council—was not only something of an historical accident in the United States; it was also a striking anomaly in a country in which the most distinctive political institution is the elected chief executive as the keystone of political, governmental, and managerial progress. The mayor manager idea," he continues, "has the great and lasting value that it brings the reorganization of our city governments back into a familiar focus, consistent with our efforts in the national and state governments. In this respect it is an indigenous political idea."

Despite the fine dash of patriotic fervor in this peroration, perhaps one may be permitted to ask certain questions. How old does a political idea have to be in order to be "indigenous"? If the council-manager idea of the twentieth century was an historical accident, was not the elected Presidency of the late eighteenth century equally an historical accident— especially since the makers of the Constitution did their best to protect the Presidency from the evils presumed to be inherent in popular election of the chief magistrate? Or, having once made that accidental but unquestionably happy discovery, must we stigmatize all future and variant avenues toward "political, governmental, and managerial progress" at whatever level of government as nongenuine?

These questions begin to have more force when one reflects on the failure of most states to develop the office of governor in the image of that of President. The recent report of the Commission on Intergovernmental Relations points out that "today, few States have an adequate executive branch headed by a governor who can be held generally accountable for executing and administering the laws of the State."[5] In other words, very few *states* have anything analogous to the strong mayor plan that Mr. Sayre finds so natural to the American scene. As already suggested, an examination of the charters of mayor-council cities would also show that there is only a relatively small number of cities that have as yet been prepared to entrust their elected chief executive with the powers necessary to justify holding him "generally accountable for executing and administering" the affairs of the city. The truth is that the strong mayor plan is largely a myth, or at best an objective.

Of course, it is true that state Little Hoover and economy and efficiency commissions going back almost half a century have been urging the

---

[5] *A Report to the President for Transmittal to the Congress* (Government Printing Office, 1955), p. 42.

strengthening of the office of governor. Some progress has been made in this direction. In like manner there has been a tendency in some mayor-council cities that have not gone over to the council-manager plan to add, bit by bit, new strength to the office of mayor. This is all to the good for the states and cities concerned, but one wonders why the generally more substantial and spectacular progress resulting from the adoption of the council-manager plan in approximately 1,300 communities should not be regarded as at least an equally characteristic American achievement.

Mr. Sayre is careful to avoid referring specifically to the American doctrine of the separation of powers as a justification for the strong mayor plan. Yet what he is saying in effect is that the separation of powers between independently elected legislative and executive branches, which is one of the prime characteristics of the United States government and a theoretical characteristic of all our state governments, should be embraced at the municipal level. This justification, naturally enough, has not escaped the attention of persons advocating adoption of strong mayor-administrator charters.

For example, the final report of the Newark Charter Commission, dated September 3, 1953, lists "a *clear separation of powers* between the council as the legislative body, and the mayor as the head of the city administration" as the first of "six basic principles deemed essential to efficient and responsive local government." The second principle is that the mayor "be the chief policy maker" and the third calls for "unified administration of all local services" under the mayor. The council is, however, supposed to "serve as an independent critic of the exercise" of the mayor's executive power and checks and balances between the mayor and council are stressed. The commission's own words reveal the dilemma that is inherent in the separation of powers system. In the policy area, for example, the commission declares that the council "will legislate on matters of public policy," but "the mayor, who will be directly accountable to the people, . . . will be the chief policy maker." Although the record of the first year of Newark city government under its new strong mayor-administrator charter is generally a good one, the check and balance system has already produced some unfortunate conflicts between the mayor and council and the council has succeeded in preventing the mayor from appointing certain well qualified persons of his choice to important posts.

But the deadlocks, the buck-passing, and the evasions of responsibility that are common occurrences in governments organized on the basis of the separation of powers are too well known to need recounting here. Nor is this the occasion to argue the ultimate merits of the separation of powers principle for the higher levels of American government. It may be appropriate to observe, however, that the circumstances that led to incorporation of the separation of powers into the United States Constitution were of such a special character that they do not necessarily indicate it as a principle of universal or even of wide application. It probably was and still is the most practical solution of the complex problem of organizing government at the federal level. It may be the best solution for most states despite the fact that few of them have followed the national model closely enough to give it a good try.

A basic reason for resort to the separation of powers is to compensate through the elected chief executive for deficiencies in representativeness and leadership in the legislature. Such deficiencies are perhaps unavoidable both in the Congress and in many state legislatures. The bicameral system is an almost insuperable obstacle to responsible government based upon legislative supremacy. Fortunately all but eight American cities have found that they can get along very well with a one-house municipal legislature and the overwhelming majority of them have discovered that it is not necessary to have a large and unwieldly body in order to achieve representativeness. The improvement in the quality and effectiveness in city councils has assuredly been a major element in the general improvement in the quality of city government which has occurred since James Bryce pronounced the government of cities to be the American people's "one conspicuous failure." While much of the improvement of city councils has been associated with the spread of the council-manager plan, it has also occurred in many mayor-council cities.

It seems hard to believe that if Mr. Sayre had taken full account of this phase of municipal history, he would have embraced the conclusion that the most promising if not the only road to municipal progress lies in maximizing the office of the elected mayor both as chief executive and as chief policy maker.

II

Let us now turn specifically to the problems involved in strengthening the governments of our largest cities. First, it is clear that the choice of means for improving management must depend heavily upon the kind of city council it is deemed desirable and possible to have. No one, for example, would suggest trying to make an appointed manager responsible to the present bicameral New York City Council. If the council-manager plan were ever to be considered seriously for the city of New York, it would have to be on the assumption that the present City Council would be replaced by a reasonably wieldy and representative one-house body. It would also be hopeless to try to base a council-manager operation on the present 50-member, completely ward-elected, Chicago City Council. It is almost equally impossible to imagine a sound council-manager government with the 35-member council, composed of 25 ward representatives and 10 aldermen elected at large, proposed by the recent report of the Chicago Home Rule Commission.[6]

Large cities are complex entities. If there is any representative pattern or formula that will work best in all cases it has not yet been discovered or generally agreed upon. The tailoring of a city council to the needs and political realities in such a city is, therefore, one of the most difficult problems in representative government and one which calls for a certain amount of boldness and willingness to experiment. It is well worth the effort, however, because a sound city council is the surest first step toward good management, as it is toward wise policy making.

Mr. Sayre seems to suggest that there is something inherent in the nature of large cities that requires the leadership of an elected mayor who holds the principal prerogatives of a chief executive—"extensive powers to appoint, to remove, and to direct the heads of administrative agencies."

Of course policy leadership is necessary in large cities. It is also necessary or at least highly desirable in medium-sized and small cities. Fortunately, out of the richness of American municipal experience, we have learned that there is more than one way of providing for it. There are, for example, some pretty big council-manager cities that have not suffered for lack of policy leadership. In Cincinnati a number of vigorous personalities, beginning with Murray Seasongood, elected by their council colleagues to serve as mayor, have been more effective policy leaders than many a separately elected mayor enjoying substantial prerogatives of the traditional chief executive. Since the fall of Pendergast the same thing has been true of Kansas City where the mayor is elected separately from his colleagues on the council and has proved to be a political leader in the best sense of the word.

Before comparing the relative leadership potentialities in the strong-mayor and council-manager plans more closely, we should, perhaps, pause to consider just what we mean by leadership in city government. Much that passes for leadership in politics is strangely reminiscent of the sound and fury that accompanies a battle between two bulls. It is a matter of great importance to the contestants and may be to their more ardent partisans, but it has very little to do with the public interest.

Admittedly, this personalized counterfeit of public-oriented leadership may appear in connection with any form of government. But surely no sophisticated student of politics or administration now doubts that form has something to do with selecting the people who choose or qualify to play the game, and even more to do with the rules by which the game

---

[6] *Modernizing a City Government* (University of Chicago Press, 1954), p. 320.

is played. This unstated assumption, indeed, underlies Mr. Sayre's whole thesis.

Our common objective must be to find the formal or structural framework that will be most conducive to municipal progress. This means that we should seek a structure that will be as favorable as possible to the rise of elected leaders who are more concerned with municipal objectives than with their own future, more anxious to achieve substantive results than to wield power.

Experience indicates that, on the whole, the council-manager plan has certain positive advantages over the mayor-council plan as a vehicle for such constructive leadership. The basic reason for this is that the design of council-manager government is essentially functional. It is the simplest available structural arrangement for obtaining representative decisions on policy and competent execution of those decisions.

The structure of the strong-mayor, separation-of-powers plan, however, reflects the preoccupation of its designers with power and the struggle for power. In the endeavor to control the lust for power, it actually diverts attention from the public objectives to the private or personal perquisites and incidents of politics and limits participation by those who are unwilling or unable to compete on these terms. Even in the absence of strong personal or partisan rivalry, the normal interaction of the parts of the system tends to generate unnecessary friction and conflict. These tendencies adversely affect both short- and long-term policy planning and continuous, skilled administration.

The mayor in council-manager cities is usually chosen by his colleagues on the council because they deem him their most effective spokesman. If he is separately elected, he is likely to have been nominated to lead the winning slate of council candidates. In either case, there is no built-in invitation to bickering between the mayor and the majority of council. Moreover, the fact that the mayor has no personal appointments of consequence to make and no orders to issue to administrative personnel eliminates patronage as a potential source of discord between him and his associates. And since the mayor is the leader only as long as he speaks for the majority, he can be replaced or by-passed by a new mayor or *de facto* leader if he gets hopelessly out of line. All of this helps to account for the fact that issues of policy, including the basic issue of maintaining or of raising the quality of administration, tend to loom larger in comparison with mere questions of personality in elections in council-manager cities than they do in others.

Another advantage of council-manager government is that it does not put all its leadership eggs in one basket. Neither the city charter nor the fact of popular election can be counted on to endow a legally strong mayor with the skill and wisdom to be the kind of leader in policy and administration that a city should have. But, if a "strong" mayor fails to provide proper leadership, there is generally no one who can fill the breach. Members of the council are in no position, legally or politically, to compensate for his deficiencies. They are on the other side of a wall and their natural bent is to throw bricks at the mayor and make political capital out of his weaknesses, not to bolster him. An ambitious council-man or a leader in a rival faction or party may be grooming to succeed the mayor, but until he has the office his efforts are likely to be disruptive rather than constructive in terms of their effect on both policy and administration. This tendency of the separation of powers system has been demonstrated repeatedly at all levels of government.

In a council-manager city, however, the mayor is simply the first among equals. He is presumed to be the chief policy spokesman of the majority in council, but leadership can be and often is shared by several council members in a manner that would be difficult or impossible in a mayor-council city. Deficiencies on the part of the mayor can thus be made up by, literally, putting leadership in commission.

In addition the council-manager plan has the manager, a leadership asset of no mean importance. There are no people more firm in their determination to keep managers out of politics in the ordinary sense of the word than the managers themselves. On the other hand, the manager is recognized not only as the council's agent for executing policy but also as the council's servant in developing plans and proposals for its consideration. While responsibility for public advocacy of proposed policies is vested in the council and in the mayor as its chief spokesman, the manager is responsible for maintaining a continuous flow of public information of the kind that provides a basis for public understanding and evaluation of policy proposals. Thus the code of ethics adopted by the International City Managers' Association describes the manager "as a community leader" who "submits policy proposals to the council and provides the council . . . a basis for making decisions on community goals." Speaking of the same function of the manager, Leonard G. Howell, city manager of Des Moines, Iowa, and former president of the International City Managers' Association, listed as one of the obligations of the manager a duty to "assume his role as a responsible civic leader—not a political leader—and act accordingly." Elaborating on this point, Mr. Howell declared that "a manager must be more than a technical administrator . . . he must find out the needs and desires of the people of his community and recommend to council solutions to those problems, including the ways and the means to accomplish them—he should be able to carry to the people of his city by word of mouth an accurate and competent account of what his city is doing—never as a political proposition, but as one primarily interested in and responsible for the civic welfare of his community."[7]

Anyone who has taken the trouble to follow the voluminous professional literature that flows from experience with council-manager government knows that an increasing amount of attention is being devoted to this aspect of the manager's function as it relates to his dealings with the council, with municipal employees, and with the general public.[8]

It is now clear, if there was ever any doubt about it, that when a city hires a manager it should expect to hire not only a good generalist in municipal administration but also a sensitive civic and public relations consultant to the city council. Thus the manager is to the city government something like what an efficient executive secretary is to a large voluntary civic, welfare, or other community agency.

It was suggested earlier that leadership in council-manager government could be and often is shared by the mayor and other members of the city council. Actually, it is also shared between them and the manager. The mayor and council members handle the conventionally political aspects of the task and the manager plays a role in the area of public information, the visible dimensions of which will depend to a considerable extent on how much of the limelight the mayor and council want to reserve for themselves.

It is sometimes true, as managers themselves have complained, that mayors and councilmen are too ready to let the manager carry the ball. Whether or not this is a special weakness of the council-manager plan as some have suggested is open to question, for many a "strong mayor" has failed equally to give effective attention to the constructive aspects of political leadership. In any event, in a council-manager government inadequate leadership on the part of the people's elected representatives can at least to some degree be compensated for by an articulate and effective manager speaking with the knowledge and consent of the council which may fire him any time it feels he is not representing it properly. It is safe to say that many a city has been saved from civic or governmental stagnation because of the professional civic leadership that the manager has been able to bring to bear in the making and explanation of public policy.

[7] *What Are the Elements of Continued Successful Operation for the Council-Manager Plan of Municipal Government?* published by the Colorado Municipal League as a contribution to the thinking and action of the citizens, elected officials, and administrators for the council-manager cities of Colorado, 1951.

[8] See especially numerous articles in *Public Management*—for example, "Relations of the Manager with the Public," a report prepared for discussion at the 40th Annual Conference of the International City Managers' Association held at St. Petersburg, Florida, December 5–8, 1954, in 37 *Public Management* 77–83.

This brings us to consideration of the "politics-administration dilemma which," according to Mr. Sayre, "increasingly bedevils the council-manager plan in operation" and also is a problem for the mayor-administrator plan. Mr. Sayre is able to comfort himself with the thought that the mayor-administrator plan may have the advantage in the ultimate resolution of this dilemma by imagining that "council-manager doctrine emphasizes council monopoly over policy while practice underscores the necessity for policy leadership by the manager. . . ." The council-manager plan is today a going operation of some 40-odd years' standing. Many theories, appropriate and inappropriate, have been propounded in connection with it. The plan continues to gain ground, however, on the basis of practice, and the practice is essentially that described in the preceding paragraphs. This practice, more naturally and efficiently than that of any other plan, reflects that "unity of the governmental process," which the Temporary State Commission to Study the Organizational Structure of the Government of the City of New York accepted as fundamental to a sound system of government.[9] In developing its concept of this essential unity the commission asserted that "politics and administration are not airtight departments separated from each other by clearly identifiable walls. They are merely phases in the continuous process of government, which, in itself, is a phase in the process of social organization." Splendid! No better justification for the council-manager plan in practice has ever been written. The commission was able to fall into the trap of using this as an argument for preferring the strong mayor plan to the council-manager plan because it saw the council-manager plan through the haze of the curious notion about council-manager doctrine or theory that Mr. Sayre later expounded in his article.

III

The foregoing observations on the practice as distinct from more or less gratuitous theories of council-manager and mayor-council governments do not, of course, tell us what form of government most of the country's dozen or so giant cities will or should have in the future. The purpose of this article has been primarily to try to keep the record straight and see to it that the claims of America's distinctive contribution to municipal government, government based upon the marriage of legislative supremacy with professional competence, shall not be sold down the river.

---

[9] *Four Steps to Better Government of New York City: A Plan for Action.* Report of the Temporary State Commission to Study the Organizational Structure of the Government of the City of New York, 1953, p. 33. Devereux C. Josephs was chairman of the commission and Wallace S. Sayre was director of research.

The present writer is inclined to believe that most of these largest cities will continue to operate with some variation of the mayor-council form. In some cases the great unlikelihood of reorganizing the city council so that it would provide a safe basis for administration by a manager solely responsible to it is reason enough for this prediction, though it may be hoped that political ingenuity will not cease to work with the problem of giving our largest cities, as well as our states, more effective and more representative legislatures. In other cases, tradition and entrenched political interests would make a break to the council-manager plan pretty difficult to achieve.

Mr. Sayre points out that in some large cities the office of mayor is very "important as a prize in the party battle, its possession one of the significant keys to state and even national party power." He adds that "it would seem unlikely that any large city would abandon such a governmental and political asset." Maybe so, but it should not be imagined that mayors and council members in council-manager cities, whether elected on party or on nonpartisan ballots, have no influence in behalf of their cities in Washington or the state capitol. The recent past president of the American Municipal Association, for example, was Mayor William E. Kemp of Kansas City who, though elected mayor on a nonpartisan ballot, has been a highly effective leader in the dominant national party in his city and state.

Assuredly there will continue to be mayor-council cities. Let us hope that more and more of them will give their mayors the prerogatives necessary to be effective chief executives and policy leaders. This writer shares with Mr. Sayre the hope that those cities will learn how to make the maximum use of professional managerial talent. Mr. Sayre believes he sees a trend toward appointment by the mayor of a single general administrator to be his second in command with respect to the entire city administration. Actually, the number of cases that it is yet possible to analyze is so inconclusive on this point that it is far from certain that the single top administrator is necessarily better for every large city than some variation on the Philadelphia plan of providing the mayor with several high-level administrative aides.[10] The problem of providing the mayor with an adequate professional staff is not altogether different from that of staffing the office of governor or of President, or even that of manager. What is needed is continuing experimentation and objective analysis of experience with various methods of staffing the chief executives in our larger governments. Mr. Sayre disclaims any wish to develop a new cult interested in

---

[10] Charlton F. Chute, *Modern Ideas on Administrative Assistants for the Mayor in Large American Cities,* (privately published, May 17, 1954).

promoting the mayor-manager or mayor-administrator plan. Premature identification of a "trend" in that direction might conceivably tend to discourage further progress by making it appear that "the way" had already been found.

There are, of course, many matters in connection with the government of our cities that cry out for further research, as Mr. Sayre himself has suggested. Some of these have to do primarily with the best ways to organize professional assistance for elected political and citizen officials. Some of them have to do with the relation between form and structure, on the one hand, and political organization and leadership, on the other. Some of them have to do with the ways and means by which citizens may best organize and conduct themselves through voluntary political and civic organizations to get and maintain good government. Some of them have to do with the relations between local and state and national politics.

There is special need for increased attention to research on many problems of political and civic leadership, organization, and action. In the long run no government will remain permanently far above the level of the capacity of a fairly good cross section of the citizens to work together through political and civic agencies for sound, common objectives.

Steve Matthews
38. Types of Managerial Leadership*

Political disagreement and conflict at the local level have been generally replaced by a discussion of the issues. People are more and more concerned about needed public improvements, better schools, better garbage service, better utility service, bigger and better airports, planning for the future, an ample water supply, and many other policy issues. However, an intelligent discussion of the issues is possible only when civic leaders and citizens in general are informed.

Just what is the city manager's role in leadership? Before analyzing this subject, it should be remembered that the art of management applies to city managers, and airport administrators alike with only slight changes from time to time and from one situation to another. The three basic positions which a manager can take in leadership involve many factors relative to his success or failure.

NECK MANAGER. The first type of manager is the neck leader or neck

---

* From *Public Management.* March 1957, pp. 50–53. Reprinted with permission of publisher.

manager. He is the man who leads with his neck most of the time. There are many actions which mark him as such. For example, he makes a recommendation on all agenda items. In order to eliminate all doubt, he likes to write on the agenda: "Recommended by the City Manager." He recommends policy to the council in public meetings without prior discussion with the council. He presents engineering facts and figures to prove everything that he places on the agenda. There is little alternative except to accept that which is placed on the agenda by the city manager. Many times, however, he is statistically right and politically wrong.

The neck leader settles all controversial problems with citizen groups prior to the council meetings. The neck manager also makes all administrative and committee appointments authorized by the charter without consulting the council in advance. After all, the charter gives him authority for appointments. As you can see, the neck leader sometimes heads for trouble.

Council members never like to pick up their evening paper and learn for the first time about the manager firing the police chief. But in following such procedure, the neck manager feels that councilmen need a good jolt now and then, and he seems to enjoy the technique of surprise. The neck leader can always point to the charter provision that the manager can hire and fire department heads.

The neck leader generally speaks to the press for the entire city government, including the council and the mayor. He always knows what the mayor and council will do and say. When he gets the council out on a limb, there is always someone standing by to conveniently saw it off.

FANNY MANAGER. The second type of manager is the fanny leader. The fanny manager's attitude is, "Let the mayor and council do all the thinking and all the work. If they want something, they can mention it to me and I will get the job done." The fanny manager generally takes action on major projects and matters only at the insistence of the council.

This manager operates the city by ear. He does little advance planning and seldom anticipates problems. Unfortunately, a lot of cities are run by ear.

The fanny manager does only those things that people call him about. The telephone is thus a pretty good indicator of the type of manager he is, and whether he is a fanny manager. At the same time, the quality of services in a city can generally be judged by the presence or absence of the telephone call.

SHOULDER MANAGER. There is another type of leader; the manager who leads with his shoulder. He leads through the council. He develops the management team through the department heads and the council, and he leads through direction. He pushes occasionally, but seldom pulls, realiz-

304 / Urban Government

ing that he has to stimulate action and desire in the city personnel and in the council.

Naturally, the personality of the manager generally determines the approach in leadership. While there are undoubtedly many other types, we can all agree that most managers use a combination of the three types of leadership mentioned. Experience changes us from time to time and as we move from city to city. Yet, no two of us fit the same pattern because we are all different.

Digressing on this point, I would like to note that in my 17 years as a manager, I have taken action indicative of all three types of managers. At times, I've been quoted on matters that strictly involved council policy, and I have been severely criticized for it. I will be frank and admit that the newspaper always quotes me right; it just doesn't always come out in print the way I *meant* to say it.

It is amazing how much time we can spend figuring out ways to avoid facing problems we don't like to work on. For example, what manager likes to initiate tax surveys; recommend the annexation of a large area against the residents' will; work on building or electrical codes; or fire an employee? There are a number of things that we do not like to do, and these often require a push from the city council. But, there are a lot of things about management that we have to do, whether we want to or not. We must learn to face the issues.

Undoubtedly, there are numerous actions which do not appeal to airport managers: (1) Come in as a new manager and recommend a planning and financial survey be made. Even though an airport manager fully realizes that such a report is most desirable because of the weight it carries with banks and investment firms, he may hesitate to recommend such action in that it might reflect on his own ability to conduct such a survey; (2) Negotiate leases with airlines and locally based operators; (3) Ask a restaurant concessionnaire to improve his service and clean up the premises; (4) Get caught in a campaign from the local businessmen demanding additional airline service for the city.

Any manager or administrator could make a long list of things he dislikes to do. But failure to do them is what makes a fanny manager. We ultimately have to face the issues—whether we are pushed or go voluntarily. The best course is to be well prepared, have the facts, know with whom you are dealing, and go to it.

CITY COUNCIL LEADERSHIP. Shoulder leadership is by far the most desirable type, with its philosophy of working *with* people and *through* the city council.

How can a city manager share his experiences with his council? First, he lets the council help him develop his ideas. Private council sessions are the best for this type of discussion because they afford the manager the opportunity to study the council's weaknesses and strong points. He helps them bridge over their weak points.

It is the shoulder manager's job to develop key civic leaders as future councilmen. He stimulates their interest and keeps them informed. Good training grounds for future councilmen are the city planning commission, civil service board, and the park and recreation commission.

Strong leadership involves salesmanship. Equally important is the ability to set goals, that is to determine the final objectives which underlie any successful program. The shoulder manager will lift the council's sights. The size of the city is not important. Actually, the smaller city may require more vitality of leadership. In a larger city the manager leads through others because he has more personnel and a better trained staff. In many respects it is thus easier to manage.

In educating his city council to good management practices and policies, the city manager has a big job. New councilmen are generally inexperienced. The manager is placed in the position of leader and educator. Somehow, he must relay his years of experience to his council in a matter of a few weeks or months.

The early experience of the public works director in a large city illustrates this point. Soon after he went to work as chief of an engineering field party for the Texas State Highway Department back in the early 1930's, he was promoted to construction inspector for a 50-mile concrete highway project. Though he was well qualified, he had never had any previous experience as an inspector. The district engineer of the state highway department called in the general contractor for the project and introduced the new inspector with these words: "This is Mr. Oldham. He's going to be the state inspector on this highway job. He hasn't had any experience on this type of work. But, you'd better do a bang-up job of training him because in two weeks he will be telling you what to do!"

This situation is equally true of a city council. When a manager starts out with a new council, he had better do a pretty good job of helping them and letting them know what their job is. After three or four weeks in the job of policy-making, the new councilmen will have felt the pulse of the public, and will have all kinds of ideas. The matter of selling your bosses on consistent policies is vitally important.

City managers spend the bulk of their time educating the public, the city council, the city staff and employees, and influential groups in the city. A shoulder manager tries to win acceptance for the council's program and goals.

A shoulder manager knows that he has to have close associations with his council. Perhaps the best means of developing such an association is through the techniques of "off-sessions" and special luncheons. One of the most difficult problems to be faced in this situation, however, is that the newspapers need to be sold on the necessity of such sessions. To accept this arrangement, the manager will need to gain the support of the papers by keeping them informed as to where such sessions are held and, in all likelihood, what matters are being discussed. Caution must be used to assure that no formal action is taken at such meeting and definitely that no final decisions are made. Rather, such meeting should be used for informative purposes, where all views may be aired without worry of repercussion. Such informal meetings, with their benefits of understanding and mutual confidence, can be developed as a principal source of council harmony. The council must plan and know where it is going. "Off-sessions" are the only way of accomplishing this purpose.

A shoulder manager discusses major problems in advance with his council, employees, and the citizens. He tries to anticipate things before they occur. For example, you can usually anticipate whether or not the public will accept an ordinance before it is passed. You can gain a lot of good experience from other cities. An off-street parking ordinance is always difficult to pass; the churches come in and say you are stopping all church growth. They may have you down to a point where you are an infidel before it is over. Whenever you get into the rights of individuals and private interests, you must anticipate a variety of stock questions. Brief the council on the answers before the private interests come in with their side. If by anticipating the questions you have reasonable answers ready, the battle is half won.

Most problems can be anticipated. You know when a bond issue will be needed for expansion of facilities. Does everyone else? You know when a board or particular group in the community is going to ask about certain major problems. Do you have the answers ready?

There are a number of other problems you have to anticipate. For instance, on streets with a high traffic count, a congestion problem may develop from cars piling up for a left turn. This is obviously a traffic engineering problem, but it may be larger in scope if you are forced to remove curb parking in front of business houses to gain additional traffic lanes. In one such situation after talking with the city council about it, the manager decided not to make the change immediately. Sometimes you can be too efficient and anticipate a problem too soon! As a result you may get ahead of the people. So, in this case it was decided to let the traffic stack up two or three blocks. Pretty soon, citizens started calling to tell the city to put in left turn lanes. You have to let the situation get bad sometimes before people will realize that something must be done. Then, the solution is easier to sell.

These examples may sound elementary, but they do stress the importance of timing. Timing has a lot to do with public acceptance, and favorable public opinion is what keeps a city council in office. This same proposition of timing can be applied to airport management. In negotiating with airlines for increased revenues on municipal facilities, talk to them at a time of the year when traffic is good and income is high.

We do not remove curb parking on streets during slow business months; neither do we establish one-way street patterns at that time of year. Merchants will say that it is ruining their business. We can do it better during the Christmas season when everyone is downtown and business is good. You can take such action strictly in the interest of the Christmas rush.

DEVELOPING POLICY. The underlying principle of all decision making should be consistency of policy. But, change the policy if you cannot follow the one which you already have. This is extremely important. Don't keep it forever just because someone else had it.

Policy must be flexible. It must fit the case at hand as well as the case down the road. Good policy can be judged on this basis. Sometimes a group will come and make a request in regard to a specific problem. The decision rendered should be based on the idea of what will be done when similar requests are made by other groups in the future. Future needs must be anticipated so that policy may remain consistent. The answer given to one group must be consistent with the one given to the next group.

Survey other cities as to policy. Then, frame policy to fit the specific needs of your city. That is the way the best policy is created—by studying other policies and tailoring them to your situation.

Stay in the background. Push and lead through the council and the staff. The council is elected for its leadership. Get things done through others, but avoid differences. It is practically axiomatic that in most council-manager differences, the manager generally comes out second and goes out first. When you are right, few people remember. When you are wrong, no one forgets. Keep the citizenry with you.

Develop and share your ideas with the council. Give them credit for a good idea. Pass the glory on to the team; there is enough glory for everyone. Generally, the more you try to pass on glory to others, the more comes to you. And in the end, credit is shared by the entire group.

A person's success and tenure always depend on how well he can develop cooperation and unity. In municipal affairs, people will not tolerate leadership that cannot get along with itself and develop "community thinking." What do people look for in their community leaders? They respect most those persons with definite opinions but who can reason and compromise in the spirit of progress. Citizens always recognize results. They notice lack of cooperation and conflict. They respect cooperation and unity. They expect progress and, finally, they expect a spirit of optimism and cooperation among their leaders.

Robert Moses

39. Are Cities Dead?*

I picked up a New York City paper one morning recently and was appalled by the space and emphasis given to an obscure assistant professor with no record of administration, who, enjoying a foundation grant and speaking for a regional civic organization, prophesied imminent chaos and the early disintegration of our metropolis. He maintained that there are 1467 municipal agencies, fiercely independent, viciously uncoordinate, and shamelessly spending taxpayers' money in frantic insanity.

These counsels of despair come just as the Congress plans a Department of Urban Affairs of Cabinet rank. If the new Secretary begins by believing that American cities are doomed in spite of the increasingly rapid shift from rural to urban centers, he will accomplish little. If emphasis is on anything but local initiative, the effect will be zero, and we shall have merely elevated a bureau to an expensive department and put another bureaucrat in orbit. Anyway, if we are to have a new Secretary, let us see that he believes in cities.

There are plenty of things that are wrong with our cities. These things should not be slurred over or forgotten. There are many failures which should be appraised. But why exaggerate? Why imply that the faults are beyond redemption? Why minimize evidence of progress? Why ignore the remarkable people and achievements which make our big cities the powerful magnets they are?

One of the most-quoted Jeremiahs who inveigh against the condition of our cities is Lewis Mumford, author of *The City in History*. He is widely acclaimed in the academic world. I object to these Jeremiahs primarily because they attempt to poison a rising generation of ordinarily optimistic young Americans. There is another good reason for deprecating this school of thought: those who undermine the very foundations and *raison d'être* of cities, and not merely the incidental mistakes of individuals, make municipal administration increasingly unattractive and relegate it finally to the lowest politics and the poorest talent.

* From the *Atlantic Monthly*. January 1962, pp. 55–58. Reprinted with permission of publisher and author.

Suppose we were to ask some of our best and most ambitious mayors, battling valiantly for limited, immediate objectives, whether concentrations of population are beyond improvement, whether the *raison d'être* of the metropolis is gone, and whether their plans for redevelopment are essentially futile. I mean men like Lee of New Haven, Dilworth of Philadelphia, Miriani of Detroit, and former Mayor Morrison of New Orleans. Are the citizens who believe in such men now to be told that their trust has been betrayed?

There is, indeed, much wrong with cities—big and little—but the answer is not to abandon or completely rebuild them on abstract principles. Only on paper can you disperse concentrations of population and create small urban stars with planned satellites around them. In the course of many years devoted to reclamation of water front, manufacturing of topsoil to cover thousands of acres of new parks, buying and preserving large areas of natural woodlands and shores in advance of the realtor and subdivider, planting thousands of trees along parkways and expressways, building hundreds of playgrounds, planning cultural centers in place of decaying tenements, tightening zoning and building laws, restricting billboards, opposing entrenched power companies and other utility corporations to keep the basic natural public resources inalienable, and stopping water pollution, I never caught a glimpse of the breast beaters who are now touted as pundits in this field. I saw none of them in our long battle to establish eleven thousand acres of Jamaica Bay with New York City as a permanent, protected unspoiled natural game refuge. Is Jamaica Bay a symbol of urban rot, or is it just too small and obscure to attract the attention of the critics?

Recently, a number of planners and civic leaders in New York wrote a letter to the press advocating the conversion to a park of the whole of Welfare Island, a wedge in the East River presently occupied by hospitals. I tried this twenty-five years ago, before new hospitals and a bridge on the wrong side of the river were built, but the hospital commissioner poured abuse on me and was supported by the then mayor. It is too late now, because of the huge investment in modern institutions and vehicular access. Meanwhile, we have built adequate parks on Randall's and Ward's Island a little way up the East River and a pedestrial bridge to Ward's, which the paper planners never mention.

In his Baccalaureate Address for 1961, President A. Whitney Griswold of Yale said, among other things:

"I shall not attempt to recite here all the worst things that are said about us or to refute them by pointing out that just as bad (or worse) things go on in the countries which say them. Neither shall I attempt to itemize the shortcomings which we ourselves acknowledge. It is enough to remind ourselves of the nature of the great, national, hundred per cent

American jeremiad. It goes like this. We are soft. We are spoiled. We are lazy, flabby, undisciplined, in poor physical condition, poorly educated, beguiled with gadgets, bedazzled by sex, uninterested in anything but our own comfort, unprepared for the responsibilities fate has placed upon us, unready for our destiny. In a word, we are decadent. Do I exaggerate the case? Listen to an American voice in the chorus of American self-criticism. I quote.

"The arena, the tall tenement, the mass contests and exhibitions, the football matches, the international beauty contests, the strip tease made ubiquitous by advertisement, the constant titillation of the senses by sex, liquor and violence—all in true Roman style.

". . . These are symptoms of the end: Magnifications of demoralized power, minifications of life. When these signs multiply, Necropolis is near, though not a stone has yet crumbled. For the barbarian has already captured the city from within. Come, hangman! Come, vulture!

"This is not an editorial from Pravda or one of the lighter touches from a tirade by Castro," President Griswold continued. "It is a view of present-day American life by Lewis Mumford in his most recent book, *The City in History*. It is a view that is shared, or at any rate expressed, by many Americans from pulpits, classrooms, editorial offices, and high places in government.

"Are things really that bad? If they are, heaven help us—and heaven will not help us until we help ourselves. If things are not that bad, why do Mr. Mumford and so many of his fellow citizens say they are? Perhaps they haven't got the facts straight. . . . Maybe the whole of Western civilization is decadent and, since we are the leaders of it, we are the most decadent of all."

The physical beauties of a city can, no doubt, be exaggerated, but no balanced observer will ignore them. Europeans coming to New York City for the first time are ecstatic about the view of lower Manhattan in the early morning from a great liner as it passes through upper New York Bay; mid-Manhattan seen from the Triborough Bridge at sundown; the jeweled diadem spread before the jet flyer at night; the clean gossamer cobwebs of its suspension bridges; the successive bustle and tomblike silences of its streets; the fantastic daring, imagination, and aspiration of its builders. Visitors are, of course, aware of New York's congested traffic, but is the slowdown any worse than that in London or Paris?

Admittedly, the gasoline motor has provided us with problems which did not exist in ancient Rome. But the jaundiced eye of the city historian sees no signs of achievement and progress. He is obsessed with the harlotry and the decline and fall of Rome and Babylon, and the beams and motes blot out Jones Beach.

Here is one example of this counsel of despair: "Such form as the metropolis achieves is crowdform: the swarming bathing beach by the sea or the body of spectators in the boxing arena or the football stadium. With the increase of private motor cars, the streets and avenues become parking lots, and to move traffic at all, vast expressways gouge through the city and increase the demand for further parking lots and garages. In the act of making the core of the metropolis accessible, the planners of congestion have already almost made it uninhabitable. . . .

"We must restore to the city the maternal, life-nurturing functions, the autonomous activities, the symbiotic associations that have long been neglected or suppressed. For the city should be an organ of love; and the best economy of cities is the care and culture of men."

Nowhere does the author even remotely tell us how these "symbiotic associations" can be revived and encouraged or where he would start with this renaissance.

As to housing, we read many similar grotesque misstatements. For example, Mumford says: "Stuyvesant Town was built by a private insurance company with generous aid by the State: but its residential density of 393 per acre remains that of a slum. Despite its inner open spaces, this housing would require eighty additional acres to provide the park and playground space now regarded as desirable, nineteen more than the entire project without buildings."

Here are the facts. The state had nothing to do with this project. It is not a slum in any sense. It is not overpopulated. New York City and the Metropolitan Life Insurance Company substituted for filthy tenements excellent, modern, low-rental housing with plenty of light and air and views all around on less than 20 per cent land coverage. Everyone familiar with housing and recreation knows that no such huge additional space as eighty acres is needed for parks and playgrounds in a project totaling seventy-two acres.

Similar distortions appear in dicta regarding traffic.

"In the interest of an unimpeded traffic flow highway engineers produce vast clover leaves even in low density areas with limited cross traffic, where there is no reason whatever why the arterial flow should not be occasionally halted as in a city street."

Every competent engineer knows that halting through traffic at a clover leaf would produce strangulation and is the negation of all accepted standards for limited-access highways.

The prosperous suburbanite is as proud of his ranch home as the owner of the most gracious villa of Tuscany. In the suburbs the hiker finds the long brown path leading wherever he chooses, by day, in filtered sunlight, or by evening, in the midst of the rhythmic orchestration of tree frogs. The little identical suburban boxes of average people, which differ only in color and planting, represent a measure of success unheard of by hundreds of millions on other continents. Small plots reflect not merely the rapacity of realtors but the caution of owners who do not want too much grass to cut and snow to shovel—details too intimate for the historian.

The real-estate subdivisions east of the city are not all there is to Long Island. The South Shore is my home. It is still mostly unspoiled, well protected, and largely in public ownership. Those of us who work at the problems that critics chatter about go down to the sea in cars and ships for respite, to fish, swim, soak up sun, and refresh our spirits, and in off seasons to wander in the anonymous enveloping ocean mist. Our fog appears, not stealing in on cat feet, but as a ghostly emanation of the sea, in silence punctuated only by the muffled bell and intermittent warning of the buoys along the hidden channels. Here we knit up the ravell'd sleeve of care. Who are these pundits to say we have neglected our problems or that others might solve them better?

The cultures, amenities, and attractions of cities, suburbs, exurbs, and open country are manifestly different but complement each other. The sanest, best-balanced people are those who spend part of the year in each area and do not stay continuously under urban pressure. In that way they get the best of the city and of the more or less open spaces. A shack nearby or shelter in some vast wilderness will shortly be within the reach of most families.

In Mr. Mumford's recent gloom book, Baron Haussmann, a giant among planners, who saved Paris and turned it into a modern city, is contemptuously dismissed as a bulldozer and sadistic wrecker of fine old neighborhoods.

Here is some further pontification:

"To keep the advantages first discovered in the closed city, we must create a more porous pattern, richer in both social and esthetic variety. Residential densities of about one hundred people per net acre, exclusive of streets and sidewalks, will provide usable private gardens and encourage small public inner parks for meeting and relaxing. This can be achieved without erecting the sterile, space-mangling high-rise slabs that now grimly parade, in both Europe and America, as the ultimate contribution of 'modern' architecture."

Can anyone possibly believe that garden apartments housing over one hundred persons an acre are uncivilized and that small public inner parks have not been repeatedly considered and found wholly unworkable?

To sum up, let me ask the Gamaliels of the city a few pointed questions.

By what practical and acceptable means would they limit the growth of populations?

How would they reduce the output of cars, and if they could, what would take the place of the car as an employer of workers or as a means of transport in a motorized civilization?

If more cars are inevitable, must there not be roads for them to run on? If so, they must be built somewhere, and built in accordance with modern design. Where? This is a motor age, and the motorcar spells mobility.

13

METROPOLITAN
PROBLEMS

The rapid growth of metropolitan areas has been a prominent characteristic of recent United States history; approximately two thirds of the population of the United States live in the 212 Standard Metropolitan Statistical Areas (SMSA), and there appears to be no end to the growth of these areas in sight.

Governmental problems have multiplied with the development of metropolitan areas: some services often are inadequate whereas other services are duplicated, metropolitan planning commonly is lacking, many local governments have serious financial problems, conflicts of authority between different units of government are common, traffic and parking problems become acute, the ballot is long, and health problems are sometimes serious.

In 1961 the Advisory Commission on Intergovernmental Relations, established in 1959 as a permanent bipartisan commission of twenty-six members to study intergovernmental problems, recommended the enactment by each state legislature of "a 'package' of permissive powers to be utilized by the residents of the metropolitan areas as they see fit." While it is apparent that the adoption of the commission's recommendations by the various state legislatures would not be a cure-all for the complex problems of metropolitan areas, these areas would be in a position to arm themselves with weapons that would alleviate many of their most acute problems.

Extraterritorial or extramural powers refer to the powers that a city may exercise outside its boundaries. The Advisory Commission on Intergovernmental Relations in 1962 issued a report that catalogues the uses of extraterritorial powers, their strength and weaknesses, and recommends that state legislatures grant extraterritorial planning, zoning, and subdivision regulation powers to municipalities where effective county powers do not exist in unincorporated areas.

The experiment with commission-manager government in Dade County, Florida, is attracting wide attention among students of metropolitan areas. In November 1956 the voters of Florida approved a constitutional amendment that provided a broad grant of home rule and local autonomy to Dade County. In May 1957 the voters of the county approved a new county charter that provided for a commission-manager form of metropolitan government. The metropolitan government of Dade County was challenged during its first year of existence by 155 suits that were brought against it. None were successful. Robert Nelson, a staff correspondent of *The Christian Science Monitor*, presents a progress report on the Dade county experiment.

The Lakewood Plan, an outstanding example of interlocal cooperation, represents another attempt to solve some of the problems of metropolitan areas. Like the commission-manager plan in Dade County, the Lakewood Plan involves the county, in this instance the county of Los Angeles. The city of Lakewood was incorporated in 1954 but instead of providing all government services itself it contracted with the county for the provision of nearly all of its municipal services. The Lakewood Plan has been adopted by twenty-seven other new cities upon their incorporation. The plan according to Arthur G. Will, county-city coordinator for the county of Los Angeles, has been a success, yet is still in the stage of development and modification.

40. *Vigorous Action Required—Recommendations to the States**

In the recommendations which follow, the Commission sets forth no single "pat" solution for easing the problems of political and structural complexity at the local government level. The Commission is convinced that no single approach can be identified as the most desirable, whether from a national standpoint or within a given State. Neither does the Commission believe it can be a profitable effort for the legislature of any State having within its borders a number of metropolitan areas to endeavor to legislate a single solution; rather, the approach recommended in this report is one of legislative provision by the State of permissive authority to all of its metropolitan areas to employ whichever of these principal methods is determined by the residents of the areas and their political leaders to be the preferable one in the light of all the attendant circumstances. . . .

In brief, the Commission is proposing the enactment by State legislatures of a "package" of permissive powers to be utilized by the residents of the metropolitan areas as they see fit. Additionally, the Commission is proposing that States establish within the structure of State government a dual function of oversight and technical assistance to local units of government, thereby asserting a determination to assist continually and to intervene where necessary in ameliorating political jurisdictional problems in the metropolitan areas.

PROVISION BY THE STATE OF "ARSENAL" OF REMEDIAL WEAPONS TO BE DRAWN UPON BY METROPOLITAN AREAS

1. Assertion of legislative authority regarding metropolitan areas

The Commission subscribes firmly to the principle of maximum flexibility and freedom of action for local units of government in meeting the needs of their citizens; however, the Commission also believes that certain limitations must be introduced against the historical concepts of home rule as applied to political subdivisions located within metropolitan areas. The Commission recommends that the States, when considering either

---

* Advisory Commission on Intergovernmental Relations. From *Governmental Structure, Organization, and Planning in Metropolitan Areas* (Washington, D.C.: U.S. Government Printing Office, 1961), pp. 19–21, 24, 26, 30–33, 37, and 39–41. Footnotes in original omitted.

general constitutional revision or undertaking constitutional changes with regard to local home rule, reserve sufficient authority in the legislature to enable legislative action where necessary to modify responsibilities of and relationships among local units of government located within metropolitan areas in the best interests of the people of the area as a whole. . . .

2. Authorization of municipal annexation of unincorporated areas without consent of areas annexed

The Commission recommends that the States examine critically their present constitutional and statutory provisions governing annexation of territory to municipalities, and that they act promptly to eliminate or amend—at least with regard to metropolitan areas—provisions that now hamper the orderly and equitable extension of municipal boundaries so as to embrace unincorporated territory in which urban development is underway or in prospect. As a minimum, authority to initiate annexation proceedings should not rest solely with the area or residents desiring annexation but should also be available to city governing bodies. There is also merit to the proposition that the inhabitants of minor outlying unincorporated territory should not possess an absolute power to veto a proposed annexation which meets appropriate standards of equity. The Commission further urges States generally to examine types of legislation which in certain States have already been adopted to facilitate desirable municipal annexations, with a view to enacting such facilitative provisions as may be suitable to their respective needs and circumstances. . . .

3. Authorization of interlocal contracting and joint enterprises

The Commission recommends the enactment of legislation by the States authorizing, at least within the confines of the metropolitan areas, two or more units of local government to exercise jointly or cooperatively any power possessed by one or more of the units concerned and to contract with one another for the rendering of governmental services. . . .

4. Authorization for the creation of functional authorities

The Commission recommends that States consider the enactment of legislation authorizing local units of government within metropolitan areas to establish, in accordance with statutory requirements, metropolitan service corporations or authorities for the performance of governmental services necessitating areawide handling, such corporations to have appropriate borrowing and taxing power, but with the initial establishment and any subsequent broadening of functions and responsibilities being subject to voter approval on the basis of an areawide majority. . . .

5. Authorization for voluntary transfer of functions from municipalities to counties and vice versa

The Commission recommends the enactment of legislation by the

States authorizing the legislative bodies of municipalities and counties located within metropolitan areas to take mutual and coordinate action to transfer responsibility for specified governmental services from one unit of government to the other. . . .

6. *Authorization for creation of metropolitan area study commissions*

The Commission recommends that where such authority does not now exist, States enact legislation authorizing the establishment of metropolitan area commissions on local government structure and services, for the purpose of developing proposals for revising and improving local government structure and services in the metropolitan areas concerned, such commissions to be created, optionally, by either mutual and concurrent action of the governing bodies of the local units of government within the area or by initiative petition and election of the voters of the metropolitan area, and with the proposals developed by such commissions to become effective if approved at a special election held for the purpose. The enabling legislation should contain provisions designed to assure that the membership of such commissions is balanced in such a way as to provide general equity of representation to the population groups and governmental constituencies making up the metropolitan area as a whole. . . .

7. *Authorization for creation of metropolitan area planning bodies*

The Commission recommends the enactment of legislation by the States authorizing the establishment of metropolitan area planning bodies to comprise representatives from the political subdivisions of the metropolitan area. The functions of such a planning body should consist at least in providing advisory recommendations to the local units of government in the area with respect to the planned development of the metropolitan area; desirably they should include the development of areawide plans for land use and capital facilities and the review of zoning ordinances proposed by the component units of government in the area. . . .

DIRECT STATE ACTION—ASSISTANCE AND CONTROL

1. *Establishment of unit of State government for metropolitan area affairs*

The Commission recommends the enactment of legislation by the States to establish (or adapt) an agency of the State government for continuing attention, review, and assistance with respect to the metropolitan areas of the State and associated problems of local government, planning, structure, organization, and finance. . . .

2. *Establishment of State program of financial and technical assistance to metropolitan areas*

The Commission recommends that the States take legislative and administrative action to establish a program (or to expand existing programs) of financial and technical assistance to metropolitan areas in such fields as urban planning, urban renewal, building code modernization, and local government organization and finance. . . .

3. *Control of new incorporations*

The Commission recommends that where such authority does not now exist, States enact legislation providing rigorous statutory standards for the establishment of new municipal corporations within the geographic boundaries of metropolitan areas and providing further for the administrative review and approval of such proposed new incorporations by the unit of State government concerned with responsibility for local government or metropolitan area affairs. . . .

4. *Financial and regulatory action to secure and preserve open land*

The Commission recommends the enactment of legislation by the States (a) to provide for acquisition by the State of conservation easements designed to remove from urban development key tracts of land in and around existing and potential metropolitan areas and (b) to authorize local units of government to acquire interests and rights in real property within existing metropolitan areas for the purpose of preserving appropriate open areas and spaces within the pattern of metropolitan development. . . .

5. *Resolution of disputes among local units of government in metropolitan areas*

The Commission recommends that the States, where necessary, take legislative or administrative action to encourage and facilitate exercise of discretionary authority by the Governor and his office, to resolve those disputes among local units of government within metropolitan areas which (a) cannot be resolved at the local level by mutual agreement, (b) are not of sufficient scope or subject matter to warrant special legislative action and (c) which, however, in the determination of the Governor, are of such moment as to impede the effective performance of governmental functions in the area. . . .

41. *The Use of Extraterritorial Powers**

Extraterritorial powers as defined in this report are powers which a city exercises outside its ordinary territorial limits to regulate activity there or to assist in providing services to its citizens within its own boundaries.

* Advisory Commission on Intergovernmental Relations. From *Alternative Approaches to Governmental Reorganization in Metropolitan Areas.* (Washington, D.C.: U.S. Government Printing Office, 1962), pp. 20–25. Footnotes in original omitted.

Regulatory powers of an extraterritorial nature commonly include control over possible threats to health and safety, abatement of nuisances, and regulation of zoning and subdivisions. The use of extraterritoriality for providing services to the city's residents is most commonly connected with water supply, sewage treatment, recreation areas, and rubbish dumping sites outside city boundaries. The term "extraterritoriality" is also frequently used to refer to the power of a city to furnish services to areas outside the city. In this report such action is covered in the next section on intergovernmental agreements.

1. SCOPE AND TREND OF USE

Use of extraterritorial powers by cities varies among the States and by the type of power authorized. State legislatures have been relatively generous in granting cities power to go outside their boundaries to help in providing a service to their residents. In most States cities are particularly allowed to obtain their water and treat and dispose of sewage outside their boundaries, because of the frequent difficulties of providing these important utility services within their own boundaries.

Cities quite commonly exercise police power beyond their borders for health purposes—the protection of milk and meat supply, especially. About one-third of the States authorize cities to exercise extraterritorial powers to abate nuisances, such as slaughterhouses and soap factories. However, only a small portion of the cities exercise their nuisance abatement authority, leaving regulation mostly to the State. Few States grant localities the power of extraterritorial regulation of morals, such as gambling and the sale and use of liquor, and fewer cities exercise such powers. These are generally regarded as State-wide problems.

About 30 States have given cities jurisdiction beyond their boundaries for regulating subdivisions. To some extent, the increased establishment of county planning and zoning in unincorporated areas is reducing the need for such extraterritorial power. Few States have given cities power of extraterritorial zoning.

As a method of helping to meet governmental problems in metropolitan areas, the planning, zoning and subdivision regulation facets of extraterritoriality have received most attention in recent years. They can be effective in dealing with the problems of haphazard growth in the unincorporated fringe areas of municipalities, particularly where counties do not have such regulation in unincorporated areas. Thus, zoning divides an area (usually a municipality) into districts and within those districts regulates the height and bulk of buildings and other structures, the percentage of a lot that may be occupied, the size of required yards and other open spaces, the density of population, and the use of buildings and land for trade, industry, residence, or other purposes. Subdivision regulation controls the arrangement and width of streets, length and depth of blocks, provision of public open space, provision of sewer and water distribution systems, grading and surfacing of streets, and sufficiency of easements for utility installations. Such subdivision regulations are frequently required to conform with the provisions of the comprehensive plan of the municipality concerned, as in Wisconsin, in order to assure orderly development of the entire area.

A survey conducted for the *Municipal Year Book 1954* gave an indication of the extent of use of extraterritorial zoning and subdivision regulation powers. The survey covered 174 cities over 5,000 population out of a total of 2,527 cities.

While about 85 percent of the responding cities had zoning ordinances in effect within their boundaries, only about 10 percent had such ordinances effective outside their boundaries. Of the latter, only one-half were effective up to three miles outside the boundaries, one-fourth up to five miles, and one-fourth up to one or two miles. The principal reason for this relatively small use of zoning outside the city boundaries was the lack of statutory permission. To some extent the cities' lack of extraterritorial zoning was offset by county zoning laws in the unincorporated areas, particularly around big cities, but county zoning tended to be less comprehensive.

Extraterritorial subdivision regulation was more common than zoning. Seventy-seven percent of the cities surveyed had subdivision regulation within their borders, and 37 percent had extraterritorial authority. Of those with the power, two-fifths exercised it up to five or six miles beyond the city limits, another one-third exercised it up to three miles, and the remainder exercised it up to one or two miles. Counties participated only slightly more often in the areas not touched by extraterritorial subdivision controls than they did in areas not touched by extraterritorial zoning controls.

2. STRENGTH AND WEAKNESS

a. As an aid to providing service

A city's use of extraterritorial power is a way of extending its geographical jurisdiction. As a means of providing or improving city services, as in the case of water supply or recreation sites, it is a logical and frequently necessary way for a city to discharge its responsibility to its citizens. From the standpoint of the metropolitan area as a whole this may prove a disadvantage if it deters the city from cooperating with other communities in an area-wide approach yielding greater overall benefits. This approach also raises the possibility of creating intergovernmental friction if the city is not careful to be a "good citizen" in the way it carries on its activity in the outside area. The maintenance of refuse dumps and correctional institutions are examples of activities susceptible to complaints by the outside areas.

b. As a regulatory device

The use of extraterritoriality as a means of extending a city's geographical boundaries can be more important in the regulatory field, particularly in planning, zoning and subdivision regulation in unincorporated areas. Uncontrolled development at the fringes can have deteriorating effects on property values in the established neighboring areas of the central city, and can complicate the provision of certain services within the municipality, such as fire protection, crime control, traffic control and disease prevention. The use of extraterritorial zoning and subdivision regulation in unincorporated fringe areas can bring these conditions under better control by the adjoining municipality. By so doing it strengthens the movement toward area-wide land use planning.

Extraterritorial planning, zoning and subdivision regulation may also serve as a step toward annexation by giving the fringe area characteristics harmonious with those of the adjacent city. Such an effect seems most likely in such States as Virginia, North Carolina and Texas where the cities have considerable initiative in annexation proceedings and fringe areas can not exercise a veto over annexations. On the other hand, the threat of extraterritorial controls may stimulate hasty and ill-advised incorporations as a "defensive" measure, particularly in States where incorporations are easily accomplished.

From the standpoint of political feasibility, the use of extraterritorial controls has the advantage of creating relatively little disturbance in the political status quo. Unincorporated territories usually have only "rudimentary government," so that the officials and employees whose positions are threatened are few. Moreover, while the extraterritorial controls represent an exercise of governmental power from outside, it is the very lack of exercise of such power by the residents of the territory which frequently moves the adjoining city to exercise its power there. Thus extraterritorial regulation represents a new exercise of power, rather than a shift of an existing power.

A major weakness of extraterritorial regulation as an approach to reorganizing local government structure in metropolitan areas is its limited applicability. Many States do not give localities adequate authorization for the most important regulatory powers from the standpoint of dealing with metropolitan growth: planning, zoning and subdivision regulations. Even where the powers exist they are useful only when there are unincorporated areas adjacent to municipalities, a condition which is long past for many urban centers. Moreover, to the extent that these controls help ease the problems of fringe areas, they relieve the pressure for more basic solutions, except where the fringe area cannot veto a proposed annexation initiated by the adjoining city.

While extraterritorial regulation as presently authorized in most States enables the central city to protect itself it deprives the residents of the outside areas of a voice in determining their own affairs. This is contrary to the principle of local self-determination. It also can generate resentment, to the detriment of the cooperation required for satisfactory intergovernmental relations in metropolitan areas, as well as continued working for more comprehensive approaches to reorganization.

3. RECOMMENDATIONS

The Commission recommends that where effective county planning, zoning and subdivision regulation do not exist in the fringe area, State legislatures enact legislation making extraterritorial planning, zoning and subdivision regulation of unincorporated fringe areas available to their municipalities, with provision for the residents of the unincorporated areas to have a voice in the imposition of the regulations.

It is the Commission's view, that while extraterritorial power holds no great potential for resolving basic intergovernmental problems in metropolitan areas, such potential as it has should be made available to localities. Where counties are not already exercising effective control of the unincorporated fringe areas, extraterritorial planning, zoning and subdivision regulation can be important tools for preventing the development of problem areas around individual cities, and for easing the transition to a sound governmental structure.

The content of legislation authorizing municipalities to exercise such extraterritorial powers is suggested by the model draft statute attached in the form of an amendment to existing State statutes on planning, zoning and subdivision regulation. The proposed statute is adapted from a 1959 North Carolina statute on extraterritorial zoning recommended by the Municipal Government Study Commission of the North Carolina General Assembly and an earlier North Carolina statute on extraterritorial subdivision regulation. The suggested draft provides for the inclusion of residents of the unincorporated territory on the planning commission and zoning adjustment board for participation in making recommendations on planning, zoning and subdivision regulation matters applying to the "extramural" territory in which they reside. The fact that the municipality and unincorporated area have equal representation on the extraterritorial matters gives the unincorporated area some protection against arbitrary action by the municipality. Adoption of the zoning ordinance and approval of zoning adjustments, however, are still left to the municipal governing body.

Even with the provision for equal fringe area representation on the planning commission and the zoning adjustment board, the granting of extraterritorial zoning authority might stimulate a movement toward "defensive" incorporations. This is a risk that seems worth taking in view of the possible advantages to be gained by orderly fringe development and the stimulation of greater county-wide interest in zoning. Also, as the Commission pointed out in its report on *Governmental Structure,* any action directed toward greater control over the unincorporated area, whether it be giving municipalities greater initiative in annexation proceedings or, as in this case, greater control through extraterritorial zoning, should be accompanied by simultaneous strengthening of the State's regulation of new incorporations.

The minimum size of municipality and the distance of extraterritorial jurisdiction from the municipality's boundary for the zoning and subdivision regulation statute is not specified in the draft legislation because of varying State needs and conditions.

Robert Nelson
42. Regional "Metro"*

Just five years ago this past spring, voters in Dade County, Florida, authorized an era of local government reform that has become a national pace-setter. They allowed a burgeoning metropolitan area to shake itself free of an antiquated county government structure and to begin to base an area-wide local government on economic rather than strictly political needs.

They replaced a county government originally created for a small community and ended the jurisdiction of the state Legislature over strictly local affairs.

Metropolitan Dade County's government "Metro," as it is called, has faced rough buffeting at times from civic hurricanes as racking as the

---

* From *The Christian Science Monitor.* June 11, 1962, p. 9. Reprinted with permission of publisher and author.

tropical blows that sometimes menace Florida. But after each storm of criticism passed, Metro remained—frequently stronger than before.

Anti-Metro petitioners have, in fact, mounted literally dozens of lawsuits and three threatening county-wide referendums to try to smash this government reform showcase. Last fall, they came extremely close, falling only 6,000 votes short of upsetting the unique Metro home-rule charter.

SUPPORTERS REASSURED

But to supporters, survival is important in these early years of Dade County government renovation, by whatever margin.

Critics are quiet at the moment, having long held that enlarged authority for the county excessively and unfairly dilutes the powers of the county's 27 municipalities—including glittering Miami. But Metro backers are conditioned to expect a repeat attack some future day.

The narrow vote of confidence last fall is counted a one-man victory for an affable, fluster-free man whose gentle speech enfolds a steely resolve to make government function with economy and efficiency.

His name is Irving G. McNayr. He is Dade County Metro manager. He serves at the will of a 13-man board of county commissioners who pay him $25,000 a year to administer services for 900,000 people and 2,054 square miles, large zones of which are unincorporated.

FEDERATION GOAL

A native of Massachusetts, former city manager of Columbia, South Carolina, and a two-degree graduate of the University of Alabama, Mr. McNayr looks at Dade County in these terms:

"My concept of metropolitan government is that of a federation calling on all its individual members rather than that of a supergovernment encompassing all within its bounds.

"I have no other aim or objective than to get everybody pulling to-gether for a common purpose."

Despite his very recent arrival in Dade County—early 1961—Mr. Mc-Nayr seems to have mustered an impressive force of pullers already.

Dade has the chartered power to plan and act for the entire county —the unincorporated areas, for the most part, but also in behalf of or in conjunction with municipalities as they desire.

TRAFFIC CODE REVISED

For example, the county has invoked a county-wide uniform traffic code, installs and maintains all traffic lights and signs. At one time, Dade used 27 different sets of motor traffic regulations, some of them in Spanish.

Water supply, communications, public safety have yet to be consolidated under the county authority, but steps in that direction are being considered.

Once beyond its first year, when the Dade County legal department had to defend itself against 155 separate lawsuits, Metro government began to roll. Some contend that it rolled too fast, making more enemies than friends, and foreshadowing such referendum crises as last year's. Many residents of the county simply objected to such drastic changes being made at a gallop.

Mr. McNayr's unhalting but easygoing gait now sets the pace and the upset may be easing ever so slightly. As a result, centralized purchasing, machine records, data processing, and performance budgeting now move ahead impressively.

A $20,000,000 seaport for Miami is being transformed by Metro planners from a 32-year dream into a commercially bright reality.

AIR TERMINAL OPENED

A $26,000,000 terminal opened recently at Miami International Airport —it, too, under the supervision of the Dade County Port Authority.

Metro is overseeing a 200-mile county expressway system. County freeholders voted last year even to increase their county taxes one mill to boost the program.

Last summer, Metro's trash trucks began the county's first once-a-month refuse collection throughout unincorporated areas.

If there is one common principle that links all of these advancements, it is a commitment to save money without jeopardizing progress.

The recommended road department budget for the current fiscal year, for example, is $1,048,367 and includes more services and more facilities for more drivers on the roads but still adds up to less than the combined municipal-county total for 1958.

COSTS REDUCED

The cost-conscious Metro Purchasing Division reported savings of $400,000 during the first year of operation and a total of $1,500,000 through 1960, thanks to blanket contracting, centralized purchasing, waiver of performance bonds, encouragement of more competitive biddings, and simplified internal operating procedures.

As a result, Metro is buying traffic paint priced 85 cents lower than for any other municipality in the United States and paper cups for less than the federal government pays.

Honolulu, Milwaukee, Hartford, Houston, San Diego, Green Bay and several states have written to Dade County officials to ask just how they do it.

By establishing the county's first fulltime law department in 1957, the Metro government saved taxpayers $245,109 in three years, based on fees the county used to pay on an actual cost basis compared to what Metro now pays for the same service.

ACCEPTANCE GAINING

"This great bold venture in modern government," Mr. McNayr wrote The Christian Science Monitor recently, "is slowly, but surely, finding acceptance throughout Dade County. Its list of accomplishments far out-weighs any disadvantages claimed by its critics. And Metropolitan Dade County has made these advances while holding the line on taxation. We have cut the number of departments from 34 to 18, eliminating what the Research and Planning Council of San Antonio, Texas, once called 'fuddy-duddy administration.'

"The same organization, upon completing a survey of Metropolitan Dade County government recently, reported: 'Metro officials were not content with improving service and efficiency. They cut costs where it could be done without impairing service to the public.'"

Mr. McNayr is particularly grateful for an increased spirit of give and take between county and municipal governments and cites downtown Miami's new Federal Building, for which ground was broken April 2, as an example.

"In order to have the new building constructed in Miami," he explains, "Dade County donated a site at its civic center, a complex of city, county and state buildings approximately a mile from the downtown area."

MOVE PROPOSED

The Miami-Dade County Chamber of Commerce, however, desired to have the Federal Building go up downtown as the first unit of a proposed city center development to spur a revitalization drive for the downtown area.

"To work this out," says Mr. McNayr, "the city gave up its claim to a downtown site opposite the courthouse. The property in turn was donated to the federal government with the city getting in exchange the tract previously given to the federal government, plus $800,000 in rent in a proposed city-county office building to go up near the courthouse."

This mood of co-operation has proved appealing to private interests also. The Dade County Development Department claims it recently led the nation with 289 new plant arrivals and major plant expansions on record in a single year. As much as $45,000,000 in new payrolls may have been added to the local economy in just one year.

New plants mean new jobs—a commodity in high demand in Dade County, where, by one calculation, a new resident arrives every 12 minutes. By national standards, this population growth should be matched by a new school per month, one new fireman every seven days, and one new policeman every five days. The magnitude of the challenge to metropolitan government could hardly be more vividly portrayed.

Decrying "the indescribable government confusion" and "the jungle of intertwining powers and authorities of administration" in countless American urban areas, former Milwaukee Mayor Frank P. Zeidler has appealed for a "new philosophy of life as a basis for city development."

A definite majority in Dade County, Florida, is clearly bending every effort to measure up to just such a mandate.

Arthur G. Will
43. Another Look at Lakewood*

First and foremost, a little background may be helpful to you in understanding not only our past history in this operation but also in some of the predictions we are making for the future. As may be known to many of you, the County of Los Angeles is one of the largest local governments in the country, covering an area of over 4,000 square miles and with a population of 6,400,000, of which approximately 80% are within the boundaries of 73 incorporated cities. Effective political and administrative leadership enabled the county to develop a highly sophisticated management and service organization very early, placing it in a position from the beginning of being able to meet the demands for many services from cities and districts. Contract services have been provided by the county to incorporated cities since the turn of the century, with the first service being assessment and collection of taxes. This program grew as the county and the cities grew until 1950, when we were providing approximately 400 services to the 45 cities existing at that time. In April 1954 the City of Lakewood incorporated and inaugurated a whole new concept of the contract services program by receiving virtually all of its municipal

* Paper presented at the 27th annual conference of the National Association of County Officials, New York, July 11, 1962. Printed with permission of author.

services from the county in a package. This became known as the "Lakewood Plan" and was duplicated in 27 city incorporations between then and the present date.

Today the county provides services under 1300 individual service agreements to all 73 cities, with services ranging from microfilm record storage to construction of city streets and police and fire protection. There are many reasons for this growth in the number of cities and the subsequent growth in contract services provided by the county, a few of which are worthy of discussion here. A literal flood of incorporations took place in the County of Los Angeles beginning in 1954 and covering virtually every urbanized area of the county. Twenty-eight cities were formed, encompassing a combined population of 651,133—or 10% of the present total county population. Prior to this time, no incorporation had taken place since 1939 and there was neither great public demand for new cities nor was it very easy to do financially. With the great post-war population growth, however, many square miles of citrus groves and farm land were swallowed up in residential subdivisions and many country communities in unincorporated territory found themselves large, thriving cities overnight. As these communities grew and developed, community pride, a strong urge for preservation of identity, and resistance to annexation to adjoining cities built up, and these desires centered upon the formation of a city as the means of achieving community goals. In 1955, the Legislature of the State of California enacted a uniform 1% local retail sales and use tax for both cities and counties. Many cities had levied sales taxes prior to this date but several others did not, and counties had no authority to get into the sales tax field. As a result, mere incorporation of an area and execution of a contract for administration of sales and use tax with the State brought a considerable amount of immediate revenue into the new city's treasury. This became a major enabling factor, then, for those communities which wanted to become cities but did not think they could afford it. Right at this time also the incorporation of Lakewood, with the retention of all county services under contract, provided the final impetus for the large number of incorporations which subsequently took place.

This development has made Los Angeles County probably the largest laboratory in the world for the extension of local services across jurisdictional lines and has given us an opportunity to review these services in several different environments and come to some conclusions as to which service areas are successful, which are not, and what this portends for the position of the county in a rapidly expanding urban area.

Basically, the plan provides for the performance of all essential municipal services by the county under contract or by special district. It is a partnership of cities and the county to provide joint services at the least cost while both agencies retain the power of self-determination and home rule. It is further a voluntary partnership under which cities may establish and maintain local identity without heavy initial investment in capital plant, equipment and personnel. Thus, neither agency loses any of its powers but cooperates for the provision of the services at a mutually satisfactory level. . . .

What has happened to the program—what is Lakewood like several years after incorporation—what changes, if any, have taken place—and what directions, if they are discernible, is the program beginning to take?

1. GROWTH THROUGH NEW INCORPORATIONS

The first and most obvious change is, of course, the growth of the program. As I have indicated earlier, the number of service agreements has increased from around 400 in 1950 to 1300 today. By far the largest portion of this growth is due to new incorporations whereby anywhere from 20 to 30 county services are continued in the newly incorporated city.

2. GROWTH IN OLDER CITIES

Another significant factor has been the growth of contract operations in the older cities, or those incorporated prior to Lakewood. Close to 200 new service agreements have been entered into with these cities within the same period. This definite growing tendency for older cities to request contract services from the county probably has more significant implications for the future than the development of the Lakewood-type operation. Many of these cities have been critically reviewing their service operations each year and more and more have asked the county to submit proposals for the provision of certain services and subsequently have requested that they take them over. Therefore we find a gradual breaking down of some of the old attitudes and a growing view that many services can be shared or cooperatively provided without affecting the basic independence of the city or the power of the city council to freely exercise the right of decision.

3. CHANGING SERVICE PATTERNS IN NEW CITIES

While some older cities are seeking services from the county, we find the beginnings of what may be a very important development in the new cities. We have determined a definite trend in many of the new cities to revise the level, extent, and degree of service from that provided in the early years of their incorporation. Many of these now have come through the initial adjustment stage and have grown in both years and stature. They are now reviewing their entire service operations as provided by contract and are making several changes. Thus, while the initial approach to the provision of services to newer cities was a "package" including all municipal services, we find now a tendency towards selection of the service by the city from the county, other cities, private contract, or the establishment of their own service organization. We feel that this has a decidedly strengthening effect on the system since many of the services which we continue to provide in these cities are those apparently most conducive to contract operation while those we lose through cancellation or revision of service level are those with which we may have been experiencing problems. This further emphasizes the voluntary nature of the program and the fact that the County is not demanding that the cities take these services under any and all conditions but is flexible enough to adjust to individual circumstances.

4. CHANGING ROLE OF COUNTY DEPARTMENTS

These changes which are taking place in our contract service operations have had a major impact upon the various county departments involved in providing the individual services. The change from serving one master to serving many has brought about a number of major revisions in attitude and policy in all of these county departments. In many instances the personnel in the various departments have been "jacked up" and made more alert and responsive to the service needs, not only in incorporated cities under contract but also in communities in unincorporated territory. The operation of services in the various cities and the differing experiences within each of them have caused a considerable amount of soul-searching on the part of departmental personnel, and a real effort to either provide the service requested in each city or determine why it cannot, or perhaps should not, be done.

5. CHANGES IN POLITICAL PICTURE

Probably the most important trend in the contract service program since the incorporation of Lakewood are the implications in the local political arena—City Councils and the Board of Supervisors. There has been a serious question in the minds of many students of government that the tie-in of services between the county and cities may also automatically fuse political policies of the Board of Supervisors and the various new city councils. The program in operation in its various environments has proved instead that a new and quite constructive type of relationship has developed between the city councils and the Board. Rather than fusing political policies along a pattern set by the Board of Supervisors, there is rather a tendency to better understanding of common problems and a compromise of political attitudes along workable lines. Because of the existence of major county operations within the cities, more opportunities have been presented for these city councils to meet with their representative Board members, thereby creating a more frank interchange of ideas, information and negotiation of common problems. There has been no noticeable difference in the degree of independent action taken by the newer city councils as compared to those of the older established cities. There has, however, been more of a movement toward getting the two political organizations together to work out differences. The Board of Supervisors has also shown a noticeable trend to rely upon the city councils for leadership within each of their communities, thereby reducing the number of individual citizen contacts necessary within each supervisorial district. This has been particularly beneficial to the Board, considering the large number of people—over one million—contained in each of the five supervisorial districts.

We have briefly reviewed what we think are the principal changes which have taken place in the last few years. Now let us investigate some of the specifics of the above and a few of the practical aspects of operation of the system within cities.

Intergovernmental cooperation has been a tradition in Los Angeles County for many years. We have been used to solving a number of our problems by joint action of cities, the county, school districts, and other public bodies, and should have a sufficient amount of experience to approach any problem arising in the metropolitan area. As an example, the problem of water supply to the area was partially solved by the establishment in 1928 of the Metropolitan Water District which brought a major water supply from the far-distant Colorado River into the counties and cities of Southern California. Within the county, major sewage disposal problems have been met by the establishment of County Sanitation Districts, and the very difficult problems of air pollution resulted in the creation of an Air Pollution Control District. While these have all been cooperative ventures of cities and counties, they have, however, been separate agencies, and though governed by representatives of the cities and/or county, have had their own service organizations. . . .

It is very difficult to systematically categorize each of our "lessons" so to speak, since the problems vary with locality, the service rendered, the people involved with rendering the service, and the political situation in the community at any given time. We can, however, arrive at some general conclusions and perhaps some criteria to guide us in the provision of these services in the future.

The two parallel developments of increasing contract activity in older cities and changing emphasis in the new cities is obviously the most significant indicator of future trends. The services involved also give an equally significant clue to where the program is going. The older city with an established service organization is primarily interested in augmenting its service capacity and acquiring technical and specialized talents which it may not be able to obtain due to small size and/or financial resources. Thus the services of recruitment, selection and training of personnel; preparation of master plans of zoning and land use; specialized public works maintenance such as traffic signals, traffic striping and sewer maintenance; engineering services such as subdivision map checking and storm drain design; cooperative purchasing; mental health services; and election services, to name a few, are being requested on a more and more frequent basis.

Conversely, the new cities are beginning to set up service departments of their own to operate those functions which appear to them to be more appropriately performed at the city level. This has not occurred, as yet, on a wholesale basis as certain of the services, by their very nature, still provide overwhelming advantages in a "package." Law enforcement, fire protection, and others consequently remain essentially unchanged and continue to grow both in numbers of cities and scope of service.

Many services are conducive to fractioning, however, such as public works, and many of the new cities are moving into these areas on a highly selective basis. A good example of this is one city's approach to public works by the establishment of a department for provision of the more routine maintenance and engineering services, leaving to the county the services involving specialized equipment and personnel. Thus the city sweeps the streets, posts signs, performs routine patching, curb repair, and certain engineering functions, while the county continues major construction, traffic signal maintenance, building inspection, sewer maintenance, and some specialized engineering work. This results in a mutually satisfactory allocation of functions *on the basis of experience,* and provides us with a good foundation for evaluation of our services in other communities. Interestingly enough, it will be noted that most of the public works services the county retains in this example are the same services being requested with growing frequency by older cities.

We have had similar experience in the planning service where new cities have employed their own personnel for handling the routine requests for zone changes, daily contacts with the public, and working with the city planning commission, and have retained our planning department for investigations, reports, and the more extensive research in preparation of master plans for land use, streets, parks and other matters. City planning is, of course, a very sensitive area in any community and it is probably better that the city exercise more control over this service.

What are some of the criteria used by both the cities and the county in making the decision to either obtain a new service or change an existing one? Our experience during the past few years has shown the following to be the most influential factors and present in varying degrees in each transaction:

1. Local identity and home rule is far and away the most important consideration from the standpoint of the city. Older cities are not at all interested in diminishing their control of local affairs and new cities are constantly seeking means of further establishing their identity. As a home rule county under California law, the Board of Supervisors strongly supports the cities in this matter. Consequently, any service agreement entered into between the county and a city has been thoroughly reviewed from this standpoint and the city has made the determination that their power of home rule is not affected.

2. Cost and service level are, of course, basic factors in any service contract and are controlling in many, though not all, cases. In all negotiations in our experience, the cost considerations have involved the most time and extensive research on both sides. Since the standard set by the Board of Supervisors for service in county departments is full cost as determined by cost accounting methods, there is little flexibility for negotiation in this segment of the program. Rather, the level of service comes in for the most attention. The Board has been extremely careful that no subsidy exists in contract services for one group of cities at the expense of others.

3. Responsiveness and the time factor in performance of the service on a continuing basis appears to be one of the most frequent considerations in revision or cancellation of a county service. A new city, particularly, will usually desire to change the patterns of service of county departments operating in the area prior to incorporation. Different time standards will be requested which can usually be met by rescheduling work and adjusting assignment of personnel. We have found, however, that there is a limit to the variety of standards which can be accommodated by a county department without adding personnel and thereby increasing costs. As a result, some service agreements have been revised because the time element could not be satisfied.

There are many other considerations to decision making in this area such as availability of service, community demands, etc., but the above represent the major pivot points around which all of our negotiations turn one way or the other. Further, they are not mutually exclusive but depend upon one another to some degree in each case. For instance, cities have elected a more expensive alternative in some services where the matter of home rule is paramount or the county has declined to provide a service where a too-extensive change is required in our organization or service level. . . .

We feel that the cities have performed an admirable job in assisting us to study the effects of these services within each community and in virtually all instances the decisions have been made on the basis of objective findings mutually agreeable between our offices and the city administration. Not all has been sweetness and light, however, and there have been instances in abundance where a county service has become the center of an emotional issue within a community. There are several examples also, where a local dispute, not related to a county service, has caught up one or more departments as innocent bystanders in the maelstrom. In defending the position of the department and the county employees providing the services within the community, the county is in the unenviable position of stepping in as a third party between two local disputants and becoming involved itself. It must be remembered that the county provides many, many State services county-wide without respect to city boundaries, such as welfare, operation of county hospitals, etc. In such instances, therefore, the county is actually in two positions: one of representing the area-wide operation in the performance of statutory services and therefore impartial in any local problem, and two, of being driven onto one side or the other of a local controversy.

Discounting the incidents where political dispute has arisen, our first impressions from the above are that we are now well into the process of natural selection between the county and the various cities for allocation of the local services between the two agencies. Our first conclusion is that cities very probably will amend our contract operations over the years to provide for themselves the primary services involving identity and direct and frequent contact with their citizens. These services will generally be the bread-and-butter public works services such as responding to complaints for repair of streets and other public works facilities, the handling of routine day-to-day planning and zoning matters, the handling of certain engineering design functions, and many others. The county will more and more step back and assume those supporting functions requiring highly specialized personnel and equipment and less direct contact with the public. . . .

It has been stated by many observers in the past that the Lakewood Plan is not the final answer to the problem of provision of services in a metropolitan area. It has been stated further that the program provides an excellent transition from one step to the next in our urban growth. We feel that the Lakewood Plan has been an extremely strong and virile program to date and has solved a number of extremely difficult problems for new cities in this area. The best features of the plan will combine with the changes described herein to solve most of our interjurisdictional service problems *without changing our basic city or county organization or powers*. We are seeing the beginnings of this change and are entering a new era of operations with contract services. If we can maintain the same objective approach to the analysis of each of these services which we have in the past, we will be able to seek out and settle these service areas within the not-too-distant future. We think that much of what is going on in our county right now is an accomplishment of what has been stated academically in studies of metropolitan area problems throughout the country in the matter of allocation of functions. Rather than talking about them, we have been in the process of actually making these allocations by experience and settling these service areas into the proper location in our local government structure. The County of Los Angeles has a great deal of work to do and we hope other counties can very materially benefit from our experience.

part seven

STATE AND
LOCAL ACTIVITIES

14

EDUCATION

Education is the most expensive local activity and has been growing in importance. The financing of education has been a source of considerable debate. The Committee for Economic Development, composed of 180 leading businessmen and educators, through its research and policy committee offers four recommendations designed to solve the principal problems associated with school finance.

Dr. James Bryant Conant, formerly president of Harvard University, has studied thoroughly the public school system in the United States in the post-World War II period and through his books probably has had a greater impact upon the public school system in recent years than any other individual. Mrs. Agnes E. Meyer, a staunch defender of public schools, evaluates Dr. James Bryant Conant's book entitled *Slums and Suburbs,* which is concerned with schools in metropolitan areas.

44. Paying for Better Public Schools*

We need better schools and we can have them. The essential requirement is that we should want them strongly enough. The "We" in this case is the American people. Nobody can give the American people better schools. But we can afford better education and will get it if we recognize the need.

The recommendations in this statement are based on the belief that the American people value education, can be brought to value its improvement and will be willing to pay for it. The record of the postwar years supports this belief. Faced with an enormous increase in the school-age population we have made a great increase in expenditures for public schools. Contrary to many gloomy predictions, the public school system has not been overwhelmed by the crisis of rising enrollments but has probably been somewhat improved in the face of it. . . .

Many of the steps that must be taken to improve our school system lie in the field of school finance, the subject of the present statement. This statement recognizes the importance of other kinds of action, but concentrates upon these financial matters. It considers only the publicly operated elementary and secondary schools. It does not examine the serious questions of finance that are raised by the increase in the proportion of our population receiving formal education beyond the high school.

This Committee recommends four kinds of action to overcome the main financial obstacles to the improvement of the public schools.

1. NEW ATTACK ON REDISTRICTING—BY STATE LAWS. Immediate reorganization of small school systems into effective units of local government is required in most states, including almost all of the most populous states. This is an old situation, widely appreciated by experts for many years in which progress, though real, has been slow. We urge a fresh attack upon it.

A large proportion of the school systems in the country are much too small to provide good schools at all or to provide any kind of schools efficiently. They can't provide an adequate curriculum. They are highly wasteful of school personnel and typically offset the high costs this entails by maintaining low salary scales and by absorbing an exorbitant share of state school funds. In the great majority of instances, school districts with small enrollments are not the necessary result of population sparsity.

* Committee for Economic Development. From *Paying for Better Public Schools.* (New York: Committee for Economic Development, 1959), pp. 5–12. Reprinted by permission of publisher.

Rather, they reflect the fact that the school system covers only a tiny area. In only 19 states is the average geographic area covered by a school system as much as 225 square miles—equivalent to an area 15 miles square. In 21 states it is less than 49 square miles.

A complete school program can hardly be conducted by a unified school system with much less than 2,000 students. Substantial educational advantages continue to accrue until a school system has perhaps 25,000 students. There are financial advantages of many kinds in even larger units, although other problems begin arising in an extremely large system.

In early 1957 only 2,000 school systems had as many as 3,000 students. Less than 3,000 more had as many as 1,200 students. Thirty thousand districts had less than 50 students. Schools in such small systems are doomed to be inferior.

The present 45,000 school districts should be consolidated into something less than 10,000 systems. The exact number of school systems that would provide the most effective organization, and their boundaries, can be determined only on a state-by-state basis. In most states the county provides a convenient and suitable geographic area for the administrative unit. Separation of cities, subdivision of counties into two or three areas, or combination of two or more counties into a single school district also may be found desirable in particular situations.

All experience shows that effective consolidation cannot and will not be achieved by the local units themselves. Even under rather strong state pressure, "voluntary" reorganization requiring approval by voters in the local districts not only has proceeded at a snail's pace, but has usually resulted in consolidated districts that are still too small to provide an effective program or a sufficiently broad tax base.

On the other hand, many states have achieved school systems of appropriate size by mandatory state legislation. The practicality of reorganization by compulsory state law is demonstrated by the fact that 23 states have at some time reorganized their school districts in this way. These include all the Southeastern and New England states and such sparsely settled Western states as New Mexico and Nevada. Most of them succeeded in eliminating or almost eliminating small districts.

The reorganization plan in a few of these states was not fully adequate, and in the New England states reorganization was carried out so long ago that redistricting is again needed. Despite this, these 23 states together contain fewer school districts with less than 1,200 pupils than do any of ten individual states that have not adopted compulsory state plans.

The state governments created the existing multiplicity of units, and it is their responsibility to create units of school government that can operate effectively and efficiently. Achievement of effective school district reorganization requires mandatory action by the state government.

Once sufficiently large school districts are established, small schools within them must be consolidated into schools of efficient size. It is usually necessary for a state reorganization plan to include provisions to facilitate the consolidation of individual schools.

2. STATE ASSISTANCE TO LOCAL SCHOOL DISTRICTS. *In most states the state government should take over from the local districts a larger share of the financial burden of schools.*

For all practical purposes the local district has one source of revenue —the property tax. Although a district may have adequate economic resources to support improved schools, it will often be unable to tap these resources through the property tax. Increasing the property tax rate will further increase the already excessive burden on real property as compared with other sources of income and magnify the consequences of inevitable inequities in assessments. Moreover, property is less equally distributed among districts than other potential tax bases such as income or sales. The inherent limitations of the property tax, as well as other limitations imposed by state law, are serious obstacles to the flow of funds into education. These will become more serious as financial needs increase.

State funds should be distributed to local districts through a "foundation" program that insures each district within the state the financial ability to support its schools. The program we recommend requires that the essential ingredients of a satisfactory school program be established and kept current as costs change. While the ingredients are uniform, certain of the costs, such as transportation, may vary somewhat per pupil from school district to school district. The state would then provide each school district with funds equal to the difference between the cost of the "foundation" program and the amount that would be raised in the district by a property tax levied in all districts at a moderately low, uniform rate, based on full or at least equalized valuation of property.

It is important that the assumed tax rate be low enough to leave the local districts with some fiscal capacity to go beyond the "foundation" program in supporting aspects of the school program that they deem desirable, and thus to leave real scope for local variation and choice in establishing the level and use of school funds. It is also important—though this is a condition already met by most states—that state revenues not be obtained from a state property tax that competes with local governments.

This second recommendation is closely tied up with the first. Unless the basic school districts have achieved reasonable size and financial strength, such a foundation program is extremely difficult to operate. *Both sensible school district organization and an appropriate state foundation program are essential. Together they are capable in most states of eliminating the numerous local pockets of substandard education, meeting the financial requirements of a still-greatly-expanding public school enrollment, and providing the financial base to permit most school districts that have the leadership and desire to do so to move forward to establish better educational systems.*

3. FEDERAL SUPPORT FOR EDUCATION IN THE POORER STATES. In a number of states, mostly but not exclusively in the South, school expenditures per child in public school are much below the levels prevailing in the remainder of the country. While there are notable local exceptions, teachers in these states are poorly paid and often are less qualified than elsewhere; the better teachers are hard to retain; classes are large; school retention rates are low; and education appears to be generally inferior.

Per capita incomes in these states are low and the proportion of the population in public school is large. Inferior education prevails even though a higher percentage of the community's income goes into education than in other sections of the country. Under the pressure of financial necessity, most of these states have already largely effected the savings, additions to effective tax resources and educational improvements that school district reorganization brings, and they are supplementing local funds with large state programs. Additional state and local support is possible. But we believe that it is not realistic to expect that the poorer states will bring their schools up to nationally acceptable standards out of their own resources.

These facts provide no rationale for further Federal participation in support of schools throughout the country, and *we oppose any proposal for general support of school systems on a nationwide basis.* We believe the national interest in adequate education will best be served by continued reliance upon state and local governments, which are capable of meeting the schools' needs and for the most part are, in fact, responding to the requirement for sharply rising expenditures.

While we regret the necessity for any further expansion of the Federal role, *we do find Federal supplementation of state and local funds necessary for the improvement of schools in the poorer states. We recommend that the Federal Government make financial grants to support public schools in those states where income per public schoolchild is substantially below the national average.* The formula we suggest for apportioning these grants would involve an annual Federal cost of about $600 million at present. The program we propose contains safeguards to ensure a reasonable level of school support from the state's own residents and to prevent the substitution of Federal funds for local funds presently expended.

Some members of this Committee would prefer to go beyond Federal assistance to the low-income states and would favor a program of Federal participation in the general costs of education throughout the country. Others believe that Federal support—in addition to what is now being done—is unnecessary or unwise, whether it is nationwide or confined to the low-income states.

4. CITIZEN EFFORT TO IMPROVE THE SCHOOLS. *The numerous citizens throughout the country who appreciate the need for improved education must be better organized to bring this need to bear at every level of government—local, state, and Federal. This is the way to generate the energy necessary for results.*

Outstanding examples of effective local action for better schools show what can be done, and how. Organized citizen interest will attract and stimulate strong professional leadership in the schools, which will in turn elicit further public support. Public participation in school elections and budget hearings is essential; many non-partisan groups, such as the League of Women Voters, have shown capacity to generate such participation. In thousands of areas citizens' committees to study school programs and school needs have guided public discussion and government action. These committees have been most effective when organized on a permanent, representative basis, in good working relationship with other local bodies and with a state committee, and with professional assistance.

BUSINESS, ECONOMIC DEVELOPMENT, AND THE SCHOOLS

We believe that businessmen have a responsibility, as citizens, to participate in the local, state, and national effort to improve the schools. But we would like to state specifically why we, the Research and Policy Committee of the Committee for Economic Development, a group consisting largely of businessmen, place high priority upon the improvement of education.

To start with the narrowest reason, we recognize that one important source of economic growth is improvement of the skills and adaptability of all groups in our labor force. Within most occupations the skills required for useful performance are increasing and changing. Employment opportunities for the illiterate and the semi-literate are dwindling. Occupations requiring major skills and long training are expanding. We expect the schools to provide the necessary groundwork both for acquisition of skills and for adaptation to changing requirements. Special importance from the standpoint of economic growth, as from other standpoints, attaches to the education of individuals of exceptional ability, those with capacity for leadership and the potentiality for new inventions, discoveries, and innovations. Such contributions raise the income and living standards of everyone.

America's past accomplishments in raising productivity, of which we are justly proud, were not obtained without greatly increasing the average number of years spent in formal schooling. Since 1880 we have doubled the average number of days that pupils enrolled in public schools spend in school during the year. We have broadened and enriched the school curriculum, and greatly raised the standards of school staffs. If this has been a main factor in our past economic growth, even the continuation of our past rate of economic progress would seem to imply continued rapid improvement in education.

But economic development is not in itself a sufficient goal. It is a means for expanding the range of choices open to men. This range has already become very large, and we may confidently expect it to become larger. The need and the opportunity for wisdom and discrimination in the exercise of these choices become correspondingly greater. It would be shortsighted for anyone concerned with economic development not to be concerned with its uses and consequences. A proper aim of education is to prepare the individual to make wise decisions—both in the private use of his income and leisure and as a participant in the democratic process.

The whole nation has been shocked into awareness of a great threat to our national security. That a connection exists between our precarious security position and our educational system has become widely appreciated. This connection is sometimes found in the training of scientists and engineers. It is sometimes found in high rates of draft rejection for illiteracy and the inadequate background of many who are accepted into the military services. But the connection between education and security is even more general and basic than this.

We have not sufficiently valued intellectual achievement—either in what we paid for it or in the respect and freedom we gave it. This applies to all fields of intellectual endeavor, and not merely to the sciences. Education's responsibility for national security extends far beyond the training of scientists and servicemen. It extends to the influence that education exerts upon the ability of people to understand the alternatives before them and choose wisely among the real alternatives. The real danger to our security arises from the fact that we are not using our resources as wisely as we could. . . .

The education of the people to improve the quality of the choices made and thus to make the best use of the power of our economy and of our government is not a responsibility of the schools alone. The responsibility is shared by all the institutions and processes that form peoples' understanding—families, churches, adult education programs, the media of public information and the course of life itself. But the schools are basic.

MORE THAN MONEY IS REQUIRED

In this statement we concentrate on problems of school finance because we believe we are better qualified to consider these problems than other aspects of education. But we must emphasize our conviction that the provision of more money, while essential, will not of itself satisfy the nation's proper aspirations for its school system.

The schools need as clear a view as they can obtain of what they should be trying to achieve and of the scope of their responsibilities; a view adapted to the requirements of modern life and to the potentialities of education. What is the proper balance of courses for students of differing abilities, interests, and expectations of education beyond the high school? What should be the content of individual courses? What, in brief, do we expect students to obtain from their public education? How much stress should be placed on physical and social development, character building, or citizenship training? How far does the responsibility of the schools extend for the provision of facilities for community activities and of public athletic and other entertainment, or for the custody of children unable to benefit from school but dangerous to the community if released from school supervision?

We applaud the steps some localities are taking to obtain broad community participation to study and resolve priorities among school objectives. Determination of objectives and responsibilities is no easy matter, but conscious decisions are likely to lead to a more coherent and effective school program than will be obtained in their absence.

The schools need to use more efficiently the resources available to them to meet their objectives. Securing efficiency in public education has many aspects, but perhaps the most important questions concern teacher training and compensation policies, instructional methods, the effort made by the students themselves, and the allocation of funds among different types of expenditures. It is important to stress that erroneous decisions with respect to many of these most important aspects of school operations cannot possibly be overcome by larger expenditures alone, however generous we might be.

The nation is not getting the full benefits that a decentralized school structure was intended to, and could, provide. In the first place, local school systems and the public are often too reluctant to experiment with new approaches and techniques. This does not appear to be the greatest difficulty, however. Nearly every alternative that has been responsibly suggested anywhere has been tried out in a number of school systems —frequently over periods covering many years. What is lacking is the development of appropriate standards to judge success or failure; methods for systematic, objective appraisal of experience in different areas to determine what has worked and what has not, and why. Even when experience has led to a consensus among informed individuals that an idea is a good one, it often takes decades before it is generally adopted. Clearly, we need better channels for disseminating ideas and objective appraisals of them.

We do not mean to disparage the good work in those fields that is now being done. But it seems clear that in education there is inadequate attention to what in business would be called research and development, and to the application of research findings. Private foundations and professional associations, and the schools of education, could do more in this field. The United States Office of Education has recently secured additional resources for this purpose, and the importance of its leadership is clear. State departments of education are especially well positioned to disseminate research findings to local school systems, and urgently require a directive and funds to engage in these activities on an adequate scale.

Local school systems might now consider the appointment of a special official to encourage experimentation and to be responsible for the adoption of tested improvements.

A more receptive attitude toward new ideas must be cultivated in school administrators—at the state as well as the local levels, in the schools of education, and among parents. *Methods of determining what is useful and accelerating the adoption of proven ideas may well be the greatest need of all in our educational system.*

Agnes E. Meyer
45. *Slums and Schools**

In his study of education in American high schools, entitled *The American High School Today*, Dr. James B. Conant encountered the wrath of the teaching profession, largely because he proved that our bright students were not working hard enough. With his latest book, *Slums and Suburbs,* in my opinion the most important of Dr. Conant's reports on education, he has brought down upon himself the wrath of Negro leadership and that of our sentimental liberals who, with more heart than head, favor

---

* From the *Atlantic Monthly.* February 1962, pp. 76–79. Reprinted with permission of publisher and author.

desegregation of our public schools regardless of its effect upon the education and the welfare of Negro children. In addition, he has shocked those who wrongly believe that the Supreme Court decision of 1954 makes all segregation in our schools illegal.

I have long admired Dr. Conant's courageous defense of our public schools and his insight into their fundamental importance to the future of democracy. We met on various occasions many years ago, when he was president of Harvard University, sometimes at huge national conventions of teachers, sometimes at small suburban gatherings, and in the halls of Congress, where we were both arguing for higher standards of public education and for federal aid to the public schools. It was heartening to me that the president of Harvard University, who, as a distinguished chemist, was also deeply involved in the development of atomic energy, could find the time to take an active part in the struggle to improve the schools and to express his conviction that higher education could not be improved unless the foundation of our educational system, the public schools, was strengthened throughout the nation.

Let me confess that his initial report was a disappointment to me, largely because the title, *The American High School Today,* promised too much. Obviously, Dr. Conant was obliged to set limits to his task. He chose the comprehensive high schools, which enroll a third of the high school population and exist chiefly in smaller cities, of ten to sixty thousand inhabitants. I rebelled against Dr. Conant's arbitrary figure of 15 per cent of the student body as comprising the gifted ones who alone should be encouraged to pursue an academic career. The other 85 per cent were brushed off as fit only to be trained in "marketable skills" with as much academic work as such a vocational curriculum would permit. The Council on Basic Education has just issued a report that 35 per cent of our schoolchildren are seriously retarded in reading, and 40 per cent more are not reading as well as they might. Surely these children, with remedial-reading lessons, could learn even in high school to prepare themselves to cope with academic work instead of being relegated to Dr. Conant's 85 per cent who are to be excluded from the elite.

I agreed enthusiastically, however, with Dr. Conant's just criticisms of the curriculum in our large high schools, his insistence on continuity of study in the fundamental academic subjects, his accusation that our bright boys, and especially our bright girls, are not encouraged to work hard enough, and instead of doing homework are allowed to fritter away their energies in senseless afterschool activities. These accusations, made by so distinguished an educational authority, stung the pride of the teaching profession. Instead of admitting these shortcomings, the educators pounced on Dr. Conant's call to greater excellence and greater student motivation by denouncing his program as "aristocratic," because he insisted that any bright high school student could readily carry five, rather than the traditional four, academic subjects a year.

In his new book on schools in the metropolitan areas, *Slums and Suburbs,* Dr. Conant fills the lacunae of his first volume and, by citing the records of six so-called lighthouse schools, confounds the critics who maintain that his demands on American youth are too severe. For these six high schools, and he could have cited more, prove beyond doubt that five academic subjects can be carried successfully by any bright boy or girl without undue tension and strain.

His latest volume has met with sharp criticism from another direction. It has aroused the indignation of Negro leadership. Since the education of Negro children should progress with all deliberate speed, their parents ought to realize that Dr. Conant's advice for the improvement of education in the large Negro ghettos of our big Northern cities is sound. In fact, of his several valuable treatises on American education, *Slums and Suburbs* is the most important one Dr. Conant has written.

He points out that the prime responsibility of schools, instruction and learning, is hampered if students—white or Negro—are disturbed, sick, or hungry and their parents are irresponsible or, worse, in prison or on probation. Dr. Conant dismisses as irrelevant the academic curriculum demanded of the comprehensive high schools. "The nature of the community," he says, "largely determines what goes on in the school. Therefore to attempt to divorce the school from the community is to engage in unrealistic thinking, which might lead to policies that could wreak havoc with the school and the lives of children. The community and the school are inseparable." Given the unavoidable social responsibilities of the urban slum school, what becomes of our democratic boast of equality of opportunity when the wealthy suburban communities spend $1000 a year per child and the large cities less than half that amount?

Dr. Conant's book is thus a powerful appeal to the American conscience, an appeal for justice to our Negro fellow citizens all the more effective because it is based on his scientific analysis of grim facts. But the calm objectivity of the scholar is shaken by the shock of discovery, of his exposure to the sordid living conditions in the slums and their effect on the process of education. As a result, he makes a passionate appeal for equality of opportunity for the Negro child, which brings into sharp focus the heights and depths of American culture.

"I have walked through school corridors in slum areas and, looking into classrooms, have seen children asleep with their heads on their hands. Is this situation the result of poor teachers without either disciplinary control or teaching ability? No, the children asleep at their desks have been up all night with no place to sleep or else have been subject to incredibly violent family fights and horrors through the night. Checking into one case, a principal told one of my staff that after climbing six flights of a tenement he found the boy's home—one filthy room with a bed, a light bulb, and a sink. In the room lived the boy's mother and her four children. I might add that it is not unusual for teachers in these schools to take home with them children with no place to go at night." Seeing through Dr. Conant's eyes, I felt as if I were being confronted with such misery for the first time. I share his indignation when he adds: "It is after visits to schools like these that I grow impatient with both critics and defenders of public education who ignore the realities of school situations to engage in fruitless debate about educational philosophy, purposes, and the like. These situations call for action, not hair-splitting arguments."

The actions he prescribes are definite and salutary.

The most acute problem in Negro slums is unemployment of youths between sixteen and twenty-one. It ranges from 17 per cent on a nation-wide average to 70 per cent in some areas. This is social dynamite, says Dr. Conant. It is not the sole cause of delinquency and crime, but it is a major contribution to them. The educational experience of youth should fit their subsequent employment. Vocational training should be upgraded. One solution lies in study and work programs. An auto-mechanics shop for boys should exist in every metropolitan high school. But the best vocational training does no good whatever when it prepares boys and girls for nonexistent jobs. Indeed, highly trained Negro boys and girls who cannot find a market for their skills are apt to become all the more embittered.

Racial discrimination now makes unemployment chronic for the Negro male, North and South. In the largest cities, the employment of youth is literally nobody's affair. Discrimination extensively practiced by employers and unions is a serious roadblock. Effective placement services and the cooperation of labor-management committees are essential; the obligation of the school should not end when the students drop out of school or graduate. Guidance officers ought to be given the responsibility of follow-up from the time pupils leave school until they are twenty-one years of age. This total program will cost money for additional staff. Not only more guidance officers but more teachers, and higher salaries for them, are necessary, as well as special training programs for teachers in slum schools. They must enlist the interest of parents in the slum areas through adult-education programs.

Indeed, the whole problem of financing public education in the large cities is a major national concern. Federal aid to improve education in our urban slums is essential if we are to avoid serious social unrest. For a mass of unemployed and frustrated Negro youth in congested areas of a city may be compared to the piling up of inflammable material in an empty building in a city block. Potentialities for trouble are surely there. What can words like "freedom," "liberty," and "equality of opportunity" mean to these young unemployed Negroes? How well prepared are they to face the struggle with Communism, which shows no signs of abating? Our success against the spread of Communism in no small measure depends upon the successful operation of our own free society.

Dr. Conant makes it crystal clear that he is much more concerned about the plight of urban parents whose children drop out of or graduate from school without prospects of further education or employment than about the plight of suburban parents whose chief ambition is to enter their children, regardless of intellectual qualifications, in prestige colleges. Moreover, he urges suburbanites to take an active interest in improving urban education.

> I have sought to create anxious thoughts in the minds of the conscientious citizens who, while living in the suburbs, work in the city. To improve the slum schools requires an improvement in the lives of the families who inhabit the slums; but without a drastic change in the employment prospects for urban Negro youth, little can be accomplished. We need to know the facts of urban educational problems. When these facts indicate a dangerous social situation the American people should be prepared to take prompt action before it is too late.

Without becoming an alarmist, Dr. Conant, in *Slums and Suburbs,* makes a most ardent and effective plea for equal educational opportunities for Negro children and for their parents. Nevertheless, he has been severely criticized by Negro leaders, by "professional" friends of the Negro, and by many other advocates of school desegregation who feel that he has hurt their cause by his treatment of this stormy, emotion-laden problem. What does Dr. Conant actually say? First, he makes the point that the Supreme Court decision declared "the segregation of children in public schools *solely* on the basis of race" illegal. In other words, *de jure* segregation as practiced in the South is condemned by the Court, but *de facto* segregation, which is unavoidable in huge Negro ghettos, is a very different situation. "The justices," he points out, "appear to have expressed no view as to whether the pupils in a completely Negro school are deprived of equal educational opportunity if they are not assigned solely because of their race. In short, if one group of children is separated from another group because of the neighborhood in which they live, the fact of this separation is, of and by itself, no evidence of an inequality of education." Whether the facilities and instruction are equal is to be determined by examining the schools. To assume that Negro education can be satisfactory only if in each schoolroom there are some white children, in Conant's opinion, to take a defeatist view of Negro education in our large cities. I agree with him in his belief that a sense of inferiority can be removed by the expenditure of sufficient money to augment staff and facilities and by an integrated staff of white and Negro administrators and teachers.

The situation in New York City, where Negro children have been transported by bus to distant white schools, has proved that this is a trivial, costly, ineffective solution to desegregation, and in the case of the elementary-school children, may even be detrimental. There are in the New York City school system about 170,000 Negro children in the kindergarten and grades one to eight. Of these, slightly more than 6000, or a little more than 3 per cent, are transported to white schools. How was this token group chosen? I do not know, but if such an experience is essential for all Negro children, it seems a great injustice to the vast majority, since tossing 170,000 children around the city is impossible. Why make an exception for a handful? Why not use the money, instead, for improving the schools?

Moreover, is it not too great a strain for Negro children to have to journey every day to a remote white school for a few hours, and then return to their Negro neighborhoods? I discussed this procedure with some Negro high school students in another city, who, after attending a distant white high school, had returned to their Negro high school, and I am convinced that artificial desegregation is harmful. "When I left my friends and went to the white high school," said one tall young athlete, "it made me so nervous to compete with white children who are strangers to me that my hands would sweat." What, then, does being tossed between a strange white school and a familiar Negro neighborhood do to a little boy or girl?

Another point is of major importance. How can the teacher in some remote white school know the imported Negro child's home and background? Yet, without such knowledge, she is handicapped in teaching the child. No, the little elementary-school children are much better off in their community schools, with their friends, in a familiar background, even though it may be a slum.

Take, for example, the situation in Washington, D. C., where *de jure* segregation used to exist. The schools have now been integrated as far as this was possible. But the Capital still has, and always will have, all-Negro schools, because 81 per cent of the children are Negroes, and their ratio to white students has been increasing annually. Many schools cannot be desegregated except as to the teachers, since there are not enough white students to make it possible. This does not mean that these Negro children are receiving an inferior education. More of them go to college every year. This fact proves Dr. Conant's point that the Negro child in an all-Negro school does not suffer from a harmful sense of inferiority, provided that the children and their parents realize that they are not segregated on the basis of race, but out of sheer necessity.

The attacks on Dr. Conant's position are unjust. He is as much opposed to *de jure* segregation as any other law-abiding truly democratic American. Gerrymandering a district is just as abhorrent to him as *de jure* segregation. But I agree with him that "it would be far better for those who are agitating for the deliberate mixing of children to accept *de facto* segregated schools as a consequence of a present housing situation and to work for the improvement of slum schools whether Negro or white." This is in the best interests of the Negro and of the nation. It is, indeed, the only hope for upgrading the education, both academic and vocational, of the total Negro population in our Northern cities.

Since these cities contain almost half of our Negro population, the improvement of Negro education and job opportunities is the quickest route to raising the economic and social status of the race.

These improvements cannot be achieved as rapidly as they should without federal aid. The Negroes should not be afraid to use their considerable political power to urge passage by Congress of a bill for federal aid to public schools. Nor should they fear that segregation will be strengthened in the South if the all-Negro schools benefit by federal assistance. If the segregated Southern schools were made wholly equal in the quality of staff and facilities, white children would not travel for miles to go to a white school. They would go to the nearest Negro school and thus contribute in many areas to a voluntary process of desegregation.

But Negroes should insist that federal aid be refused to all private and sectarian schools. For nothing would segregate the Negro more effectively and permanently, both in the North and the South, than the proliferation of private schools, which are free to select their student bodies, and which, in any case, most Negroes cannot afford to attend. If the federal government should yield to the pressures, now heavier than ever before in the nation's history, for the support of private schools, the public schools would become pauper schools in our large cities, attended only by Negroes and poor whites.

The struggle to improve education of the urban slum schools, Negro or white or desegregated, will triumph more quickly if Dr. Conant attains his goal of arousing the conscience of our country.

Equality is the moral imperative of our era. The problem is how best to achieve it. If Negro leaders and Negro parents accept Dr. Conant's sage advice, I am convinced that his latest book, *Slums and Suburbs,* will prove to be a turning point in the history of their race, and eventually they will be grateful to him.

Not satisfied with the wound stripes he has already earned, Dr. Conant is now engaged in a study of teacher education and training. Other people have been known to step into a hornet's nest, but not deliberately. I can only say with more devoutness than I usually feel: I pray the Lord his soul will keep.

15

PUBLIC HEALTH, PUBLIC WELFARE, AND PUBLIC PROTECTION

Increasing longevity has raised the associated problem of financing the medical expenses of our senior citizens who have an average annual income of approximately $2,000. In 1956 the voters of Colorado approved a medical care program for senior citizens which provides that any resident drawing a pension from the state is eligible to receive free medical care. James Harwood, a staff reporter of the *Wall Street Journal,* writes of the problems that have beset the Colorado program.

Approximately seven million citizens are welfare recipients. A controversy has developed over the effectiveness and usefulness of the welfare system as now constituted. City Manager Joseph M. Mitchell of Newburgh, New York, touched off a nationwide furor in 1961 by his "get tough" program with welfare recipients. A. H. Raskin of the staff of the *New York Times* scrutinizes the Newburgh program, its proponents and opponents, and concludes that a re-examination of welfare programs is needed.

In an attempt to cut the expense of protective functions, a number of communities have been organizing public safety departments whose members are qualified to provide police and fire services; this relatively new development has been a controversial one. Mitchell Gordon, a staff reporter of the *Wall Street Journal,* records the problems associated with the integrated police and fire department.

James Harwood
46. Health Plan's Ills*

A little more than three years after it began, Colorado's once widely heralded program of medical care for the aged is undergoing emergency surgery.

Officials in this so-called "welfare" state issued orders earlier this year barring oldsters covered by its program from entering hospitals except in emergencies. In addition, they cut the maximum free hospital stay from 21 to 18 days, eliminated free ambulance service and limited nursing home care to only the most feeble of the aged.

The cutback in benefits followed disclosure that costs for the old-age medical program were far outstripping the $10 million budgeted for the fiscal year ending June 30; a $1.4 million deficit was looming. Even the recent cutbacks are not going to save the program from being splattered with red ink; state officials look for a deficit of more than $600,000 by the end of the fiscal year.

Increasing charges for hospital and medical services are contributing to Colorado's woes. Hospital fees have risen an average of 8% annually in each of the past four years. But over-utilization of facilities—as welfare workers term the problem—is blamed by many for the bulk of the plan's fiscal ills.

"When the state put up that money, it was like everybody had come into a big inheritance," says Walter R. McKinstry, chairman of the State Welfare Board which oversees the medical program. "Too many pensioners with colds and hernias decided it was time to go to the hospital. It wasn't long before we reached the bottom of the barrel."

IMPACT ON OTHER STATES

At a time when many other states and the Federal Government are considering the problems of paying old folks' medical bills, the troubles of Colorado's program are worth a close look. Already, they have helped bring about a re-evaluation of plans in some states engaged in setting up similar programs in order to get matching funds authorized by Congress last year. . . .

Partly because of Colorado's troubles, North Dakota is building strong safeguards against over-use into its new medical-care-for-the-aged program

---

* From the *Wall Street Journal*. June 9, 1961. pp. 1 and 14. Copyright 1961 Dow Jones & Company, Inc. All Rights Reserved. Reprinted with permission of publisher.

scheduled to go into effect July 1. Ralph M. Atkins, director of public assistance in North Dakota, reports his state will require prior authorization from a county welfare board before any pensioner is eligible for treatment. The state will also demand contributions from a patient's family when it is able to chip in.

In Tennessee, Mrs. C. Frank Scott, commissioner of the Department of Welfare, says Colorado's experience is also playing a role in shaping her state's medical program. "Don't think that Colorado deficit doesn't scare a person," she declares. Mrs. Scott says the state's plan will contain tight restrictions on entrance to hospitals. The Tennessee program is slated to go into effect July 1.

NEW MEXICO CUTS BACK

Colorado isn't the only state having trouble with existing medical care programs. On March 1, New Mexico reduced its program's benefits, limiting hospital care for the elderly to a "life-endangered-only" basis. In other moves, the state said it would only pay an oldster's expenses for a maximum of six home or office visits with a doctor a year, and limited any one hospital stay to 21 days. Previously, such benefits were unlimited. Murray A. Hintz, director of public welfare, explains: "We had to do something. We saw we were rapidly exceeding our budget."

Colorado's current cost-cutting move marks the first reduction of any part of its old age program since it was set up in 1936. At that time "all needy persons over 60" in the state who met residence requirements set by the legislature were guaranteed a pension. From time to time, the pension benefits were liberalized until today a Colorado resident 60 or over is entitled to a monthly payment of $108 from the state. However, any outside income, whether it be from the Federal Social Security program or other sources, is deducted before the payment.

To qualify as a "needy person," an applicant for a pension must not have property worth more than $1,000, aside from his residence, and his spouse must not have property worth more than $2,000. To get a pension at age 60, a person must have lived in Colorado for 35 consecutive years. To qualify at age 65, however, a Coloradan need have lived in the state for only five of the previous nine years.

In 1956, voters approved the medical program for the state's oldsters and made any person drawing a pension from the state eligible for free medical care. Of 220,282 Coloradans over 60 years of age, more than 52,000 were entitled to the medical benefits.

When voters approved the plan, they authorized a budget of $10 million annually. Hardly anyone at the time expected costs to approach such a figure for many years. "It sure looked like a lot of money then," states one legislator.

Almost immediately, spending on the program ran higher than expected. In fiscal 1957-58, first full year of the plan, costs totaled $6,500,-000; the next year they climbed to $8,151,000. By the third year, actual costs shot up to $10,246,000 but the Welfare Board avoided a deficit by postponing some spending until the current year. Early this year the problem no longer could be sidestepped. Benefits were cut sharply.

In addition, the state began a crackdown on abuses which had crept into the program and were siphoning off a growing share of the medical funds. For example, in March the Welfare Board snapped up the license of one nursing home for falsifying reports. The state bases its payments on the classification of the home, which is determined by the size of its staff and its facilities. "This home was reporting a larger staff of professional persons than it actually had in order to be paid as a top-grade home," reports Guy R. Justis, director of Colorado's Department of Public Welfare.

Welfare officials also have been vexed by the large number of pensioners who have used the program to take care of needs other than medical. Frequently cited by officials are the lonely old ladies who go to the hospital as often as possible to revel in free food and attention. Also mentioned are couples who have used the plan as a handy "sitter" for parents who couldn't be left alone.

"When the cutback first began," Mr. Justis recalls, "I received a call from a woman who chewed me out because she and her husband wanted to attend a convention and had planned to put his father in the hospital until they got back. With the rules changed, they couldn't do it."

CHECKING ON DOCTORS

The Welfare Department also swung an ax on some of the broad powers exercised by physicians under the medical program. In a move that has stirred the anger of many physicians, the state ordered hospitals to establish admissions committees of three staff doctors to rule on the conditions of all patients.

"Many physicians were being far too easy-going in determining whether an elderly patient should go into a hospital or not," says Mr. Justis. "It's much easier for a doctor to treat them in the hospital than to go traipsing around the town on house calls. So some doctors send them all to the hospital and treat them on a mass basis. This sort of thing had to be stopped."

State officials hope to get physicians to cooperate voluntarily in holding down costs of office treatments and drugs for pensioners. Claims Dr. John

E. Robbins, a Denver doctor who also serves on the State Welfare Board: "If the physicians don't cooperate, we're stuck." But Dr. Robbins isn't overly optimistic. "Take the doctor in the small town, for instance. He's got to live in that town. It's hard for him to turn folks down. And even the city doctor has to remember that each elderly patient has about 15 members of his family who are also patients and who won't be too happy if the old man isn't treated well."

Though the state's medical societies have pledged their support to the Welfare Board's efforts, many individual doctors are holding back. In private conversations, some of them jealously oppose the idea of having their diagnoses picked over by other physicians. Some also fear the possibility of public and professional criticism for "violating" the current rigid admissions requirements may make them dangerously over-cautious. Also, they blame the state for cutting back on hospital treatment without making more provisions for office and home care. . . .

BLAME PUT ON PENSIONERS

Many physicians are ruffled by the charges that they're to blame for the program's ills. Instead, they point to the pensioner. At a recent hearing of the state medical advisory board, Dr. Vetalis V. Anderson, president-elect of the Colorado Medical Society, accused healthy pensioners of "shopping around" until they found a doctor willing to put them in the hospital. At the same meeting, Dr. H. M. Husted, a Denver osteopath, told the board he has checked hospital charts and found "many who had no business taking up hospital beds."

As might be expected, some of the most vocal criticism of the recent cutbacks in the medical program is coming from the group most directly affected—the pensioners. "Medical care has been cut back to where the program is almost useless as far as old people are concerned," grumbles Charles E. Bloedarn, president of the National Annuity League.

A. H. Raskin

47. Newburgh's Lessons for the Nation*

Seven turbulent months have passed since a declaration of war on the welfare state thrust this drowsy Hudson Valley community into national prominence. Its City Manager's "get tough" program for cutting relief

* From the *New York Times Magazine*. December 17, 1961, pp. 7 and 57–59. Copyright by the New York Times. Reprinted by permission.

rolls has made Newburgh both symbol and battleground in a national conflict over the $4 billion a year American taxpayers provide for public assistance to the needy.

Ranking public officials, industrialists, union leaders, university professors, social workers, white supremacists, Negro organizations, political extremists of Right and Left, citizens worried about the high cost of government and citizens worried about the high cost of human misery have condemned or applauded the Newburgh plan with a vehemence normally reserved for debate on such cosmic matters as nuclear bomb tests or the fate of Berlin.

The noisy tide has attained such force that an earnest Newburgh youth in a checked mackinaw, standing where George Washington once made his headquarters and wrote his declination of a throne, now gives a visitor this quavering appraisal of the city's new-found celebrity: "No little town ever got so famous so fast except Little Rock, and no other town ever had so many people fighting about what it did and whether it should have done it."

Newburgh's total population of 31,000—rich and poor, employed and unemployed, sick and well—is less than one-tenth the number of persons receiving public relief in New York City, sixty miles away; all the Federal, state and local money Newburgh spends on welfare in a year would scarcely meet New York's relief bill for a single day. What significance can the success or failure of an attempt to make such a small welfare system still smaller have for the nation and its seven million relief recipients?

The seeker after answers goes first to the program's author, now the center of a storm as violent as the one that has engulfed his brain child. He is City Manager Joseph McD. Mitchell, a 39-year-old professional bureaucrat turned crusader against "bureaucrats, do-gooders and bleeding hearts." Last May he started his campaign to banish "chiselers, loafers and social parasites" from the relief rolls by ordering a surprise muster of welfare recipients at police stations. All who could walk, including the aged, the blind and the disabled, hobbled to precinct houses to identify themselves and pick up their checks. Result of the round-up: not one case of fraud.

Mitchell's next move was more comprehensive. On the strength of a special study of relief operations, he charged that shiftless migrants from the South were flooding the relief rolls and that the city was subsidizing crime, immorality, slums and a general "pollution" of social standards. This was the jumping-off point for thirteen new rules, all aimed at putting more pressure on people to quit relief.

The rules ranged from cutting off assistance to unwed mothers who bore any more illegitimate children to compelling all able-bodied men on relief to work full-time on municipal projects. Senator Barry Goldwater quickly announced that he found the Newburgh approach as exhilarating as an Arizona breeze, but his enthusiasm was not shared by the State Board of Social Welfare, which regulates basic relief policy in New York.

The board got a court order to stop the Mitchell program after denouncing it as illegal, inhuman and unnecessary. Statistics prepared by the state agency indicated that Newburgh, far from being crushed under the weight of its relief burden, had a much lighter load than other comparable cities. Even the supposed deluge of migrants flocking to Newburgh to luxuriate on relief took on less ominous dimensions in the cold light of the state report. It showed that only $205 had been spent last year on aid to new arrivals, with every penny of it reimbursed by the state.

Today, undaunted by the injunction or the state's suggestion that he has neither chiselers nor crisis to combat, Mitchell insists that his economy program is making headway through a combination of "psychological warfare" and "thought control." The psychology is directed at making life on relief as unpleasant as possible so people will be more eager to get off. A state report says the effect has been to turn welfare into a "chamber of horrors" for those seeking help.

The thought control measures are aimed at the Welfare Department staff. Mitchell believes all graduates of professional schools of social work are indoctrinated with the "maternalistic" notion that people should do nothing for themselves but leave everything to government. His remedy is to try to infiltrate the department with enough officials who are innocent of any knowledge of social work to set in motion a kind of reverse brainwashing.

In Mitchell's office at City Hall, serenity about the rightness of his program is so pervasive that he answers a question about it by turning on a wire recorder. His voice booms out an announcement that "The Newburgh Plan Continues to Succeed" and proceeds, with the mellifluous detachment of a radio commentator, to tell how the city's people fought for home rule in a revolt against the welfare state.

It is a simplistic recital, in which relief is blamed for every community ill from social disease to increased fire hazards. The fight over his program permits a clear differentiation between good guys and bad guys. Allied with Mitchell are "politicians of principle, taxpayers, the man on the street, the working man and the business man." Against him are unscrupulous politicians and assorted eggheads who dwell in a "fairyland" unrelated to real life.

Mitchell put his program to the test of the voters last month by offering to resign if two incumbent Republicans were not re-elected to the City Council. They squeaked through by narrow margins in the face of a general Democratic trend. Thus encouraged, Mitchell has been showing so many signs of eagerness to run for state-wide office that some of his closest backers have called on him to stop campaigning and spend more time on the job. His foes would be happy to have him go—but not to a higher post. They assert that the whole drive to slash relief was a cynical hoax, devised to advance Mitchell's political fortunes at the expense of the needy.

The City Manager, impassive as an Ivy League Buddha in button-down shirt and tweed sports jacket, answers such imputations with a fresh sheaf of statistics. He reports that the number of persons on relief dropped from 1,382 in February to 900 in October, without the exclusion of any-one in genuine need. The resultant savings, he says, will help give the city its first tax cut in eight years.

As usual, the figures do not go unchallenged. The state notes that wel-fare rolls in the rest of Orange County dropped even more than those in Newburgh and that fifteen other upstate welfare districts also showed bigger declines. Seasonal factors, not the Mitchell program, are held responsible for the drop.

Mitchell's assertion that his plan will make it possible to run the relief system next year for $92,000 less than the $1,000,000 in Federal, state and city funds originally projected for this year also provokes an argument. The state contends that Newburgh's share of its relief bill has been stand-ing still at a little under $340,000 a year for the last three years. Under Mitchell's new budget estimates, it says, the local contribution for 1962 will be up $40,000, not down.

The bickering over figures fades when the visitor gets away from the embattled politicians and wanders into the slum districts, where most of the relief families live. He walks past a church, with a sign proclaiming that it is a "soul saving station," and he is reminded that welfare is not merely caseload and money but also people.

He climbs inky stairs and knocks at the doors of a dozen cold-water flats. Behind each is a story of defeat—the wrecking of a life or a family by disease, desertion, lack of educational or economic opportunity, and sometimes by manifest personal inadequacy or maladjustment.

A 42-year-old father, just released from a Veterans Administration hospital after treatment for epilepsy, stares emptily into space. He worked steadily as a machinist until periodic seizures forced him to stop two years ago. "I was brought up to work," he says. "I want to take my wife and the four kids to a real house. This rathole is falling down and the landlord won't fix it up. I can't work; I just sit and shake."

A 33-year-old ironworker with one eye, who attained local fame last July as the only able-bodied man the Welfare Department could find when it tried to set up a work relief program, shivers with his wife and six children in a house that has no stove, heater or hot water. He freed himself from relief in October by earning $400 in ten days on a school construction project. Now he is having trouble getting back on the rolls because he cannot explain where $90 of his pay went. His wife is worried that the city will institute court action to put the children in foster homes.

"I have faith in The Man Upstairs," she says quietly. "He wouldn't send us children if he didn't want us to have them. We are not unfit parents, and we are not vegetables. We will fight in court to keep our kids, and we won't be in contempt because we ought to have them."

A similar determination to resist any effort to take away her children is expressed by a 28-year-old mother, whose husband has left her and who cheerfully admits that the last two of her nine children were not his. Each relief household adds a tile to the dark mosaic of lives misshapen by a boundless range of afflictions, weaknesses and social pressures. The only integrating factor in the list is the welfare check as a shield against destitution.

How does the 97 per cent of the city's population not on relief feel about the City Manager's campaign? An inquirer quickly discovers that those most ardently on Mitchell's side believe the real problem in Newburgh has been the increase in its Negro population in the last decade— from one-sixteenth of the total population in 1950 to one-sixth last year.

A retired grocer sums up his feeling this way: "The Negroes who are moving up here these days want everything for nothing; they have no respect for anybody; they knock you right off the street." A construction worker voices the same idea: "Mitchell is right in keeping the riffraff out. They come in here by the truckload, get in a house and have kids of all colors and force all the decent people to move away."

Such sentiments draw a sharp rebuke from Mayor William D. Ryan, the lone Democrat on the City Council. Ryan feels so strongly against Mitchell that he had bought a one-way bus ticket to New York to present to the City Manager on Election Day if his candidates lost. Ryan praises the desire of Negroes to move North in search of a better life as a product of the same impulses that brought the early colonists to America.

"This whole welfare fiasco was set up to frighten the Negro from coming to Newburgh," the Mayor says. "Are we to tell these people they can't seek a better way of life? We'd be playing right into the hands of the Communists if we did. We have no problems here of migrants going on relief. In fact, we have no serious welfare problem at all. The situation has been blown up out of all proportion. We are just an ordinary city as far as welfare is concerned."

For many in Newburgh, the question does not lend itself to resolution in elementary terms. They see a slow decay in their 250-year-old city and they are convinced that something needs doing to keep it healthy. They feel that the Mitchell formula is wrong in that it blames the poor for all the evils that produce poverty. They think a better approach to lower relief is to grapple with the roots of social neglect.

This means an intensified drive to attract new industries and a better coordination of community agencies to fight for more schools, improved housing and better intergroup relations. Newburgh's biggest industries now are in relatively low-paid fields like handbags and garments. Rigid patterns of segregation exist in housing. New bridges must be built between the races to prevent color conflict from taking violent expression.

The political tensions and frustrations that are reflected in Newburgh exist in a thousand other communities. Those who feel relief programs have become instruments of moral and financial bankruptcy clash with those who see in the drive to cut relief spending a general right-wing assault on all the social reforms ushered in by Franklin D. Roosevelt's New Deal.

But, even among those who consider the Newburgh plan a return to the Dark Ages in avoidance of social responsibility, there is a willingness to acknowledge that relief programs need a basic overhaul. No significant re-examination of the welfare system has been made since the depression of the Thirties brought into being, almost overnight, a host of new Government agencies to provide emergency aid to millions of jobless workers and their families.

In every major city and state, questions have been raised about the extent to which abuses have crept into relief administration, about whether enough is being done to discourage habitual dependency, and about the possibility of reorganization to guarantee that communities receive maximum social good for their welfare dollar.

One of those who believes most emphatically that relief policies have been in a state of drift and require a new look is President Kennedy's chief patrolman on the welfare front, Secretary Abraham A. Ribicoff of the Department of Health, Education and Welfare. His approach is 180 degrees different from that taken by Newburgh; he considers the Mitchell formula "heartless" and wants a vastly increased stress on positive measures to prevent people from needing relief and to rehabilitate those already on the rolls.

Mitchell has no appetite for the rehabilitation idea. He regards it as a dream word invented by "welfare bureaucrats and empire builders" to encourage taxpayers to pour more money down the drain. His theory is that the country should get back with all practicable speed to the assumption of primary responsibility for welfare by families, churches and private charities.

The heart of the difference between the Mitchell and Ribicoff schools lies in whether the main object of relief reorganization should be saving money or saving people. Ribicoff argues that a great new mission of human renewal must replace the notion that the relief rolls are a social scrap heap. This would take the accent off the search for "chiselers" and put it on the regeneration of the will-to-work and the ability-to-work of the needy.

The chief defect of existing welfare systems, in the opinion of state and Federal officials, is that most case workers are too overburdened with duties and too undersupplied with professional training. Thus they are unable to do anything worth-while in the way of analyzing the myriad problems that stand between their clients and a return to self-respect and self-support.

This is especially true in the program of aid to dependent children, which has been the target of severest criticism on the charge that it encourages illegitimacy. The question is how to curb the multiplication of children out of wedlock without punishing the children for the sins of their parents.

In the worst cases of immorality and neglect, the right answer is court procedure to place the children in institutions or foster homes, even though such care involves a tripling or quadrupling in cost to the taxpayers. But, in many cases, removing the children from an atmosphere of maternal affection, even in a broken home, is much more likely to produce disturbance or delinquency than letting children and parent stay together as a family.

Through expanded guidance and training services, unwed mothers can often be helped to lift themselves out of the need for relief. Washington, D. C., already has pioneered in this field by setting up a residential training center to instruct young mothers in trades that would enable them to become self-reliant again.

A similar broadening of family and job counseling facilities in all phases of relief, establishment of more day-care centers for children of working mothers, more stress on mental health programs—all these are part of a course that combines a recognition of human dignity with society's need for the soundest development of all its resources.

One reform that is sure to be recommended by Secretary Ribicoff is Federal participation in the financing of local work relief programs. Now such programs are authorized by state law in New York and many other areas, but no Federal money is available to help pay the bill. How great the effect of this change will be no one knows. Many communities have found work relief too expensive to be practical, and some, like Newburgh, have been hard-pressed to find anyone on their rolls physically able to man the projects.

A special committee has just submitted to Ribicoff a blueprint for changes that go far beyond the simple addition of work programs. Its aim is to turn welfare into "a positive wealth-producing force" for the nation through new preventive and protective services. Under such a plan, more money might have to be spent now, but the committee is convinced it is the only sound long-range way to cut the rolls and restore families to financial independence.

Thus, the result of the furor stirred by the Newburgh experiment may be Administration proposals to increase the range of Government activity in the welfare field. Such a solution will generate in Congress and in legislative halls an even more sonorous debate than rages here. The last has not been heard of little Newburgh as the nation strives for a welfare program that will balance the requirements of hardheadedness and warmheartedness.

Mitchell Gordon
48. Firemen-Cops*

Pressed by the soaring cost of police and fire services on one hand and by public demand for more effective protection on the other, a growing number of U. S. communities are attempting a highly controversial solution. They are combining the two public safety functions into a single department whose members are trained to perform both jobs.

In the past five years, more than a dozen U. S. cities have put their

---

* From the *Wall Street Journal.* November 27, 1961. pp. 1 and 12. Copyright 1961 Dow Jones & Company, Inc. All Rights Reserved. Reprinted with permission of publisher.

policemen and firemen into the same uniforms and have sent them out to patrol the streets until summoned to a blaze. An almost equal number of cities have had the plan in operation for a longer time. Proposals for additional police-fire mergers are in various stages of study and debate in a number of other cities.

Communities now operating under the single department plan range in size from Sewickley Heights, Pa., with a population under 1,000, to Dearborn, Mich., and Winston-Salem, N. C., both with populations of more than 100,000. It is generally agreed that the system is more applicable to small towns than to big cities, but such major municipalities as San Diego (population: 600,000) and Seattle (575,000) in recent years have become embroiled in controversies stemming from police-fire merger proposals.

The opposition to these mergers usually is led by the policemen and firemen themselves. They are not particularly attracted to the other fellow's job and contend both services are likely to suffer when departments are integrated.

BIG BUDGET ITEMS

Police and fire protection are usually the two largest items in city budgets. According to the U. S. Census Bureau, police and fire services absorbed 18% of the $11.8 billion American cities spent in their fiscal years ended during 1960. Since personnel costs take $8 of every $10 spent by the two departments, substantial economies appear to be impossible without a more efficient use of manpower.

A strong appeal of police-fire integration, its advocates contend, is that it turns the idle time of firemen to useful purposes. A survey of firemen's time, published in June by the San Diego municipal government, showed that in the period under study the city's firemen spend only 1.3% of their work week responding to alarms. . . .

This reasoning understandably brings angry rebuttals from fire officials. Firemen generally concede they spend only a small part of the time actually fighting fires, but they argue fire-fighting skills cannot be developed by men who must do police work part of the time. The firemen say that in combined departments teamwork suffers, with potentially dangerous consequences in the handling of major fires.

Firemen also contend they work considerably longer hours than policemen and that the reduction of their work week to police levels would cancel many of the alleged economies of a combined service. According to the International City Managers Association, the work week last year for firemen in most cities of more than 10,000 population was 63 hours, compared with 40 or 42 hours for patrolmen. . . .

HOW INTEGRATION WORKS

The degree to which police-fire integration is practiced varies widely from place to place. But the concept of the single safety department is a relatively simple one. In its purest form, practiced by Oak Park, Mich., and Sunnyvale, Calif., among other cities, it calls for the manning of fire stations by only the number of men needed to drive fire trucks to a blaze. There, the trucks are met by public safety officers summoned to the scene by radio messages received in their patrol cars.

The public safety officer usually wears a police uniform but is equipped with a fireman's helmet, coat and boots, which he carries in his patrol car and dons at the scene of a fire. The officer also customarily carries a fire extinguisher and may have hydrant wrenches, rope and other gear useful in emergencies.

There are several variations on this system. Occasionally, cities lump police and fire forces into a single public safety department although there is no real integration of personnel. In these cases, one individual, perhaps called the public safety commissioner, may head both forces. Another variation is followed by a number of Illinois communities, Champaign, Rock Falls, Park Forest, Glencoe and Evanston among them. They maintain permanent, unintegrated police and fire forces and also have a group of public safety officers trained to serve with either force, wherever they are most needed.

There appears to be considerable enthusiasm for police-fire integration among officials of some cities where it has been in operation for a long time and among taxpayer and citizens' groups which have studied the plan. . . .

In Sunnyvale, which has had a combined department since 1957, City Manager Perry Scott figures the unification is saving more than $300,000 a year from what it would cost to maintain separate departments. Although most of this saving comes from a greater efficiency in the use of manpower, Mr. Scott asserts, some of it results from not having to maintain two sets of buildings, two communications centers, record departments and similar facilities.

Sunnyvale officials recently published a brochure in which they made the point that public safety officers touring in patrol cars usually arrive at fires ahead of the fire trucks. In a six-month period to Dec. 31, 1959, the city found, the first two patrol cars were at the scene of a fire on an average of 2.6 minutes after the alarm was turned in. The average for the city's fire trucks was 3.3 minutes after the alarm. Proponents of police-fire mergers argue that the arrival of help a minute quicker could mean the difference between a life lost or a life saved.

On the other hand, critics of the combined departments claim it takes longer to assemble a full fire-fighting force when the men are scattered around a city and that public safety officers are less effective in working together than full-time firemen would be. These critics also recall one case in which thieves set several diversionary fires in a Canadian city with a combined department, then proceeded to help themselves to $120,000 from a credit union. Proponents of unification say this should not happen if the single department is adequately manned. . . .

POORER FIRE RATINGS?

It is a commonly heard contention of opponents of police-fire integra-tion that the mergers of these departments usually lead to poorer fire ratings. The California Fireman, a monthly publication of the California Firemen's Association, recently claimed that "fire insurance rates are far higher in cities with integrated departments" than in communities with separate forces. . . .

But the Missouri Public Expenditure Council stated after a recent survey that it was unable "to find one city that had been penalized" in its fire rating because of a police-fire merger. And an official of the National Board of Fire Underwriters in New York recalls no such case. On the contrary, the fire grades of Sunnyvale and Oak Park have improved since these cities combined their departments, though officials say this might be due to better water supplies as much as anything else.

Last summer, an unsuccessful effort was made in the Illinois legislature —reportedly with the backing of the Illinois state chapter of the Inter-national Association of Fire Fighters—to outlaw combined police and fire departments. . . .

BAY STATE PROHIBITION

In Massachusetts, the IAFF has been more successful. In 1959 the legislature there passed a law prohibiting combined departments in cities of more than 40,000 population. There were no integrated departments in the state at the time and there is none now.

An IAFF pamphlet, Fight Back! seeks to present the case against police-fire mergers. On the first page there is this statement: "Almost without exception, those communities that have given the plan a trial have returned to separate fire and police departments. The experience of seven California cities is typical. The cities of Buena Park, Chico, Fremont, Hawthorne, Monterey Park, Sanger and San Marino tried combining the two departments and reverted to separate fire and police departments. It may have taken a disaster to prove the unworkability of the scheme; in most cases, however, it was community dissatisfaction with lowered fire and police service that brought the return to separate departments."

According to a tally published in October by the Cleveland Bureau of Governmental Research, Inc., only 15 of 88 cities credited with some form of police-fire integration have abandoned it. A Wall Street Journal check on the seven California cities mentioned in the IAFF pamphlet shows that three of the communities—Chico, San Marino and Fremont—never carried police-fire integration beyond the stage of a single safety director heading both forces. And in at least two of the other communities, according to public officials there, unification was abandoned principally because of dissatisfaction among department personnel rather than among the citizenry. . . .

16

PLANNING AND
URBAN RENEWAL

Although city planning can be traced to an early origin, only in the post-World War II period has it begun to receive proper attention.

Zoning, a tool of plan implementation, refers to the division of a community into zones and the establishment of regulations governing the use of land within each zone. New York City in 1916 was the first city to adopt a comprehensive zoning ordinance.

Mr. Dennis O'Harrow, executive director of the American Society of Planning Officials, illustrates zoning principles by discussing the result of zoning a 160 acre tract for residential, commercial, or industrial use and the impact upon the community of each type of zoning.

Robert L. Zion, an architect and site planner, offers several unusual ideas for the improvement of cities including gallerias, parklets, zoolets, and water squares. Although Mr. Zion's article is entitled "Some Impractical Ideas for the Improvement of Cities," a serious study of his suggestions reveals that they may not be as "impractical" as the title of the article implies.

The automobile has had a greater impact upon cities than any other development of the past seventy-five years; it has been primarily responsible for urban sprawl, deterioration of downtown areas, traffic congestion, and parking problems. Frederick W. Roevekamp, a staff correspondent of *The Christian Science Monitor*, views the program of Henry A. Barnes, head of New York City's traffic department, to relieve the City's traffic jam.

Dennis O'Harrow
49. Steps to Secure Sound Zoning*

I am inclined to be dubious about step-by-step instructions on anything. I have at home one of these interlocking wooden puzzles which came with a set of step-by-step instructions on how to put it together. However, the instructions omitted one very vital step: they forgot to tell you how to take the thing apart before you started putting it together.

So I will give you my version of how to get a good zoning ordinance for a city. But I am afraid it is not going to be quite the conventional How-To-Do-It set of instructions.

It seems to be a common characteristic of human beings—perhaps more so of American human beings—to want to get things done as rapidly as possible. And when we see something being done by an expert, it always looks so easy.

When you see the piano being played by Hoffman or Fats Waller (perhaps that dates me) you think "Gee, that looks easy! Maybe I could do it." But when you come out of the dream world, you know very well that you can't hope to play the piano like one of the experts unless you are willing to spend the years of eight-hour practice days that those men have spent before you saw them. Maybe the reason that you are more willing to concede the pianist's unusual ability is because you recall some grueling childhood hours of piano practice or practice on some other instrument.

Well, let me ask you then to transfer some of that realization of the difficulty in musical performance over to the arts of city planning and zoning.

In fact, in some ways the musician has an easier job than does the city planner. The musician knows that the notes of his copy of Beethoven's or Gershwin's music are not going to jump around and change completely the next time he has to perform the composition.

The city planner has no such assurance. In fact, just the opposite, he is quite sure that the problems he solved in writing the zoning ordinance for the last city will be quite different from the problems he meets when he goes to the next city.

My first instruction, then is this: Don't be in too much of a hurry, be-

---

* National Industrial Zoning Committee (Columbus, Ohio: National Industrial Zoning Committee, no date). Reprinted with permission of publisher and American Society of Planning Officials.

cause the construction of a good zoning ordinance is a very difficult undertaking.

Now I want to talk about zoning on a specific piece of land, and I want to use as an illustration a tract of land that each of you knows. In order to do this I am going to ask each of you to recall a specific tract of land that he is familiar with lying outside his home city. Of course, each of you will have a different tract, but I hope you will be able to translate the things I say and apply them to that tract of land.

Here are the specifications: It should be a quarter section of land, 160 acres. It should be outside your home town in the direction in which the city seems to be growing. It should lie alongside a principal highway and should be a half-mile to a mile-and-a-half beyond the area that is now built up.

I hope that you can recall such a piece of land, if not such a specific quarter section at least an area in which such a specific quarter section could be found. The topography should be reasonably flat so that there are no particular construction problems involved. Incidentally, I want it a little beyond the present built-up or building-up section so that there is not an obvious pressure on the land at the moment for classification in any certain type of zone. But it should be land that will be developed within the next ten or twelve years.

Now let's take your 160 acre tract and try out some zoning on it to see what is involved. First let us zone it for residential use.

It would undoubtedly be single-family residence since that is almost the universal type of residential development in a fringe area. At the current popular density of residential development, the quarter section will eventually house 750 families—slightly less than 5 families per gross acre. In 750 families there will be 2,500 to 3,000 persons. What does this mean?

Well, it means a lot of things. For one thing, it means that you will have about 750 school children in that area. To meet the needs of these school children for reasonable standards of education you would need 16 to 17 new primary school rooms and 10 to 12 new high school rooms. You would need 15 to 20 acres of school land. At the current costs for building schools you would need an investment of somewhere between $600,000 and a million dollars. Your school budget for these children would be around $200,000 per year.

And don't forget! All of this school plant and school budget is *in addition to your present school plant and school budget.* All for the people who are going to live on your 160 acre tract that you have zoned in single-family residence.

Schools aren't the only thing that you need to serve this residential area, by a long shot. You will need to add three to four more policemen on your force, three to four more firemen and another piece of fire equipment. Your water supply plant must be ready to supply about one-third million gallons of water per day over and above what it now supplies. You should have (and this is one community facility that is being most neglected in today's residential expansion) about 15 acres of parks and playgrounds, just for the 750 families. *Additional* parks and playgrounds, remember! Of course, if you want to zone the 160 acre tract for apartments, say up to a density of 20 families per acre, you would multiply all these figures by four—two and a half to four million dollars in school plant, 12 to 15 additional policemen, and one and a third million gallons of water per day.

Let's try out another classification on your quarter section of land. Let's try commercial zoning. Let's make full use of the 160 acres as a regional shopping center.

If you provide the proper amount of off-street parking on the tract you would be able to get *only* about 35 to 40 acres of retail sales space, approximately one and one half million square feet. For such a center to be successful it would need to be the primary shopping center for a population of approximately 200,000 people living not more than 30 minutes driving time distance and not separated from any of its potential customers by a major natural boundary such as a river. Nor should there be any serious competition for shopping goods within that distance.

If this shopping center is going to be successful, I will tell you what must take place. 5,000 to 6,000 automobiles must drive into and out of the parking lot each day. These automobiles will bring 10,000 customers. Each day these 10,000 customers will spend $50,000 and over the year they will have spent some $15,000,000 in your 160 acre shopping center tract.

That is a lot of people, a lot of money, and a lot of automobiles and auto traffic. Your roads to the center must be able to handle that kind of traffic. And I have a hunch that you will need at least as many traffic policemen to handle the crowds on the 160 acre commercial tract as you would have needed patrolmen to take care of the 160 acre residential development.

Let's try a third alternative on the quarter section. Let's zone it for industry. As I am sure you know, we can't generalize as well about what will take place under industrial development, or what is required, as we can with residential or commercial development. Industrial types are much too diverse. Nevertheless, we can give some ranges.

With modern practices in factory design and location, the quarter section of land would end up with somewhere between a half million and three million square feet of factory floor space. The number of employees would range somewhere from 2,000 to 15,000, give or take 10,000 employees one way or the other.

The facilities that are needed to supply an industrial development also will vary widely. For example, take water. You may need only enough water for domestic use of the employees while they are on the site, which would run 20 to 40 gallons per day per employee, plus enough reserve water for fire protection. Or you might get in a heavy water using industry requiring a supply on the order of 50 million gallons per day. (The tract is too small for an integrated steel plant. Otherwise, we would be up in the range of 750 to 1,000 million gallons per day.) You have the problem of industrial waste disposal, which again might be nothing more than minor sanitary waste or something requiring a phenomenal engineering structure.

No matter what industries go in there, you have to be sure that you have rail and truck facilities to handle raw materials in and finished products out. Again, you have a whale of a traffic problem.

I am sure that most of you here are familiar with the latest in the series of studies on "What 100 New Factory Workers Mean to a Community." This was issued by the United States Chamber of Commerce just last year. Now, whether or not you agree with the U. S. Chamber's exact figures, I am fairly confident that each of you would fight to the death for the axiom that new factories bring in new people, new business and new money. So we will just adapt a few of those figures to our new 160 acre industrial development.

If we assume toward the bottom of our employee range that there would be 5,000 employees on the site, the U. S. Chamber of Commerce says that this would mean 15,000 more people, 5,600 more households, and 5,035 new automobile registrations.

Take the 5,600 new households alone. That is just about eight times as many as we figured would be on this quarter section of land if we zoned it for residential use. That means two square miles of new residential land, 5,000 more school children, 175 more school rooms, and so on and so on and so on. I don't think we want to go through all *that* again.

Maybe you can see from this conglomeration of figures I have been tossing around why certain New England towns are desperately seeking for some legal method (they don't even care too much whether it's legal) to halt development of all kinds completely. I wouldn't blame you if you decided that the highest and best use of your particular quarter section of land is its present use as sheep pasture.

But we might as well be realistic about this thing. Except for a few ifs: if you selected a quarter section of land that is in the logical path of development, if economic blight does not descend on your particular city, and if we keep the H-bomb under wraps, that 160 acre tract of land *will* be developed. So we are going to have these problems, whether we like them or not.

The second point that I want you to recognize is that zoning is not and cannot be an isolated operation. I have tried to illustrate this by referring zoning to an undeveloped tract of land. Zoning in a partially developed city takes on exactly the same type of inter-relationships, perhaps on a lesser scale. Rezoning a fully developed area brings up some other problems which are even more difficult to solve, but I don't think that we need to go into details here.

This is part of the ever repeated and desperate cry of the planners. Zoning is only part of the job. Unless a zoning ordinance is tied in with comprehensive planning, planning for streets, for public transit, for water supply, for sewers, for schools, for parks, for playgrounds—the so-called "protection" given by the ordinance will disappear within a year.

This brings me to the third point of zoning, which is perhaps the most difficult one to explain. It is difficult because it is a request that you discard some basic notions about zoning which I am sure most of you have. One of these basic notions is contained in the word which I used before, "protection." It appears enclosed in quotation marks. It symbolizes a negative approach to zoning.

What do I mean by "negative"?

It means that we look at a zoning ordinance with the idea that it is a long list of "thou shalt not" commandments. "Thou shalt not build a slaughter house in my industrial district." "Thou shalt not build thy house nearer than 25 feet to a property line." "Thou shalt not put up a store building unless thou providest a stall to park my automobile." And so on.

How would I word these?

I would like to think of these statements in the positive form: here will be a district of unobnoxious and pleasant factories. Here we want broad streets with green lawns that are pleasant to drive through. Here we want a shopping area which is pleasant, convenient and efficient to use.

Now this may seem to you as merely two ways of saying exactly the same thing. But that isn't true. Negative zoning is an attempt to prevent people from doing the things they want to do.

Positive zoning, on the other hand, is an attempt to help people to do the things that they want to do. A negative zoning ordinance acquires, by accretion, a longer and longer list of prohibitions. Positive zoning is a legal tool used to carry out a positive land use plan for development of the city. And a land use plan is the positive expression of the people, through their plan commission and through their city council, of the type of city they wish to live in.

The third requirement in the zoning process, then, is that we think of it as a legal tool used to help guide the development of our city, not as a law designed to take away property rights. You can be sure of a positive zoning ordinance *only* if you have an acceptable and accepted land use plan.

This brings me to a point of technique in the zoning ordinance itself, a weakness that is found increasingly in newer zoning regulations. It is also a weakness, sad to say, that it has been introduced into the ordinances by planners and zoning experts themselves—not excluding the speaker.

In the most modern and modernized zoning ordinances we are trying to do too much. We are trying to include in one legal document enough subject matter and regulation for six or a dozen laws. We are trying to establish controls and standards in many fields which are not properly within the sphere of zoning and land use regulation. Most of the time, I fear that we are doing only a half-baked, inadequate job of regulation in these outside fields, in these subjects which have no business being forced into a zoning ordinance.

For example, take the subject of off-street parking. Any zoning ordinance which makes any pretense of being up to date includes requirements for off-street parking. There shall be one off-street parking space for each dwelling unit. There shall be one off-street parking space for each 100 square feet of retail sales space. There shall be one off-street parking space for each two employees on the largest shift.

I think that we will all agree that the automobile is here to stay. It is an integral, important, and even necessary part of modern life. Any structure which does not provide for the necessities of modern living is a substandard structure. Substandard structures create blight and slums and unpleasant cities. Any structure which does not provide off-street parking is substandard and will inevitably create blight.

A dwelling or a store or a factory without inside toilet facilities is also substandard. But we do not write into our zoning ordinances a requirement that all structures built in the future shall have inside toilet facilities. We leave that requirement where it belongs, in a sanitary code or a building code. For this same reason, off-street parking requirements should not be in a zoning ordinance, but should be in a traffic control ordinance.

Now right here, I am going to make a contradictory statement and then try to explain it away. Whenever I am asked to criticize a zoning ordinance, one of the first things I look for is off-street parking provisions. If I do not find them I say that the zoning ordinance is inadequate and will not work. I do this because, so far as I know, there is no city with a traffic ordinance which contains adequate off-street parking standards. In the current state of our municipal ordinances, the only place that this very important problem is recognized is in the zoning ordinance. This also explains why planners have gone so far out on the limb in loading a zoning ordinance with all sorts of extraneous material. These regulations that are quite necessary for the intelligent development of a city are not being handled anywhere else. In some cases, the planner may have been able to slip into the zoning ordinance regulations which would not be accepted as separate ordinances. I fear that in many cases the planner has not even tried to discover whether a separate control ordinance would be accepted.

For this reason we find in many zoning ordinances elaborate regulations and controls for air pollution, noise abatement, housing, trailer camps, tourist camps, drive-in theatres and drive-in restaurants, filling stations, and a host of other matters.

Again, to soften any criticism of planners, I will say that through the zoning ordinance the planner has pioneered in a great many things establishing standards for new and different uses. He will probably always do so. Nevertheless, when these ideas are beyond the experimental stage and well established they should be the subject of separate ordinances.

One of the essentials of zoning is that it establishes different regulations for different zoning districts, although in each district the regulation is uniform. This is one clue to extraneous material in a zoning ordinance. For example, gasoline storage tanks for a filling station are properly located underground whether the filling station is in a neighborhood commercial district, a central business district, an industrial district, or even as a non-conforming use in a residential district. This requirement does not vary from district to district but it is uniform throughout the city, wherever a filling station is to be located. Therefore, this type of regulation does not need to be in a zoning ordinance, but should be in a general code regulating construction and safety for filling stations. The same thing can be said of requiring off-street parking space for each dwelling unit, whether it be located in a single-family residential district, two-family residential district, apartment district, commercial district, or industrial district (if you are going to permit residences in an industrial district).

The fourth requirement then is that a zoning ordinance should properly embrace only zoning, and should leave smoke control to an air pollution ordinance, sirens to a noise abatement ordinance, and trailers to a trailer ordinance.

Finally, I would draw the obvious inference from all that I have said before. I have said that the preparation of a zoning ordinance is difficult and time consuming. I have said that zoning is bound to be improper unless it is part of a study and plan for the entire city. I have said that zoning should be a positive thing, an expression of a land use plan. I have said that zoning should stick to zoning and not try to cover every conceivable regulation needed for the proper growth of a city.

To me this adds up to just one thing: the zoning ordinance must be prepared by the co-operative efforts of the people of the city, the city's legislators and administrators, and the best professional planning help you can get. In zoning and planning, just as in most other services in the world today, you are generally going to get just about what you are willing to pay for. That is not quite true, because in the long run you pay a lot more for a cheap job than you do for one that was done right in the first place. This is such a well-known principle that I am sure that I do not need to explain it.

If you are going to ask that your zoning ordinance be done by the city attorney in his spare time, or by a local surveyor, it is my advice that you forget about it entirely and get along with your 1923 version or with none at all.

But if you really have the idea that you would like to help your city become a better place in which to live and to work, that you would like to see rational progress into the future, then I recommend that you approach land use planning and zoning as a creative process which is worth all the time and money and intelligence and patience that you can dig up to put into it.

Robert L. Zion
50. Some Impractical Ideas for the Improvement of Cities*

In these days of cholesterol panic, one insidious ailment has spread rapidly and unremedied among planners in high places. Its common name: "Hardening of the Categories"—a sort of total occlusion of the imagination.

Victims of the disease are stricken first in their vocabulary—an increasing recurrence of certain telling words: *extravagant* (in the sense that the grand boulevards of Paris and the parks of London take real estate off the tax rolls), *impractical* (as the canals of Venice), *unfeasible* (as the breath-

---

* From *Journal of the American Institute of Architects*. February 1962. pp. 25–29. Reprinted with permission of publisher and Robert Zion-Harold Breen, Site Planners —Landscape Architects, New York City.

taking siting of San Gimignano), *uneconomical* (as Tivoli, Copenhagen's in-town amusement center).

No cure is yet known, and though therapy can now restore most coronary cases to normal lives, the insidious combination of flattery and fear which surrounds all political jobs induces sick planners to continue useless and, in many cases, destructive careers.

With the exception of certain sections, perhaps, of Boston, Philadelphia, Savannah, San Francisco and New Orleans, American cities have "designed" pleasure right out of their lives by using efficiency and economy as their sole design criteria. Anyone who lives or works in our cities today will attest that they neither work efficiently nor charm effectively. If they are to survive, we must introduce some of the "impractical" amenities and pleasures of urban life which Europeans have treasured for centuries. Here are a few such conceptions which would add to the pleasure of life in New York or any other city:

INSTANT GALLERIA

What American tourist sipping expresso at a cafe in Milan's Galleria or strolling through the GUM Store in Moscow hasn't wished for a similar place at home? Easily done! The recipe: Take one crosstown street (predominantly low brown-stones) and close to auto traffic; pin aluminum frames to the walls of buildings on both sides (greenhouse construction); span street and roof with lightweight transparent plastic; install sidewalk cafes. Heat with braziers for winter; air-condition for summer. Cut service alleys from two adjoining streets; season lavishly with potted palms; trail flowers from upper story windows; add pools and fountains to taste. Then, enjoy the mad scramble for leases at astronomic rentals in this in-town all-weather shopping center.
Arrivederci Milano!*

LOST OPPORTUNITIES

Every true New Yorker has at some time looked with nostalgia at a midtown building site newly cleared by demolition crews and imagined it a tree-filled square. How tantalizing was the abandoned Astor Plaza site for almost a year—begging to be filled and planted to trees, which New York needs so desperately. Imagine the Seagram Building on a pedestal overlooking "Seagram Park" (a Madison Avenue adman's dream). Costly?

---

* Strangely enough, Cleveland and several other American cities already have arcades, which they have allowed to deteriorate. These facilities can be turned into priceless advantages in the new struggle to revive the Central Business District.

Perhaps too much to expect of private industry—though the advertising possibilities of such a donation are limitless—but not too much to expect of the city. The outright cost of the land and its removal from the tax rolls would be more than repaid by the inevitable increase in the taxable value of surrounding properties overlooking the new park.

PARKLETS (THE KINNEY SYSTEM)

It is a certainty that New York City can never acquire too much park land. We desperately need every parcel we can get, but not every acquisition need be a Central Park or a Bryant Park—not every park must have a meadow or lake or ramble—or even grass. Webster defines a park as "a piece of ground, in or near a town or city, kept for ornament and recreation and usually enclosed." Central Park fits this definition. But, so does the 50' × 100' site of a deteriorating brownstone, leveled, paved and planted solidly to trees and enlivened perhaps by the splash of a wall fountain. Fifty or one hundred such parklets scattered throughout town would add immeasurably to the pleasure of life in the city.

If the Kinney Parking Systems were converted into the Kinney Park System—each parking lot made in a "parklet" as described above—New York City would be the greenest city in the world with adequate space for Mr. Hartford's "Memorial" well outside Central Park and, perhaps, even a new home for evicted folk singers. Our choice for the next park commissioner: A. H. Kinney, for the keen sensitivity with which he has unwittingly assembled a perfect urban park system for New York City.

ZOOLETS

Any New Yorker who has ever dined on the terrace overlooking the seal pool in Central Park will assure you that this is one of the most delightful experiences in our city. It isn't the food, certainly, so it must be the animals. And anyone who has worked on lower Broadway for a time will recall with a sigh the pleasant lunch-hours spent in the aquarium (seals again!).

If animals bring such pleasure, why not scatter them throughout the city in little "zoolets" or one-ring zoos. A seal pool at one location, a monkey cage or aviary of brightly colored birds at another.

The "parklet" which houses a "zoolet" will be fenced to protect the animals and a subway token or more charged for admission to defray maintenance costs (an attendant). Perhaps a municipal band made up of golden-aged musicians might oom-pah-pah during the lunch hour.

DOWN TO THE SEA AGAIN

New York City is an island, yet how seldom in our daily living are we aware of or able to enjoy this delightful fact? We have turned our backs to the water, ignoring the excitement, the color, the sound, and the romance of the busiest harbor in the world. Strange, when we all know of the delights which the Seine brings to Paris, the canals to Venice and the Thames to London. What traveler to Naples can forget dinner at a harbor restaurant set to the music of strolling mandolinas?

Except for a narrow linear park along Riverside Drive and a very grand bland bore at the Battery, we enjoy no social use of our waterfront; we have handed it over to commerce without a whimper. Let's take it back and treat ourselves to some hotels and restaurants (municipally owned concessions, perhaps) on those abandoned piers. Or flatten the roofs of some of the active piers to accommodate glass-walled restaurants with ceilings open to the sky in the summer. Perhaps the steamship companies can be induced to supply the cuisine so that atop the French Line pier one could dine and dance as aboard the Liberte while watching the great liner being loaded under floodlight. This ought to give ocean travel a boost. And while they're at it, why not revive the midnight sailing with band music and color streamers?

Why not river barges (reconditioned sand and gravel scows) equipped as restaurants or dance pavillions moored during the spring and summer along the East and West Side Drives? It's done in Rome and even in Moscow.

WATER SQUARES

Let's allow the river to come back into the city as it used to and recreate the old water squares or "slips" as waterfront parks where downtown workers can dine alfresco at the water's edge.

Many of these old slips are surrounded by blocks of early nineteenth-century buildings intact but deteriorating rapidly. Too little of our past is allowed to remain, as housing projects and commerce centers require that entire sections be destroyed to make room for characterless immensities. That we miss the past can be seen from the annual tourist trek to the old cities of Europe. Museums don't help. It's the living, *working* past that charms. Let the city recondition some of the old buildings that cluster around the east-side slips. One slip could become a gourmet square where the ground floors would be equipped and rented to the finest seafood restaurants in town. And during the spring and summer, there could be dining at the sidewalk under trees (autos would be excluded). Another slip could become the antique center of the city, the ground floors being rented exclusively to antique dealers. How much more suitable to use these buildings of the past than to scatter antique shops haphazardly along Second and Third Avenues. And how much better for business and tourist trade this picturesque concentration could be—an elegant "Flea Market" to vie with Paris, Rome and Madrid. And the upper stories could be restored to apartments. A delightful place to live!

THE CITY AFTER DARK

Such a plan would bring life to a section of the city which few New Yorkers ever visit—a dead city after dark. The city of Philadelphia is sponsoring a large restoration program, but we can learn from the Philadelphia story that the restoration of isolated buildings as opposed to clusters or entire districts takes on the lifeless character of a museum.

THE COMPLEAT TRANSPORTATION CENTER

History nowhere records an attempt of the Doges to suspend bocce courts or bowling alleys from the ceiling of San Marco. But New Yorkers have recently been told that this is the only means of saving Grand Central Station.

If a town square must produce income to survive (Grand Central is, after all, a town square) then let's eliminate the cheap shops that clutter the interior, and those giant cigarette ads. Rip the automobile chassis from the walls, and in their place—along the grand balconies—accommodate ticket offices of all the airlines, steamship companies, travel agencies, etc.—everything to do with travel. It will perhaps be possible to utilize the abandoned train tunnel on Park Avenue south of the terminal to bring in airline buses, thus eliminating any need for the East and West Side Terminals. Rentals now accruing to these inconveniently located (and ugly) facilities would certainly keep Grand Central afloat without hanging anything from the ceiling unless it's a ticket agency for trips to the moon.

We're all for a grand equestrian statue of St. Jane Jacobs in Washington Square Park—with lots of pigeons on it—for her lonely crusade to preserve neighborhoods for the underprivileged! But, Jane, let's not abandon the privileged and the overprivileged who are always with us. Along with Mrs. Jacobs' corner candy store let's have some waterfront hotels and restaurants, gallerias, sidewalk cafes, parklets, zoolets, etc.—"impractical concepts" only if the word *pleasure* is no longer a part of the planner's vocabulary.

If a piece such as this must have a conclusion, it is this: American city life is clearly not the delight it should be. Yet, we can't place all of the blame on the "constricting regimentation" of the gridiron plan. Some goes to the designers who are thinking "too big"; they are redesigning huge areas but ignoring eye-level details and the pleasures of the pedestrian. But largely responsible for the plight of our cities are the all-too-practical planners. If our urban designs are to revive our ailing cities, we must first revive or replace our ailing planners and city officials. When "imaginative" and "impractical" are used synonymously around City Hall it's time to open the windows and air the rooms.

Frederick W. Roevekamp

51. Traffic Boss Sees the Light*

NEW YORK JAM

Henry A. Barnes, the man who has set out to disentangle New York City's traffic jams in the next five years, pointed out of his tenth-floor office window down at the two unbroken lines of cars whose rooftops glinted in the morning sun as they crawled across Brooklyn Bridge like a procession of multihued centipedes.

"The average speed at peak traffic hour down there now is three to four miles an hour," he said. He swiveled his chair back to his desk in one quick movement, answered a question from his secretary on the intercom, and then said:

"We can push that up to 30 miles an hour if we replace the traffic signals in the areas at each end of the bridge by systems that adjust automatically to traffic demand."

The thickening traffic jams in American cities, Mr. Barnes said, result from the stepchild treatment traffic departments get compared with housing, health, and sanitation.

"The future of our cities will depend largely on whether traffic can be made to flow more rapidly and more safely," he said. Within traditional

---

* From *The Christian Science Monitor*. June 9, 1962. p. 1. Reprinted with permission of the author and publisher.

limitations, however, cities such as Houston, Los Angeles, Atlanta, Baltimore, and Denver have made substantial progress.

PROBLEM EASIER ELSEWHERE

In other countries, the problem is still in an earlier stage and thus easier to solve, he said. Tokyo has the worst. London, on the other hand, which he visited some time ago, "would not faze me. They have 575 traffic lights; we have 9,000. Europe has the traffic problems New York had 25 years ago."

Last January, when Mr. Barnes took over as the city's new traffic commissioner, preceded by his reputation as an internationally known get-things-done man in traffic, the question seemed to be "when" instead of "if."

But Mr. Barnes had not changed his mind about the practicability of his ideas. He has merely found that over the past five increasingly controversial months in his new post that double-parked cars and inflexible lights may not be the worst obstacles in the path of his sweeping improvement program.

No doubt Mr. Barnes was aware of this to some degree before he came. But the complexity of this city government and politics has a way of taking even a well-prepared newcomer by surprise.

This may partly explain why his public emphasis on priorities in his triple-phased program (construction of off-street parking space, electronization of the signals system, and conversion from two-way to one-way arteries) appears to have shifted somewhat in recent weeks.

The park commissioner, Newbold Morris, does not want garages under the parks. The City Planning Commission and its chairman, James Felt, does not want them in midtown. Businessmen and motorists resist one-way avenues. Borough presidents protest when another borough gets more traffic money than their borough gets.

Confronted with this multiple threat in a city famed for the ferocity of its devotion to protesting against government, Mr. Barnes apparently has decided on a beachhead strategy: He now aims to achieve striking results in one phase—signals—which will help him gain support in tackling the rest.

"We'll build garages everywhere except midtown," he said in an interview this week. "We'll build anywhere except under the parks. We won't make big directional conversions for the time being, and we'll try to spread the money around the boroughs without thinning it out to the point where it becomes useless."

AN UNBLINKING RED LIGHT

"But one thing we shall do and that is the lights," he said—leaving no doubt that this is the point where his opponents will find an unblinking red light.

Mr. Barnes's reputation has been built primarily on what he has done elsewhere through installing traffic-signal systems capable of adjusting their cycles constantly to the changing flow of traffic.

The length of cycles in these lights is changed by a central computer which, in turn, receives its information about the current traffic flow from an electronic detector. Lights change simultaneously in each control area after information from all detectors has been evaluated by computers. Baltimore has eight such control areas; New York would have about 25.

In Baltimore, from where Mr. Barnes came, it took commuters 1½ hours to drive into town over a certain major artery. New traffic lights cut that down to 25 to 30 minutes.

In Denver, where he served as traffic chief from 1947 to 1953, a pair of two-way streets that was used by no more than 400 cars in an entire day was streamlined to handle 2,000 in a single peak hour. This was done by banning parking on both sides, building a bridge across a creek, installing 44 traffic-sensing signals lights, and creating one-way streets.

Ultimately, a "thousand per cent" improvement is possible provided all three phases of his program are carried out, he asserted.

In addition, mass transportation such as trains, subways, and buses also must be improved to reduce the number of those who clog the streets.

"Most of our streets are nothing but parking lots. You've got to get those cars off the streets if you want to achieve anything."

ANOTHER FINANCIAL LEAGUE

As the first immediate actions after taking office, the new traffic commissioner launched a program for larger, more legible street signs; converted two downtown Manhattan arteries into one-way traffic effective early in June; initiated a test program of new signal-light cycles (popularly called "Barnes dance") at some intersections; ordered double center lines on major arteries to separate traffic more effectively; set up a new radio network which keeps department inspectors in instant touch with headquarters; and doubled the volume of the painting program for school crosswalks.

His timetable for the next five years alone—leaving out improvements in other areas—calls for more than half of all major arteries in Brooklyn,

Queens, and the Bronx to operate under the higher-speed system and for "considerable improvements in Manhattan."

Just to cover the first year of his program for replacing New York's 9,000 signals will run $15,000,000 to $20,000,000.

"If we don't get that, we might as well settle down to becoming the best maintenance department in the country," he said dryly.

"The public does not expect me to be a 'yes' man," he said. "If I have to disagree with long-established views and programs, I'll say so. While I don't intend to become known by my public arguments, I have to be permitted to do the job I was asked to do."

17
REGULATION OF BUSINESS

State and local governments regulate business more closely than the federal government. Acting under the police power, state and local governments regulate business in order to protect and promote public health, safety, morals, welfare, and convenience.

Sunday closing laws, popularly known as Blue Laws, have been a subject of considerable debate for many years. Such laws are found in every state and within each state do not require all businesses to close on Sundays, although they usually restrict the commodities that may be sold. Mr. Clarence Newman of the staff of the *Wall Street Journal* has written a case study of a Brooklyn grocer who was issued a summons charging him with violating the Sabbath. Since this article was written, it has become legal in New York City to keep small, family-operated businesses open on Sunday if the proprietor observes another day of the week as the Sabbath.

Citizens generally are aware that licenses are needed for hunting and fishing, driving an automobile, and marriage, but usually have little conception of the variety of licenses issued by state and local governments. Richard Haitch of the staff of the *New York Times* has compiled an interesting and informative list of the types of state and city licenses needed by residents of New York City.

Building regulation is one of the most sensitive activities of city governments. Corruption can creep into the administration of the building code as Ed Cony, staff reporter of the *Wall Street Journal,* points out in describing the building situation in New York City.

Clarence Newman
52. Sunday-Closing Laws*

Charles Pam, a ruddy-faced, rotund proprietor of a small food store in the Brownsville section of Brooklyn, appears to have started a legal ball rolling which may make revision of many, if not most, of the Sunday closing laws a necessity.

The possibility of his setting a legal precedent traces back to a sunny Sunday morning last July when, at about 10:30, he made a sale of a can of tuna and a jar of baby food. Taking the transaction out of the routine category was the presence of Patrolman James J. Dalton of Brooklyn's 69th Precinct who handed the grocer a summons charging him with the violation of the Sabbath. Article 192 of the New York State Penal Law makes it a crime to perform work or conduct business on Sunday with, of course, certain specified exceptions.

Like most so-called blue laws, Article 192 is a curious mixture of dos and don'ts. Gas stations can sell gasoline, oil and tires, but not batteries. Newspapers and magazines can be sold, but not books. And real property can change hands, but not personal.

In the case of grocers, they can sell cooked and prepared food only before 10 a.m. and between 4 p.m. and 7:30 p.m. Thus Mr. Pam obviously violated the law by a 30-minute margin. But he balked at paying a $5 fine, asked that the constitutionality of the law be tested and enlisted the aid of the American Jewish Congress which has provided him with free legal counsel.

Nor has Mr. Pam been passive in the Sunday law skirmish he's stirred up. The 47-year-old proprietor of an old fashioned delicatessen complete with barrels of pickles and sauerkraut has fired off telegrams to Gov. Rockefeller, addressed the Democratic State Committee and picketed in Albany. His theme: Sabbath laws are unfair, unjust and conflict with our principles of religious freedom.

CONSTANTINE'S SUNDAY LAW

Mr. Pam's persistence initially stemmed from his rejection of the charge that he was a Sabbath violator. Rather he regarded himself as a strict observer, since as an orthodox Jew he closes his grocery store every Friday evening until Sunday morning.

---

* From the *Wall Street Journal.* January 16, 1963. p. 18. Copyright 1963 Dow Jones & Company, Inc. All Rights Reserved. Reprinted with permission of publisher.

Individual citizens like Mr. Pam have been having problems with Sunday laws for centuries. "Sunday in the Sixties," a pamphlet distributed by the American Jewish Congress, says the first compulsory Sunday law in recorded history originated with the Roman Emperor Constantine who decreed "all judges and city people and the craftsmen shall rest upon the venerable day of the sun." His choice of days was a shrewd one, for both Christians and Mithraists (sun worshippers) observed Sunday.

Interestingly, even Constantine was forced to make exceptions so country people could plant or reap when the season and the weather demanded it, regardless of the day.

And from Constantine's time until the present the bane of Sunday law writers and enforcers has been exceptions. Even now in the 37 states that restrict Sunday commerce there are exceptions, some of which seem to defy logic or reason. For example: In Pennsylvania, shoe polish may not be sold, but shoeshine boys can work; South Carolina swimming pools are allowed to stay open, but the lifeguard who works at one risks a fine, and in New York bread and cake may be purchased but not fresh meat.

A BASIS FOR ATTACK

Mr. Pam's legal aides hope to upset the case against the grocer on the basis of too many businesses which seem to be unwarranted exceptions to the New York State Sunday law. Their hopes are pinned on the case of the State of New York vs. Utica Daw's Drug Co., Inc., in which the Appellate Division held last February that a showing of discriminatory enforcement of the New York Sunday law is a valid basis for attacking the constitutionality of the law's enforcement.

In the last major Sunday law test in New York State, the Friedman case of 1952, the argument was principally based on the Constitutional ground that asking an orthodox Jewish grocer who observed the Saturday Sabbath to also observe Sunday violated the First Amendment on two counts—it interfered with freedom of religion as well as the prohibition against state establishment of religion.

This argument was unsuccessful then as it was more recently in U.S. Supreme Court decisions dealing with Sunday laws in Pennsylvania, Maryland and Massachusetts. Also in the Friedman case, evidence of alleged discriminatory enforcement was ruled inadmissible.

However, the unanimous decision in the Utica Daw's case changed the legal climate. It said in effect that if a defendant can prove there has been discriminatory enforcement of Sunday laws he is entitled to a dismissal, and such proof of discrimination should be presented in a pre-trial hearing. Mr. Pam's attorneys have adjusted their court room strategy to this finding.

392 / Regulation of Business

Calling for a pre-trial hearing last month, they fired off 36 subpoenas at New York's major media of communications and other well known commercial operations. On the list were the three major networks—ABC, CBS and NBC, all the morning newspapers, R. H. Macy & Co., Gimbel Brothers, Inc., major theater chains, sightseeing facilities, Hertz Corp. and others.

Marvin M. Karpatkin, an officer of the American Jewish Congress metropolitan council who heads up Mr. Pam's defense, said "that the police department by cracking down against a grocery store operator like Mr. Pam, while ignoring other and far more serious violators of the statute, is guilty of discriminatory enforcement of the law, thus causing a denial of equal protection as guaranteed under the Fourteenth Amendment."

TOYS AND BINGO

"If the law is to be enforced," he continued, "it should be enforced against all who violate the statute—among them: Every radio station that broadcasts on Sunday; every newspaper whose editorial and mechanical staffs work on Sunday; every drug store that sells cosmetics, toys and similar items on Sunday; every newsstand that sells on Sunday; every sightseeing bus or boat that operates on Sunday; every church or other operator of Sunday bingo games, and every other public or private facility that—wittingly or not—violates the New York Sabbath laws."

At the pre-trial hearings spokesmen for the subpoenaed companies testified their Sunday operations had never resulted in summonses for law violations. In contrast, the AJC notes that in 1961 there were some 20,000 cases of alleged Sabbath law violations involving smaller businesses, and they constituted the second largest category of summonses (traffic violations led).

Although the Kings County (Brooklyn) District Attorney's office regards the Pam case as a straightforward, obvious violation of the statute that merits prosecution, the AJC is hopeful.

Feeling that they have enlisted many important allies in the pre-trial hearing, the AJC plans to use the same legal technique against Sunday closing laws in other states.

Discriminatory enforcement of Sunday laws is general in most states, the AJC claims, although there are 12 that grant exemption to Saturday-Sabbath observers and two more states that give stores the option of closing on Saturday or Sunday.

Various Protestant church groups have supported the exemption of Saturday observers from provisions of Sunday laws. And sharing this point of view are not only Jews but also Seventh Day Adventists and Seventh Day Baptists.

"A DAY OF REST"

On the other side of the issue, support of Sunday closing laws tends to be less on a religious basis these days, since this would put the state in the position of enforcing one particular set of religious tenets. This is the case despite the U.S. Supreme Court decision that it's Constitutional for state governments to impose Sunday laws.

The court's reasoning has been that such statutes reflect legitimate state interest in public welfare. In a majority decision, Chief Justice Earl Warren wrote that although such laws had religious origins, they've lost their religious cast and now merely reflect society's interest in "a day of rest."

However, in a vigorous dissenting opinion when the high court declined to consider a challenge to the constitutionality of Kentucky's Sunday closing law, Justice William O. Douglas asked, "By what authority can government compel one person not to work on Sunday because the majority of the populace deems Sunday a holy day?"

Although there appear to be religious overtones to the Pam case and his attorneys will argue that the law infringes on his religious freedom, their main argument will be based on the Utica drug store case, which in turn hinges on something exotically known as the Yick Wo doctrine.

It was enunciated by the Supreme Court in 1886 and involved a laundry regulating ordinance adopted in San Francisco which was enforced mainly against Chinese launderers, but unenforced against Caucasian laundry owners. The Supreme Court's judgment was that although the law was impartial, it was applied with an "evil eye and an unequal hand" so as to produce discrimination between persons.

It is on the basis of alleged discriminatory enforcement that the Brooklyn grocer's lawyers have argued the case. A verdict is expected soon, and one in favor of Mr. Pam would undoubtedly be a forerunner of similar cases in other states and probably set the stage for the modification of many present Sunday laws.

Richard Haitch
53. About: Licenses*

Cabaret and other night-spot employes in New York City, swept up recently in a whirlpool of controversy over the merits of a law requiring that they be licensed to work, need not feel lonesome in their plight.

* From the *New York Times Magazine.* March 5, 1961. p. 100. Copyright by the New York Times. Reprinted by permission.

Nearly 1,400 categories of activity or employment are listed by the city as requiring licenses, permits, certificates or other official approval.

The regulations, enforced by city, state or Federal agencies, cover the alphabet from A to Y—everything from able seamen and abandonment-of-business sales to wrestlers' seconds and yacht-club sites.

Most of the regulations are taken for granted—birth certificates, marriage licenses, burial permits, driving licenses, hunting and fishing licenses and the like. Others are relatively obscure. But they remain on the statute books, ready to be enforced when a need arises or when some patrolman on the beat feels particularly astute and well-read in the licensing laws. Here is a sample of who and what are affected by these laws:

Barbers, barbers' apprentices and barber-shop owners need personal licenses from the New York Secretary of State. To operate a barber shop, the proprietor also needs a store permit from the city's Board of Health. Barber-shop quartets must seek a Department of Parks permit if they would do their harmonizing formally in a city park.

Psychologists, podiatrists, optometrists apply to the State Education Department; psychiatrists, to the State Mental Hygiene Council; pharmacists, to the State Education Department and the State Board of Pharmacy; cosmetologists, to the Secretary of State; embalmers and funeral directors, to the State Department of Health.

Planning to erect a bandstand outdoors? See your Borough President if you want to put it in the street. If you prefer the sidewalk, see the City Department of Buildings. To hold a dance "to which the public may gain admission," be sure to get a special police permit if the affair is on licensed premises.

Not many people know it, but the simple act of taking a photograph in the city is fraught with license-law undertones. You should, for example, have a permit from the Department of Public Works to take a photo from the Brooklyn Bridge—or from any other city-operated bridge, for that matter. The odds are that no one will hustle you off to jail if, without a permit, you are caught in the act with a camera; but, in the strict sense, it's still not legal.

The Port Authority and the Triborough Bridge and Tunnel Authority, on the other hand, don't mind if you take photograps from their bridges so long as you stay on the sidewalk, behave yourself and don't distract motorists.

Fire sales, bankruptcy sales, alteration sales, reorganization sales and loss-of-lease sales require a license from the city's Department of Licenses; otherwise, the authorities have learned, a few sharpies inevitably will hold daily distress sales of inferior merchandise at exorbitant "giveaway" prices.

Don't make a pet of a robin or a wren. Wild migratory birds are a special concern of the State Conservation Department, and no one can take either the feathered creatures, their nests or their eggs without express permission.

Speaking of birds, if you are hauling a truckload of feathers to a dump, you need a license from the Department of Licenses. But if the load is for the manufacture of pillows, no license is required.

Never, never drive cattle through the streets of the city without first notifying the Police Department. One of the steady applicants for this seemingly eccentric privilege is the circus, which annually drives its animals from the railroad yards to Madison Square Garden—and back again when the circus is over. The circus, of course, cannot hold performances without a number of licenses from the Department of Licenses.

No cannon firing is allowed in New York City unless the Department of Licenses says it's all right—and then the caliber of the artillery is not to exceed that of a four-pounder.

If you have on hand or are planning to store more than 500 gallons of alcohol or distilled liquor, please notify the Fire Department. Solicitation of donations almost anywhere requires the sanction of the Department of Welfare. And don't cut into or lower a curb unless the Department of Buildings approves.

If you employ shipping clerks, maintenance men, factory workers or porters and want to pay them their wages by check, you need a permit from the State Labor Department, Division of Industrial Relations. But you can pay office help, sales people and other white-collar employes by check (or in cash or barter) and no permit is required.

Even the humble newsboy needs a certificate to operate. He gets it from the Bureau of Attendance of the City Board of Education after first receiving a medical examination from the Board of Health. Girls, including so-called tomboys, need not apply. No girls are permitted to be newsboys.

Ed Cony
54. Builders & Boodle*

The most common building material in this city is neither steel nor concrete, brick nor wood.

* From the *Wall Street Journal.* May 16, 1961. pp. 1 and 22. Copyright 1961 Dow Jones & Company, Inc. All Rights Reserved. Reprinted with permission of publisher.

It is graft.

This at least is the conviction of many contractors, architects and engineers who are putting up new structures or remodeling existing ones in the nation's largest city. "For seven years I haven't been on a job here where we didn't have to make payoffs to city employees," says a veteran construction superintendent who watches over about 20 jobs a year in New York City.

The New York State Commission of Investigation spent 10 months recently looking into the administration of building regulation in the city. Its findings: A pattern of corruption is saddling New York's construction industry with extra costs. These costs add millions of dollars annually to building outlays, now running at a rate of $1.4 billion a year. And by and large these costs are passed along to the consumer—the apartment dweller, the business firm renting office space, the manufacturer who builds a new factory, the retailer who remodels his store.

Who gets paid off? "Almost everyone," the commission said. "Clerks, plan examiners, multiple dwelling examiners and plumbing inspectors." . . .

"You run into graft and corruption in every big city in the country, at least every one we've worked in," says an executive of a large national contracting firm. "But," he adds, "it's more widespread in New York than in any other city, in my opinion. It's more systematic and solid here."

So entrenched, in fact, have under-the-table payments to city workers become that the recurrent investigations of the problem seem to be having less and less effect. The state's probe of New York City's Department of Buildings was the second investigation in four years. And yet interviews with builders and architects here indicate that though barely five months have passed since the state investigators turned in their report, payoffs once again are becoming about as common as they ever were.

"For a time, while the heat was on, we had some relief, but it's getting back to normal fast," says a contractor.

REVENGE AGAINST REFORMERS

Investigations are hampered by the fact that the builder who admits he has made payoffs incriminates himself. He may as a result lose necessary licenses to operate in the city. Or the aftermath of his testimony as an informer may be agonizing delays by vengeful city employes in processing paperwork on his construction projects long after the investigation itself is ended.

The report of the State Commission of Investigation is pretty much dismissed by Buildings Commissioner Peter Reidy and his aides. Mr.

Reidy notes the testimony was "unsworn" and says he couldn't get witnesses to repeat it under oath, on grounds of self-incrimination. Deputy Commissioner William Kane is more outspoken. The investigation was "politically motivated," he says, and the results were "a lot of malarkey."

Nevertheless, a Brooklyn judge this month urged Mr. Reidy to bring departmental charges against 27 of his inspectors. Although a grand jury reported it lacked sufficient evidence to indict them on criminal charges, Brooklyn's district attorney declared the testimony of these men "to say the least stretches credulity far beyond the breaking point."

PAYOFFS BEGIN EARLY

According to construction men, the sequence of bribery begins weeks, and sometimes months, before the first shovelful of dirt is turned for a new building. The initial payoffs occur when a would-be builder tries to get his plans approved so he can get a building permit. The motive in most cases: To short-circuit the lengthy delay in getting a permit.

An executive of a small engineering concern describes what happens: "Your architect files a set of plans with the Buildings Department, and they are given to an examiner. Then you wait, two to four months, until you get a card saying the plans have been examined. In 999 cases out of 1,000, the plans are disapproved."

The disapproval is usually based on technical violations of New York's cumbersome, ancient building code, which runs to 794 pages and hasn't been thoroughly revised since the mid-1930's. The code is a vague document, subject to widely different interpretation—"like the Constitution, only not nearly as well written," complains an engineer.

When plans are disapproved, the architect must make an appointment with the examiner to go over his objections. "Usually, he has to submit the plans again and again," says a man who has had this experience. "Typically, it takes six months to a year to get plans approved through normal channels in Manhattan. Recently it took us nine months to get plans approved for a $17,000 remodelling job on a laundry. By that time the client no longer was interested," he adds.

Such frustrations lead directly to bribery, according to builders. The State Commission of Investigation asked one architect what would happen if he stopped paying off department employes. His answer: "Well, you just wait and wait till you get your plans approved."

While the payments are petty—in the order of $5 to $10—they are frequent. And contractors say the wide prevalence of bribery adds substantially to building costs. "Even the clerk who just stamps 'approved' on your plans has a sliding scale of fees," says one architect indignantly.

Not all employes in the department have their hand out, of course, nor do all architects accept them, contractors and architects say. But they add that the architect who refuses to go along with the system pays a penalty. Listen to one such architect:

"I'm known down at the department as a 'non-payer.' Several times plans of mine have been 'lost.' I have had to redraw the complete set of plans. Then my folder is 'found' again."

A CONVENIENT OUT

Architects and engineers says some of their colleagues who have no stomach for passing money to city workers find a convenient out among a group of practitioners known as "expediters." An expediter will file an application for a building permit, oversee its progress through the Department of Buildings and guarantee its final approval.

The expediter's bill may run $150 or $200 for "services rendered," with no precise breakdown as to the nature of the services. One architect describes a well-known firm of expediters: "They have a couple of men at the building department, each with a pocket full of money. One quoted me a flat fee of $150; he said if he had to pay off more than that, he'd stand the loss."

Some expediters may perform a legitimate service. But some present "curious credentials," according to the investigating commission. For example, one expediter is a waiter in a dance hall off Times Square. He once worked as a clerk in the Buildings Department, the commission says. . . .

MONEY IN FOLDERS

Money usually is passed to city workers in envelopes or in the "job folders" containing the plans which are being expedited, the State Commission of Investigation reports. An architect who has spent hundreds of hours at the department describes another popular method: "You can actually see money changing hands—a $5 or $10 bill in a match book."

In fairness to the Buildings Department, it must be said it has to administer an outmoded building code. Some critics of corruption claim the code is primarily at fault. "The code is over-regulation at its worst," says a construction executive. "It creates a climate for corruption. If inspectors really followed the letter of the law, you'd never get any building done.". . .

Currently, Buildings Commissioner Reidy has a committee studying the need and the most feasible way to rewrite the code. A new code is at least two years away, however, according to architects. . . .

MORE MONEY AND MANPOWER

Commissioner Reidy has been aggressively seeking more money and more manpower. He has raised salaries so that a plan examiner now starts at $8,200 a year. Also, he has increased his plan examination staff to 76, about 20% more than two years ago. These men still carry a staggering load, however, in view of the 75,000 plans filed in New York City last year.

Mr. Reidy maintains he's doing all possible to "eliminate the possibility of corrupt activity" in his department. In the past year he has held 22 disciplinary hearings "resulting in six dismissals," he says.

The struggle to get a building permit, however, is only the beginning. During construction, as many as a dozen city inspectors will check on the work in such areas as general construction, steel, plastering, plumbing, electrical work, boilers and fire protection.

After all work has been finished, it is important for a contractor to have a document indicating the city approves the work. This is known as the certificate of occupancy; without it the contractor usually doesn't get paid. The going payoff rate for a "C. of O." according to one of the city's largest builders, is $10 an apartment—"that's $1,000 for a project with 100 apartments." On a really big project, with 1,000 apartments, he says, it is sometimes possible to get a volume rate of $6,500 or $7,000.

"When you start to build, you make the deal with the field inspector, who normally speaks for his boss too. You pay 25% on approval of the foundations, 25% on completion of the superstructure, 25% on approval of a temporary C. of O. and the final 25% on getting your permanent C. of O.," the builder says.

The evidence is that a goodly proportion of city inspectors can be—and are—bought. One investigator who has spent considerable time looking into this field says there are "three purchasable commodities" from heavily-overworked inspectors: "One is prompt inspection, two is prompt approval of the work, three is overlooking work which does not measure up to the standards."

PREMIUM ON PROMPTNESS

Prompt inspection can be worth a good deal of money to a contractor. Plumbing, for instance, normally is inspected at the roughing stage, just before it's enclosed with plaster. "The plasterers may be waiting to go ahead. If you don't get prompt inspection, the contractor has to hold up the work or go ahead with the risk that when an inspector does show up he will tell him to tear out all the plaster so he can do a proper inspection on the plumbing," the inspector says. . . .

As a recent public hearing on the activities of New York City's Department of Water Supply, Gas and Electricity, the State Commission of Investigation offered evidence naming 70% of the city's electrical inspectors as having received illegal payments from contractors. Eight contractors swore that paying off inspectors has been the accepted way of doing business in New York. . . .

Carl Cook of Cook Electrical Co., Haworth, N. J., explained that customers do not pay the contractor in full until a city inspector approves the work. He said this made it vital "to get the final inspection over with."

He testified it may take two months to get the final inspection of electrical work unless you pay off. Asked how long it takes "if you meet the inspector on the job and give him a sum of money," he replied: "You get it right away."

During construction, "the police are the biggest pests of all on shakedowns," says one contractor. "Two hours after the first truck arrives on the job, cops will be around dreaming up some violation," he complains. "We had a job recently where the police wanted $80 a car for six patrol cars in the precinct; we settled for half of that price," he adds. Such bargaining is common. Says another construction man: "A cop was around the other day demanding a 'Grant' (a $50 bill). I gave my foreman $5 and told him to tell the cop he'd have to settle for a Lincoln."

When a policeman wants $10 to $15 to overlook a violation, one of his favorite approaches is to tell a foreman, "I need a new pair of shoes," says a job superintendent, raising his voice over the clatter of a construction job. Police payoffs are so institutionalized that Friday, the day petty cash is replenished on construction jobs, is commonly recognized as "pay day" for the police. "They practically line up for it," says one investigator who has been studying the system.

A COMPARISON OF COSTS

The alternative to paying off the police may be a series of summonses. One gray-haired job superintendent recalls he once successfully contested a summons in court. But later, when he figured the time he spent away from the job, he realized a bribe would have been cheaper.

This soft-spoken veteran says contractors usually are violating some city regulation and thus are vulnerable to shake-downs. Frequently, they store building materials in city streets without a permit—or beyond the limits authorized by their permit. "When material is delivered to the job late in the afternoon, your contractor may prefer to pay off the cops rather than to pay overtime wages to his workers to get it off the street," he says.

Graft extends to other city departments. Fire Department inspectors often are "on the take," contractors say, and it isn't confined just to city employes. Elevator operators, labor union officials and the contractors, engineers and architects themselves are enmeshed in corruption.

"There are a great number of payoffs to the Fire Department, to get inspectors to approve your building," says one architect.

Police and Fire Department officials deny such charges in similar language. Fire Commissioner Edward Cavanaugh, Jr., says he's done "everything possible" to stamp out graft. He adds that it is "disgraceful" for anyone to give money to a fire inspector and not report it to him or to the district attorney.

Contractors complain about private employes. Says one: "If you're remodeling in an upper floor, the elevator operator and the building superintendent will demand money—or they'll hold you up when you want to haul materials in the elevators. One superintendent recently told me right out he wanted $60."

The power of labor union officials is attested by a remarkable reluctance on the part of contractors to talk about payoffs, even anonymously. But several do say payoffs to union business agents do occur. "Let's say you need 20 men of a certain trade right away—or your whole job is held up. You go to the business agent and pay him so much per man, and he'll get them off another job." This situation is made possible, contractors will tell you, because some building union locals in New York limit membership to the point where labor shortages occur with regularity.

CORRUPT CONTRACTORS

There's every indication, however, that a certain element among the contractors is equally corrupt. The hearings on electrical inspections, for instance, turned up cases of contractors getting shoddy work—so bad as to be a fire hazard—approved by bribing the inspectors.

A top executive in a big construction firm which does business all over the country says flatly: "You could clean this whole thing up here in New York by making some needed reforms, but soon you'd have contractors going around at city hall looking for an edge, asking 'who do I take care of around here.'"

The petty nature of most payoffs disguises the extent to which corruption pads construction costs. One architect says, "On a $20,000 remodeling job, I've had contractors put in $1,000 for 'fees, permits, etc.' The

402 / Regulation of Business

actual cost of the fees might be $100. So you have almost 5% added to construction costs, because of the bribery that goes on."

The most serious expense for the honest contractor is the delay built into the present system of corruption, suggests the State Commission of Investigation. "By far the most staggering cost is the hidden cost to builders and property owners whose projects remain idle while the Buildings Department wheels slowly grind out the approval essential to their building permits," says the commission.

One engineering executive comments: "Your property taxes go right on during construction." And a construction man says: "On a $10 million construction job, the interest on your construction loan may cost $50,000 a month. Figure out what a month or two of unnecessary delay costs."

part eight

STATE-LOCAL PERSONNEL AND FINANCE

18

STATE-LOCAL PERSONNEL

Attention has been focused upon the manpower needs of municipal governments by the Municipal Manpower Commission, which spent two years studying the manpower needs of municipal governments and found a serious shortage of manpower. The Commission in its report makes a series of recommendations designed to solve the problem. It is reasonable to assume that a study of the manpower needs of state governments would lead to conclusions similar to those reached by the Commission.

The question of unionization of state and local government employees and their right to strike has been a source of considerable controversy. Some have maintained that public employees who perform duties similar to those performed by employees in private industry should have the right to strike. Others maintain that no public employee has the right to strike against the government. This question and its ramifications are examined by Mr. A. H. Raskin of the staff of the *New York Times*.

Public concern over the morality of public employees has led to the drafting and adoption of codes of ethics that set forth in detail standards of behavior for public employees. The International City Managers Association has prepared "A Suggested Code of Ethics for Municipal Officials and Employees" that is relatively brief yet has a wide coverage. Mr. James P. Clarke, a social administration advisor in the Social Security Administration of the United States Department of Health, Education, and Welfare, prepared the original draft of the

406 / State-Local Personnel

code on the basis of his doctoral dissertation. The code deserves careful study by all city councils that are convinced of the need for a written code of ethics.

On the seventy-fifth anniversary of the adoption of the civil service laws of the federal government and New York State, Mr. H. Eliot Kaplan, a past executive secretary of the National Civil Service League, took stock of the achievements and the shortcomings of the merit system and predicted that significant changes in the system would occur in the future.

55. Governmental Manpower for Tomorrow's Cities—a Summary*

THE PROBLEM: THE METROPOLITAN AREA

The vitality of America's metropolitan areas—home of nearly two out of every three citizens—is one of this country's most important domestic concerns. A swelling tide of growth poses mounting problems: congestion, slums, water pollution, juvenile delinquency, racial tension, chronic unemployment, rising tax rates, suburban sprawl. By 1980, there may be 190,000,000 persons—more than our entire population today—living in vast metropolitan complexes.

These conditions should make even the most complacent American recognize that the battle for a better urban environment may be won or lost within the next two short decades.

Local governments, especially the 18,000 which serve metropolitan residents, will feel the immediate impact of this growth and its consequences. While the federal and state governments also have important roles to play in shaping tomorrow's metropolitan habitat, citizens depend upon local government and its decisions as never before. It must provide something more than the artesian wells, compost piles, and bucket brigades characteristic of an earlier, less complex civilization.

DEMAND GROWS STRONGER

Metropolitan residents loudly demand from their governments education for their children, road and transit facilities, sewage treatment plants, clean water, unpolluted air, police and fire protection, parks and playgrounds, regulation of public utilities, and protection from fraud and the unscrupulous.

They are also affected by the policies of local government. To protect the value of their homes, businesses and jobs, they need sound planning, zoning, and tax administration.

To provide these essentials, local government faces a never-ending series of decisions: Shall there be bridges or tunnels, superhighways or

* Municipal Manpower Commission (Washington, D.C.: Municipal Manpower Commission, 1962). Reprinted with permission of publisher.

mass transit, better trained police or bigger jails, more welfare money for indigent families or for retraining the jobless?

These decisions will be made by, and depend on, people—hopefully the best equipped, the most imaginative, the strongly motivated; not the cast-offs, the security-seekers, the disinterested. The urban public service, staffed by superior persons, can go far to ensure the vitality of metropolitan America. If superior talents are not at work on these critical problems and decisions, the quality of daily living in metropolitan areas faces a steady and inevitable decline.

Unfortunately, too many people still think of local governments as made up of trash collectors, police and firemen, and fail wholly to realize the range of tasks to be done and of human talents required.

A VITAL GROUP IS IGNORED

Largely overlooked is the vital corps of people who man our urban front lines. They are the Administrative, Professional and Technical people (we call them APT for easy identification) who must face the problems of local governments day and night, who—in addition to providing highly specialized services—must search out the facts, list and evaluate alternative courses of action, advise local legislators, resolve many questions within prevailing policy directives and laws, carry out policy decisions—and then start the process all over again.

In the course of a two-year investigation, we examined the quality of today's APT personnel, their role, and the need for increased competence on the part of local governments.

We have focused our attention on manpower as a key ingredient to a better urban habitat. We have dug deeply to find answers to two critical questions: What are local governments doing to attract and hold able people? What needs to be done to overcome the difficulties now encountered?

THE FACTS: SHORTAGE OF ABLE MANPOWER, ANTIQUATED PERSONNEL PRACTICES

The first nation-wide study of local governments' APT people accumulated massive evidence to support the following observations. Research by professional organizations, extensive questionnaires, and hundreds of first-hand interviews with civic leaders and local government officials left little doubt of the critical prospect ahead.

1. SHORTAGE OF ABLE MANPOWER. There are able, dedicated persons in key positions in local governments—but not nearly enough. And, as the

national shortages of APT talents increase, the local governments will experience more acute shortages of these talents.

More than one-third of all municipal executives will retire within ten years. By 1980, local governments may have to recruit as many as 300,000 APT people.

The over-all quality of today's APT personnel is inadequate to cope with emerging metropolitan problems—and the quality of "back up" strength is even more suspect. Today, division heads and their chief subordinates are not well-trained in breadth or depth. Today, department heads are not trained to deal with ever-broader problems of public policy.

2. INADEQUATE RECRUITMENT PROGRAMS. Recruiting efforts are feeble, underfinanced, unimaginative, and are considered to be ineffective—even by personnel directors. Only a small minority of all local governments conducts campus recruiting regularly. As a consequence, these local governments have not attracted at the entry level a fair share of able young people.

Only one in every twenty units has anything like a formal plan to foresee future manpower needs.

3. LACK OF OPPORTUNITY FOR CAREER DEVELOPMENT. Promotion from within does not produce quality among key APT officials: those covered by civil service have less formal education than those who are exempt.

The average municipal executive has considerably less varied experience than his counterpart in private business: more than four out of five municipal executives have worked for only one city.

Career development programs are almost non-existent: there are virtually no opportunities for excellent advanced training of APT personnel who have the potential to assume broader responsibilities.

Many units are too small to provide an adequate challenge or satisfying careers.

4. INADEQUATE COMPENSATION. Professional salaries in local governments lag behind comparable employment elsewhere. The differentials tend to be greatest for public officials at the highest levels.

A Commission analysis of professional positions in 20 cities, 14 of them larger than 250,000 population, showed that in every category the average salary offered by the local governments was substantially below the national average paid to persons going into industry in 1961.

5. LACK OF DIRECT CONTROL OVER PERSONNEL. Control over the vital personnel function is denied chief executives in too many urban governments.

Those who administer independent civil service commissions are hostile to management: this is most hampering when management's search for qualified applicants conflicts with inflexible regulations and attitudes.

6. MUNICIPAL MANPOWER PROBLEMS NEGLECTED BY EDUCATIONAL AND PROFESSIONAL ORGANIZATIONS. Scarcely a handful of universities and professional associations have paid any attention to the manpower problems of local governments.

The heavy weight of this evidence cannot be ignored any longer. The public must recognize that its own best interests are not served by local governments which are poorly financed and inadequately staffed. It is manifestly clear that no easy solutions are possible; it is equally certain that failure to seek solutions is intolerable.

THE ENVIRONMENT: PUBLIC APATHY

A direct, massive effort must be launched to attract and hold more and better APT persons in local government. But, in the course of its investigations, the Commission recognized that the ability to recruit highly capable personnel depends upon a tangled web of factors:

1. The public—"Mr. John Q. Citizen"—and its attitudes

Many citizens regard local government and its people with skepticism, cynicism, or even outright hostility; among most others, apathy reigns:

2. The lack of civic interest and leadership

Without unselfish public spirited leadership, a local government's officials lack community support and thus are often unable to act in the community's best interests.

3. The need for clear, considered objectives for each local government

The broad objectives of each community give a sense of direction and purpose to the entire structure and to the staff of the local government.

4. Rising costs

The financial resources allocated to local government are seldom sufficient to provide all the services, functions, and construction demanded by citizens.

5. The fragmentation of local government

Some 18,000 cities, towns, villages, counties, special districts, authorities, and school districts operate within this country's metropolitan areas. Frequently they operate without knowledge of, concern for, or cooperation with, the policies and programs of others.

6. The relationship between levels of government

The localities, the states, and the federal government—each with a stake in metropolitan progress—have failed to develop policies which take the importance of this fact into account.

TOMORROW: MANAGEMENT, MERIT, AND MANPOWER

There is an immediate need for improving the quality of APT personnel in local government. We recommend prompt and substantial actions in five areas: the necessity for merit, the assignment of responsibility for personnel, the role of independent civil service commissions, the guide lines for personnel practices, and the obligations of colleges and universities.

1. Appointment and advancement of public personnel should be based exclusively on merit principles

The principle of "merit"—that men and women should be selected and promoted only on the basis of proved competence and accomplishment—must be observed in any enterprise faced with great changes and public responsibilities. Modern personnel administration can build a merit system based on ability, performance on the job, and capacity for growth.

Professional personnel staffs are able to establish well-defined criteria of merit. Advancement, for example, should not depend upon military service, union membership, political allegiance, or seniority without a requirement of objective evidence of ability.

2. The chief executive should be given clear-cut authority for personnel administration

Government, like business, has moved beyond the stage where it can afford the uncertain performance of weak management.

The executives of growing, changing, urban governments must have authority over the personnel on whom they depend to get their work done. Mayors, city managers, department heads and others of like rank in urban counties must have greater authority to hire, to promote, to discipline, and to fire. It is particularly important to place control of the key APT personnel in the executive.

Where patronage and spoils still prevail, or threaten, means should and can be devised to safeguard personnel from arbitrary or discriminatory treatment, but without depriving the chief executive of the essential authority to hire, promote, discipline, and dismiss personnel.

3. The independent civil service commission, where it exists, should be abolished or limited to an advisory function

The *independent* civil service commission, a foundation-stone of the movement for better government for three-quarters of a century, has outlived its usefulness as an instrument of personnel management. Today, we must look to responsible mayors, city managers, and department heads to seek out and provide the experienced administrators, and the qualified professional and technical personnel that are required.

Hence, where an *independent* civil service commission now controls the recruitment, selection, compensation, training or promotion of personnel, it should be abolished or its administrative authority and functions should be limited to an advisory role.

The mature urban units of this country—those that have grown up politically and administratively—can operate perfectly well without an independent civil service commission. For those lacking maturity, or where some local situation of a compelling nature exists, a civil service commission can be used to perform important functions apart from personnel management.

The benefits of an independent body are in the realm of non-partisanship and integrity. Drawing upon the public acceptance and confidence it has in many places, such a civil service commission can well be vested with advisory powers to audit, review, and report on the government's personnel policies and practices. An independent commission used in such a way could quickly become a strong ally to administrators in search of quality, and a powerful adversary of those officials who would misuse the personnel power.

4. Personnel practices must be revitalized to provide rewarding careers

a. Urban local governments must raise their present salary schedules to compete successfully for relatively scarce APT personnel.

The total compensation of APT personnel must be comparable to that enjoyed by men and women of like skill, and bearing like responsibilities, in private employment and the more advanced public enterprises. This principle of comparability is, in the long run, economical in its application and is in the public interest. In a growing number of units, it has been applied to the compensation of rank-and-file employees. But APT personnel also have a right to expect that urban service will permit them to live with a dignity appropriate to their position.

No local government should have to depend on men and women who are satisfied with less compensation because they can afford the luxury of public service.

b. Local governments must develop APT personnel for broader professional and executive duties.

Furnishing greater opportunities for personal growth for every person in an APT position must be recognized as a public responsibility for the public's benefit. It is essential that each administrative, professional or technically trained person keep abreast of advances in his field. His continuing growth will be furthered by application of the full range of training techniques, instructional methods, and materials. In addition, incentives for training should be established as an inducement to APT personnel.

c. Broader career opportunities must be provided for APT personnel.

A career system that relates advance to personal growth and to that alone is the only career system that will meet the needs of local governments. They must single out especially able employees and utilize their talents fully, ensuring that their careers are not limited to a single department or division, but that their growth is facilitated by a diversity of experience.

d. Mobility must be greatly facilitated.

Local governments can stimulate mobility by:

1. The abolition of restrictions based on the residence of prospective employees which close many doors for talents which are not locally available;

2. The maintenance and use by local governments of a central roster which informs able men and women of job opportunities throughout the country. Professional associations can help, in collaboration with federal, state, and local governments, by working out an effective system for creating regional and national manpower pools to promote interchange of APT personnel; and

3. The establishment of a nationwide retirement program for local government employees so that the shackles of local retirement systems can be done away with. This is especially important, and will require significant collaboration by all levels of government.

e. Recruitment practices must be thoroughly renovated.

Local governments should first undertake long-range manpower planning, guided by a personnel agency adequately financed and staffed to recruit with the best techniques, stimulate personal development, and evaluate how well APT people are utilized after they are employed.

5. Colleges and universities must meet the needs of an urban society

A rapid expansion of the total supply of APT personnel is fundamentally the role of the colleges and universities. Their output of trained men and women must be promptly and significantly increased. Executives of local governments in every metropolitan area should work with colleges and universities to acquaint them with governmental manpower needs and the educational programs that are needed to meet those needs.

In addition, universities, particularly state universities and other universities based in metropolitan areas, must take the lead in helping to close the gap between research studies and the use of that research in urban areas.

SPECIFICALLY, THE COMMISSION RECOMMENDS THESE ACTIONS:

a. Colleges should acquaint undergraduate students with the new urban America, and the challenges of local government service.

b. Universities should revise and expand graduate programs which will better equip more men and women for careers in urban governments.

c. State universities, and other institutions of higher education based in metropolitan areas, should transmit knowledge of urban affairs to government officials.

d. All educational institutions should give greater status and recognition to programs of training for urban careers, particularly in the professional associations of university administrators, professors, and their respective disciplines.

The Commission urges that a national organization be established to assume responsibility for identifying and focusing attention on the major, unsolved problems of urban communities such as the need for total metropolitan planning, for new approaches to metropolitan transportation, for greater understanding of urban renewal, and of other social, economic, and physical problems.

What is needed in an urban civilization is the analysis and illumination of new and critical problems by some of the society's best minds. That need constitutes an unmatched opportunity for the existing associations, the independent research or planning institution, or for a major university.

AGENDA FOR COOPERATION

The challenge of metropolitan problems is formidable enough to stretch the minds, test the skills, and give satisfaction to able individuals. But this challenge has not been translated into attractive individual opportunities for the persons best-equipped, by training, experience, and motivation, to deal with them. Instead, this working environment has operated as a devastating obstacle to the getting and keeping of able and trained men and women in the local public service. Today, only 17 per cent of this nation's municipal executives would recommend a career in local government to a son or daughter.

The solution of the critical manpower problem cannot be solved apart from the vital problems of binding the governments of metropolitan areas into effective working teams, and of the need for imaginative, civic-minded leadership to establish metropolitan goals that will attract, provide incentive for, and set clear directions for able APT personnel.

RESHAPING THE ENVIRONMENT

Reshaping the local governmental working environment calls for actions by governmental units and by civic and political leaders.

LOCAL GOVERNMENTS SHOULD: Cooperate with each other in metropolitan areas to devise effective arrangements capable of resolving metropolitan-wide problems while preserving neighborhoods and communities.

Seek necessary legislative and administrative support from state and federal governments to permit greater ability to meet problems at the local level.

STATE GOVERNMENTS SHOULD: Revise constitutions and laws to give local governments more opportunity to provide and finance essential public services.

Encourage new governmental arrangements in metropolitan areas for the effective handling of area-wide problems.

THE FEDERAL GOVERNMENT SHOULD: Make a strenuous effort to coordinate all federal programs which have an impact on the development of metropolitan areas.

Continue to stimulate metropolitan planning and follow-through by extending the "workable program" concept to grants-in-aid aimed at communities.

ALL GOVERNMENTS SHOULD: Cooperate with the various levels of government to improve coordination of programs and policies which have an impact on the planning and development of metropolitan areas.

CIVIC AND POLITICAL LEADERSHIP SHOULD: Organize on a metropolitan-area-wide basis, formally or informally.

Study, define, and promote metropolitan community objectives.

Propose actions which would achieve these objectives.

ACCEPTING THE RESPONSIBILITY

The task of this Commission has been to identify the importance of administrative, professional, and technical personnel in local government and to confirm that a distressing manpower situation currently prevails throughout the country. In its recommendations for widespread action, the Commission has gone far beyond matters of personnel administration. But such recommendations do not require the Commission's long-range participation in political give-and-take.

No commission, study group, or national organization can prescribe all the ingredients to improve the manpower in a single local government. No government can force a community to accept them. Therefore, any commitment to better manpower and better local government must rest on the public and its leaders. It is their task to ask the questions and analyze the hard facts about manpower.

There are trouble spots in our emerging metropolitan habitat, and they are growing more severe. Americans deserve better communities in which to live and work. A strong team effort by civic leaders of all segments of the community, political officials, and local APT personnel can build these communities. It is high time we got on with the job.

A. H. Raskin
56. Do Public Strikes Violate Public Trust?*

Should government employes have the right to strike? The debate has been renewed and the State Legislature will carry it forward in the next few weeks when it considers changes in a state law that prescribes automatic dismissal as the penalty for strikes by public employes.

For many citizens all that needed to be said on this subject was said by Calvin Coolidge in 1919 when he was Governor of Massachusetts. Coolidge then backed the firing of Boston police strikers with the declaration that "there is no right to strike against the public safety by anybody, anywhere, at any time." This affirmation of the state's sovereignty over any strike challenge helped carry him to the Presidency. It also provided the basis for an increasing tendency to write into law the proposition that no civil servant could strike.

Now insistent questions are being asked about whether such an absolute ban is justified when one out of every six workers in the country is employed in Federal, state or municipal agencies and when their activities range from coping with disasters to selling whisky across the counter of a state liquor store.

Labor's general status has changed enormously in the four decades since the Boston police walkout. However, the officials who contributed most extensively to building up legal safeguards for unionization, collective bargaining and the freedom to strike of workers in private industry did not deviate from the Coolidge doctrine that strikes by public employes represented illegal insurrections against the structure and security of government.

The father of the New Deal, Franklin D. Roosevelt, set forth in 1937 his conviction that it was "unthinkable and intolerable" for civil servants sworn to support the government to seek to paralyze it as a means of achieving their demands.

The co-author of the Norris-La Guardia Anti-Injunction Act, Fiorello H. La Guardia, was equally hostile to the idea. When strike threats arose during his Mayoralty, the Little Flower's response was blunt: "The city does not and cannot recognize the right of any group to strike against the city."

---

* From the *New York Times Magazine*. January 8, 1961. pp. 12, 78, 80, and 82. Copyright by the New York Times. Reprinted by permission.

Similar statements still come each year from Democratic and Republican officials at every level of government. Men elected with strong union support have been as vehement as those on labor's blacklist in denouncing strikes by civil-service workers as acts of treason. The same philosophy has been repeatedly upheld in court decisions.

But the question never stays snugly buried. Periodically some group defies the prohibitions. Then, embarrassed administrators must often pretend the strike never happened to avoid imposing punishments that would cripple government processes even more than would the stoppage itself.

What has made the problem particularly complex is the mushrooming of government functions and the attendant growth of the public payroll in bad times as well as good. The State Department under Thomas Jefferson consisted of four clerks, a French interpreter and two messengers. The department Dean Rusk will take over Jan. 20 has 23,455 employes all over the world. The combined personnel of all Federal, state and local agencies is 8,675,000—double the figure of twenty years ago.

True to the precepts of Parkinson's Law, the scope of bureaucatic function has increased as rapidly as its size. The boundary line between what is a distinctive responsibility of government and what is the proper bailiwick of private enterprise becomes more and more shadowy.

A member of the Transport Workers Union driving a city-owned bus on Second Avenue is legally estopped from striking; his union brother at the wheel of a privately owned bus on Third Avenue is under no comparable restraint. Traffic on the two avenues flows in opposite directions, but that may not seem an adequate explanation to the two unionists of why a similar contrariness should regulate the legality of strikes.

In a real sense there are three categories of government service, each operating at a different level of urgency. One is made up of jobs on which there is no basic argument about the propriety of a no-strike mandate. This includes such agencies as the Police Department, the Fire Department, the Federal Bureau of Investigation and other groups concerned with law-enforcement and the protection of the community against emergencies.

Crime never takes a holiday. When a fire breaks out on a new aircraft carrier or a jet plane crashes in the middle of a city, government disaster services must be on the job. In recognition of this most unions operating in the law-enforcement and fire-fighting fields have voluntarily incorporated in their charters a renunciation of the right to strike.

How far the emergency category should extend beyond policemen and firemen is subject to some debate. Garbage collectors in New York and other cities have struck for short periods, but there is a general conviction that functions of this type belong in the essential, no-strike category. This feeling is not diminished by the apparent paradox of situations such as that in which workers in Consolidated Edison have the right to strike while employes of the Department of Water Supply, Gas and Electricity are forbidden to do so.

The second category of government jobs embraces such routine day-to-day assignments as filing real estate deeds, issuing death certificates, keeping tax records, and typing reports. Unglamorous as many of these tasks are, they are clearly indispensable to the state's performance of its obligations to its people.

The third category of government jobs stirs the most substantial controversy in the strike debate. It is made up of services that are interchangeably performed by public or private workers.

For an example, a warship may be built in a navy yard or a private yard. Some of the men who perished in the Constellation fire had worked in private shipbuilding establishments until they got jobs on the ill-starred carrier in the Brooklyn navy yard. They could have walked out in the private yards if they were dissatisfied with safety standards. At the navy yard they had no such option. Again, in Michigan, Ohio, Pennsylvania, Virginia and twelve other states liquor clerks are state employes. In New York, New Jersey and the rest of the country, a strike of liquor salesmen can put an effective damper on bottled comfort. But in the states with liquor monopolies the serious drinker is assured of an uninterrupted flow of liquid cheer.

Those who subscribe unreservedly to the doctrine that there is no right to strike against the Government see no incongruity in enforcing the anti-strike rule in all these categories. Their contention is that the nature of Government, as the embodiment of all the people, makes it insupportable for any group to force its will on the people by coercive means. By this yardstick, the important thing is not what specific things Government does but the fact that it is government.

By all odds, the most effective statement of the case for a total ban on stoppages in the public service was made by Gov. Thomas E. Dewey when he signed the Condon-Wadlin Act after a Buffalo teachers' strike in 1947. This is the law New York's legislators are taking a fresh look at this month after receiving private intimations that Gov. Nelson A. Rockefeller feels its provisions are too arbitrary.

Governor Dewey held that public service was a public trust not only for elected officials but also for every employe of a public agency. He noted that the employer was not a profit-making enterprise but the people, and that the people could not tolerate an attack upon themselves.

All this led Mr. Dewey to the thesis that paralysis of Government represented anarchy and in anarchy all liberties became useless.

"Government is not an end in itself," he observed. "It exists solely to serve the people. The very right of private employes to strike depends on the protection of constitutional Government under law. Every liberty enjoyed in this nation exists because it is protected by Government, which functions uninterruptedly. The paralysis of any portion of Government could quickly lead to the paralysis of all society."

The law passed in consonance with this philosophy holds that any public employe who stays away from work or slows down to induce a change in pay or privileges "shall thereby abandon and terminate his appointment or employment." If he is rehired, he cannot get any raise in pay for three years and he must stay on probation for two years after that.

These penalties are theoretically self-executing, but New York's Mayors, from O'Dwyer through Wagner, have managed to pass through dozens of mass exoduses by groups of city employes without ever applying them. Officials elsewhere in the state have shown a comparable lack of enthusiasm for cracking down on strikers in the rigorous fashion supposedly made obligatory by the Condon-Wadlin Act.

Despite this record of non-use, the New York ban is by no means the most restrictive in public employment. Last March, Birmingham outlawed picketing as well as strikes by its municipal workers. As part of a pattern of total inhibition, its ordinance forbade the use of "abusive or opprobrious words" calculated to block or discourage the performance of service to the city.

For the last five years the Federal Government has had a special law prohibiting a job for any person who asserts the right to strike against the Government or who belongs to an organization asserting such a right. Far from opposing this limitation when the bill was before Congress, all the major unions and associations of Federal employes testified in its favor. Most had long had specific provisions in their own constitutions renouncing strikes, picketing or other harassing acts against their boss, Uncle Sam.

The chief challenger of the notion that "you can't strike against the Government" is that old champion of unpopular causes, the American Civil Liberties Union. In a statement drafted by the chairman of its labor committee, Prof. Walter Gellhorn of the Columbia Law School, it takes an irreverent view of the theory that every strike of public employes smacks of revolution.

It notes that many posts manned by public workers now bear no resemblance to the traditional exercises of sovereignty. It finds inconvenience or annoyance no more valid a basis for outlawing public-work stoppages than for imposing a total prohibition on private strikes.

Only where maintenance of uninterrupted services is essential to the community are limitations on the right to strike justifiable, the civil libertarians believe. Even in such cases the union has some emphatically expressed caveats. Underlying them all is the notion that the strike right of workers should not be curtailed unless adequate mechanism for redress is provided.

To guard against injustices of this sort, the union recommends effective appeals procedures, with arbitration as a final step, to handle complaints of administrative abuses. It also wants machinery for discussing pay scales and working conditions through organizational representatives of the workers' own choosing and the appointment of fact-finding boards to inquire into basic morale problems that might otherwise find expression on the picket line.

Many critics of the present strike ban feel a start toward a more selective application of the rule could be made by sifting out those government-operated functions also widely performed under private auspices.

An indication of the possible merit of such an approach came in a recent decision by the California Supreme Court. This decision affirmed the legal right to strike of bus drivers employed by the Los Angeles Metropolitan Transit Authority. The court found the warrant for its ruling in the fact that the law establishing the authority specifically included clauses guaranteeing its workers freedom to organize and to engage in concerted activity for mutual aid and protection.

In terms of community welfare, however, it is obviously much better to figure out ways to make public employes want to stay on the job than to give them more opportunity to strike. This is a task to which many branches of Government have addressed themselves with both vigor and ingenuity in the last few years.

All these efforts stem from a belief that it is unfair for the community to insist that its employes surrender the economic weapons all other workers have at their command unless ample impartial machinery is provided for adjudicating employe grievances and improving labor standards.

In line with this belief, such key cities as New York and Philadelphia have refused to take refuge in the exemption of public employes from all the protection of the national and state labor-relations laws. They have played a pioneering role in adopting comprehensive programs of union recognition and collective bargaining within the framework of civil-service laws and regulations.

In this city eighty bargaining certificates were issued in municipal agencies in the first twenty-two months of a program initiated by Mayor Wagner on March 31, 1958. The New York plan was evolved by Miss Ida Klaus, former solicitor of the National Labor Relations Board and now counsel to the City Labor Department, after the most definitive study in any community of how employer-employe relations could be conducted most fruitfully in public service.

Her conclusion was that the city's business would be run most efficiently if machinery were provided for collective bargaining.

"Human nature is such that paternalism, no matter how bounteous its gifts, may be of less real satisfaction and advantage to both sides than the process of reasoning together around the family table, no matter how meager the fare," Miss Klaus told the mayor.

She might have added that excessively harsh penalties for civil-service strikers are as ill-calculated to improve Government operations and enhance Government prestige as is paternalistic largess.

Too often the penalties fail to overawe those they are designed to keep on the job. Government employes know that interrupted service must be promptly restored. They also know that an avalanche of mandatory dismissals would probably hamper or prevent such action. In the end the inability to enforce an unworkable law wounds the very sense of sovereignty the law was designed to sustain.

The experience with the Condon-Wadlin Act points not to stiffer sanctions but to better grievance machinery and more extensive bargaining procedures in all branches of public employment. This is the moral Governor Rockefeller appears to have drawn. President-elect Kennedy has made it plain, too, that he favors a law to give recognition to unions of Federal employes and to set up bargaining devices.

Out of such developments can come meaningful cooperation to raise the standards of service to the public as well as the standards of equity to those who supply the service. It is visionary to expect that all grievances will evaporate and all explosions be averted. But a better balance will be established between the compulsions of freedom and of authority. The dividends should benefit all of us, the people.

57. A Suggested Code of Ethics for Municipal Officials and Employees*

Be it resolved [enacted] by the Council of the City of_____ _
that the following be a "Code of Ethics for the Public Service of the City
of_____."

1. DECLARATION OF POLICY

The proper operation of democratic government requires that public
officials and employees be independent, impartial, and responsible to the
people; that government decisions and policy be made in the proper
channels of the governmental structure; that public office not be used for
personal gain; and that the public have confidence in the integrity of its
government. In recognition of these goals there is hereby established a
Code of Ethics for all officials and employees, whether elected or appointed, paid or unpaid. The purpose of this Code is to establish ethical
standards of conduct for all such officials and employees by setting forth
those acts or actions that are incompatible with the best interests of the
city and by directing disclosure by such officials and employees of private
financial or other interests in matters affecting the city. The provisions and
purpose of this Code and such rules and regulations as may be established
are hereby declared to be in the best interests of the City of_____.

Commentary. A declaration of policy should be included as a preamble to the Code
of Ethics. This validates the historic function of the legislative body in setting governmental policy.

The basic policy objectives of democratic government are: (1) governmental efficiency; (2) equal treatment of equal claims; (3) public confidence; (4) preventing the
use of public office for private gain; and (5) preserving the integrity of governmental
institutions. Each of these concepts is contained in the Declaration of Policy.

1. The emphasis on efficiency in government has been strong since 1900 and is an
area where municipalities have helped to shape the structure and functions of all
modern governments. A corrupt or unethical government is inefficient by definition,
since self-interest rather than efficiency will be the primary motivation of its officials
in conducting public business.

2. Equal treatment always has been part of the historic philosophy of American
government. It means equality before the law as part of democratic government.

3. Public confidence in established government is essential to survival of that
government. Government predicated on consent of the governed is endangered if

* International City Managers Association. "A Suggested Code of Ethics for
Municipal Officials and Employees." (Chicago: International City Managers Association,
1962). Reprinted by permission of publisher. Mr. James P. Clarke prepared the working
draft of the code.

officials' self-interest is put before the public interest. This concept is highly pragmatic as well as idealistic.

4. The use of public office for private gain is contrary to the concept of public office as a public trust. Confidential information is available to public officials by virtue of their official positions. Misuse and abuse of this power violates the historic concept of trusteeship and the fiduciary.

5. Governmental integrity depends upon decisions being made by established governmental policy-making institutions. Changes are made officially and for the benefit of all, not for the private gain of a few.

A declaration of policy or statement of purpose for a Code of Ethics often has been included in governmental codes. This is also a legislative practice to give a synopsis of the purpose and content of proposed and enacted bills. The states of New York, Ohio, Texas, and Washington and the city of Los Angeles, for example, have included a preamble or statement of purpose in their codes.

2. RESPONSIBILITIES OF PUBLIC OFFICE

Public officials and employees are agents of public purpose and hold office for the benefit of the public. They are bound to uphold the Constitution of the United States and the Constitution of this State and to carry out impartially the laws of the nation, state, and municipality and thus to foster respect for all government. They are bound to observe in their official acts the highest standards of morality and to discharge faithfully the duties of their office regardless of personal considerations, recognizing that the public interest must be their primary concern. Their conduct in both their official and private affairs should be above reproach.

Commentary. This article states what may seem obvious—that public officials and employees should carry out their duties fully and in accordance with law. They must "discharge the duties of their office" because failure to act may at times be as damaging to the public as unethical acts. This section stresses the concept of public office as a public trust, loyalty to the form of government, and the primacy of the public interest over the self-interest of the agents of government.

The most difficult question is to determine the "generally accepted" standards of morality of the community. A start can be made by studying controlling laws and local customs. It may be helpful to formalize this more by assembling a representative group of citizens as a board of ethics to develop precedents on a case-by-case basis. (This is discussed in Chapter 3 under the heading, "The Board of Ethics.") A board of ethics should have expert help in arriving at advisory decisions; its membership therefore should include one or more persons skilled in law and in municipal government service. One of the most important functions of an advisory board of ethics may be to interpret prevailing standards of morality. This would provide a practical way to recognize regional and local differences in cultural and religious attitudes and to anticipate conflicts of interest.

3. DEDICATED SERVICE

All officials and employees of the municipality should be loyal to the political objectives expressed by the electorate and the programs developed to attain those objectives. Appointive officials and employees should adhere to the rules of work and performance established as the standard for their positions by the appropriate authority.

Officials and employees should not exceed their authority or breach the law or ask others to do so, and they should work in full cooperation with other public officials and employees unless prohibited from so doing by law or by officially recognized confidentiality of their work.

Commentary. A section of this kind should be included in all or most codes since public management is a vital part of ethical government. It should be recognized that this is a new departure, although not an original idea, in public service codes.[1]

4. FAIR AND EQUAL TREATMENT

A. INTEREST IN APPOINTMENTS. Canvassing of members of the council, directly or indirectly, in order to obtain preferential consideration in connection with any appointment to the municipal service shall disqualify the candidate for appointment except with reference to positions filled by appointment by the council.

Commentary. Members of the city council have an important role in the conduct of municipal government affairs. It is natural and proper for councilmen, who often are life-long residents of a community, to be approached by persons interested in municipal employment. But the motivation for such an approach is important. Persons who express interest and wish additional information about municipal employment should be encouraged in their interest. It is quite another thing to seek preferential treatment in violation of the concept of fair and equal treatment.

Many city councils appoint certain officials directly. In these cases of course it is both necessary and desirable for them to be involved directly in the appraisal and selection of officials.

B. USE OF PUBLIC PROPERTY. No official or employee shall request or permit the use of city-owned vehicles, equipment, materials, or property for personal convenience or profit, except when such services are available to the public generally or are provided as municipal policy for the use of such official or employee in the conduct of official business.

---

[1] See Phillip Monypenny, "A Code of Ethics for Public Administration," *George Washington Law Review,* March, 1953, pp. 423–44, for reference to loyalty to program and political objectives and use of the administrative chain of command. See also William Beyer, "Ethics in the Public Service: Proposals for a Public Service Code," *The Annals of the American Academy of Political and Social Science,* Vol. 101, 1922, for suggested "canons" governing working in full cooperation with other public servants and use of administrative channels in case of disagreement on policy or procedure.

This section is intended to encourage constructive and evolutionary changes in governmental institutions. How well such a provision can be put into practice is not clear. The one major code that includes a management concept, that of the United States government, House of Representatives Concurrent Resolution 175, 1958, has no machinery to put it into effect.

Commentary. This section is part of the concept of fair and equal treatment. It also applies to the responsibility of the holder of a public trust to exclude personal benefit from public trusts. In some municipalities a provision of this kind has been enacted by ordinance or by administrative regulations issued by the chief administrator. In such cases a provision in the code of ethics may not be needed.

No one would question the importance of this section in reference to extremely valuable property or large amounts of money, but it is significant also with reference to the cumulative waste of small items which can amount to a large amount of money. The section permits flexibility in the use of city-owned automobiles by authorized officials and employees. This is provided by the statement ". . . except when such services are available to the public generally or are provided as municipal policy for the use of such official or employee in the conduct of official business."

C. OBLIGATIONS TO CITIZENS. No official or employee shall grant any special consideration, treatment, or advantage to any citizen beyond that which is available to every other citizen.

Commentary. This section also is part of the concept of fair and equal treatment and the responsibility of public office as a public trust. This section is a restatement in the context of fair and equal treatment of the principles included both in Article 1, "Declaration of Policy," and in Article 3, "Dedicated Service."

5. CONFLICT OF INTEREST

No councilman or other official or employee, whether paid or unpaid, shall engage in any business or transaction or shall have a financial or other personal interest, direct or indirect, which is incompatible with the proper discharge of his official duties in the public interest or would tend to impair his independence of judgment or action in the performance of his official duties. Personal as distinguished from financial interest includes an interest arising from blood or marriage relationships or close business or political association.

Specific conflicts of interest are enumerated below for the guidance of officials and employees:

Commentary. Conflict of interest is at the heart of governmental ethics. Based on extensive experience in government, it is the kind of provision that should be precise and clear and should avoid rigid application in an attempt to cover every possible kind of situation.

Conflict of interest has been covered by federal law since 1853 and by some municipal ordinances as far back as the 1830's. In the 19th century some of these conflicts in the United States involved some of the most corrupt actions—the grossest kinds of theft that would be inconceivable today. This historical context means that conflict of interest usually has been dealt with in criminal law. In recent years there has been some shift of emphasis, in recognition of improved ethical standards, toward covering conflict of interest through civil law and administrative control.

A. INCOMPATIBLE EMPLOYMENT. No councilman or other official or employee shall engage in or accept private employment or render services for private interests when such employment or service is incompatible with the proper discharge of his official duties or would tend to impair his independence of judgment or action in the performance of his official duties.

Commentary. This provision not only is the most frequently occurring prohibition in operating and proposed public service codes of ethics but also has the longest acceptance historically. This concept is traced to the Sermon on the Mount and the warning against attempting to serve two masters, which was incorporated in the English common law. It has been a strong prohibition ever since in the legal profession. Even if the public official is of the highest integrity, the presumption of conflict continues. The experience of centuries is that when in an equivocal position it is human nature to decide in favor of one's own interest.

A provision on incompatible employment almost always is needed in a governmental code of ethics. It does not work undue hardship on the great majority of employees because it does not prohibit *all* outside employment—only incompatible employment. Some cities have adopted ordinances and regulations controlling and regulating outside employment, but very few have attempted to prohibit all outside employment. Where outside employment is regulated by ordinance or regulation, these controls usually have two principal objectives: (1) to prevent employment that has an actual or potential conflict of interest between off-the-job and official duties, and (2) to prevent an excessive amount of outside work so that the employee is unable to render good service in his regular, full-time job with the city.

B. DISCLOSURE OF CONFIDENTIAL INFORMATION. No councilman or other official or employee shall, without proper legal authorization, disclose confidential information concerning the property, government, or affairs of the city. Nor shall he use such information to advance the financial or other private interest of himself or others.

Commentary. This article, which is clear, comprehensive, and brief, covers the most frequently occurring provision in operating public service codes of ethics. There is widespread acceptance of the concept that confidential information is the property of the government, not of the individual. Any use of such information for private profit is unthinkable and, in cases of national security, could be subversive.

C. GIFTS AND FAVORS. No councilman or other official or employee shall accept any valuable gift, whether in the form of service, loan, thing, or promise, from any person, firm, or corporation which to his knowledge is interested directly or indirectly in any manner whatsoever in business dealings with the city; nor shall any such official or employee (1) accept any gift, favor, or thing of value that may tend to influence him in the discharge of his duties, or (2) grant in the discharge of his duties any improper favor, service, or thing of value.

Commentary. The mink coat and freezer episodes of the late 1940's and early 1950's focused public attention on the problem of gifts for governmental officials and employees. Controlling this practice can range from absolute prohibition to no control whatever. The prudent course is to make a differential evaluation. What counts is the expectation of the gift-giver and the commitment of the person receiving the gift. The practical criterion is to prohibit gifts "of value" that might influence him. Some cities require that any official or employee who receives a gift must report it to his supervisor.

One of the benefits of a board of ethics is its ability to evaluate gift-giving incidents and thus to develop standards. It is possible, for example, for an officer or employee to accept a gift in good faith without knowing that the giver has business dealings with the city.

In drafting this section of the Code of Ethics an analysis was made of the following sources: the 16 available operating codes of ethics in governmental jurisdictions in the United States, three proposed codes for governmental jurisdictions, all federal statutes on conflict of interest (based on the published report of an intensive two-year analysis by the Association of the Bar of the City of New York), the findings and report of the U. S. Senate Committee on Labor and Public Welfare, Subcommittee on Ethics (Douglas Committee), and the report of the Committee on Conflicts of Interest of Montgomery County, Maryland.

Analysis showed 17 major items within the general area of conflict of interest. The specific areas of conflict of interest most frequently found were the following:

1. Incompatible employment—holding a position in addition to a public position which interferes, or may interfere, with the proper discharge of the public duty.

2. Use of confidential information, obtained as a result of public position, for personal gain.

3. Acceptance of or soliciting of gifts and favors by a public official or employee.

4. Any use of official position for personal gain.

5. Holding (possession) investments which interfere, or tend to interfere, with the proper discharge of public duty.

6. Representation by public officials or employees of private interests before government agencies, courts, or legislative bodies, and participation in the profits from such representation.

7. Participation in transactions as a public representative with a business entity in which the public official or employee has a direct or indirect financial or other personal interest.

8. Personal interest in legislation, to the extent that private interest takes precedence over public interest and public duty.

9. Entry into contracts or other conduct of business for profit by a business in which a public official or employee has a substantial or controlling interest, especially when the public official or employee can influence such contract or business because of his public position.

10. Soliciting or accepting future employment with a business doing business with the government over which the public official has some control in his official capacity at the time of the transaction.

In addition to the 10 most frequently occurring conflict-of-interest provisions in public service codes of ethics, the following topics also are covered in one or more such codes:

1. Mandatory disclosure of sources of income by public officials.

2. Representing private interests before the courts, where official position or information is presumed to exert an undue influence or to give advantage.

3. Prohibition against any impression of corruptibility by a public official as a result of the official's conduct or other act.

4. An injunction to the public official to adhere to ethical or right conduct in his official and private conduct.

5. Prohibition against *ex parte* (unilateral) communications or applications to the exclusion of other interested parties.

6. Prohibition of political activity for appointed officials where such activity may be

a cause of favored treatment or undue influence on official position, action, or judgment.

7. Disclosure of interest in legislation divided to specifically apply to appointed officials or employees as well as to legislators. This prohibition occurs more frequently with respect to legislators.

D. REPRESENTING PRIVATE INTERESTS BEFORE CITY AGENCIES OR COURTS. No councilman or other official or employee whose salary is paid in whole or in part by the city shall appear in behalf of private interests before any agency of the city. He shall not represent private interests in any action or proceeding against the interests of the city in any litigation to which the city is a party.

A councilman may appear before city agencies on behalf of constituents in the course of his duties as a representative of the electorate or in the performance of public or civic obligations. However, no councilman or other official or employee shall accept a retainer or compensation that is contingent upon a specific action by a city agency.

Commentary. The intent and application of this article seems clear. It is based on the following concepts which usually result in prohibitions or restrictions on public officials and employees: (1) incompatible employment, (2) the use of official position for personal gain, (3) confidential information belonging to the city not the official, and (4) acceptance or solicitation of gifts, favors, or services for which some return is expected.

This section is useful as a prohibition against bribery or the solicitation of bribes. This is one of the few prohibitions that is not being liberalized in proposals for updating and streamlining conflict-of-interest statutes. The intent is not to restrict basic rights but to prohibit improper representation and the solicitation of business or profit from such representation. One exception is that an official or employee may represent a parent, spouse, child, ward, or other person for whom he is a personal fiduciary. In doing so, however, he must (1) disclose his interest, (2) obtain information from the appropriate city official in advance of his participation, and (3) provide evidence that he is not officially involved in the transaction.

E. CONTRACTS WITH THE CITY. Any councilman or other official or employee who has a substantial or controlling financial interest in any business entity, transaction, or contract with the city, or in the sale of real estate, materials, supplies, or services to the city, shall make known to the proper authority such interest in any matter on which he may be called to act in his official capacity. He shall refrain from voting upon or otherwise participating in the transaction or the making of such contract or sale.

A councilman or other official or employee shall not be deemed interested in any contract or purchase or sale of land or other thing of value unless such contract or sale is approved, awarded, entered into, or authorized by him in his official capacity.

Commentary. The first paragraph of this section, or a similar provision, generally is found in most city charters, and the charter also may contain the following provision: "Any officer or employee who willfully conceals such a substantial financial interest or willfully violates the requirements of this section shall be guilty of malfeasance in office or position and shall forfeit his office or position. Violation of this section with the knowledge express or implied of the person or corporation contracting with or making a sale to the municipality shall render the contract voidable by the manager or the city council."

A San Francisco charter amendment adopted in November, 1959, defines "remote interest," as: (1) the ownership of less than 5 per cent of the shares of a corporation for profit; (2) a nonsalaried officer or a nonprofit corporation; (3) an officer being reimbursed for his actual and necessary expenses incurred in the performance of official duty; (4) an employee of the contracting party having 10 or more other employees, provided that the councilman or officer was an employee of the said contracting party for at least three years prior to his acceptance of such office; (5) a landlord or tenant of the contracting party; or (6) an attorney of the contracting party.

The purpose of this section is not to prevent or prohibit local businessmen from bidding on municipal contracts or participating in other business with the city, nor to make it untenable for local businessmen to become officials or officers of the city. In small cities such prohibitions would be ridiculous and perhaps a hardship resulting in loss of economy or efficiency. Instead the section covers substantial or controlling interest and leaves the decision on personal participation in such transactions with the official or employee concerned through the alternative of self-disqualification. This should be considered a sufficient safeguard of official integrity and the public interest.

This section also clarifies the point that a conflict must demonstrably exist, that presumption is insufficient evidence of a real conflict of interest. It is the official's participation in the transaction as representative of the city and private interests that is the central issue.

The problems covered by this section are historic at all levels of government, but each city must decide for itself whether it is a current problem. It is based on important concepts of public service and prohibitions upon the exercise of a public trust. It is, however, one of the less frequent provisions in present and proposed codes of ethics for government service.

F. DISCLOSURE OF INTEREST IN LEGISLATON.

A councilman who has a financial or other private interest in any legislation shall disclose on the records of the council or other appropriate authority the nature and extent of such interest. This provision shall not apply if the councilman disqualifies himself from voting.

Any other official or employee who has a financial or other private interest, and who participates in discussion with or gives an official opinion to the council, shall disclose on the records of the council or other appropriate authority the nature and extent of such interest.

Commentary. Three policy choices must be resolved in this section as follows:

1. Should disclosure be permissive or mandatory? Mandatory disclosure is recommended so that the extent of personal or private interest is known. The official or employee still has the choice of disqualifying himself or not participating to avoid disclosure of his interest.

2. Should disclosure be confidential or public? This section probably will be more acceptable if disclosure is kept confidential. It should be emphasized, however, that such disclosure is a matter of city council or other city record. An oral statement is not sufficient.

3. Should disclosure be required on a continuing or periodic basis? A periodic statement may suffice, but care should be exercised with ordinances and other matters before the city council.

6. POLITICAL ACTIVITY

No appointive official or employee in the administrative service shall use the prestige of his position in behalf of any political party.

No appointive official or employee in the administrative service shall orally, by letter, or otherwise, solicit or be in any manner concerned in soliciting any assessment, subscription, or contribution to any political party; nor shall he be a party to such solicitation by others. Such appointed officials and employees shall not take an active part in political campaigns for candidates.

No official or employee, whether elected or appointed, shall promise an appointment to any municipal position as a reward for any political activity.

Commentary. The purpose of this article is to help develop and maintain an impartial municipal service. The first two paragraphs apply only to appointed officials and employees, thus recognizing that elected officials do and should participate freely in politics. The central issue is to preserve the nonpolitical character of the administrative or civil service.

This article raises a difficult question in the minds of some who hold that it impinges on the civil rights of municipal employees by forbidding or severely limiting their participation in political activities. The question, however, is not the civil rights of employees with respect to participation in politics. The question revolves rather around the point of maintaining an impartial municipal service for the administration of all municipal programs for all citizens. Of course the municipal official or employee has the right to be active in politics, but he does not have a correlative right to municipal employment. Very few governmental codes of ethics include a provision of this kind, but many cities and other governmental jurisdictions make substantially the same provision through statutes, city charters, and civil service or merit system rules. This is an area of considerable controversy and legal dispute. Care therefore should be taken in drafting this article to meet state and local legal requirements.

This article is needed, irrespective of the form of municipal government, to work toward the ideal of the public service that is dedicated to all citizens. Both "fair and equal treatment" (Article 4) and avoidance of "conflict of interest" (Article 5) are more easily achieved and maintained in the city that has abandoned patronage and other attributes of the spoils system. This article attempts to strike a balance between the right of the employer (the municipal corporation) to require a neutral and impartial civil service and the right of employees to vote and exercise other basic rights of citizenship.

The third paragraph of this article is intended especially for cities with council-manager government, although it should be considered by other cities as well. Its purpose is to prevent flagrant abuses of public service through patronage and the spoils system. As worded above, it applies to all municipal positions, including appointments to boards and commissions where the service is part-time and there is little or no salary. As an alternative this paragraph could be modified so that it applies only to positions in the classified civil service.

7. APPLICABILITY OF CODE

When a councilman or other official or employee has doubt as to the applicability of a provision of this code to a particular situation, he should apply to the authority on ethical conduct constituted for the implementation of this code for an advisory opinion and be guided by that opinion when given. The councilman or other official or employee shall have the opportunity to present his interpretation of the facts at issue and of the applicable provision(s) of the code before such advisory decision is made. This code shall be operative in all instances covered by its provisions except when superseded by an applicable statutory or charter provision and statutory or charter action is mandatory, or when the application of a statutory or charter provision is discretionary but determined to be more appropriate or desirable.

Commentary. This article states the rights of the official or employee to a fair hearing and to participation in the decision-making process. It clarifies the fact that a code of ethics is part of rather than something foreign to established law, customs, and practices in a community.

A statement of this type should be included since it informs persons covered by its provisions of that fact and what is expected of them in relation to the code. The statement also covers implementation and individual rights. This is a minimum requirement of law and is desirable also in a code of ethics.

8. SANCTIONS

Violation of any provisions of this Code should raise conscientious questions for the councilman or other official or employee concerned as to whether voluntary resignation or other action is indicated to promote the best interest of the city. Violation may constitute a cause for suspension, removal from office or employment, or other disciplinary action.

Commentary. This article is a succinct statement of the remedies that may be invoked for violation of the Code of Ethics. Administrative remedies are proposed in preference to criminal penalties. Governmental codes increasingly stress that codes should be a part of the civil law with administrative remedies. Criminal penalties are not recommended. They are too severe, especially if they involve jail sentences. As a consequence they seldom are enforced except in cases of gross malfeasance. Thus no action is taken on many violations of codes of ethics because appropriate administrative sanctions are not available.

This is practical recognition that a code of ethics should be a means of administrative control. It asserts the rights of the city, as the employer, to require certain standards of behavior and to discharge any employee or to take other appropriate action against one who does not or refuses to meet those standards. This kind of control is more effective; it also is more acceptable to officials, employees, and the public.

This article also emphasizes internal control through self-discipline by providing for "resignation or other action" on a voluntary basis. "Other action" might include restitution or recovery of any loss to the city that resulted from violation of the code.

In the long run this will encourage a professional sense of responsibility, based on pride of service instead of fear of reprisal. It may even in time appreciably reduce the need for external control. Appropriate voluntary action taken by a person who violates the code also avoids embarrassment for the city government and unnecessary hardship for the person involved. Voluntary action eliminates the need for drawn-out administrative or legal procedures that create a poor public impression. The emphasis is on self-enforcement and discretionary rather than mandatory administrative remedies.

H. Eliot Kaplan

58. Civil Service 75 Years*

The 75th anniversary of the adoption of civil service laws of the federal government and New York State is a propitious occasion to take inventory of the accomplishments and shortcomings of the administration of the merit system and to prognosticate future developments.

We have come a long way in improving administration of the civil service merit system since its adoption in 1883. Like most radical reforms it started with a rush in the federal service and in some larger states and cities, halted precipitately to consolidate its gains, lagged for a considerable time and, since 1936, resumed its inevitable advance. It hesitated again during World War II but has resumed its forward march. There were only nine states operating under a formal civil service law up to 1935. There are now 24 states under merit system laws; and every state is now required to select on a merit system basis employees of their agencies paid in whole or in part out of federal funds.

At the same time the public rosters—national, state and local—have swelled at an accelerated pace—from about 3,250,000 civilian employees in 1935, with an annual payroll of $10 billion, to over seven million and a yearly payroll of $30 billion. The likelihood is that our public services will expand by 1975 to about eight million with an annual payroll of over $35 billion.

This huge expansion of governmental services has placed a responsibility on personnel agencies. The failure of half the states to join the merit system brigade must prove disheartening to many. They may take solace in the knowledge that even in such "non-conformist" jurisdictions the devastating influences of the patronage system have long abated in the face of obvious need for competent administrators and employees. . . .

The temptation in observing a landmark anniversary is to point glowingly to the advances made and ignore or gloss over frustrations and weaknesses. Because the merit system is a generally accepted principle we are prone to assume that administration is more or less sound and effective.

We are likely to overlook the fact that much public support for the competitive examination system is founded on a somewhat negative attitude rather than on a conviction of its effectiveness. No one has been able successfully to defend—or rather to undertake publicly to defend—the

* From *National Municipal Review*. May 1958, pp. 220–225 and 250. Reprinted with permission of publisher.

patronage system as desirable or as effective. This has proved advantageous to complacent advocates and practitioners of the competitive examination system. Attacks on the effectiveness of the competitive system are easily thwarted by charges of partisan exploitation of the public service and other ulterior motivation. There has been lacking, therefore, an aggressive and militant approach toward determining the validity of our testing processes and improving methods and techniques of examinations.

One of the most devastating aspects of the examination process is the long delay between recruiting candidates and certifying eligibles for appointment. No other factor is more responsible for discouraging the competent to seek careers in government service; none is more prolific of attracting mediocrity through failure of effective competition. We may even need to discard our concepts of determining comparative potentialities for successful performance on the job.

SYSTEM WELL ROOTED

There need be no fear on the part of personnel administrators and technicians that weaknesses revealed in a study of testing methods would lend comfort to opponents of the merit system. The system is too well rooted in our present governmental processes to be endangered by lack of public support. Our democratic institutions have too much vitality to be shaken by pseudo claims of charlatans among professional patronage dispensers. The hesitancy of legislatures to weaken civil service laws attests to the regard the public has for the merit system.

Over the years there has been built up a congeries of local civil service agencies operating under general civil service merit laws, notably in Illinois, New Jersey, New York and Ohio. The home rule principle needs to be respected, but extension of the principle to administration of civil service laws has become a smoke screen to obscure the ineffectiveness of local administration in many smaller municipalities. In Illinois, New York and Ohio, for example, local personnel agencies are completely autonomous, with most of them acting primarily as cloaks for political exploitation of the public services rather than being concerned in staffing their agencies with competent talent. Fortunately, this has not been the experience in the large cities but in the smaller municipalities it is quite prevalent.

This may be due in part to failure of adequate appropriations for such agencies—some deliberately designed to assure innocuous application of the local civil service rules. It is questionable in light of experience whether it would be effective even if adequate funds were made available.

Certainly it would be uneconomical as contrasted to centralized administration in the state personnel agency.

This is not to advocate direct administration of the civil service law by the state agency as in New Jersey. It is rather to advocate direction and supervision in the smaller municipalities by the state agency through a personnel officer in each municipality with dual responsibility to the state commission for enforcement of the law and rules and responsibility to his municipality for other phases of local personnel administration.

No longer content with or able to depend on orthodox methods of recruiting for administrative and executive talent, personnel agencies have been forced to adopt more aggressive means of attracting university graduates. Emulating private industry, the campuses have been invaded to lure promising graduates to make government their careers. To accomplish their objective of competing with private agencies for such talent, competitive examination procedures have been short-circuited. Testing methods have been geared more practically to bring candidates and positions closer. Opportunities for appointment were heightened by confining competition for internships to such graduates.

ATTRACT COLLEGE GRADUATES

These departures from traditional policy of waiting for candidates to seek out the personnel agencies have had a salutary effect. One obstacle to greater appeal of these internships to college and university graduates is the lack of a positive program of accelerating their promotion or, perhaps more correctly, their absorption in the regular competitive service after completion of training and orientation.

This trend toward encouraging young college graduates can, however, be overdone and, in some cases, has become a fetish. The notion that only those with formal education should be inspired to seek careers in our public services, to the exclusion of others perhaps less fortunately situated, may not appeal to our democratic ideals. Nor would it be wise or politic to advance a policy of looking with a jaundiced eye on non-college-bred potential leaders. We need to have both if we are to be realistic and maintain a balanced perspective. It will be impossible to wean the American public from its deep-rooted desire for "representative government"—distinguishable from partisanship—even in the permanent career civil service.

We have gone a long way in inventorying our manpower in the public service through classification of positions based on duties and responsibilities. Salary schedules have been established on more equitable premises. But have these devices remedied the basic difficulty of leveling all incumbents in the same class, regardless of competency? Rigidity of salary classifications tends to level all in the class to a common denominator. In this respect private industry has a decided advantage over the civil service. The latter is usually inhibited from making any distinctions among its employees. Recognition of unusual talent or industry or initiative is denied the public administrator. . . .

A LOOK TO FUTURE

What apparitions appear with respect to the future of personnel administration as we gaze in the crystal ball? What developments may we expect during the next score years? One may be reasonably sure that government personnel administration will undergo vast modification. Personnel agencies as now constituted will have to measure up to much greater responsibilities or be superseded by other more dynamic and practical administrative devices.

With more and more functions placed on personnel agencies, most of them only collateral to their primary one of recruiting, examining and certifying for appointment, many agencies have been taking on responsibilities for which they are inadequately equipped. Many of these functions, such as administration of pension plans, group life insurance plans, accident and sickness insurance protections and other fringe benefits, have been dumped in the laps of these agencies because there appeared no other place to allocate them. Dealing with affairs of public employees, it would appear logical for the personnel agency to assume such responsibilities.

From a practical point of view it seems of doubtful wisdom to saddle agencies with these added functions when they have had all they can do to administer primary functions adequately, particularly with their paucity of professional technical staffs woefully unfamiliar with such new functions and inadequate appropriations. The personnel agencies will probably of necessity neglect their primary functions of staffing operating agencies, so preoccupied will they become with the new ones. This may encourage more extensive and radical reorganization of personnel functions.

If the emphasis of personnel administration as an integral part of management has the validity professed for it, the trend may well dispel the fiction of the personnel agency continuing as an independent agency of government. The multiple commission form of direction will probably be abandoned in favor of a personnel manager responsible to the "general manager," the head of a comprehensive department of administrative management. The fact is, multiple commissions have outlived their original purpose. Concern as to nonpartiality of the direction of the merit system by assurance of a bipartisan commission has been dissipated by sad experience. Impartiality has come not by such device but by the public's vital stake in its growing public service and the inherent complexities of government.

RESPONSIBLE ADMINISTRATION

Our university and college facilities will be such that none but their graduates will be among competitors for executive and administrative posts. This will probably force abandonment of our traditional "practical" examinations in favor of broad examinations to determine capacity for responsible administration. To accomplish this successfully we will need to reorient our concepts of testing techniques and procedures and drastically revamp the professional and technical staffs of the personnel agencies. More comprehensive in-service training programs must be developed.

More likely to go overboard is our present practice of filling higher executive and administrative positions by competitive promotion examinations. Appointing authorities will have far more responsibility and control over promotions, with the personnel manager having at most only a veto power over them. On the other hand, personnel managers will have added responsibility with respect to facilitating transfers from one agency to another. There will be greater flexibility in the assignment of generalists as well as specialists among the agencies of government. There will be an ever growing recognition of "expertise" in the know-how of government operation. This will perforce reduce to a minimum turnover in such personnel on change of political administration.

NEW CONCEPTS

With increasing public confidence in the impartiality of appointive heads of departments and agencies, with attendant more enlightened political leadership, it is likely that governmental personnel programs and policies will be decentralized and delegated to operating departments. A department of administrative management, to embrace the personnel agency, will be responsible for establishing standards of personnel practices and post audit actions of operating departments. The lessened pressure for partisan patronage will encourage public opinion to abandon the false notion that public administration needs the myopic supervision of a bipartisan independent personnel agency.

Position classification based on duties and responsibilities will take on an entirely different concept. In spite of probable short-sightedness of employee organizations imbued with the spirit of "equality of pay for equal work," more consideration will be given to superiority of performance. The era of mediocrity oozing to the top because of overemphasis on seniority and longevity is slowly waning in favor of greater incentives for those achieving unusual results. The pace in that direction will quicken as we turn more and more to government to solve our complex problems and to serve more effectively our expanding public services. . . .

It is safe to conjecture that there will be far greater gains in the public personnel field during the next score years than have occurred during the last 40. It is equally safe to prophesy that every state, and every municipality of substantial size, will function under a reasonably sound civil service merit system. Utopia, civil-service-wise, appears still far off on the horizon; but our sights will have been raised to much greater heights of hopeful accomplishments.

19
STATE-LOCAL FINANCE

One of the most perplexing problems of state and local government is finance. Most state and local governments have been experiencing serious financial problems as the result of inflation and the expansion of activities and have been searching for new sources of revenue.

In developing a tax program consideration should be given to the criteria of a good tax. A tax should be fair, certain and not arbitrary, convenient as to time and place of payment, have a low administrative cost, produce a stable yield, and conserve tax resources.

In 1958 the American Federation of Labor–Congress of Industrial Organizations advanced a program for state and local taxation. The AFL-CIO is highly critical of the existing state-local system of taxation and makes specific proposals for the reform of state and local taxes.

Grants-in-aid have assumed an increasing importance since 1945. An Advisory Committee report on local government submitted to the Commission on Intergovernmental Relations in 1955 maintained that the term "intergovernmental payments" is a more accurate term than grants-in-aid. The report also discusses the purposes, for which grants are made and the major problems associated with grants.

59. The AFL-CIO Program*

. . . There are only a few economically acceptable taxes and a system that confines itself to these few is a better system and one that is easier to maintain in good working order than one which utilizes many taxes.

Our revenue system is too demanding and too complicated a problem to expect, at least immediately, that all its needs can be met by a single tax based on income. Among the respectable supplementary sources are the selective consumption taxes on gambling, liquor and tobacco, the motor vehicle taxes (largely correlated with special benefits) and a local property tax at reasonable levels. All of these are vastly superior to general sales or payroll taxes which are based on pure opportunism or worse and have no rational defense where other sources are available.

Let us now try to summarize the basic tax principles . . . and propose ways to begin the job of making our state and local tax systems more equitable and more productive.

A STANDARD FOR JUDGING STATE AND LOCAL TAXES

In the first place, we must begin with the basic principle which underlies any equitable tax program—that the load which each of us must bear should be related as far as possible to our relative economic position in the community. The best way to judge an individual's economic "ability to pay," of course, is in terms of 1) his net income and 2) the number of people who must depend upon that income for their support.

Unfortunately, most state and local taxes, as we have seen, violate this basic principle. Regressive taxes like those on sales and payrolls, and the variety of business taxes which so easily can be passed on to the consumer, actually have their greatest impact on the families who are least able to pay. This is even true of the property tax on which local governments must continue to so largely depend and which we must substantially overhaul in order to make them somewhat fairer.

Since all taxes ultimately must be paid out of someone's income, why shouldn't a much larger part of the revenue needs of the states and localities be raised in the first place from taxes imposed on the net incomes of individuals and the profits of corporations?

. . . it is often argued by reactionaries that since the federal government

* From *State and Local Taxes*. (Washington, D.C.: American Federation of Labor and Congress of Industrial Organizations, 1958). pp. 105–114. Footnote in original omitted. Reprinted with permission of publisher.

already gets much of its revenue from progressive income taxes, the states and localities should emphasize the use of taxes like those on sales, excises, property and the like in order to keep the total tax structure of the nation in "balance." To extend progressive taxation to the state and local level would practically confiscate the incomes of the high income group, they claim.

This position . . . is just not based on fact. Wealthy individuals and corporations can substantially reduce their federal taxes because of the privilege Uncle Sam gives them of deducting many state and local taxes from their incomes *before* figuring their tax to the federal government. Because of this "deductibility" privilege, progressive state and local taxes can be introduced without in any way extracting unreasonable amounts from the well-off. Similarly, state gift, inheritance and estate taxes can also be increased . . . without any confiscatory result. The tax credit afforded in this case gives even greater protection than deductibility and this greater protection should be extended to the income tax field.

No similar adjustments, however, are provided by the federal government in behalf of the millions of low and moderate income families who now carry so much of the burden of unfair state and local taxes. It is these families—who should be required to bear only a very light tax burden or none at all—who are truly being subjected to confiscation under regressive state and local tax laws; even before their incomes are whittled still further by sales taxes and other regressive levies that have no bearing on "ability to pay," there often is too little family income to support the necessities of life.

It just does not make sense to argue that state and local taxes that penalize the very poorest can be morally or economically justified simply because our federal tax system is reasonably progressive and fair.

Our real problem is not whether an overhauling of the tax systems of many states and localities is necessary; the question is how the changes should be made and how to begin. We cannot hope to scrap all the regressive taxes and substitute sufficient progressive new ones all at one time; politically this would not be feasible. We can hope, however, to work slowly and persistently at two objectives: progressive taxes can be initiated or improved where they already exist; at the same time, we can begin to eliminate the worst aspects, at least, of many of the regressive taxes even if it will take a long time to completely end them. . . .

THE LONG RANGE CHALLENGE

An informed public can achieve several important tax reforms on the state and local levels in a reasonably short time; many vital changes, however, will depend on our ability to rewrite the state constitutions themselves. This is a long, hard job and must not be minimized. But we must plan for the long range objectives as well as for the more easily obtainable ones if effective tax reform is to be achieved.

LEGALIZE INCOME TAXES. While by 1958 about two-thirds of all the states had some kind of income taxes on their books, 17 had no tax on individual incomes and 14 had no levy on corporation profits. Some of our most industrialized states, like Michigan, Illinois and Ohio, collected no income taxes at all.

In most of the states where this unfair situation exists, it is an outdated constitution which perpetuates the crime. Therefore, if progressive taxation is to be achieved—most of these states now raise the greater part of their revenue from general and selective sales taxes—a ceaseless campaign for constitutional reform must begin. This campaign must also aim to secure the legal right of local governments to institute their own progressive income taxes. Unfortunate situations such as exist in Pennsylvania—where the municipalities may levy an income tax on payrolls but are prevented from taxing investment income, corporation profits, or using progressive rates—must be eliminated.

END PROPERTY TAX LIMITATIONS. There are also several other undesirable restrictions on the taxing power of the states and localities which are required by the provisions of state constitutions or by statutes passed by the state legislatures.

In some states, limitations are placed on the right of local taxing districts to establish their own property tax rates, thereby limiting local revenue and stifling tax reforms.

While at least 20 states have already relinquished the use of general property taxes in favor of their localities, and most others have drastically reduced the use of this tax as a revenue source, state imposed restrictions on local property tax rates should be ended. . . .

INCREASE THE RIGHT TO BORROW. Constitutional or statutory restrictions which either outlaw or too narrowly limit the right of states to borrow should be ended in order to permit the states to increase the flexibility of their taxing and spending systems. . . .

Rigid restrictions on the right of the states to borrow forced the enactment of general sales taxes in many states during the depression; in most cases, the tax never was removed when the special emergency which brought it into being had ended.

STOP SEGREGATING STATE FUNDS. In 27 states the constitution requires that funds from taxes on gasoline and motor vehicles—which accounted for almost 29 percent of all state tax revenues in 1957—must be "ear marked" for exclusive use for highway construction and maintenance. In many other states, this segregation of highway funds is similarly required by state law.

Since either method deprives the elected legislature of its democratic right to use public tax revenues where they may be most urgently needed at a particular time, these constitutional or statutory restrictions should be ended as fast as possible. . . .

THE SHORTER RANGE OBJECTIVES: STATE TAXES

Whenever a state legislature convenes, an opportunity arises to modify, at least in some degree, the existing tax structure. A good place to begin is with the two-thirds of the states where income taxes are already sanctioned by the state constitutions and are on the books.

IMPROVE EXISTING INCOME TAXES. Income taxes aren't necessarily progressive; in most states, they are not. Often exemptions and dependents' allowances are so low that families who shouldn't be forced to pay are victimized while at the same time a combination of very low and flat income tax rates, or ones that are only slightly graduated, keep the cost to the well-off down to a minimum.

In some states, on the other hand, the exemptions for individuals and corporations are so high and the tax rates are so low the revenue yield is insignificant and other levies, like a general sales tax, are resorted to in order to increase state revenues.

In almost every income tax state, a revision of both the exemptions and the rate structure is critically needed to make the tax truly progressive and more productive. This can be done without unduly burdening wealthy individuals and corporations since the tax that is paid to the state can be deducted before figuring taxes due to the federal government. Under this "deductibility" allowance the tax to the federal government goes *down* as state income taxes levied against individuals and corporations go *up*.

The existence of this deductibility privilege gives the states an opportunity to sharply increase their own income tax levies with very little extra cost to wealthy individuals or corporations. Likewise, the states can increase their death and gift taxes without encouraging well-off individuals to move to another state, since the federal government allows a large part of his tax from these sources to be paid off with receipts that show that death and gift taxes have already been paid to the states.

While AFL-CIO supports deductibility, since it is a device through which the federal government helps all states to increase their revenue from progressive income taxes, we emphatically oppose the "double" deductibility which now is allowed by many states. Under this handout an individual or corporation can also deduct their federal income tax payment before figuring the amount of their state income taxes. . . . this double deal practically reduces the impact of state income taxes to zero in the case of very wealthy individuals and the most profitable corporations. Still worse, the tax savings from this handout are a direct loss of income to the states.

Is it any wonder that with the allowance of unreasonable exemptions, very low tax rates and double deductibility privileges under so many state income tax laws, only 17.6 percent of the total tax revenue of all of the states comes from the income tax? In Oregon, New York and Wisconsin where genuinely progressive income taxes exist, 58.3 percent, 50.5 percent and 42.3 percent respectively of the total tax revenues of these states came from income taxes in 1957. Oklahoma, Louisiana and New Mexico also have individual and corporate income taxes on their books; but they raised only 9.7 percent, 7.9 percent and 5.3 percent respectively of their total tax revenue from these levies. The three states with genuine progressive income taxes have no general sales tax; as we could readily anticipate, the last three states do. . . .

REDUCE THE SALES TAX IMPACT. If we set to work to substantially increase state revenues from income taxes, it stands to reason that the impact of regressive sales taxes can be reduced, even though it may not be feasible to eliminate them completely or as quickly as we would wish.

In 1957, 33 states collected general sales taxes. A reduction in this tax could be accomplished in two ways: 1) By reducing the tax rate and 2) by excluding food and drugs from the tax in the 24 states where these items are now covered. Perhaps both methods can be combined by reducing the sales tax from two percent to one percent, for example, and simultaneously removing food from taxation; perhaps the change can only be accomplished one step at a time.

Of course, in the states where general sales taxes still do not exist, any effort to introduce them must be vigorously opposed. . . .

BUSINESS MUST BEAR A LARGER SHARE. The fairest tax to impose upon any business is one that is related to its net profits. Unfortunately, fourteen states still levy no income tax on corporations and in states that do, the tax generally is extremely low. As a consequence, in all states many other special levies are charged against business. These include severance taxes, gross receipts imposed upon public utilities, insurance companies and other enterprises, business activity taxes, licenses of various sorts, chain store taxes, etc.

Besides the confusing variety of these special taxes and the fact that enforcement is often difficult, their inadequacy grows out of the more important fact that: 1) instead of being levied on net profits, they generally tax the value of gross sales, the number of units produced or sold, or the nature or size of the business enterprise, etc., 2) very often they are not a charge against business profits but are easily passed on as business "cost" in higher prices levied against the ultimate consumer, and 3) while they raise more revenue than all the state corporate income taxes, they are not an acceptable substitute for a truly progressive corporate income tax and the substantially larger yield that it would provide.

In states where corporate income taxes are now on the books, exemptions and rates should be carefully examined and every possible corporate enterprise should be subjected to coverage. Because of "deductibility," rates can be substantially raised without hardship to business. In the case of corporations operating in several states, the Massachusetts Formula or a variation of it . . . should be introduced to measure the net profits originating in a particular state for purposes of taxation.

In states without corporate profits taxes and in others where this tax doesn't effectively reach certain forms of business enterprise, a variety of other tax approaches must be undertaken. Severance taxes on the extraction of natural resources from land or water have been productive in many states. Substantial income can be obtained from license taxes in cases where special privileges and services are given by the states. As a group, the utilities, banks, finance and insurance companies have probably enjoyed greater tax freedom than other businesses and a careful check-up should be made. . . .

THE SHORTER RANGE OBJECTIVES: LOCAL TAXES

Our cities face three major problems: 1) the increased demand for services, 2) the spread of taxable resources beyond municipal limits, and 3) the failure of property tax receipts to keep up with rising revenue needs. Other local taxing units—the school districts, townships and counties— face similar problems in varying degree.

In planning to meet their financial problems the cities are hamstrung at the outset by their captive status. As "creatures" of the states almost every local action—a new tax levy, a move to consolidate with a neighboring local unit, etc.—must be taken to the state capitols for final decision. But even in the states where some "home rule" has been allowed, the limited tax base available to most local governments and the administrative difficulties involved in trying to collect taxes in a small jurisdiction leave the local units harassed and without adequate income.

Nevertheless, some important tax reforms can begin at home.

IMPROVE THE LOCAL PROPERTY TAX. Even though property taxes are, on the whole, regressive, as we have seen, they now provide about 86 percent of all local tax income and they unquestionably will continue as the most important source of local revenue for many years to come. Therefore, we must undertake the job of trying to make them both more fair and more productive.

In most communities the present assessed value placed on properties is far below their current real values. A thoroughgoing re-assessment is in order and should thereafter be repeated at reasonable intervals. In addition a complete inventory of all property should be made to make sure that none have improperly escaped from the tax rolls. Furthermore, the value placed upon industrial and commercial properties is often shockingly low and out of line with the assessments on residential property; this favoritism must be ended.

To establish property tax procedures on an efficient and honest basis, the assessor's office must be removed from politics, and the personnel involved must be properly trained. The states should assume leadership in helping their localities to improve assessment procedures by conducting training services and perhaps, as in some states already, the assessors should be put under Civil Service System.

All states should set up "equalization boards" or similar bodies with authority to require their local units to enforce uniform assessment procedures. This is mandatory if property tax burdens are to be fairly distributed among all of the property owners in the state.

LOCAL SALES AND PAYROLL TAXES MUST BE OPPOSED. By improving property tax procedures local revenues may be substantially increased; even so, much income will still escape local taxation and more revenue, particularly in the cities, will be required to meet local needs. While state permission to levy non-property taxes as an aid to solving local financial problems is of little help where an adequate local tax base just does not exist, in some of the larger cities an increasing amount of revenue is being raised from non-property taxes. . . . .

The increasing burden of municipal sales and payroll taxes bears hardest on the poorest families in the community. The payroll taxes are all levied at flat rates and most of them allow no personal exemptions and make no allowance for dependents; furthermore, the major sources of income of the wealthy—dividends and interest and often rents and capital gains—are excluded from the payroll taxes entirely. Local sales taxes, of course, simply heap another inequity on top of the general sales tax burden already imposed so unfairly by most of the states.

Genuinely progressive individual and corporate income taxes are the fairest levies on the local level as well as in the states and in Washington.

But if income taxes are to be used locally the states must grant not only legal sanction but administrative help in collecting them as well.

Without much greater state and local tax coordination, which must include a variety of forms of local aid, many municipalities, even in prosperous times, just cannot carry the burdens placed upon them.

HOW THE STATES MUST AID. Help from the states, in addition to methods already enumerated, is critically needed. It should take three different forms:

1. *The use of state-collected, locally shared taxes must be increased.* We have seen how jurisdictional problems make it extremely difficult and expensive for cities to collect most non-property taxes. The states can and must help them tax their own citizens more fairly and efficiently by extending the use of *shared taxes.* Under this process the state levies and collects the tax, as for instance, the Wisconsin State income tax, and then returns a certain percentage of the revenue to the local units in proportion to the origin of the revenue. The localities then can use their share as they see fit.

Another variation of the shared tax device which gives more scope to local autonomy is the *tax supplement* whereby a city is given the opportunity to add to an existing state tax a certain percentage to be collected from their own residents and then returned to it for local use. In view of the difficulty of imposing progressive income taxes on the local level, the tax supplement provides a way by which the states can and must cooperate with the cities in order that genuine progressive income taxes can be levied locally and then be efficiently collected.

2. *The states must extend direct financial aid to poorer local units.* Grants-in-aid are a device whereby the state enables a relatively poor municipality or other local unit to furnish at least a minimum service that is deemed essential, such as education. When state grants-in-aid are extended, they should be related to some fair standard of need. To give all local units a flat grant on the basis of a matching formula does not perform the equalizing purpose which is desired.

3. *Some of the services that have been administered and financed on the local level should be performed and financed by the states.* The performance of some services, such as the Social Security aids under which state-wide standards of public assistance are established, are not subject to local variation or discretion. In these types of cases the states could well assume complete responsibility for the service and thereby free local tax resources for the performance of other functions.

A guiding principle in extending this form of tax relief to local governments should be that the state only assume functions which do not require local direction to be effectively administered. . . .

60. Grants-in-Aid*

The term "grants-in-aid" is misunderstood. Basically it means monetary payments by one government to another. "Intergovernmental payments" might be a more expressive, and scientifically more objective, term because of the erroneous connotation attached to each part of the term "grants-in-aid." A "grant" implies a gift, a certain benevolence on the part of the paying government, and casts the grantor in the role of "lady bountiful," and the recipient in the role of the needy, the receiver of a gift or windfall. Addition of the term "in-aid" strengthens this connotation because the implication is that the payment is in aid of the program of the recipient government. Actually, a substantial portion of so-called "grants-in-aid" are transfers in order that the recipient, as an agent, may carry out the grantor's program. Instead of the grantor aiding the recipient, the opposite is true—the recipient is aiding the grantor by implementing the latter's program, receiving only reimbursement for its expenditure outlays. The aid may really be a burden; the function may not be a local responsibility at all but an imposed agency relationship on behalf of the State or National Government. Ironically, in State-local relations the political subdivisions often have no choice; they are mandated to act as agents. Also some of the so-called Federal aids to local governments are really channeled Federal expenditures used to implement Federal programs imposed upon the local units by agreement between the National and State Governments.

The term "grants-in-aid" is also misleading because in financial reporting it is necessarily restricted to direct monetary payments. To illustrate. If the State gives a city or county some cash from the gasoline tax to build a city street or county highway such payment is called a "grant-in-aid." But, if the State takes the same amount of money from the same pocket and spends it directly to build the identical road or street in the same city or county, this is treated as a State expenditure for highways and not a grant or an intergovernmental payment. For this reason, comparisons between States as to grants-in-aid lose some validity just as the total expenditure and revenue figures do. Since the arguments for and against grants-in-aid center around the amounts involved, still more refined statistical work is needed to obtain a clear picture of the facts.

* From *An Advisory Committee Report on Local Government Submitted to the Commission on Intergovernmental Relations.* (Washington, D.C.: U.S. Government Printing Office, June 1955), pp. 33–41. Footnotes in original omitted.

448 / State-Local Finance

The local officials want a clearer understanding of this whole area of intergovernmental relations. The difficulty is that assistance can be given by one government to another in several ways. The first is through the payment of cash which is labeled a "grant." Help can also be given, as seen above, by direct expenditures of the State or National Governments through their own employees. Technical assistance in the form of loans of expert personnel and the supplying of free information and technical advice is a common form of Federal nonmonetary assistance to State and local governments. Aid can also be extended by giving assistance in a variety of ways to the private industries of a city or county, such as placing war orders in an area of unemployment, thereby indirectly relieving the local government of some of its welfare relief burden. In the case of the National Government, aid may also come from monetary, fiscal, or other broad policies. But only the direct, monetary payments are now labeled as grants.

So far the inherent difficulties in the term "grants-in-aid" have not been surmounted. Few writers have been willing to switch to "intergovernmental transfers" or "intergovernmental payments," which admittedly are colorless words. Yet the term "grants-in-aid," probably ill-chosen in the first instance, has now become so burdened with semantic barnacles that the very use of the term distorts our thinking. Despite all warnings to the contrary, the word "aid" is more often than not construed literally. Even high-ranking public officials at all levels of government often place in their thinking all grants in one category and fail to distinguish between true aids and other types of transfer payments.

Grants-in-aid are made for a variety of purposes some of which directly contradict the others. These purposes are not always mutually exclusive; it happens that one type of aid program may comprise a complex of objectives. A list of purposes would include the following:

EQUALIZATION. If the grants are true fiscal aids to the recipient government, an attempt is made to apportion funds in accordance with need and the ability to support the program. Payments, therefore, constitute a geographic redistribution of wealth for a particular purpose and a transfer of revenue from an area with an above-average income to one with a below-average income.

STABILIZATION. The grant-in-aid device can be used to stabilize local revenues. When receipts from local taxes and public-service earnings fluctuate due to changes in the cycle of business activity, the State or National Government with a broader economic base can, by increasing or decreasing grants, stabilize the total revenue receipts of the local governments. With fairly constant and recurring expenditure burdens, local governments require some stability in their revenues.

ASSISTANCE IN PERIODS OF SERIOUS DEPRESSIONS. While akin to the preceding purpose, the difference in degree seems to warrant a separate purpose category. The objective is to absorb the shock of extraordinary depression expenditures. In depression periods, State and local financial powers could be extremely limited so that an actual breakdown in State and local government might occur unless the Federal Government came to its financial rescue. Some important grant programs have been started to cope with a national crisis which neither the States nor localities could finance. The prime example was Federal financial assistance for taking care of unemployment relief in the 1930's.

DISTRIBUTION OF TAX PROCEEDS BY THE GOVERNMENT BEST ABLE TO COLLECT SUCH TAX REVENUES. This is a device for utilizing the superior fiscal capacity of the National or State Government while at the same time preserving local government autonomy and administration. So-called "higher governments" often have a greater ability for efficient collection of taxes than they do for performing certain services and handling the expenditures therefor.

Some so-called State grants to local governments exist solely because the State government has taken over collection of certain taxes previously collected at the local level. This is illustrated by the California procedure of returning the personal property tax on motor vehicles to the local governments. The latter collected the tax until it was discovered that better results could be obtained by State collection. And yet the present return of the collections from this tax to local governments is labeled as a grant-in-aid. The significant thing to be noted here is that changes in State and local economies have made it desirable from the standpoint of administrative convenience and fiscal expediency to transfer collection of certain revenues to higher levels. Yet the higher levels have no greater proprietary rights to the revenues than they did when the lower governments collected them.

STIMULATION. Grants are sometimes given to start new types of services or activities. For example, the National and State Governments have started new programs in the fields of social welfare and health. These programs originated through pressure on the Federal and State legislative bodies by some groups of enthusiasts. As a means of getting a program started, the Federal or State Governments offered part or all of the money to accomplish a specified purpose. Such grants are generally classified as stimulating or promotional. The recipient government is induced by this method to enter fields not formerly a part of its governmental services. The offer of a new aid stimulates a matching appropriation lest the proffered funds be "lost." The danger is that once the new program becomes established the grants will be reduced or withdrawn. Citizens generally will not permit a reduction in scope of the new program to fit funds available, nor are they willing to finance the growing deficit through additional local taxation. The local government is "in the middle" and may have to reduce appropriations to other services below the desirable median with the result that the entire service program suffers. An example illustrative of this is the Federal grant to Kansas City, Mo., used to pay salaries of personnel in venereal disease, industrial hygiene, and convalescent home inspection. In 1952 this grant totaled $42,000, and in 1953 it was reduced to $24,000. Not only must the city itself finance the $18,000 reduction, using funds previously budgeted for other equally necessary activities, but ironically the industrial hygiene and convalescent home inspection employees enforce State health division regulations and not local ordinances.

SUPPORT OF A MINIMUM PROGRAM IN A FIELD IN WHICH THE GRANTING GOVERNMENT HAS AN INTEREST. The objective in establishing a minimum program is usually to raise the standard of performance. This has been true of some of the public health and public welfare grants.

SUPPORT OF A PROGRAM IN WHICH THE GRANTOR HAS THE MAJOR INTEREST. For example, Federal grants have been given to accomplish a national need common to all or most of the States, or for the construction of facilities crossing State lines or existing in most individual States. Thus the National Government came to aid highways as part of a national highway system for purposes of national defense and national convenience. The airport program exists because only the National Government can properly control air traffic. There is the further justification of national defense.

Although only a few of the Federal grant programs which affect local governments originated through pressure from the local governments, once the programs were started local officials have generally supported them.

As between the States and the localities, most of the grants are made either because the State has legal or moral responsibility for a function such as education or because the State is better able than the local governments to collect revenue.

Grants-in-aid are an important revenue source to States and local governments. Federal grants constituted 17.3 percent of State revenues in 1952. For the same year local governments received 26.1 percent of their revenues from State payments. Of great significance is the fact that the States, in 1952, received from the National Government $2,329 millions in grants-in-aid which was 17.3 percent of State revenues but the States made grants to local governments totalling $5,044 millions which was 31.9 percent of all State payments. Although it appears that local governments as a whole received 26.1 percent of their revenues in the form of State payments, this figure will be misunderstood and misinterpreted unless it is known that public welfare, education, and highways received $4,229 million of the $5,044 million State payments to local governments. To complete this picture, it should be noted that $1,855 million out of $2,329 million Federal grants in 1952 were made for public welfare, education, and highways. Thus it appears that Federal aid and State aid are not so much "aid to local governments" as they are "aids to selected functional activities" in which the granting governments have a major interest.

GENERAL OPINIONS ON GRANTS

Already in defining "grants-in-aid" certain implications in the minds of the public have been pointed out. There is a tendency to regard such moneys, collected over a broader area, as a windfall or gift which cannot be passed up and which need not be spent very carefully because it "did not cost anything." On the other side of the coin, the strings attached to the grants, the conditions to be met and the red tape of conforming to standards and of accounting and reporting have made grants-in-aid seem a real threat to home rule and a symbol of centralization. The degree of truth or falsehood in these opinions is beside the point. The existence of these opinions is itself a potent fact.

With a variety of grants and with multiple objectives, it is understandable that public attitudes toward grants is divided. The use of a common term to designate so many different types of payments does not make for clarity. In addition some programs start with one avowed purpose but continue under an entirely different philosophy. The school-lunch program, for instance, started as a means of disposing of surplus agricultural commodities. The program now continues with cash payments by the National Government on the theory that all school children should be well nourished.

Much of the opposition to grants-in-aid arises from the failure of so-called equalization grants to achieve their purpose. Frequently, the grants appear to have made more money available for a service in all areas instead of equalizing opportunity or establishing a desirable minimum level of service in all places. Probably this accounts for the attitude of most of those who protest strongly against grants-in-aid.

Others are really not as much opposed to grants-in-aid as they are opposed to government spending generally. These opponents of grants-in-aid feel that if the grant is eliminated and the next lower government must support the service alone, then the activity formerly supported will be greatly reduced in scope and the total public expenditure will be far less.

This last idea should be assigned considerable weight in evaluating the opposition to grants-in-aid.

MAJOR PROBLEMS

Much of the difficulty with Federal grants-in-aid arises from one or more problems which have not been properly resolved:

1. Some Federal grants are inherently arbitrary because the laws upon which they are based make arbitrary requirements necessary.

2. Lack of coordination in the administration of the various types of grants. It is understandable that Federal grants-in-aid lack cohesion and consistency because almost all of the 40 grants were created separately, are being administered separately, and are appropriated for separately, whether or not they are related programs or could be better administered collectively.

3. Administration has not been fully decentralized to Federal offices close to the point of actual expenditures. District offices of Federal agencies, and State offices beneath them, could be of greater help in bringing the national programs down to the State and local level if they were given wider discretion in adjusting the programs to local conditions. Their inability to make discretionary decisions limits their usefulness and causes much of the State and local friction in the Federal programs. Inflexible national rules are established to obtain national uniformity. Such uniformity is not necessary to accomplish the purpose of the Federal grants. It would appear better to permit variations within a general objective in order to stimulate experimentation and competition.

4. Grants-in-aid are sometimes used for indoctrination of State and local officials with ideas originated by Federal officials. This has been true particularly in the health field where Federal funds have been spent upon the training costs of State and Territorial health departments.

5. Functional autocracies have grown up in certain of the grant areas, which has resulted in functional pressures and functional loyalties.

6. The bases for distributing Federal grants need reexamination. It may well be that a number of grants for specific purposes could be consolidated into more general purpose grants based on a combined index of need and ability. Some modification of the British block grant might be the proper approach. The block grant resembles sharing in that it leaves local governments free to spend at their own discretion. It differs in not returning revenues to the place of collection. Grants for broader purposes might not immediately reduce the amount of Federal grants, but this shift would simplify administration, reduce the number of administrative employees and likewise reduce the impact of pressure groups which now support many of the highly specialized grants.

7. The requirement of matching sometimes defeats the equalization objective. Most Federal aid programs require the benefited local government to match the Federal grant according to a percentage sometimes as high as 100 percent. Too frequently, the size of the grant depends almost entirely on the local government's ability to raise matching funds. The more the local unit has, the more it can get. This may result in one of two conditions, neither of them favorable. The local government may be unable to produce local revenues for matching purposes and thereby lose a program or facility which is greatly needed, or it may secure its matching funds by reducing the budgets of other vital municipal services: police, fire, recreation, etc. If Federal funds are to be used to equalize opportunities, new formulae should be developed which recognize local needs as well as local ability to pay.

8. Rulings by Federal agencies often add to the cost of capital projects. Several examples from Kansas City, Mo., will illustrate:

The Civil Aeronautics Administration, which administers Federal airport aid, requires that before a project is advertised for bids, labor rates, as predetermined by the Secretary of Labor for all classes of labor likely to be required, be included in the specifications. These rates may not be more than 90 days old. Kansas City recently forwarded to the Civil Aeronautics Administration for approval specifications for a project when 60 days validity remained on the labor rate list used. Approval was granted on the 91st day and new rates were required. This delayed the project 6 or 7 weeks and the new rates were identical with the old.

The Federal Bureau of Public Roads agreed to participate in the right-of-way costs for a new expressway. The city was to be permitted to purchase property by negotiation based on a real estate board appraisal before resorting to condemnation. The appraisal was made in 1950, but the flood in 1951 placed a premium on all available rental space and caused a general increase in property values. As a result the appraisal was out of date. Although the city asked permission to make a new appraisal, the Federal administrators adhered rigidly to their original decision that property could not be purchased for more than its 1950 value. They did agree, however, that Federal grants would be paid on the basis of condemnation awards. The city was required, therefore, to condemn much property which could have been purchased at a small increase over the 1950 appraised values. The condemnation awards were considerably higher than the cost of the properties if they had been acquired by negotiation.

In preparing plans for the replacement of portions of a concrete airport apron, the Civil Aeronautics Administration insisted on use of a rock subbase, although local engineers stated such a base was neither practical nor necessary. During construction, after watching an abortive attempt to place the rock subbase, Civil Aeronautics Administration officials reluctantly agreed that this was an impossible requirement and that a sand base should be used. Although the apron rested on river sand, the Civil Aeronautics Administration inspectors required that 4 inches of sand be dug out and replaced with 4 inches of sand, which was hauled to the job. It is estimated that the cost of the unnecessary pavement base amounted to 10 percent of the total cost of the project.

Certainly, some control is needed to assure the Federal authorities that Federal grants are used honestly and for the purpose intended. But sometimes unnecessary costs are injected, particularly in engineering and construction projects.

The extension of local taxing powers is one alternative to grants-in-aid. The larger cities and counties which have larger per capita operating expenses but which also have large resources which they cannot now tax locally would profit from such a change. The granting of such powers would do away with raising revenue from all to serve a few and, in some cases, from a few to serve all. Even though these larger cities and counties were to levy the same kind of taxes as the State or National Governments, the total tax burden would probably be less if the larger cities and counties which appear to have the greatest present needs could raise directly a greater portion of their own revenue.

Another alternative to grants-in-aid is the transfer of activities or functions from the local level to the State or National Governments. This has already been done with respect to some activities in some States. While this may be the most simple alternative and while it may be the least expensive method of operation, it is not entirely consistent with the theory of federalism in the United States nor consistent with local responsible democracy. Perhaps the transfer of functions and the improvements of the revenue system could be accomplished simultaneously by enlarging the areas of government and/or the areas of taxation so that there would be less need of equalization by providing larger areas with greater breadth of taxation.

Greater State and local shares in federally collected revenues is another possible approach but one restricted in applicability. The difficulty with this alternative is that the point of collection of revenues does not always constitute the proper basis for the distribution of funds. Many of the purposes of grants-in-aid would be defeated by the use of this basis. Too often also the collecting government attaches to shared revenues the requirement that the receipts be earmarked for particular purposes when they should go into the general fund subject to unrestricted uses by the local government.

In some cases a better integration of the revenue system would help